MADNESS
UNDER THE
ROYAL PALMS

MADNESS UNDER THE ROYAL PALMS

Love and Death
Behind the Gates of Palm Beach

Laurence Leamer

HYPERION
New York

 Printed in the United States of America. For information address Hyperion, 114 Fifth Avenue, New York, New York 10011.

Paperback ISBN: 978-1-4013-1011-0

Hyperion books are available for special promotions and premiums. For details contact the HarperCollins Special Markets Department in the New York office at 212-207-7528, fax 212-207-7222, or email spsales@harpercollins.com.

Design by Renato Stanisic
Title page photograph © Jerome Olivier

FIRST PAPERBACK EDITION

10 9 8 7 6 5 4 3 2 1

To

JAMES JENNINGS SHEERAN
(1931–2008)

Contents

Prologue: A Stranger in Paradise *1*

1. A Small Dinner Dance 5
2. A Royal Ascent 14
3. Palm Beach Millionaire Seeks Playmate 24
4. Illusion of Sex 36
5. Hope Is Not a Diamond 46
6. The Evening Is Only Beginning 56
7. A Road That Led Elsewhere 65
8. Triumph of the Nouveau 78
9. King of the New Yorkers 97
10. "Nice *Nothing*!" 106
11. Half of Everything 114
12. The World Turned Upside Down 127
13. Outside the Guarded Gates 137
14. The Shiny Sheet 147
15. Winter Dreams 159
16. The Dance of Wealth 167
17. Palaces of Privilege 177
18. Spinning and Spinning and Spinning 193
19. A Bird of a Different Feather 201
20. Pierced by Sorrows 214

21. Goblets of Revenge 228
22. Dirty Energy 237
23. Cowboys and Indians 249
24. The Most Precious Asset 261
25. The Golden Ring 268
26. Two Wild and Crazy Guys 278
27. Everybody Hurts 287
28. Regrets Only 297
29. The Entitled 309
30. Epilogue: Crimes and Misdemeanors 322

Acknowledgments *331*
Notes *335*
Bibliography *355*
Index *359*

It is difficult to describe the rapacity with which the American rushes forward to secure the immense booty which fortune proffers to him. Fortune awaits them everywhere, but happiness they can not attain.

—ALEXIS DE TOCQUEVILLE IN *DEMOCRACY IN AMERICA.*

MADNESS
UNDER THE
ROYAL PALMS

Prologue: A Stranger in Paradise

I have lived all over the world, from the mountains of Nepal to the provinces of France, a city in southern Peru to a town in Japan, but Palm Beach is as exotic and as hidden a place as I have ever resided. I first visited the island in December 1991. I drove east on Okeechobee Boulevard from West Palm Beach and across the middle bridge onto Royal Palm Way.

The island, off the east coast of South Florida, is faultlessly beautiful, with a sense of solitude and security all its own. There are flowers everywhere and the Atlantic Ocean lies nearby, but the air is so pure and pristine that there is no scent at all. The tall palms lining Royal Palm Way are the descendants of trees born of twenty thousand coconuts from the cargo hold of a ship that smashed against the shore in 1878. The scene could have been Cannes or Nice, except for the fact that there are no shops, no cafés, and no blissful boulevardiers along the street. Instead, imposing vault-like private banks line the street. Welcome, they say silently, to wealth—*real* wealth.

I drove a few blocks south to Worth Avenue, which, along with Fifth Avenue and Rodeo Drive, is one of the most celebrated luxury shopping streets in America. I got out and walked along its three blocks. Even though this was a few weeks before Christmas, there was only a handful of shoppers. At the eastern end of the street stood a splendid public beach, but there were no restrooms and few parking spots, nowhere to eat, and only a few people scattered on the beach. Everything conspired to tell the visitor he or she was not welcome.

There is no luxury trademark in the world quite like Palm Beach. For over a hundred years, the wealthiest Americans have been coming here for the winter season, living lives of exclusivity and privilege apart from the rest of us. As I drove the length of the thirteen-mile-long island, I tried to see as much as I could, but most of the estates stood behind walls and manicured hedges, and everything seemed shrouded from view.

I wanted to find a place away from the winter gloom where I could write my books in solitude and sunshine. For some unfathomable reason, I kept thinking, why not live here? I cannot quite explain it, even today. It would have been more like me to buy a bungalow in Key West or a cottage in Naples.

In 1994, my wife, Vesna, and I purchased a duplex in a condominium on South Ocean Boulevard, a block north of Worth Avenue. Edward Durrell Stone, architect of the Kennedy Center, designed the elegant, modernist building that is the most architecturally significant apartment building on the island. I found everything about it spectacular, from the way I could lie in bed looking out on the ocean, to my office overlooking the inner courtyard and atrium pool. When I got up early in the morning and sat in my office looking down on people coming in and out of their apartments, I felt like Jimmy Stewart in *Rear Window*.

We had been there less than a week when there came a knock on the door. A committee from the board presented themselves. I thought they were there to welcome us to the building, but that was not why they stood there in an unsmiling, stolid line. I was told I could not sit in my bathrobe in my office without blinds. I apologized. We were redoing the apartment and our new blinds had not arrived. I had no idea that I had scandalized my neighbors. I found it odd that they felt they needed to show their strength of numbers, when all it would have taken was a phone call from one board member.

A little later, I noticed a wet spot high on the living room wall that, day after day, grew larger. The swimming pool is on the roof, and I assumed that it had leaked. Once the stains dried up, I asked the building to pay a few hundred dollars to have that part of the wall repainted.

The board president came to inspect the purported damage. There is a sartorial progression in Palm Beach. Men of a certain type deal with aging by dressing in wilder and wilder colors. Blue is good for the sixties, green for the seventies, and for the eighties a red so vibrant that these gentlemen look like walking fire hydrants. The board president was old beyond his years. Though barely in his fifties, he wore the reddest of pants. He surveyed our apartment with a face that matched them and refused to sit down, as if that would mean he had accepted some sort of commonality with me.

Our apartment was furnished with art from Peru to Yugoslavia, and rugs from Tibet to Russia. Many of our guests thought that it had been professionally decorated. The president surveyed the room as if under siege.

"It must be like living in a trailer park," the president sniffed.

"The reason you don't like me is I don't wear red pants," I told him, equally candidly. "My wife's name isn't Muffie, and I don't have paintings of sailboats on my walls."

I had never met anyone quite like this blustery Tidewater aristocrat, and I was more intrigued than irritated. Little did I know that what I was experiencing was the tip of a submerged world, which when fully explored, would yield as strange and, in some instances, as decadent a culture as one could find on or off this continent . . . a place of passions and obsessions not even hinted at by its too-perfect exterior. But somehow the anthropologist in my journalistic makeup must have sensed what lay beneath, because I not only stayed, but I began to explore, to poke around and pursue the answers to my questions. It led to many strange, twisted byways and eventually to Bernard Madoff, the darkest and deadliest financial criminal in American history.

What mysteries lay behind those foreboding walls? Who truly were these people? Why were many of them so hostile to anyone they perceived as different? And, perhaps most of all, where exactly did their restless pursuit of happiness take them?

Getting at the answers turned into as fascinating, in some cases as shocking, and always as unexpected a journey as I have ever taken.

I

A Small Dinner Dance

Barbara Wainscott blew out all the candles on the birthday cake except for one and motioned to her dinner companion, Prince Edward Windsor, to do the honors. It was not only Barbara's fiftieth birthday this evening in March of 1997, but in three days it would be Queen Elizabeth and Prince Philip's youngest son's thirty-third birthday. The guest of honor doused the candle without puckering his princely lips. It was as if Edward had been practicing all day. The sixty-five other guests applauded as much their good fortune being in the presence of a Windsor as commemoration of the dual anniversaries.

The tall prince had a newborn's pink skin and a demeanor of almost feminine refinement. His looks set him apart from everyone else at the Palm Beach party, and were another reason why many of the guests were nervous to have a conversation with him. Barbara and Prince Edward continued whispering tête-à-tête, with her occasionally giving out the throaty laugh that was her verbal signature. Her horsey chortling advertised that the prince had bestowed yet another wry jest on his hostess.

Barbara had blue eyes so large that it was as if she had no eyelids. These eyes saw everything of social consequence, judged all and forgave little. She was five feet ten inches tall, and would have been a strikingly handsome woman had she not weighed over two hundred pounds. She was as shrewd in her dress as in every other element of public life, and despite her heftiness, she projected an image of class and wealth that few women of any size could have equaled. That evening in her gold chiffon gown and multilayered, shimmering diamond necklace borrowed from Van Cleef & Arpels, she had the magisterial presence of a monarch.

Barbara sent out heavy, hand-engraved invitations "for a small dinner dance in honor of His Royal Highness The Prince Edward," from the society printer, Mrs. John L. Strong, in New York City. That was the first of the exquisitely rendered elements for this dinner dance at Elephant Walk, the estate she shared with eighty-four-year-old David Berger, her longtime lover. She had a fastidious sense of detail, a mosaic of concerns that came together into a seamless whole. Barbara could have hired Bruce Sutka, the leading event planner, but he was too flamboyant.

Barbara and David's home stood at 109 Jungle Road, on the corner of South County Road, a block away from the ocean, just south of the town center. The house was a Palm Beach regency, a style ubiquitous in parts of the island. There was a marquee tent affixed to the back of the house. This permanently tented pavilion was a discriminating setting for parties, but not quite large enough for the event Barbara was planning. Thus she attached to the marquee two temporary tents for the orchestra and the dance floor.

The hostess ensured that the lighting was gently forgiving to the imprecations of age, yet bright enough to highlight every element. She set out mirrored dinner tables that reflected the richly appointed place settings and the glittering jewels on the ladies. She ordered a nursery's worth of roses, lilacs, crocuses, and lilies of the valley to festoon every empty space, and the white tent gave off the rich bouquet of Rubrum lilies. She spent over a thousand dollars on the centerpiece floral displays on each table. Barbara garnished every dish with a touch of luxury, such as smoked trout mousse with caviar and beef tournedos with foie gras, all served with superb French wines.

Barbara saw to it that the temporary dance floor would not hobble ladies in high heels. Nor would she have her guests assaulted with the blaring blast of brass, sounds that overwhelmed talk at so many Palm Beach parties. She told band leader Bob Hardwick that she wanted a rich overlay of strings and no microphones or speakers. With the eight violins and gently muted brass, her company conversed without shouting while the shimmering, scintillating music practically lifted people out onto the dance floor. Senator Claiborne Pell, a blueblood Rhode Island politician who had just retired from office, hardly left the dance floor.

As Barbara surveyed the gathering, she was observing what might appear glorious frivolity but was one of the most important and calculated endeavors of her social career. In fact, Barbara had been preparing most of her life for this. She came from a family that traced its lineage back to the Jamestown, Virginia, colony in the seventeenth century. Her mother's family, the Buckleys, had lost everything in the Great Depression. Her father, Desmond Simmons, had made a good living as a project manager on major buildings in Manhattan, but Barbara grew up learning that her family had once known rich, advantaged times that seemed forever lost.

In 1965 when Barbara Simmons was attending Mary Baldwin, a Virginia women's college, former Vice President Richard Nixon introduced her to another college-age Republican, Jeffrey Wainscott. After graduating, the tall, well-born gracious Republican activist married the tall, wealthy, handsome navy lieutenant who flew off to fight for his country in Vietnam. His bride became Pat Nixon's social secretary during the 1968 presidential campaign and served in the Nixon administration. Barbara perhaps loved the idea of her lieutenant more than the reality, and when he returned, the marriage was soon over. The young divorcée moved to New York City, where she worked in public relations overseeing events for the elite of the city.

Barbara's aged lover, David Berger, came from the small town of Archbald, Pennsylvania, where his father had been a successful Jewish merchant. David Berger had graduated first in his class from Penn Law School in 1936, eventually becoming one of the first lawyers to pursue federal class action suits, winning colossal settlements in such cases as *Exxon Valdez* and the Three Mile Island nuclear disaster. His legal achievements were well-known, but what was not widely recognized was that his specialization had netted him a fortune estimated at over $350 million. David flew first class to be met by chauffeured limousines that took him to suites in the finest hotels in the world, but wherever he went, he felt his life lacked a crucial imprimatur that could only be achieved in Palm Beach.

For a hundred years, the social elite of America and those seeking to be part of it had been coming to this island off the coast of South Florida to spend the winter season. During that time, Palm Beach became not only the most exclusive resort community in the world, but the most socially segregated town in America. When David was a young man, there were restricted clubs in many other places, but at the Everglades and Bath and Tennis, the two leading clubs on the island, that policy continued unabated and unchallenged. Even in these years at the B&T, if one of "them" somehow got onto the tennis courts or into the dining room, he might well be asked to leave. For most of his life, David could not have joined two other clubs on the island, the Sailfish Club and the Beach Club, either, but when faced with legal and political challenge, they changed their policies.

David had come down to Palm Beach as a young Philadelphia lawyer and stayed at the Whitehall Hotel. He remembered the Whitehall primarily for its old-fashioned tin bathtubs. At this time in the fifties, David and other visiting Jews were like West Berliners on the Berlin corridor during the Cold War, traveling on a narrow strip that contained the three almost exclusively Jewish institutions on the island: the Whitehall Hotel, the Sun and Surf Beach Club, and the Palm Beach Country Club. As he journeyed the route, the image of a forbidden world of glamour and elegance eternally beyond his reach was imprinted on David Berger's soul.

Now, four decades later, with a vast fortune at his disposal and with Barbara's guidance, David had set out to become the first Jew to reach the heights of Palm Beach society. "David saw a chance for social acceptance and importance that he wouldn't really have to work hard for," Barbara said. "He'd have to *pay*. He understood paying. He didn't trust favors unless they were bought. He didn't know about kindness because he had never experienced it."

THE IRONY WAS THAT David craved to win acceptance in a town that was about half Jewish. The Whitehall Hotel where David had stayed had long since been torn down. The Sun and Surf was now a largely Jewish condominium, and the Palm Beach Country Club was the leading Jewish club. Although there were Jewish homeowners throughout the island, most lived in a heavily populated strip of condominiums between the ocean and the Intracoastal Waterway at the far southern tip of town. It was so geographically separate that when one drove along a tree-lined section of South Ocean Boulevard and around Sloan's Curve, it was like entering another town.

Unlike the rest of the island where there were few large residential buildings, both sides of the road were lined with large condominiums. Middle-aged ladies walked their poodles, spouses pedaled along on matching bicycles, joggers put in their five miles, and aging gay couples paced each other for their daily constitutional. Retirees eked out their days on small pensions in modest efficiencies along the Intracoastal Waterway, but there were also superb, oceanfront apartments furnished with discriminating style. It was a vibrantly human scene that could have been any number of places along the South Florida coast.

But just to the north in the estate section practically the only human beings one saw were gardeners blowing leaves, or pool men hurrying out of electronic gates. That was what the WASP gentry considered the ideal of a proper Palm Beach life. They derided the area to the south as the "Gaza Strip," a nightmarish vision of what would happen to Palm Beach if "they" ever took over, a vulgar Catskills South that would destroy peace and property values.

THE ISLAND THAT WAS the focus of Barbara and David's ambition is America's first gated community. Its three bridges can be raised in a minute, and are as strong a barrier as the most impregnable of gates. That Palm Beach is the most controlled and exclusionary of towns is signaled in every way, from the toilet-less public beaches and the limited parking to the salesclerks with noses elevated to the sky. And on the highways leading to the island, there are no signs directing the visitor to Palm Beach, a town of thirty thousand in the winter months.

Barbara understood that life in Palm Beach is like an elaborate costume party in which one can wear whatever outfit one wants as long as the mask never falls. For over a century, people have come to the exclusive community to reinvent themselves by cloaking themselves in the illusions of wealth. They often build second acts so unrelated to the first that their biographies are like two different lives mysteriously attached to each other.

The most astute observer of the island's early years was none other than the novelist Henry James, who traveled back to America after years of living as an expatriate in England. James arrived in February 1905 by train one evening in this enclave of civilization slashed out of the jungle. There, commanding the skyline, stood the six-story, lemon yellow Royal Poinciana Hotel, at the time not only the largest hotel in the world, but the largest wooden structure ever built. The author was often appalled by the boastful grandiosity of America, but he was astounded by this visage. The Royal Poinciana was "a marvel indeed, proclaiming itself of course, with all the eloquence of an interminable towered and pinnacled and gabled and bannered sky-line. To stand off and see it rear its incoherent crest above its gardens was to remember—and quite with relief—nothing but the processional outline of Windsor Castle that could appear to march with it."

James was equally enthralled by what he saw once he entered the main portals of the hotel. There were rooms for 1,750 guests, a dining room that sat 1,800, and a veritable street of shops "dealing, naturally, in commodities almost beyond price—not the cheap gimcracks of the usual watering-place barrack."

American commercial culture was triumphant, resulting in an affluent class with the money and aspirations to vacation at the most desirable winter resort in America. James was initially delighted by the sight of these wealthy Americans attempting to learn and employ the kinds of manners that he considered the essence of European culture, indeed, exaggerating those manners as if only in overcompensating could they be sure they got it right. They had "the inordinate desire for taste, a desire breaking into a greater number of quaint and candid forms, probably, than have ever been known upon earth. And doesn't the question then become, almost thrillingly, that of the degree to which this pathos of desire may be condemned to remain a mere heart-break to the historic muse? Is that to be, possible, the American future?"

Palm Beach had become a university of taste where the new business elite arrived from all over the eastern half of the United States, often for lengthy stays. They changed their clothes five times a day, took tea at the outdoor palm garden, and attended balls and concerts. Vanderbilts, Whitneys, Cushings, Livingstons, and Winthrops stayed in the hotel, although the more typical guests were commercial gentry from cities such as Pittsburgh, Dayton, or Buffalo. They brushed against the crème de la crème, and in so doing emulated their social betters. The Royal Poinciana represented a democratization of class, the world of Newport brought south and expanded so that anyone with enough money could partake.

The author of *Portrait of a Lady* and *Washington Square* was brilliantly attuned to the nuances and subtleties of social life. Yet James was rendered dumbstruck by these hordes of people who were of a size and stature unworthy of these incredible surroundings, and distressingly similar in their demeanor and conduct. "It was the scant diversity of type that left me short, as a storyseeker or picture-maker," James concluded. "The women in particular failed in an extraordinary degree to engage the imagination, to offer it so to speak, references or openings: it faltered—doubtless respectfully enough—where they for the most part so substantially and prosaically sat, failing of any warrant to go an-inch further."

This new gentry slavishly copied the American upper class that itself had slavishly copied their European counterparts. They bowed to royalty in a gesture that some of their ancestors found abhorrent, obscuring their backgrounds and pretending to noble ancestors.

This obsession with royalty became so extreme that the *Palm Beach Daily News* editorialized in February 1898, "It is not a good sign this scouring the earth by Americans to see if they are not descended from someone who was something a hundred or a thousand years ago. Let present-day Americans stand upon their own feet. Not to our ancestors, but to ourselves let us turn for distinction."

In Palm Beach, people chased after happiness, but like dogs chasing a mechanical rabbit in a greyhound race, no matter how fast they ran, happiness was just a few inches in front of their noses. The things that were most valuable about them, their energy, initiative, and usually modest backgrounds, were covered up or devalued. The things that were ephemeral and trivial—status and social placement—were valued far beyond their worth. It was as if they feared that some untoward gesture, inappropriate dress, a crude word, a gaucherie, would expose them as the pretenders that they knew themselves to be.

A CENTURY LATER, WHAT Barbara Wainscott and David Berger were playing was still the great game of Palm Beach. Of all the aspirations that motivate humankind, none is so derided as social ambition. It is often attacked by those who pursue it most assiduously, for if you are caught striving to climb, you lose. Barbara's haughty sense of superiority did not always endear her to those she sought to impress, but she figured that the only weak card in her deck was David's Jewish heritage. Given his background, she could hardly sit back and wait for the engraved invitations to start arriving, yet she had to be subtle and shrewd.

Barbara was proud that she was the person on the island chosen to host this dinner dance for Prince Edward. She was neither a bluffer nor an exaggerator when she talked of her connections. She had befriended Prince Charles and Princess Anne when the youthful royals came to Washington during the Nixon years. Barbara's own grandmother had been friendly with *their* grandmother, the Queen Mother, and Barbara had met the former Queen Elizabeth on one of her many trips to England, where she stayed at Claridge's and missed not a single checkmark of the proper. All she had left of her family fortune was her name, her manners, and the promise of her blood. That was where David came in.

2

A Royal Ascent

As Barbara sat kibitzing with Prince Edward, what she was really doing was trumping most of the other hostesses on the island as she made an assault on the social heights of Palm Beach. Barbara had waited all these years to seek to develop a closer relationship with the Windsors, and now she did so by applying the lubricant of David's fortune liberally. By the time of the party, Barbara and David had already given three hundred thousand dollars to the Duke of Edinburgh's Award, and within the next two years they would give a million dollars more. That was an enormous sum, and without that contribution, Prince Edward would not have been sitting next to Barbara this evening.

Those who saw the Windsors in Palm Beach paid royally, and then boasted about "friendships" that were, for the most part, little more than commercial exchanges. The Windsors had been coming to Palm Beach since 1941, when the abdicated British king and his American-born wife, Wallis Simpson, arrived on a ship from the Bahamas, where the duke was governor. While Nazi bombs rained on London, the duchess complained that she had left Europe only with "refugee rags" and planned to go shopping. In the next decades, as the couple made their frequent visits to the island, they rarely indulged in the vulgarity of paying for anything, a tradition continued by the next generations.

In this less leisurely era, the Windsors rarely stayed more than two days on the island. If one wanted to be around the royals, the supplicant contributed to the charities that they used to enhance their status and pay for much of their travel. Even with his enormous contributions to Prince Philip's charity, David would have gotten nowhere by himself. It was only due to Barbara's flawless sense of protocol and manners that the couple was able to make a run at the top of the social circuit with a royal event in Palm Beach.

Barbara wended her way among the tables, talking both to her guests from New York, Philadelphia, and Texas, and to those from Palm Beach—especially the women. It is an island of matriarchs. Women commandeer the peaks of society, and Barbara was paying particular attention to those female attendees.

Most of these women either were married or had been married to far older men. A pretty young second/third/fourth wife is the defining relationship in Palm Beach—one of the perks of wealth. But these unblushing brides are of diverse and often hidden backgrounds, their only commonality being their good looks. Their husbands generally die within a few years, leaving wealthy widows with the money, time, and ambition to re-create themselves with grand new personas, sometimes taking their own younger husbands. It is these widows and wives who feed the island's ruling class of elderly matriarchs—the opposite of the world in which their late husbands had hoped to live.

For a presentable, heterosexual man looking for a rich widow, or a bisexual man capable of occasionally performing, the pickings in Palm Beach are rich indeed. It comes as no surprise that some of the worst of these men prey on the vulnerabilities and romantic dreams of the most susceptible of these aging women, just as some of these women had preyed on the vanity and declining masculinity of the elderly men who had become their husbands.

At Barbara's dinner dance, it seemed as if every Palm Beach woman was either at least two decades younger than her husband, or the widow of an elderly spouse. As the hostess looked out on the dance floor, she saw the elaborate masquerades, all so impeccably manufactured and performed. The youngest woman in the room was thirty-eight-year-old Angela Koch (pronounced Coke), who wore a plunging décolleté black gown that showed her figure off to stunning effect. The dress may have been a bit too much (or a bit too little), but Prince Edward obviously did not think so, out on the dance floor whirling the beautiful Angela around. Angela's new husband, fifty-six-year-old William Koch, one of the wealthiest men in America and a renowned yachtsman, sat wearing a very nautical white beard and a benign expression. That look was wildly misleading. He was a fiercely competitive man who in 1992 had sailed *America³* to victory in the America's Cup. He was in a brutal, interminable lawsuit with his twin brother, David, who was about to buy his own oceanfront estate a mile north of his brother's. William alleged that David and his other sibling had cheated him out of his rightful share of Koch Industries, the privately held company that was far larger than most major corporations.

Barbara could not have reporters scurrying up to Edward to ask impertinent questions about such matters as his brothers' marital problems, either Charles with Diana or Andrew with Sarah, or to query him about his own live-in companion at Buckingham Palace, Sophie Rhys-Jones. Barbara invited only one reporter, her friend Shannon Donnelly, society editor of the *Palm Beach Daily News*, who did not have to be told how she must behave.

Shannon was not yet fully aware that she was by far the most powerful reporter in Palm Beach and that within her world, she had authority that few reporters anywhere enjoyed. In this town obsessed with social position, she could anoint someone with a few words and a picture, or by ignoring, she could destroy—and within a few years she would do so with impunity. Almost everyone in town reads the "Shiny Sheet," the nickname given the daily because it is printed on paper that will not smudge the fingers of its readers. The society pages dazzlingly evoked the elaborate illusion that is the island's greatest creation. The ladies were thin, the gentlemen elegant, the jewelry real, the days cloudless, the evenings long, the laughter genuine. Those who hoped to join this ersatz aristocracy of wealth and privilege read the pages seeking to learn how they too could one day be portrayed here, or in one of the other purveyors of Palm Beach fantasy.

Shannon was a head shorter than her hostess and just about as overweight. Unlike Barbara, who had attempted to disguise her bulk in a cloaklike garment, Shannon wore a tight-fitting, short cocktail dress and heels so high they seemed less like shoes than stilts. Shannon is a witty and observant reporter who could have savaged this spectacle of Americans fawning over Edward as they awkwardly tried to follow royal protocol. But in all her years in Palm Beach, this was her first time as a guest at such an event, and in her story she would do nothing but celebrate the dinner dance.

Barbara Wainscott was acutely aware that behind the richly appointed façade of class and blood, Palm Beach is all about money. The island is full of assayers who think they can grasp a person's wealth at a glance. It takes major amounts of riches to maintain social prominence in Palm Beach, far more than most people realize even as they begin their ascents. Barbara had spent several million dollars of David's money on this goal alone, and was still having to pave the roadway with gold. She had only invited those whose mere presence could either enhance her position or in some other measure help the couple advance.

Seated to her left, Barbara placed Daniel Ponton, who owns Club Colette, a private dinner club. Dan may have been thirty-seven years old, but when he romped on the beach, he appeared no older than a teenager. Like most people on the island, Dan is as much an observer as a participant, and even as he talked animatedly to the prince, he was making his own critical judgment on the evening. David was a member of Club Colette, and the previous year Dan had catered Barbara's luncheon for Edward's father, Prince Philip. Dan was not a caterer and he had charged what even by his admission was a staggering fee, but the meal had been splendid and so was the conversation, in part, Dan believed, because *he* had been seated at the table. This evening Barbara had hired a conventional caterer and the results had been conventional food. As for the event itself, it was about as conventional as the beef tournedos, and at the earliest possible moment, Dan said his adieus.

Dan is part of a gay coterie that is the crucial element in creating the extravagant fantasy that is Palm Beach. For the most part, gay men design the houses, decorate the homes, dress the ladies, create the ambience of the balls, advise the aspiring, and escort the widows. Club Colette is one of the few private places on the island where prominent Protestants and Jews sup together without comment or concern, though generally at different tables and often on different evenings.

Dan has a brilliant sense of the social nuances of the ultra-wealthy, and is making a fortune serving their most elaborate emotional needs. He is the gatekeeper who stands in the portals turning away all those from membership who do not pass his intense scrutiny. Dan is Shannon's closest friend, and there is no venue featured more prominently in the Shiny Sheet than Club Colette.

Barbara's two closest Palm Beach friends, F. Warrington "Warry" Gillet Jr. and Elesabeth "Eles" Gillet, had good dinner seats. Eles, pronounced Liz, is a steel heiress with roots in Birmingham, Alabama. As Barbara saw it, Eles was the very model of a Palm Beach aristocrat. In 1989 the regional daily the *Palm Beach Post* had listed her among the most prominent candidates to be the new social queen of the island. ("Strong contender. Extremely attractive. Very wealthy.") Warry, her second husband, was a member of the old Maryland horse set. His wife had most of the money, a happenstance that neither ever forgot. Warry was tall and outrageously handsome. He traded on his blueblood background in the easiest and most efficacious of ways by working in real estate. He had sold David the home in which the party was taking place. Warry was in some measure continuing to broker David's social advance.

Warry had also sold the house to the previous owner, Marylou Whitney, widow of Cornelius Vanderbilt Whitney, bearer of two of the most distinguished names in American society. Marylou was herself one of the most celebrated names in Palm Beach and American society. The stunning septuagenarian continued to visit Palm

Beach each season. If she hadn't been traveling to Alaska to follow her dogsled team in the legendary Iditarod sled race, she might well have attended the dinner dance and been seated next to Prince Edward.

Barbara had shipped David off to purgatory to sit with those she considered the most dismal group of outsiders, including his brother, Harold; his younger son, Daniel; others from David's law firm; and his accountant. If he insisted on inviting what she considered the unacceptable, she would dump him off to the side with the other rejects. She was not his wife, and not even purely a lover, but also an employee hired to advance him socially, and she felt an undertone of anger toward a man to whom she considered herself overwhelmingly superior.

Three days beforehand, Shannon wrote the lead story on the front page of the Shiny Sheet about the impending occasion. The headline was enough to intrigue anyone on the island ("Prince Edward plans 'private and personal' weekend visit"). Barbara had mastered the art of understatement, and her remarks were wickedly disdainful toward the uninvited. "It's always delightful to be with him and we look forward to him meeting some new people," Shannon quoted her friend in the bylined story. "It is strictly private."

The prominent story was a manicured nail in the eye of everyone in the elite circles who had not received an invitation. It was revenge as sweet as Sauternes wine, but it came with a price. An enemy will do you ten times the harm a friend will do you good, and Barbara had most likely made some powerful enemies ready to heave their own private blackballs at the next opportunity.

In the newspaper story Barbara appeared an all-powerful, outgoing figure, but she was incredibly shy, a strange affliction for a woman who made her living in public relations. She was often late to events not because she felt superior, but because it was hard for her to face being in public. She had a certain unpredictable edginess, a hard-edged wit and candor rare in the haute WASP world. For the most part, the ladies in those circles liked both food and people without much spice, and though they tolerated Barbara, they did not embrace her.

The Palm Beach couples Barbara invited were the socially prominent individuals who could be useful to her and David. They attended the parties written about in the Shiny Sheet. They belonged to the Everglades and the B&T. They purchased tables at the most important charity balls and invited their intimates.

Among the socialites and wives of the megawealthy who were now among the ruling elite, there were those who had once been showgirls, hatcheck girls, semi-legitimate minor actresses, one woman who had been a featured player in soft porn films, and another reputed to have been a call girl.

But Barbara was immensely cautious about inviting people into her and David's world. She was not about to ask someone who might tell an off-color joke to the prince. The island was full of pretenders and frauds, and before she invited a couple to Elephant Walk, she did her due diligence.

To the cognoscenti of Palm Beach social life, those who were not invited were almost as interesting as those who were. Mildred "Brownie" McLean, the exuberant, party-loving widow of the multimillionaire John "Jock" McLean II, was one of Marylou Whitney's oldest and closest friends. If this had still been Marylou's house, Brownie would have been high on the guest list. Brownie was a blonde of blondes who in her youth had looked like a voluptuous version of Grace Kelly. She had lived with her late husband in a mansion on the ocean that she had sold to John Lennon and Yoko Ono. She thought that no one would ever cork her bottle of wine, but she was drinking from the dregs now, living in a tiny apartment in West Palm Beach and making the nightly trek over to the island to attend the party of the moment. She was still invited to many of the A-list parties, but it was yet another mark of Barbara's social savvy that she knew it would add no cachet to have Brownie as her guest.

Also not on the invitation list was Cathleen McFarlane, the emotionally extravagant, flamboyant widow of multimillionaire industrialist Norris McFarlane. Her sister, the late Margaret Hart Ferraro, had been one of the three most famous burlesque queens in America, celebrated in a song sung by Danny Kaye about farmers who "used to utterly utter when Margie Hart churned her butter." That was hardly an achievement likely to impress the gentlemen on the membership committee of the Everglades Club, but thanks largely to her husband, Cathleen had passed muster. Catholics had once been nearly as outré as Jews in Palm Beach, but they had taken on such restrained Episcopalian coloring that the term WASP should rightfully include them. But not Cathleen. Although she dined and wined among the WASPs, she had the considerable audacity to invite some of her Jewish friends to the Everglades, and had kept enough of her Irish soul to pop out with witty risqué patter that her detractors considered outrageous.

When Barbara put together the invitation list, she did not ask David for *his* Palm Beach names, for she knew that he would not have them. David had no friends, only business acquaintances. His main sources of male camaraderie were his tennis partners at the Breakers Hotel, where he played several times a week.

Among the other regulars at the Breakers courts was Eddy Louis, a middle-aged Middle Easterner married to an American woman three decades his senior. David and Barbara saw Eddy and Vera Louis often at the most exalted charity balls, where the couple put on their own command performance, dancing with endless panache. Eddy was largely unwelcome unless on the arm of his wife, and it would have been unthinkable to invite the couple.

Another man who played tennis at the Breakers and like Eddy was not a member, was Eric Purcell, a good-looking fortyish man with easy manners and quick patter. David knew little about him. He had been living with one woman in the North End and escorting several old ladies, and he would happily have donned his dinner jacket and been an exemplary escort. But Barbara did not even consider asking him, and for the last few months he had mysteriously disappeared.

I was another one of those tennis acquaintances. Soon after my wife and I arrived in Palm Beach, I joined the Breakers Club so I could play tennis and meet some of the players and pretenders off the court as well. It now costs $150,000 to join, plus $15,000 annual dues, but it was a refundable $5,000 when I signed up, with around

$2,000 in dues. It was there at the preeminent resort hotel on the island that I met and played tennis with Eddy Louis, Eric Purcell, and David Berger.

David was an avid tennis player, amazingly physically fit for a man in his early eighties. Like most of the megawealthy, David rarely traveled alone, always with at least one other person, and often with a considerable entourage. The group that arrived a few minutes before David's game seemed energized and nervous, as if around him everything proceeded in double time.

David had a chess player's approach to doubles, planning his moves far ahead and making up in finesse what he lacked in power. Playing against him, I could imagine what an opponent he must have been in the courtroom.

After our games, we often sat and had spirited conversations. David had been one of the leading Democratic fund-raisers in America, and was conversant not only about the highest levels of politics, but elite business affairs as well. David told Barbara that I was the only interesting person he had met at the Breakers. It is not quite the compliment it may appear. For the most part, the club members are narrow men who made their fortunes doing things such as building airplane hangars or buying mobile home parks. They have largely retreated into lives that begin and end with personal pleasure. Beyond talking about how they had made their fortunes, they are passionate about nothing except their own well-being.

David put me in a different category, but he and Barbara had no intention of getting to know me beyond the tennis courts. I was not part of circles to which they sought entrée. I could do them no good, and I might say or do something that would set them back in their quest for acceptance. David and Barbara were royally dismissive of those who were not part of the rarified social circles. That meant most of the residents including Fred and Rose Keller, whose presence never graced elite events. Fred was a good tennis player but David would never consider playing with him.

Barbara was not thinking about the people she had not invited. The evening had been a triumph, and she was full of an immense sense of satisfaction that she and her lover were on the cusp of achieving their dream. She had good reason to believe that she had lifted David and herself to the upper reaches of Palm Beach society, to which he so strenuously aspired and which she considered her birthright.

As she stood at the doorway gaily chatting with the departing guests, Barbara had no inkling that within a few years David's and her lives, and the lives of many of those around them, would change in ways she would have considered impossible. The old elite world that she and David were seeking to enter was dying. Weakened by inertia, self-absorption, indulgence, moral myopia, and spiritual inbreeding, it was vulnerable to being overcome by a forceful, often merciless new world of money. As much as David wanted to become part of that old world, he was one of the forces destroying the society that he sought so desperately to enter.

As Barbara said good-bye to her last guests, she had not even the slightest premonition that one of these women would be accused of poisoning her husband; one would accuse her husband of violently assaulting her; and one of her guests would fall grievously ill and miraculously recover. There would be divorces and public shame. Among the outer circle murder, suicide, humiliation, and virtual exile would ensue. As for Barbara's own fate, it would be both unthinkable and, as she saw the world, unspeakable.

3

Palm Beach Millionaire Seeks Playmate

I played tennis most of the time at the Breakers, but I also played at the Seaview Tennis Center, which sits between the private Palm Beach Day School and the public elementary school in the middle of town. When I had a game in the morning, I saw the big yellow buses bringing in brigades of kids from West Palm Beach, while a parade of Bentleys, Rolls, Lexuses, and BMWs dropped off the private school children in their uniforms of blue and white.

The public school students are bused in from across the Intracoastal Waterway. Only a few live on the island, and these are the children of servants and other workers. The two schools share the same playing field, but the children never play together. The public school is a string magnet school with a fine orchestra that sometimes gives concerts at the Palm Beach Day School, but other than that, the two schools have no contact.

The Day School teachers are often excellent, and they try to teach the children about the world beyond Palm Beach, but it is difficult. Ten-year-olds have their hair colored and go in for weekly manicures and pedicures. The private school children learn how to judge another person by his clothes, his car, and his address. Many of them are brought up more by nannies than mothers, and only toddled out occasionally to be displayed to dinner guests like a new bibelot. Many of the children, especially those who are the children of divorce, have their own therapists with whom they discuss their problems.

They live on their own island of children within the island of Palm Beach. If things go according to plan, they go to prep school and then to the Ivy League, and from there perhaps to Wall Street. As long as they live in this pocket of privilege, they are smart and adept, but step across the bridge into what most people call America, and they are confronted with a world about which they know almost nothing.

The Seaview Courts have far more affinity with the public school than with the elite private academy. For two hundred dollars a year, a town resident can play every day on both the excellent clay courts and equally good courts at the Phipps Ocean Park Tennis Center in the South End. It is the best bargain in Palm Beach, but few who play at the restricted B&T or the Everglades would be seen here. The wealthiest islanders either play at their clubs or on their own private courts.

One afternoon Herb Gray and I were having a game at Seaview. Herb is one of the first people I met in Palm Beach, and he is one of my closest friends. He grew up a poor kid in the Dorchester ghetto of Boston, and in 1998 sold his medical supply company for $131 million, out of which he netted $20 million. He had parceled out stock to many employees, a number of whom became millionaires. He is a philanthropist whose gifts the *Palm Beach Daily News* never acknowledges, and that is the way he wants it. Herb is an art collector with a passionate interest in Boston Expressionists from the twenties. He volunteers twice a week as a pharmacist at Good Samaritan Hospital. His wife, Marylou, a nurse, volunteers as well, and when she is in their Boston home, she runs a weekly soup kitchen. Herb and Marylou do not go to charity balls. His name has almost never been in the Palm Beach paper, except when he won the town senior tennis championship. He lives within an almost totally Jewish social world, yet most of those in the haute Boston Jewish world on the island have no idea who he is.

After our match, Herb and I were having yet another of our intense conversations when Fred Keller pulled up on a rusty, decrepit bicycle. The man and machine were perfectly matched. Six-foot-two Keller wore putrid-colored, threadbare surfing shorts, a ratty T-shirt, a white bonnet, and grungy tennis shoes. The mismatched tennis balls he brought with him he had picked up on the tennis court on a previous outing. The beard that covered his angular, narrow face made him look like one of the siblings on the old Smith Brothers licorice cough drops box, albeit one with a gray beard.

There are a number of impecunious, marginal people who live in the creases and edges of Palm Beach, getting by in tiny cottages or efficiencies, driving bicycles and pretending that they do so by choice. I assumed that Keller was in that group, and since he was playing on the court directly in front of me, I watched him for a while.

One can tell a great deal about a person by the way he plays. From what I saw on that court, I assumed that this was a man who once stood high up in the world. He was in his sixties and was playing a powerful, determined game against an opponent half his age who turned out to be his brother-in-law Wolfgang Keil.

I asked my friend if he knew anything about Keller. Herb said he played against him, and I should play him too. Keller, it turned out, was hardly impecunious. He was a commercial real estate magnate worth tens of millions of dollars who lived in an estate on the Intracoastal Waterway in the North End. "He complains about his young wife a lot and how she nags him," Herb said. "But you know one day we were playing and these little kids from the Day School came marching by out to the play field, and old Fred just stopped playing and pointed out there and said, 'That's my Fredchen. He's my son. I love him so much. You have to come over and see this beautiful kid.' It was touching and kind of strange."

Few people living in Palm Beach go back as far in the area as Keller did. He arrived in West Palm Beach in 1957 with his first wife, Blanch, and his adopted son, Brian, from his wife's previous relationship.

Keller was born Fred Bohlander on Long Island in 1934, the only son in a family of German immigrants who believed in Aryan racial superiority. His carpenter father taught his only son that "we of northern European heritage have intellectual genetic advantages over other races . . . [and] that we Germans are superior to others." His people had come up with an efficient way of dealing with the mentally retarded by "culling the herd," but that would never be accepted in America. Fred got tired of the constant kvetching of the Jews about the Holocaust when no one talked about how *his* people had suffered, the firebombing of Dresden, the atrocities in Russia, where German soldiers were held prisoners years after the end of the war.

Fred envisioned himself as the noble patriarch of a Germanic family, with a loyal, obedient wife and a brood of strong, stalwart children, all of whom looked up to the patriarch with deference and respect. He had been working as a surveyor on the St. Lawrence Seaway in upstate New York for the Perini Corporation when he met his first wife. Blanch Witherell was a telephone operator and had a son, Brian, who had been born out of wedlock. She was a tall, healthy, Teutonic-looking woman. "I simply felt that Blanch was good breeding stock for a future family because I had these genetic notions that I was brought up with, and she had produced a son and was physically tall and well-proportioned," Fred wrote in his unpublished memoir.

Fred liked the fact that he would get a ready-built family. He and Blanch married and moved down to Florida, where he worked for the same company as an assistant project engineer. They lived in a little house in northern West Palm Beach.

Palm Beach residents think of West Palm Beach as their warehouse, a dispirited repository of hospitals, electronics emporiums, funeral homes, antiques stores, fast food, and everything too déclassé or ordinary for their refined precincts. That is an unfair judgment on a town that has its own fascinations, but just a few blocks east of the Intercoastal Waterway lie some of the most desperate slums in the nation. To those who stop their Rolls or Mercedes at the traffic lights a few blocks across Flagler Memorial Bridge, there is always a risk of a holdup; and those who for some bizarre reason turn left into the impoverished community might be stripped of their jewelry and money.

One evening Fred stood looking across the Intracoastal Waterway from his depressing quarters. It was only a few hundred yards to Palm Beach, but it might have been an ocean distant. Another man might have looked across with awe and wonder, accepting that there were those who live so far beyond what he could aspire to or even imagine. Someone else might have looked across at that same line of great homes with anger and dismay, asserting that one day the terrible unfairness of life would end. But Fred looked across, vowing that one day he too would live there. Palm Beach was the yardstick by which he would measure his life. To him the island was the ultimate symbol of success. Three decades later, he was not only living in Palm Beach, but in an estate at precisely the spot where he had gazed with such envy and longing.

Blanch gave birth to a son, Eric, in August 1958 in West Palm Beach. Fred, his wife, and the two children returned to Long Island, where another son, Paul, was born. As the marriage deteriorated, there were several breakups and reconciliations. Keller was a proud, vindictive man who found it unthinkable that his wife would want to leave him. Each time she walked out, he considered the child support and alimony payments nothing but the punitive ranting of an intemperate judge.

Again and again, Fred tried to haul Blanch back into their marriage. When she bailed, he rose up against his wife's assaults on *his* family. Fred considered religion little more than adult fairy tales. In one angry moment, he destroyed Blanch's crucifix, an attack not only on his wife, but on her faith and even on the idea of God. In February 1962, on Brian's birthday, Blanch reported that Fred "slapped me in the head, stating that it does not leave marks that way." That action led her to ask for a final divorce and move with the children to Parrishville in upstate New York, to live near her mother.

In June, Fred arrived in Parrishville in his Volkswagen Beetle to visit his boys. Keller had run off with the sons once before, and Blanch refused his request to take the three boys alone. Blanch got into the little car with their sons, and the reconstituted Bohlander family drove to the remote rural Barnhart Island Park adjacent to the St. Lawrence Seaway, on which Fred had once worked. After an afternoon romping in the park, Fred suggested that his two older sons race him to the car. When Brian and Eric were safely ensconced in the backseat and Blanch was putting little Paul in the car, Fred pressed on the accelerator and sped away, leaving his ex-wife alone in the dusk, miles from any help.

With the secret assistance of his parents, Fred flew with the three boys to Germany, where he lived for a number of months before moving to Spain. The little group eventually settled outside Washington, D.C., in the Virginia suburbs.

Brian was the only son old enough to have vivid memories of those years, and they began with his starkly painful recollections of the boys crying in the backseat of the car, wrenched away from their mother, and forced into a new, unknowable world. Fred told his sons that their mother had died in an automobile accident. Even their name was gone—they were no longer "Bohlanders," but now were "Kellers."

Fred had no recollections of the sons feeling distraught, and felt that he was right to take the boys. "I was going to lose my kids, and Blanch was an alcoholic," Fred said. "I could not see my kids growing up in a backwoods area where hunting and logging were the big events. I wanted my kids to have more. Extraordinary circumstances require extraordinary actions. These are boys. Fathers are better bringing up boys. What choice did I have?"

Fred's parents sold their home on Long Island and moved down to Arlington to live with their son and help bring up the grandchildren. Fred lied about his education to get a good job as an engineer. He began buying cheap properties, the start of his real estate fortune. Brian was not Fred's biological son, and he treated him unlike his other sons. The boy was deeply troubled, and his stepfather eventually gave him up to a foster home. It was there that Brian's memories led to his mother. Although Fred caricatured her as little more than a pathetic alcoholic, for eight years she had been on her own single-minded pursuit for her children. She had written hundreds of letters, won thousand of dollars on two television game shows, and used the money to pay for lawyers and investigators. By the time she found her sons, Blanch was a broken woman with few financial or emotional resources, and Fred was able to pay her off with a few thousand dollars and have her leave only with Brian. All he sought were his two biological sons.

In the rapidly developing suburbs, Fred was a merciless businessman. He told with relish the story of how one day in the *Washington Post* he saw an ad in the classified section for a commercial property for sale for five hundred thousand dollars. The old lady selling the property was clueless, and as soon as Fred bought it, he flipped it for ten times that amount. In one of his apartment houses, the tenants would not leave. He had the front doors torn off and the toilets pulled out.

Brian told me how his adopted father bought a mansion and moved in, using the grand setting as a prop to sell used cars. He purchased old cars for next to nothing. One of his tenants, who ran a garage, turned the odometers back and fixed the vehicles up just enough so they would run for few miles. Fred then sold them through classified ads in the *Washington Post* as a rich man's personal once-owned vehicles. Maybe it was not big money, but he thought it was hilarious when the purchasers came back knocking on his door when their car stopped a few miles down the road.

When Fred started coming down to Palm Beach again in 1966, he was remarried, living in a modest rented house in the center of town, and buying commercial properties. When he returned to live full-time in 1984, he was newly divorced and ready for what he considered the life of a Palm Beach millionaire.

Like so many people, when Fred arrived on the island, he jettisoned his past, stripping his life of anything unseemly and unpleasant. By then he had been married four times, but he never talked of that, and especially not of the circumstances of his first marriage.

His two sons grew to be tall like their father, each over six and a half feet tall. They had the brains and the education that could have taken them anywhere. But Eric got involved in drugs and alcohol when he was in high school, and after dropping out of college a few credits before finishing his degree, had made a disaster of his life. Married and divorced twice by the time he was thirty, Eric hardly saw his two kids from his second failed marriage. It was sad, but it wasn't Fred's fault.

The same was true with Eric's younger brother. Paul worked for his dad for close to a decade. Then, against his father's wishes, Paul ordered an expensive fishing chair for Fred's seventy-one-foot Hatteras yacht. Nobody pulled a stunt like that on Fred, particularly since this act was in essence Paul's asserting his own independence. Fred ended up suing Paul to get back properties he had placed in his son's name. It broke his relationship with his son. It was sad, but it wasn't Fred's fault.

IT WAS ONLY YEARS later that I got to know Fred and saw how totally I had misread him on the tennis courts. He was disdainful of the Palm Beach world and said that he only lived there because it was safe and beautiful, a rich man's haven. He remained, however, an exaggerated version of a type of man common on the island.

Fred believed in only one God, and that God was himself. He had no use for what most people called morality, the pathetic homilies around which most men attempt to build their lives. Everyone who surrounded him was in his service: wives, women, his sons, employees. Most of them hungered for the one thing he could not give: his love. He treated them well enough as long as they did not try to subvert his sovereignty, but if they dared to attempt to circumvent him, he struck them down.

It was as if the part of Keller's brain governing moral concerns had been lobotomized. He laughed at the absurd conventions by which supposedly good people tried to live, and how they wiggled and twisted to adhere to some silly list of rules devised by priests or philosophers.

If Keller needed further proof that he was correct in his disdainful view of humanity, he could have pointed out that he played the same tricks again and again because there was an endlessly gullible audience unable to catch his sleight of hand. And each time his gambits worked, it only reinforced his belief that what most people called trust and morality was only the most pathetic credulity. It was a world of dupes out there, and he was going to play them, exploiting their naiveté and stupidity.

You can embellish it with all your pretty words, perfume it anyway you like, dress it up in gowns and jewels, but Palm Beach is a marketplace of flesh. Every man and every woman has his or her value, and the game is to trade up as best you can. Keller understood that as well as anyone. He was a shrewd businessman, whether it was commercial properties or women who took his fancy. He was as brazen and bold in asserting his own value as a man could be. He met nearly all the women in his life through personal ads in various magazines and newspapers, which stated that he was a millionaire—and now a Palm Beach millionaire—seeking young women no older than thirty who were tall, well built, and pretty ("Palm Beach Millionaire seeks slim, attractive playmate to share a lifestyle of the rich and famous"). As he saw it, it wasn't a bad trade-off. He had the money, they had the youth and the bodies he liked, and anyone who replied understood the deal.

Fred had the cynical view of women and their mercenary ways common among many men in Palm Beach, views that were borne out by the women who approached, drawn by the lure of luxury. Thus it troubled him not in the least that had he crossed the words *Palm Beach* and *millionaire* out of his ads, his mailbox would have been empty. He did not worry about them lining up like gold prospectors in front of a rich new vein. He wanted women who appreciated and deferred to his wealth. What he also got were young women with a lack of self-worth and terrible vulnerability.

Keller approached women the way he did commercial property, looking at the comparables, checking out every inch of the asset before making his first low bid. When they were local women, he arranged for blind dates three or four at a time, and had them meet him in different rooms at the enormous Breakers Hotel. That way he could peruse them first, and meet only the one who was the most attractive.

On one of the sheets that he used for keeping track of possible lovers, Fred listed thirty-two women who had contacted him, many of them through his ads in *USA Today*. They came from as far away as Pennsylvania and Massachusetts, and he did considerable investigation before he invited them to Palm Beach for a visit. Most of them were in their mid-twenties, but they ranged in age from a twenty-year-old to a forty-five-year-old. They had given him their heights and weights and almost all were tall and thin. Only twenty-year-old Heidi had given her bra size, 34C. A D cup would have been better, Fred acknowledged, but it was hardly a deal breaker.

Keller liked one of the women he invited down so much that he asked her to live with him. Her name was Shari, and she flew back to Silver Spring, Maryland, quit her job, and hired a moving company for $1,100 to ship her furniture and other belongings to South Florida. Shari was ecstatic at her change in fortune. She went out and bought expensive new clothes to look great for her Palm Beach millionaire. Then, just as Shari was preparing to fly down to West Palm Beach, Fred called and said that he had met another woman, Fran, and he was going to live with her instead.

"I am hoping that you will take part of the responsibility for my financial ruin," Shari wrote him. "I am one step away from filing for welfare. I have exactly $74.92 left to my name, without a job, and no place I can go. Please Fred, can you find it in your heart to help me out financially, because had it not been for your decision, I would not be in this awful mess. Please, Fred, help me."

But Fred was on to his life with Fran, and he could not be bothered with the past. Fran did not last either, and afterward he flew in a woman named Pene Latham, whom he had met in Texas, and who wound up moving in with Fred. He was in his late fifties and Pene was in her mid-thirties, and that was a problem because he had never dated anyone so old. She was more intelligent than many of his previous women with a wry wit and painful sensitivity. She left him once and when she returned, Fred suggested that they play a joke on his masseuse. He took out his pistol and pointedly seemed to remove all the bullets. He handed Pene the gun and said that when the masseuse arrived, she should come bursting in through the door pointing the gun at him, shouting, "You're not ever going to leave me or treat me badly again!"

It didn't feel right, and Pene gave him back the gun. He turned around and fired a bullet into the wall. Only several days afterward did it occur to her that if she had gone along with his joke, Fred would have claimed that she was serious, and when the police came, nobody would have believed her.

When Pene was about to turn thirty-five, Fred put an ad in the newspaper. "I've never been with anyone over thirty-five, and I'm not going to start with you," he told her. He soon had somebody new, a blonde in her early twenties. Fred liked young, statuesque women with large breasts and thin waists. If they did not fully meet his standards, he would get rid of them or retrofit them with breast implants. If he could have done it, he would have engineered his perfect woman, taking the breasts of one, the waist of another, the hips of a third, filling out the various body parts before he added a geisha-like personality.

The blonde was perfect except that her breasts were too small. He told her he would pay the four thousand dollars for the implants, but he wanted her to sign a note so he could take it off on his taxes as a bad debt. When he soon grew tired of her and asked her to leave, he sued her for the money—and moved on to somebody new.

The results from the ads in *USA Today* had started thinning out, and Fred had one of his relatives in Germany place an ad in a newspaper there, hoping to find some worthwhile prospects in his parents' homeland. Fred did the best he could do to winnow out the undesirables, but it was hard. The first woman who arrived at Miami International Airport was a biochemist. She was nice but a little plump, so he sent her packing. Then there had been a young dental hygienist who wanted to stay, but she cried constantly and was depressed and homesick. That would not do either. Fred had talked to the third prospect for hours on the phone. He had seen her photo, and he thought she might be the best of the lot. Her name was Rosemarie "Rose" Keil, and she said that she worked as a model. She was in her early twenties, from the small town of Dorlar, near Düsseldorf in northwestern Germany.

Although Rose had Fred's picture in her hand, when she walked into the international arrivals lounge at Miami International Airport, she sailed right past him and out the door to see if her patron was waiting at the curb. Fred told his chauffeur that they should wait and see what she did. Fred studiously observed Rose, concluding that she was the best looking of the German women, with the obligatory thin waist and ample breasts. She was tall and had a fresh, youthful attractiveness. She had paper-thin lips, a long, aquiline nose, small eyes that angled slightly downward, and a quiet, intense voice.

Only after he had checked her as best he could did he follow her out the door and touch her on the arm. "Are you waiting for someone?" he asked in German.

Fred was aggressive in his pursuit of women, but once he met them, he could be chivalrous to the extreme, not caring if it took days before the woman chose to sleep with him. It was an immensely shrewd gesture, for along with his understated demeanor, initially he came across as a man of utmost graciousness. In this instance, Fred did not have to wait long, for he told me that very evening Rose spent the night with him in the master bedroom in his Palm Beach home. His newest paramour—not unwitting in her own right—had her own agenda.

4

Illusion of Sex

The illusion of sex has always been the most useful commodity to trade in Palm Beach, but those who seem most obviously to be trafficking in it are shunned. When I arrived in Palm Beach, Eddy Louis was married to Vera Lukin, thirty-one years his senior. He was highly controversial. Even the police treated him like an undesirable, stopping his car for the most minor of matters, making it clear that he was not welcome. "The people in Palm Beach look at the externals, and nobody took the time to get to know me," he says. "They see the old masters that I paint or hear me on the Steinway. They don't believe it. I'm a genius, a successful entrepreneur, and a decent honest man. And all these bastards think it's my good looks and I'm nothing but a slut or gigolo."

When I played doubles with Eddy the first time at the Breakers, I had already heard the rumors that he had been a Moroccan waiter in Paris and had paid his way to Palm Beach with money gained from living off one woman after another. Eddy was a tall, handsome, swarthy man of strutting sexuality. He had a heavy, vague accent, and small, round eyes that darted back and forth even as he sat Buddha-like. He was naturally dark, but spent so much time sunning himself that his skin was the color of a well-done steak.

He wore old-fashioned short tennis shorts and a shirt so tight it fit like a bodysuit. Eddy was obsessed with cleanliness, and his body was sleek and hairless. He had impeccable manners until he lost his temper, and then he erupted in a mindless stream of invective in one of half a dozen languages.

Eddy was also an elegant tennis player. Although he was competitive, he appeared more concerned about his perfect technique than winning. This day, he and his partner, Joseph Idy, a French-American who was Eddy's friend and stockbroker, were giving my partner and me a battle. Idy liked to lob. Time and time again, he sent the ball high up, landing at the deepest part of the court. After an endless barrage of these missiles, Idy sent the ball above the level of the palm trees before it dropped, falling just outside the back line, giving us the game.

"Out!" I yelled with definitive pleasure. Eddy let forth a stream of French invective, accusing me of cheating on the line call. He spoke in gutter argot that I had not heard since I was a student in France, and that I'm sure he thought I couldn't understand.

Eddy's French accent is impeccable, but I knew what would set him off. "*Mon vieux*," I shouted back. "*Je parle Français aussi, mais moi, je le parle comme un français de France.*" (I speak French too, my friend, but I speak it like a Frenchman from France.)

I had hardly finished my sentence before Eddy charged. He was about to jump over the net and start punching me, when his partner held him back. Neither of us were pugilists, and we doubtlessly would have flailed away relatively harmlessly, but it would have made for a memorable morning at the Breakers.

Eddy was the scion of a well-to-do Lebanese Maronite Christian family, and had been brought up on an estate in Mount Lebanon above the Mediterranean Sea. The family built major construction projects, and his father insisted that his son attend USC to study engineering. After graduation in 1967, he got rid of his Arabic family name and changed it to the French-like "Louis." When he returned to Beirut he had a soupçon of French culture, some traditional Arab ways, and American brashness. He fancied that he would be a citizen of the world, but he discovered that the world is not one place, but an endless series of enclaves, in none of which he felt fully at home. In Lebanon, he no longer could abide the hoary traditions of his family. In Beirut, his father raged at his son's excesses. In the end, he threw Eddy out and sent him away with a tiny Fiat 125 convertible and a few Lebanese dollars. By the time Eddy arrived in Paris, he was broke. He found meals in restaurant garbage cans and slept in his Fiat. He had grown his hair down to his shoulders. He looked like an American hippie, and he began singing for coins on the street corner.

It was a long, twisted journey that led him from there to developing squash clubs in France, becoming part of the glittery world of European jet setters, and from there to life in the North End of Palm Beach married to a German heiress. He had left that relationship with nothing except Desirée, a daughter he had fathered with a surrogate mother. Although Eddy came from a wealthy family and said that he had access to their money for any of his projects, he appeared to have only modest means, and escorted elderly widows to balls and parties, where he attempted to sell investments. He was not a licensed broker; in essence, he was steering them to those who were, and getting a fee for doing so.

These rich old ladies wanted male companionship. As a single, heterosexual male, Eddy was a more valuable commodity than one of the gay "walkers." The term is a mildly derogatory one generally affixed to gay men escorting elderly ladies, though it equally applies to a motley array of heterosexual cops, auctioneers, real estate agents, and ageless adrogynes. Although the category can include practically any man owning a dinner jacket, it is largely a gay avocation. Palm Beach is nearly as gay as San Francisco, but until the mid-nineties, except for a few dress designers and gallery owners, nearly everyone stayed in the closet, a conspiracy of silence that allowed the social system to go on unchanged for decades.

Eddy wasn't gay and if he was going out with an elderly lady, he wanted to be paid in stronger currency. What was it to a wealthy lady to throw some of her money to an investment suggested by this charming gentleman?

Palm Beach counts only in twos; to be alone is social death. When Eddy met Vera Lukin, her husband had recently died in 1990. She was seventy-nine years old, doomed to join the widows escorted by gays or middle-aged stockbrokers and real estate agents, who used the occasions to press their business cards into reluctant hands. Vera could have entered their ample ranks, but that was an admission that all that she lived and loved for was over.

When Vera started dating Eddy, her sons and friends thought that she had reached an unspeakable nadir. Despite what people said, Eddy had not scooped Vera up like a treasure stumbled upon on the beach. She had wooed him, and exuding her youthful gaiety and joy, brought him closer and closer.

Eddy's greatest strength and his greatest weakness is the same quality: an immense, unfettered pride. Before the couple moved in together in Vera's house, he signed a precohabitation agreement separating their assets. That way no one could accuse him of pursuing Vera for her money.

When the couple married, Vera had everything that most women on the island desired. She had a spectacular far younger husband. She had a mansion on the Intracoastal Waterway left to her by her late husband. She had a maid, a Rolls-Royce, exquisite silver and china, and a living room so full of fine old furniture that it looked more like an antiques store than a place of habitation. She owned expensive jewelry and had enough money to attend the most fashionable balls. And she now had something else that no woman of her generation had, an adorable little child: Desirée. Although Vera did not adopt Eddy's daughter, she mothered Desirée with tenderness, teaching the girl the rudiments of manners and grace.

Vera's greatest expense was keeping up the house. Eddy saved her thousands of dollars each year by acting as a general handyman. In the damp heat of the island, the one thing that lived and thrived naturally was the jungle vegetation. Everything else rusted and rotted, steel oxidized, and wood became plagued with termites and decay.

. . .

I ALSO MET THE six-foot-two Eric Purcell on the tennis courts at the Breakers. Eric was living with a married woman, but nobody thought badly of him, and he was accepted in circles where Eddy would not have been welcome. "I wasn't really a gigolo because that isn't my style," he says. "But I was sort of in the role of it. I was trying to have fun with it, and in some ways I did."

Eric was a few years younger than Eddy and was a strong, defensive player who kept the ball in play forever until his opponent made a mistake. Like Eddy, whom he idolized, Eric was also handsome, but fair-haired, with a dapper manner and looks that exuded a sense of superiority and perhaps even a touch of cruelty when he smiled. He walked onto the courts with such authority that few would have guessed that he was not a member and had scarcely a dollar to his name.

Eric was a formidable opponent, an intriguing conversationalist off the court, and we became friends. Eric was a natural-born actor, even if he rarely performed on stage. And, like so many actors, he was introverted, though no one would have guessed it.

His thespian skills came naturally enough from his mother, Monique van Vooren, a gorgeously flamboyant actress whose major creation was herself. The Belgian-born siren with the celebrated forty-inch bust was pregnant with Eric in 1953 when she was acting in what proved to be her biggest part, playing half the title role in *Tarzan and the She-Devil* alongside Lex Barker. The role was hardly autobiographical, but Monique had a she-devil quality, a wanton sexuality that glowed overly brightly, and an obsession with stunning clothes and jewels.

If it is a curse to be the son of a famous man, it may be more of a curse to be the son of a sensuous celebrity mother seeking from each man who passes a tribute to her youthful beauty. It was impossible that a woman seemingly so young, with such an awesome figure, could have a growing child, so Monique had Eric knock a few years off his age. For a while it worked, but even Eric was not good enough an actor to convince people he was five when he was pushing ten, and at that age his mother shipped him off to school.

Eric lived an itinerant, lonely life, at one point sleeping in a makeshift bedroom in the back of Monique's latest husband's office in Manhattan. In the winters during school vacations, Monique took her son down to Palm Beach, where they stayed at the Colony Hotel or with acquaintances. As a teenager, Eric was thrown out of some of the better schools in America before finishing at the Peddie School in New Jersey.

Eric was not a good student, but he could be articulate and convincing. He went down to Washington, and in his application interview for admission to Catholic Georgetown University, played the religious gentleman of impeccable morals and the highest intellectual pursuits. Once admitted, he stopped playing that role. It would have been a stretch with a mother who during Eric's Georgetown years played the nymphomaniac Baroness Katrin Frankenstein in Andy Warhol's X-rated *Frankenstein*, a film subsequently released with the more realistic title *Flesh for Frankenstein*.

Eric became one of the leading actors in college productions. Celebrity is at its most intense in the tiniest of quarters, attested to in Palm Beach by those who think they are immortal because their picture appears in the Shiny Sheet. To be a stage star in college is celebrity of the highest order. In one production, Eric met one of the most desirable, most pursued of the coeds, Deborah Gore Dean, and fell obsessively in love.

Eric lusted after Dean's life of wealth as much as he did her body, and he could hardly separate the two. Her grandfather owned Washington's elegant Fairfax Hotel. She had been brought up at Marwood, a thirty-three-room mansion outside Washington. "It's a big mistake not to allow boys to have experience with women until they're eighteen, because a woman gets hold of them and sucks every ounce of innocence out of them," Eric reflects, the wound still festering even decades later. "This was my seduction the summer of my sophomore year in college at the Gore estate in Potomac, Maryland. At that age, you can't get enough of it. I was addicted to her. They owned the Sea Catch and the Jockey Club Restaurant. She had her own room in the Fairfax Hotel, and she was spoiled beyond belief."

After two and a half years Dean dropped Eric. He could not forget her. She haunted him, and he couldn't get over the life of luxury and privilege he would have had with her. In some ways, the rest of his life became little but an endless coda, one ineffectual attempt after another to replicate what he lost forever.

Eric was an emotional orphan. Although his last name was Purcell, his mother's husband had never adopted him. In college, he learned that his real father was David McConnell, an heir to the Avon fortune, and part owner of the Colony Hotel in Palm Beach and the then Boston Patriots football team. Far from being devastated by the news, Eric thought his patrimony might prove a blessing. He met his father in New York City, and fully expected that McConnell would give him a few hundred thousand dollars as a graduation present to send his secret son out into the world in style.

McConnell sent him nothing, and Eric took his last dollars and flew down to Palm Beach to talk to his father. The Colony sits just south of Worth Avenue, a block from the ocean. The three penthouses, the Embassy, the Presidential, and the Vice Regal, have housed everyone from the Windsors to presidents and in the mid-seventies, the boutique hotel was the apogee of deluxe accommodations.

Eric checked in, and assuming that McConnell would both pay and acknowledge his son, started living the life of the spoiled scion. However, McConnell was married for the umpteenth time, and had five daughters. He was not about to admit dipping his wick where it should not have gone.

If Eric had been a jewelry thief, he would have gone for the easily pilfered cheap items in the front cases, rather than trying to open the safe. He did not play his father for the big money, but settled for ripping him off in piddling ways, bringing women he met at the pool up to his room and impressing them by calling room service, eating at the chic Pool Room Restaurant, and buying drinks all around and putting them on his tab.

Eric was playing a cameo role as his father, a self-indulgent heir who did pretty much what he wanted to do. Although Eric's father was technically an investment banker, in actuality he was a man who, while not flying loop-de-loops in his own plane, divided his time between his two other great pleasures, Johnny Walker Scotch and Lark cigarettes. He was also used to having others handle unpleasant business for him. After a month of Eric's living at the hotel and showing no sign of leaving, McConnell was faced with removing him. He gave the job to one of his minions, who struck a deal with Eric to get him to leave. Eric settled cheaply, heading out of the Colony with three thousand dollars of McConnell's money.

The next decade and a half reads like a scrapbook in which the pictures have gotten hopelessly jumbled. There is no beginning, no middle, no end, and no logical progression. He was married for a while in L.A. and had two children, but that did not last and he was soon gone. He did some acting, most notably playing the young Orson Welles in a TV movie. He had a hustler's way with people. Wherever he was, he was selling something: investments in New York, barter exchange in Tucson, sales leads for computers in L.A., elevator advertising in Hawaii, and cars and elevator advertising in Australia.

Eric's elevator advertising business was up and running in Australia, but he only had a visitor's visa, and when he had to leave, he sold the company and flew to Miami. He did not know anybody, but he figured it was a good place to restart his business. He was soon out selling ads and getting them placed in elevators. And he started acting again, as he did wherever he was.

Eric had his ex-wife on his back for past child support payments, as well as collection letters from the IRS. When he went out, he could not pick up checks. At forty-one, Eric was older than most of the people in the clubs, but he cut a fine figure in South Beach. He had an actor's patina, and he could pretend to be an imposing, substantive character strutting along Ocean Drive.

Eric liked women who were exotic and had a touch of the forbidden to them. One evening in February 1995, at the News Café in South Beach, he met thirty-four-year-old Maria Garcia Medina, an Argentinean woman visiting from San Francisco. She was not only darkly beauteous, but had a lean, sophisticated model's look. He knew as little about her as she knew about him, but it hardly mattered, and within a few days Medina quit her accountant's job in California and moved in with him in Miami.

Eric said later that he had been "without passion for a long time," and for a while things went well, but Medina was not what he thought she was, and neither was he. After the couple had been living together less than four months, Eric returned to their apartment at about ten o'clock in the evening.

Eric had been drinking. Maria was sitting on the bed when Eric came in and asked her if she wanted to make love. That was hardly what she was thinking about.

"We should talk," he said, a strange shift from his suggestion of sex. "What do you think we should do?"

It was a question consuming both of them. "I think I should find my own apartment," Maria said, and told him she would be staying until the end of the month.

People were always leaving Eric. It was unthinkable that this should be happening to him again, and he reached toward Maria. And when he was finished she was bleeding and she was hurt. She had bruises on her legs, and worst of all, her left eye appeared as if it had been physically moved up her face, her two eyes no longer on quite the same plane.

"Well, actually, I did, if the truth must be known, I may have hit her a little bit in the closet or something, I kind of lost it, you know," Eric says. "But I never ever would be so stupid as to hit a woman in the face. I mean, I was married for five years. I used to get mad. I would never do that. That's suicide. I did not hit her in the face that caused that injury."

The police arrested Eric for assault, battery, and kidnapping, and he spent the night in jail. Maria spent the night in the hospital. She was diagnosed as having an orbital fracture that even after an operation would leave her in some measure permanently disfigured.

Eric had no money for the first-rate criminal defense attorney that he needed, and his mother refused to help him. He settled for an old prep school friend who took the case for nothing. Eric declared himself insolvent, stating that he earned $200 to $250 a week and had no property and no cash, and the court paid his lawyer's expenses. The case went on for month after month. He could have pled out and avoided prison time by accepting a guilty verdict to a major felony and paying restitution, but he could not have a felony on his record and Maria going after him in a civil suit. In addition to this, his problems with the IRS and child support made it seem as if his life was crumbling.

Palm Beach was only sixty miles to the north, a haven protected from this unseemly Miami world that had so abused him. That was his father's world, a world of luxury and privilege where he belonged, not in the vulgar, mean streets of Miami. He had no way to get there, but he was an actor and there would be a role somewhere to take him where he belonged.

5

Hope Is Not a Diamond

I had only been in Palm Beach a few months when I was invited to a cocktail party given by Mildred "Brownie" McLean in the party room at Trump Plaza, a twin-tiered condominium looking out on the Intracoastal Waterway from West Palm Beach.

The guests were an eclectic group; everyone from leading socialites, members of the old establishment, and an intriguing group of artists, PR people, antiques dealers, and interior decorators. The victuals included mini sandwiches and vegetable trays from Publix, and jug wine that also came from the local supermarket. There was only one aging bartender for the large crowd, a nearsighted man who is a fixture at Palm Beach parties.

Brownie came sweeping up to me, her words cascading into each other, and started introducing me around as an author, using superlatives that would have made Tolstoy blush. Brownie kept her age as secret as a nuclear code, but by the time I met her, she was almost seventy. Yet, there were still vestiges of the youthful blonde not only admired for her beauty, but loved for her joyous spirit. In his book *Ball*, William Wright wrote about Brownie in the early 1970s, when she was putting on the celebrated "April in Paris" ball in New York City, "people—and many of them the *right* people—don't just like her, they adore her." The author described

Brownie in her heavy black eye makeup contrasted against her white blond hair as looking like "an albino raccoon." She wore pronounced makeup so that her appearance would be unmistakable, but if she looked like an animal, it was more a Cheshire cat.

In her public mode, Brownie has a subtle, pleasurable demeanor, as if she had just heard a joke intelligible only to her. She allows herself to be gently petted, but never deeply touched. Champagne is her water. There are some who assume that this woman is a silly Pollyanna so self-absorbed and nonobservant that she notices nothing around her, but the opposite is true. If her catlike eyes cannot quite see through walls, they see to the heart and soul of any matter that affects her.

Brownie has rarely found a party she did not like. She is a philosopher of frivolity. She finds wit where others hear only dullness, amusement where others experience largely tedium.

The worst she ever says about anyone is, "I do not know her," and that was what she said about Barbara Wainscott. The comment could be taken either as a bald statement of fact, or brutally dismissive, and she usually prefers to leave the matter ambiguous. In Barbara's case, she had known her since the sixties, and her meaning was clearly the latter.

Brownie is a legendary figure, not only in Palm Beach, but in the haute world of New York and Europe. Wherever she goes, from Claridge's or Ascot in England, to the Ritz in Paris, people greet her with delight. Her life on the island goes back to the most glorious days of the fifties, and she evokes that era the way nobody else does.

Brownie has been married to two wealthy heirs, first George Schrafft, whom she divorced, and then the ultrawealthy John "Jock" McLean II, who left her a widow. By rights, she should have inherited a fortune. The rumor I heard was that she had been terribly profligate and had fallen on hard times. Living in West Palm Beach and repaying her social obligations in a cocktail party was déclassé enough, but she was not through falling. Within a few years, she had to sell her condo and move into a tiny apartment near the Intracoastal Waterway. She laughed as gaily as the first time she had visited Palm Beach, kept her troubles deeply within herself, and lived much as she had always lived, driving onto the island each evening for parties.

Palm Beach society forgets those who are sick and dying, and turns its back on those who have lost their money. Brownie should quickly have been shuttled aside, her name taken off the invitation lists, her picture gone from the Shiny Sheet. She remained, however, a ubiquitous presence at many prestigious events. The Coconuts is the most exclusive New Year's Eve party, and even today Brownie is the only invitee who can arrive with her ever-changing entourage and enter the celebration en masse.

Of course, there are some people who feel that Brownie can no longer help their social advance, and they sidle around her. Brownie's presence is no longer the imprimatur it once had been, and Barbara Wainscott was not alone in ignoring her. She is not invited to events where once her name would have headed the list, and although some refer to her as the dowager queen of Palm Beach, she is now a queen ignored by many of her subjects.

When my wife was away, word got out that there was an extra single male available. The phone would ring, and out I would go, spiffed up in black tie or a suit. I thought it would be fun, but I was a social eunuch who charmed to the left, charmed to the right, and went home alone. And there was a gruesome similarity to the events, a rote quality to the conversation, a stilted pattern to the evening, a quick and early exit

It was different when I went out with Brownie. Evening for her did not begin until the stars were rising in the heavens, and it did not end until she decided that it ended. She never had a bad time, and if you were with her, you never had one either. It was clear from what she said that the parties in her early years on the island had been far more exciting. People gave more, and they got more too, and Brownie was the very model of an exemplary hostess. She is not a woman of great intellectual depth or interests, and I might once have found her concerns trivial. But this is a superficial society given over to pleasure and amusements, and she reigns over it as does no one else.

One evening Brownie and I drove over to the Colony, where her old friend Carolyn Skelly had taken a penthouse. The oil heiress was a tiny woman with a grotesque scar that covered half her face. There were all kinds of rumors about how she been so disfigured, but it seemed like a perfect metaphor for her tragic life. People were always using her. They stole her jewels. They ate her food. They drank her liquor. They flattered her to her face and defamed her behind her back. She knew it; she let it happen, but she did nothing to circumvent her detractors.

There must have been four or five of us in Brownie's group the evening at the Colony penthouse, and when we came bursting in, the party began. Suddenly there was joy and much laughter. That was Brownie's way. She lived and died for parties, for endlessly amusing nights, and she never pretended to be anything but what she was.

Palm Beach is full of women who come from nowhere, and by marrying wealthy men, rise to the heights of what is called society. Unlike men on the island who talk in excruciating detail about how they made their fortunes, these women do not discuss the mechanics of their success. Brownie almost never talks about her earliest years, but it is not because she is ashamed of her background or her means of ascent, but because those days are reservoirs of pain.

When she was a young girl, Mildred Brownie Brown rode her horse bareback on trails in the foothills of the Allegheny Mountains of Virginia. She was a willful, determined tomboy who took no guff from anyone. Her spoiled, comely young mother died when Brownie had hardly reached the age of memory, burned to death in bed smoking a cigarette while reading. Her father was the measure of all things, both father and mother to his daughter and younger son.

Brownie's pony was an unruly beast with a temperament unfit

to be the plaything of an eight-year-old girl. The pony took no greater pleasure than throwing Brownie off its back, and when she got back on, throwing her off again.

One day Brownie walked into the barn with the firm intention of killing the pony. She jumped up above the stall and began poking at the terrified animal with a pitchfork. The pony kicked and snorted as it backed away, raising such a ruckus that a farmhand ran to the main house to fetch Brownie's father.

"Now, what's the matter, old girl?" Brownie's father said. "Can't you handle this without trying to hurt the pony? Can't you get even with it? Can't you get mad and not try to kill it?"

"But it's such a mean little animal," Brownie said, looking up at her father.

Her father looked down at Brownie and then spoke as if imparting some secret wisdom to his daughter. "Leave it alone, and it'll kill itself."

When the pony wasn't throwing Brownie, it was biting at the other horses. A few weeks later, the other animals kicked at the pony, driving it into a ravine, where it died. Sometimes the tiniest, seemingly most inconsequential moments in a person's life are the most profound, resonating forever, and her father had given her one of the essential lessons of her life. Fate took care of itself; one only had to stand aside and wait.

When she was a tall, vibrant twelve-year-old on the verge of womanhood, Brownie's father died in a farm accident, and Brownie was alone. There was not enough money for both her younger brother and Brownie to go to school and to have someone take care of them. So thirteen-year-old Brownie said that she was of age. Claiming to be twenty-one, Brownie went to work at the West Virginia Pulp and Paper Company as a page girl taking messages around the office.

"I was a big girl, and I was smart, strong, rough, and tough," Brownie recalls. "I'm a likeable soul because I'm not arrogant, demanding, or commanding. And they all loved me in that company. They sort of protected me because I was a little kid, you know. And I was cute, I guess, I had no idea what I looked like."

Brownie had a friend who dreamed of becoming a showgirl on Broadway, and the two sixteen-year-olds headed off to New York in 1943, fresh innocent young women arriving in the great, amoral city.

New York was the biggest, brashest city in the world. For a young woman of no education or background, there was the possibility in those years to marry a rich man that there never was before, and most likely never would be again.

Most single women from unprivileged backgrounds had neither the desire nor the audacity to attempt to connect with men of wealth and privilege. Those of a certain intellectual inclination headed down to the bohemian world of Greenwich Village. Others of a religious mind-set made their church the center of their lives. Then there were those like Brownie who were savvy, pretty, ambitious, shrewd, and socially daring enough to become part of a garish, flamboyant café society where they could meet socially elite men. Any number of Palm Beach society ladies had their genesis in this world.

When these wealthy young men went on their nightly rounds in the immediate postwar years, they sauntered into the back room at 21 for dinner before moving on to the Cub Room at the Stork Club, or to the other celebrated nightclub, El Morocco. And all these places were full of young, wildly attractive women. The men thought they were the hunters, but in actuality they were the prey.

Sherman Billingsley, the Stork Club's owner and impresario, admitted only those young women with enough class or beauty to add to his sparkling, nocturnal fusion. Brownie made her way there, often with her friend from Virginia. "She and I were popular because we were young, fresh, and I guess we were pretty enough," Brownie reflects. "We looked innocent enough where they'd say, 'We'll take advantage of those two chickens,' but they didn't do it." She and her girlfriend tipped the doorman in their apartment house five dollars a month to tell their escorts that they could not go upstairs, the most efficacious way to say no. That was the way she liked to do things, never raising her voice, never making a scene, but always waltzing away from trouble.

Brownie pieced together a living as best she could, doing some modeling and working for a while as a hat check girl. The wealthy young heirs Brownie was dating came from old money families that lived by the axiom: "A lady should see her name in the papers only three times in her life, when's she engaged, when she marries, and when she dies." Yet the old aristocratic imperatives were giving way to a "celebritocracy," the gossip columnists taking the place of the Social Register. Ambitious young women read gossip columnists such as Cholly Knickerbocker and Ed Sullivan to learn the players and the places.

One evening Brownie attended the tennis matches at Forest Hills with the mysterious Howard Hughes. All during the event, she kept looking down at his dirty tennis shoes and wondering why she had agreed to the date. Things changed for Brownie in the morning when she picked up the *Daily Mirror* and read in Walter Winchell's column: "Mildred 'Brownie' Brown, Virginia socialite, at Open with Howard Hughes." Winchell's column had the staccato rhythm of a telegram, and it affected people like a telegraph boy shouting the message throughout Manhattan. Now she had become just what Winchell said she was, a Virginia socialite frequenting the elite clubs of the city.

In a matter of a few years, Brownie transformed herself into an elegant, upbeat woman whom wealthy men found irresistible. To do so, she had to employ immense mimicry based on the most astute observations of the habits, manners, and mores of a whole new class of people. It took subtle empathy, and a faux intimacy, always reserving something of herself. She had always to pretend that she was something she was not or never had been. She could never drop the veil of illusion, until one day the veil became a virtual part of her skin.

In 1948, Brownie married George Schrafft, heir to a popular chain of restaurants frequented by secretaries and shop girls. The twenty-seven-year-old playboy was dependent on the erratic largesse of his mother, who wanted her son to do something other than race speed boats and fast cars. He had already been married once and had a daughter, but he was game to go at it again. The couple eloped to New Jersey and returned to stay in Brownie's little apartment overlooking Sutton Place in Manhattan.

When Brownie became pregnant, poor George no longer had a voluptuous blond playmate able to carouse day and night. George was not about to wait around for the good times to return, and he found other young playthings ready to zoom off in his Aston Martin. George had scarcely taken off his britches when his pregnant wife was onto his adulterous games.

As soon as Victoria Schrafft was born, Brownie started having her own affairs. It is unclear whether she started dating John Jock McLean II when she was still technically married to George, or after she had filed for divorce. In any event, Jock was everything George was, only bigger and better. He was richer. He was better looking. He was taller, born for a tuxedo, and a spitting image of Brownie's father. He bore a far more distinguished name. His late mother was not the owner of a chain of déclassé luncheonettes, but Evalyn Walsh McLean, whose father had discovered the legendary Camp Bird gold mine in Colorado. And he was in love with Brownie in part because he found in her his mother's fire and life.

Brownie got her divorce, and in May 1953 she married the twice-divorced, thirty-seven-year-old Jock in Las Vegas. Immediately afterward, they flew to Paris for their honeymoon.

THE WEALTHY ELITE DO not talk publicly about money, but privately it is largely what they reflect upon. Jock's mother had blown her inherited fortune. What remained was primarily the estate of Jock's paternal grandfather, newspaper magnate John R. McLean, set in an impregnable trust.

Trusts are the way great old families hold on to their money for generation after generation. With a trust fund, one profligate generation cannot dissipate the wealth. In this instance, the interest on the fortune went first to McLean's son, Ned, then to his grandchildren, to be distributed in full only twenty years after the death of

Jock, the youngest surviving grandchild. The old man was an astute judge of the family's spendthrift ways, but what Jock took away from his mother's example was that money should be spent; frugality was unseemly.

Brownie acted as if she were marrying a man of legendary wealth. Thus she cavalierly walked away from the alimony and child support that her first husband owed the mother of his child. She did not quite grasp that she was becoming the third wife of a man living on a monthly allowance—an extraordinary allowance, but an allowance nonetheless. She did not consider that if Jock died, the trust would shut its vault to her, and its doors would never open again.

Brownie and Jock set out to indulge themselves in unrelieved pleasure. "I never had a child with him," Brownie says. "I was dumb not to have, for I would have had a third of the estate." Brownie was not a great mother, but there were many terrible mothers who had children just so they could not be denied a major slice of their wealthy husband's estate. Her own daughter, Vicki, attended the private Palm Beach Day School, and in her teenage years she was sent to Hewitt School on East Seventy-fifth Street in Manhattan, out of the way of adults.

The social glitterati follow the fads, and if they are not at the right places at the right time, they are considered to be nowhere at all. During the late fifties and sixties, Brownie and Jock were almost inevitably in attendance at one of the best tables at precisely the right time at the most desired of occasions. They sped down from Palm Beach to Miami on the dirt State Road 7 to a little club in Miami where a fantastic black singer performed at two in the morning. They drove to the Golden Ox on Wellington Road in the sparsely settled western regions of the vast county, a restaurant that through Brownie's patronage turned into the place to be. On Saturday afternoon Brownie again drove west to their stables, where she and Jock kept horses, and Vicki could ride on her pony.

This pleasured world of the wealthy in Palm Beach is overwhelmingly a woman's world. "Men are lost here," Brownie reflects. "Most of the men didn't work. They didn't have to. And they had no interests. That's why I would hear them say that it's no place for a man to survive, other than on alcohol. They just burn out down here."

Jock enjoyed intimate dinner parties sparkling with frivolity, but abhorred the balls and cocktail parties that Brownie loved. They reminded him too much of his mother's overwrought life, his memories primarily of a woman in a ball gown wearing the Hope diamond kissing him good night before heading off to that evening's ball. He was not about to become a mere prop for his wife's pleasure, but she was not going to stop attending social functions.

"Now, you may sit here and drink martinis and smoke all night," Brownie said, looking down at her seated husband, "but I like people, so I'm going out. We can get divorced, or we can stay together. But I'm going to do that."

Jock said nothing. He was a three-pack-a-day man, and he sat puffing away on his Camel. Smoking was so chic that the nonsmoking Brownie used a cigarette as a prop when she was photographed. "If you don't," Brownie said finally, "I'm going to be going with somebody else and you will read about it and you'll be upset."

"Oh, darling, if I would go to one ball a year with you, would that make you happy?" Jock asked.

Brownie looked at Jock. "No, darling, you can't do that because they'd call you 'One Ball McLean.'" So Brownie went to the balls with other escorts, who deposited her home in the early-morning hours.

6

The Evening Is Only Beginning

In 1957, Jock and Brownie purchased El Solano, one of the great estates on South Ocean Boulevard. The 10,600-square-foot-home had nine bedrooms, a 40-by-26-foot ballroom, and two swimming pools—one that caught sun in the morning, one that caught it in the late afternoon.

Addison Mizner, the most important creative figure in the history of Palm Beach, built El Solano in 1925. When the forty-six-year-old largely self-trained architect arrived on the island in 1917, Palm Beach was still part of a hotel culture. Most visitors stayed at either the Royal Poinciana Hotel on Lake Worth, or the Breakers on the Atlantic Ocean. It was not until the twenties that the Army Corps of Engineers created the Intracoastal Waterway. In these years, the western shore of the island fronted the freshwater Lake Worth. The island was largely jungle, and most guests rarely ventured much beyond the confines of the hotel grounds except to go to watch Alligator Joe wrestling alligators in a dusty pit in his great thatched hut.

When Mizner died in 1933, on the grounds where Joe had fought alligators stood the magnificent Mizner-designed Everglades Club, the center of the social life of the island. Along Worth Avenue rose other Spanish/Moorish-inspired Mizner buildings, including a five-story villa with a turretlike room at the top that was his studio, like a lighthouse above the village. Beneath was a twisting narrow passageway full of small shops that evoked an image of medieval Spain. In the surrounding streets stood about a hundred homes designed by Mizner, including great mansions and petite villas. Interspersed around them were estates and homes that blended into the architect's fantasy, designed by several other notable architects, including Maurice Fatio and Joseph Urban. It was a magical scene; a bit of Spain, a dash of Morocco, a hint of Paris, a flourish of Hollywood, and something of exotic, jungle Florida as well.

The sick, rotund man who arrived in Palm Beach during World War I was an unlikely candidate to transform not only Palm Beach, but also the whole ethos of South Florida. Mizner had such a varied, contradictory existence that it was as if he lived an encyclopedia of lives. His father was a successful lawyer in Benicia, a town in northern California. His son had the soul of a bohemian and the tastes of an aristocrat. Addison was the seventh of eight children, and when the boy was sixteen, his father was named ambassador to Guatemala.

In his year there, Mizner imbued much of the cultural life of old Central America, an influence that years later he would draw upon in his own architecture. Six foot three and weighing close to three hundred pounds, he would have been an imposing figure, even without his vibrant, outgoing personality. After desultory studies in California and Spain, he set up an architectural practice in San Francisco. When that did not work out, he prospected for gold in Alaska, published a calendar in Hawaii, painted slides in Samoa, boxed in Australia, and eventually worked his way back home selling casket handles. He ended up in New York, surviving as much on his enviable charm, which he employed on wealthy ladies, as his abilities as an architect. One day in 1917, he picked up three hitchhikers in Long Island. They beat him half to death, leaving Mizner with a severely injured leg that was in danger of amputation.

In New York City, the invalided Mizner met Paris Singer, whose life was its own richly ornate biography. Singer was the next-to-youngest son of Isaac Merritt Singer's twenty-four children. The sewing machine magnate had left his son enough money so he could indulge most of his whims, including a lengthy affair with the celebrated dancer Isadora Duncan, with whom he had a child. Singer was as tall as Mizner, and was an elegant gentleman with a rakish mustache.

Singer planned to use some of his wealth to build a convalescent hospital for officers in the jungle of Palm Beach. When the new friends arrived in Palm Beach by train, Singer took the hobbling Mizner around the island. The architect was appalled at the yellow and white of the two Flagler hotels. Flagler's colors were also slapped on everything from train cars to benches.

Mizner came upon a New England–style colonial plopped down in the middle of the jungle, forlorn and bizarre, three thousand miles away from its natural northern habitat. He observed the stilted, artificial hotel life with its patrons changing their clothes five times a day, and wearing layered clothes inappropriate for the summery clime.

As the two men stood on the shores of Lake Worth a mile north of the Royal Poinciana Hotel, Singer asked the architect, "What do you see on this site?" He was not asking a practical architectural question. He was asking the man for his vision, and that was how Mizner replied. "It's so beautiful that it ought to be something religious—a nunnery, with a chapel built into the lake, great cool cloisters and a court of oranges; a landing stage, where the stern old abbess could barter with boatmen bringing their fruit and vegetables for sale; a great gate over there on the road, where the faithful could leave their offerings and receive largesse."

Mizner took what was little more than a visceral reaction and with Singer's money turned it into a dark orange fantasy that spiritually anchored the island. This dream stood far above the highest of the royal palms. Unlike most architects, Mizner was as much concerned with the interior decoration as the outside. He built a series of studio shops in West Palm Beach where he trained craftsmen to make ceramic tiles, pottery, furniture, and whatever else he needed to complete the last physical details of his vision.

Stoneworkers created discriminating objects and Mizner had them broken apart with hatchets and patched back together again, so they would appear to be old. He trained carpenters to drill worm-like holes in chests of drawers. He taught painters how to create peeling effects to make wood appear ancient. He was creating fake antiques, but to him they were not fraudulent pieces but poetic artifacts that blended seamlessly with the old to be set down in this ageless environ, outside of history, stumbled upon in the mysterious jungles of South Florida.

When one looked up at the ornate painted beams, then down at the Spanish tiles that festooned every room, at the ornate Spanish furniture and the rich damask, all that was missing was human architecture of the same vision and grandeur. The war was over and there was no longer a need for a convalescent hospital, so Mizner and Singer decided to turn the building into a private club. They named it the Everglades. Mizner and Singer were wildly opinionated men, and they ran the club like a dinner party for which they chose the guests. These five hundred members were rich and well placed, and along with their wives, they found a new quality of social intercourse at the club.

For decades, the Everglades was so much a center of life on the island that some people made the purchase of a home contingent upon becoming members. The club had its own superb golf course and fine clay tennis courts. That was part of Mizner's vision too; he envisioned that people would wear sports clothes during the day, and evening clothes at night. So they did, and their dress became both more casual and more formal.

Most of the leading characters in Palm Beach were middle-aged. They exploded in gaiety once they were released from the stuffy world of Flagler's monumental hotels. They did not walk through their evenings in humorless social minuets; they danced through them. The season lasted only six weeks, starting after Christmas and ending on George Washington's birthday in February. The brevity of the period made every day seem like a vacation.

When the obese Mizner waddled down Worth Avenue with his monkey Johnnie Brown on his shoulder, he looked out of place in the world that he had created. That was partially true. He was a gay man who was a virtual centaur, half creative genius, half hustler. As an architect hired to build their homes, he was treated as a servant of the wealthy, though he was superior in intellect to most of them. He got even by asserting his artistic arrogance, playing the prima donna. He sometimes expanded the size of a house far beyond that which his client ordered, or seemingly forgot rooms or staircases, or acted as if he cared nothing for the details of his projects when he was obsessed by them.

"Say anything you want about me," he told one interviewer. "I'll help you to the best of my ability, but remember that I am very good at faking anything."

Mizner was in the business of making fake real and real fake; of elevating the mundane into the ethereal. Mizner had an astute social sense that helped him obtain commissions from wealthy clients, and he knew that the women ruled, albeit often by seeming not to. "I aim to please the woman," he told the *Palm Beach Post* in 1926. "The man pays for the home, yes, and that is important, but it is the woman's background, and she is the one who should determine what it should be."

Mizner went on to begin to build an American Venice south of the island in Boca Raton, a planned community on a series of man-made canals. It was the greatest of all Mizner's visions, and if it had been successful, it might have changed the whole nature of South Florida history. But it was pulled down in the Florida real estate crash of the twenties, taking Mizner's fortune with it.

Mizner is not only the greatest architect in the history of Florida, but the one true architect of the Palm Beach experience. His brilliance has been bastardized and cannibalized into a Florida style found in everything from tract homes to strip malls, and the orangey hue that he favored has become practically the state color.

Most of what remains of Mizner's genius is found in Palm Beach. Many of his homes have been torn down, others have been spiritually gutted, and only a few have stayed true to his vision. These homes speak in a compelling, if lessening, voice of his dream of Palm Beach as an exquisite, timeless, sophisticated enclave.

Brownie was living in Mizner's world, and not simply because she was living in a house that he had built. In the fifties, there were no condominiums on the island, and the social life of Palm Beach centered on a few hundred homes, most of them lying between the two main clubs, the Everglades and the Bath and Tennis. Servants were the silent audience to most activities. It was a town of such formality that some couples staying home for dinner dressed formally, and an ordinance declared that it was "unlawful for anyone to walk, ride, or otherwise be conveyed over town streets without being properly dressed in customary street wear."

Jock was a member of the Coconuts, whose sole activity was to give the most exclusive New Year's Eve party on the island. The Coconuts began in the 1920s as elaborate costume parties. The invitees were as much performers as guests at these theatrical evenings. At the "Coconuts of 1924," held at the same Flagler estate where the 2008 New Year's party took place, the guests spent small fortunes both in money and ingenuity to ensure that they would have memorable outfits, most in some inspired version of a national costume. The men were as splendidly and eclectically dressed as the women, and from Pierrots to peacocks, Dutch maidens to rajahs, there was not an unimaginative costume in the room.

There was genial applause when each couple entered the French ballroom, but when the stunning, young Mrs. Gurnee Munn glided into the great room, there was an ovation celebrating the triumphant audacity of her costume. She came as a dream of an Indian princess, her whole body from the top of her head to her shoes wreathed in an incredible headdress of long white feathers tipped in azure coloring. When the applause died down and she danced with her husband, Mrs. Munn looked not so much like an Indian queen but a white bird floating across the room.

The guests danced and reveled for hours before around two in the morning, they walked in couples out to the patio, where under the palms and coconuts, they were served an elaborate supper while two costumed toreadors sang opera arias.

The Coconuts evolved into an annual event in which a group of bachelors reciprocated for the many invitations they received over the season. Twenty-five of these young men created a more formal group of Coconuts and began a tradition of annual parties known for the status of their guests and the extravagance.

Most of the Coconuts married, but they stayed Coconuts and turned the event into a New Year's Eve party. One year Brownie said that she was only accompanying her Coconut husband if her friend Estée Lauder was invited. The cosmetics magnate was the wealthiest, best-known Jewish resident on the island, but that did not mean that she was invited to the most exclusive WASP events. Jock was hardly interested in a rocking a ship that he thought was sailing along quite well, but Brownie was adamant, and Estée was invited that year and in following years.

Like most of his fellow males on the island, Jock played tennis and golf, kibitzed in the locker room and watched, bemused, as his wife traversed the island, practicing her social sleight of hand. She had her gloved ladies' lunches, her afternoon hands of canasta, and in the evening, a dinner party or a ball. It would have become boring if it lasted too long, but by mid-February they were gone, the place shuttered.

In those few weeks in Palm Beach, no one gave better, more eclectic and daring parties than Brownie. At Christmas, she invited everyone from the hoariest of the aristocrats to the Palm Beach cops, a social mélange unlike anything else on the island, a good four hundred or more filling every bit of the downstairs of the mammoth home.

"Jesus Christ, where do you know these people?" Jock asked.

"They're perfectly nice people. They have nowhere to go at Christmas, so I invited them."

Jock made a few perfunctory greetings and then trundled upstairs to read a book.

After a decade and a half of marriage, Jock's lung cancer was discovered and their last years together became a time of trial. Three years later, in 1975, Jock died, and Brownie was alone. "I'm sitting in this big house and I say to myself, 'Well, I can sit here and let the world come to me, or I can go out and find it.'" The truth was that she could not sit in the big house for long, since it was her only major asset. In 1980, she rented it to John Lennon and Yoko Ono for $25,000 a week. They were enchanted with El Solano, and Brownie ended up selling the estate to the couple for $725,000. Lennon was murdered a few months later, and the singer never lived in his new house.

Palm Beach is an island full of widows who assuage their aloneness with palliatives from booze to boys. Brownie attracted an ever-changing, eclectic entourage who were always ready to party. There were men, but they always seemed to disappear; friends were more reliable. Inviting Brownie to your gathering meant you invited her entire gang.

Brownie was never good with money. She traveled first class and stayed in only the best hotels. She tipped generously and spent carelessly. "Money doesn't make you happy," Brownie reflects. "Listen, I've had it all. I was born rich, and then you sit there and watch it all taken away. So what do you do? Why have money? If I have money, that's the way it goes. It's only the past few years that I've been watching what I spend. I've been very rich and I've been very poor. Many times, round and round we go."

Brownie decided to get groups together to travel to various exotic spots. It would be fun, and she could make a little money. Her name still had a social cachet, and wherever she decided to go, people were welcoming. She charged her friends an all-inclusive fee and took care of all the details.

The late James Sheeran, the witty publisher of *Palm Beach Society*, dubbed them "Brownie's Troop," and soon they were flying everywhere from Argentina to Morocco. One evening at the hotel in Casablanca before dinner, the troop assembled in the bar. The hostess would not think of limiting the drinks, and everyone was knocking down Dom Pérignon like keg beer. The bill was eleven thousand dollars, but Brownie paid it with a smile and a secret grimace, since there went all her profits, and more, leaving Brownie looking up out of the same financial hole, as she returned to Palm Beach and its endless round of parties.

7

A Road That Led Elsewhere

I had only seen Eddy Louis on the tennis court, and I hardly recognized him at a charity ball impeccably garbed in a tuxedo that looked as if it had been hand-fitted to his trim form. His wife, Vera, was equally well dressed in a gown that fit just as perfectly. In the half-light of the ballroom, she looked no older than fifty, the perfect partner to her handsome husband. Many of the other married couples shuffled in pedestrian two-steps as if they were counting out each move, but Vera and Eddy seemed to float above the room, Fred and Ginger among a bunch of clods.

At my table I heard a couple of men berating Eddy as a repulsive showman who should have been parking their cars or serving their meals, not waltzing with one of the ladies of the island. But Vera and Eddy danced far above their pettiness and spite.

It took an extraordinary effort for Vera to create the illusion of youth. She began each day in her dressing gown in front of a large magnifying mirror, applying makeup. Vera worked with precision and concentration for close to an hour. She was a tiny woman with birdlike bones, dyed blond hair, and a trim, supple body that matched her countenance. In the proper lighting, and that was the only lighting in which she presented herself, she appeared at the oldest a well-preserved, pretty woman in late middle-age. She was eighty-five years old, but saying so was like exposing a magician's greatest illusion and turning his masterwork into a tawdry trick.

Only when Vera was completely satisfied with her makeup did she leave her bedroom and walk into the library to have breakfast. Her morning breakfast was always two cups of black coffee followed by a glass of hot water as a constitutional. Fifty-four-year-old Eddy sat on a sofa across from her in a white fluffy bathrobe that, when he could not be naked, was his outfit of choice. Eddy was Vera's greatest youth tonic. She did not think of Eddy as three decades her junior, but as her contemporary. He was as narcissistic as his wife, and as disciplined in his lifestyle. He not only swam in the nude, he gardened in the nude, oblivious to his seven-year-old daughter, the Latina maid, or anyone else who happened to be around. Vera celebrated that aspect of Eddy's personality, taking great pleasure in looking at his tanned, naked body.

Vera was obsessed with retaining her beauty, and in that quest there was no journey too long and no act too difficult. She had waited until she was sixty to fly to London for her first face-lift. Since then she had gone through an endless series of procedures, including other face-lifts, breast lifts, tummy tucks, liposuction, and butt implants.

Not everything worked out well, and for a while her left eye would not close properly. That became something else that she had to disguise. To maintain her shapely legs, she took dance classes in which she was a good thirty years older than anyone else. She worked out in the pool every day holding a spring between her legs, an exercise that she believed kept her vagina tight.

In the mornings, Eddy often came into her bedroom for elaborate and lengthy lovemaking. Vera exalted in her sexuality, telling her husband, "I'm a lady in the drawing room, and a whore in the bedroom." Eddy said that touching Vera's body was unlike anything he had experienced before. Her breasts stood out with perfect precision and her buttocks were so firm that he was convinced he could have bounced a basketball off of them. At times, he worried that he might crush her small, fragile bones. In the end, she gasped and whimpered as they lay there spent in each other's arms.

Vera had told her closest friend, Countess Mimy Landau, that she never had an orgasm. She expressed no more regret than if she had said she had never visited Lhasa, a distant, fascinating city, but one to which she had never managed to travel. Romance was her favorite performance art, and her climaxes were as much theater as the rest of it. She was a sensualist who enjoyed the intimate play of sex, and considered it little more than an ironic quirk that climaxing was a mystery to her.

Vera saw sex primarily as therapeutic, another device to prevent her body from sending out a deceitful message. "Okay, that's my face," she said, looking into the mirror, in a monologue recorded by her granddaughter Renee Fadiman. "It's always a surprise to me that my body grows old around my very young soul."

In addition to being preoccupied with her looks, Vera was obsessed by the Shiny Sheet. Two days after Barbara's party for Prince Edward, the story of the event covered half the front page of the *Palm Beach Daily News*. At the top was the three-column photo of Barbara greeting the prince, her hands enveloping Edward's, and a second smaller photo of the royal place setting. Vera had a former lover who had been the Lord Mayor of London, and she would have conversed naturally with the prince. It had apparently been a splendid evening marred by a faux pas that Vera never would have made, and that society editor Shannon Donnelly duly noted. A number of the guests had made "three or four glances at the next table, and it was clear that the royal personage was enjoying himself in high style, and he wasn't going anywhere anytime soon. No matter. Palm Beach being Palm Beach, a few guests started quietly slipping away. Somebody had to be home before the milk truck."

If Vera had been married to someone other than Eddy, she and her husband would have been desired guests at many splendid parties. She always behaved with impeccable manners, and never would have left Elephant Walk before Prince Edward. She was full of the melancholy sense that she might never again attend such a gathering; not with Eddy, and perhaps not with anyone else.

When Vera Louis left the house just before noon in March 1997, Eddy brushed his lips against his wife's cheek and told her, "I love you."

"I love you too," Vera said in a voice that was scarcely a whisper as she hurried out the double doors and got into her Rolls-Royce. Her husband had kissed her, but nothing was the same.

Vera generally drove the British automobile with the stately slowness that seemed to be its most appropriate speed. However, she was already a few minutes late for lunch with two of her lady friends at a midtown restaurant, and she drove up Regent Park with uncommon urgency.

Regent Park made a dangerous, blind entrance onto South County Road. Vera always had a nervous moment gingerly nudging out of Regent Park, hoping that the cars cruising southward would see her Rolls and slow down. As she quickly pulled across the road and turned north, she could have driven straight into the Bath and Tennis Club, its back to the road as if it wanted no truck with the riffraff who traveled along the public highway.

In her three decades on the island, Vera had never entered the portals of the restricted B&T as a guest. Vera was a flawlessly well-mannered lady with every human attribute the club members celebrated, except for Christian faith. Her father, Mendel Racolin, had been a Menshevik, a social Democrat, in Czarist Russia. Born in 1911, Vera was brought up in an antireligious home, in which her father viewed Judaism as an anachronistic relic. Vera grew up believing in disbelief, her atheism as pronounced and as certain as her belief in gravity.

Her father had left Russia and was successful enough buying apartment buildings in New York City that he gave up practicing his profession of dentistry. The properties were worth tens of millions of dollars, and all of her adult life, Vera had been immune from most financial concerns. Her wealth and her atheism worked in tandem, giving her life an imperative to take what she wanted and to enjoy it.

Vera had no sooner passed B&T than the apricot-colored spire and red Cuban tiled roof of Mar-a-Lago loomed up, the property stretching from the ocean to the Intracoastal Waterway. Mar-a-Lago is the most famous monument on the island. The 114-room building has a mythical aura, as if somewhere in the recesses of the 62,000-square-foot mansion resides the spirit of Palm Beach's earliest years.

Vera had been to this most celebrated of Palm Beach estates many times. When she had arrived on the island in 1970, Marjorie Merriweather Post still reigned over Mar-a-Lago with an impeccable sense of propriety that had changed little since she opened the estate in January 1927. The four-times-married cereal heiress was largely deaf, but that didn't prevent her from having formal dinners for thirty-six, in which a liveried footman stood behind every chair in the gilded dining room. And she still had her celebrated weekly square dances, when notables and professional dancers mingled in cowboy garb, cloverleafing and do-si-doing until precisely ten o'clock, when the heiress ordained that it was time for everyone to leave.

Mar-a-Lago was now a club owned by Donald Trump. Vera had not joined, largely because she did not have the ready cash that everyone thought she had, but she and Eddy were frequent guests, especially at charity balls. Just the previous month, they had been there for the Heart Ball. Vera bought one new gown a year, and for this occasion she had purchased a stunning, full-length brocaded dress.

As Vera passed Mar-a-Lago and continued north on the coastal road, she drove by mansions to which she had been invited over the years. When she looked at these estates, she often thought as much of the social occasions as of the people who lived there. She had measured out her life in wine and canapés, spending endless days preparing for parties, attending parties, and reflecting on parties.

Vera's first husband, James Fadiman, was a story editor at RKO and MGM, and the father of their two sons, Jeffrey and James. Fadiman was an austere, principled intellectual, and as time went on, Vera could hardly abide him.

Vera was used to being the most beautiful woman in a room, and she was always anxious when she went with her husband to Hollywood parties attended by stars such as Rita Hayworth or Jane Russell. One evening as Vera sat before her mirror preparing herself, Fadiman paced the room looking at his watch. "Let it go," he fumed in exasperation. "You'll never be pretty enough to compare with the people at the party." Vera said nothing, but she added the brutal dismissal to her list of reasons why she was beginning to despise this unpleasant man she had married.

When young James fell sick with tuberculosis, Vera moved with her two sons to the dry air of Tucson, Arizona. Although she had no more interest in the management of her fortune than she did in the journey made by her veal cordon bleu from pasture to table, she was as much defined by money as if she had a seat on the New York Stock Exchange. Whatever the momentary vicissitudes of her life, she had a way out.

Whereas many young mothers would have accepted the tedium of their days succoring their sickly son while married to a man they no longer loved, to Vera it was a cruel attempt to block her pursuit of pleasure. She needed to have a life full of dramatic romance. She was a beguilingly feminine woman with gentle manners, and a hushed voice that men leaned forward to hear. She had the first of her many affairs in Tucson. Most of the men she loved never realized that the pursued was the pursuer, and that this was an imperious woman who sought her pleasures with single-minded purpose.

As soon as her sons were largely grown up, Vera divorced not only her husband, but everything he valued. She was not a reader of books, and found tedious the palaver of his Hollywood set. She walked away from that former sort of life for good. "My mother equated my father's ice-cold intellectuality with weakness," says her son Jeff. "She sought out men who were very different. Having bad taste in men meant choosing men who were anti-intellectual, verbally crude, and with ethics geared more toward the exploitation of women and the harming of men than the uplifting of women and the camaraderie of men."

Vera turned determinedly toward a life of pleasure. She found fascinating what others would have called only trouble. She liked wild, bad boys, and fancied that other women would have liked them too, if only they dared. Vera married one of the worst, or as she saw it, one of the best: a gorgeous impecunious young Corsican who had the morals of a pirate. That marriage did not last, but it hardly mattered, for there was always a chorus line of men waiting to step forward to whirl Vera around for a dance or two. She was rarely alone.

In 1957, Vera settled upon Philip Lukin as her third husband, a twice-divorced New York advertising man who had the brash aggressiveness that was the next best thing to a true bad boy. She entered into Lukin's hard-drinking, hard-smoking, blazingly fast world. If one party bored her, they moved on to the next.

When Lukin retired from his New York company in 1970, the couple moved to Palm Beach, where Philip purchased the *Palm Beach Social Observer*, a society magazine now called *Palm Beach Society*. The publication held more to advertising than to journalism, and was a natural for Lukin. Nary was a harsh word written about the princes and pretenders of Palm Beach. Having your photo in formal dress in the *Social Observer* granted immediate status, and there were few limits to what aspirants would pay and do to be in its pages. For the most part, Lukin celebrated many people who invited him and Vera into their homes only because of what he could do for them in his society magazine. And every evening they were part of the endless swirl of parties and balls that made up the season.

When Vera's two sons came to visit, they could not abide staying for more than a day or two. As much as they loved their mother, they despised everything they believed Palm Beach represented. Their lives became studious critiques of wealth and privilege. Jeff was one of the first Peace Corps volunteers, and after serving in Tanzania, spent most of his life in the African bush either leading wildlife safaris or pursuing academic research. James became a Jungian psychologist, and lived modestly like his brother.

Vera continued to have lovers, and as she grew older she needed them and their confirmation of her beauty even more. Men still pursued her, and she made these affairs delicious little romances that ended as gently as they began. In addition to these lovers, she succored her aging husband until his death at eighty-seven in 1990.

DURING HER FIVE YEARS of marriage with Eddy, Vera played three womanly roles: mother, wife, and daughter. She was always subtly correcting him the way a mother does her child. When he talked too loud or too long, she alerted him with a gesture. As his wife, she was his companion and lover. She played a daughterly role too, dutifully listening to him and following his advice as he watched out for the areas of their life of which she was ignorant.

Vera and Eddy had what even her sons admitted was a successful marriage. They often had loud arguments, but they appeared to be little more than lovers' quarrels. Yet within her family, there was an underlying fear that when Vera was no longer capable of managing her affairs, Eddy might try to pillage the estate.

Even though Vera's sons deplored luxury, they did not choose to facilitate Eddy's acquisition of personal wealth. The brothers felt that he performed a professional service admirably, but they didn't believe that he deserved to be remunerated with a healthy tranche of the family fortune.

When Vera and Eddy had been married about three years, he set out to organize the commercial real estate that was the family fortune so that it would bring a higher return, and he then found a buyer willing to pay sixty million dollars for the New York apartment buildings. The family turned down the offer, but Eddy believed that he was still owed a commission. Vera sided with her family and in a paroxysm of rage, Eddy vowed to divorce her.

Vera realized that nowhere would she find another man like

Eddy. To divorce him was to divorce life itself—and that was without accounting for his daughter, Desirée, to whom Vera was like a European grandmother. So she invited Eddy back into the fold of marriage, and he willingly returned.

VERA VEERED LEFT ONTO South County Road, the central north-south road on the island. Giant ficus shrubs fronted most of the houses. The road was like a tunnel through the endless foliage, spilling into the commercial center of Palm Beach.

When Vera and Eddy got back together, her son James was convinced that he must now protect not only his mother's fortune, but the family's. In October, after the death of Vera's brother, who had managed the family money, the family, including Eddy, got together to discuss the fortune. When the couple married, Vera had signed over to Eddy half ownership of the house that she and her late husband had purchased in 1985 for $2,200,000, and she had deeded him the other half in her will. Vera wanted Eddy to be taken care of, and she insisted that she receive a two-million-dollar distribution from the irrevocable trust, so that after her death, Eddy would have the money to maintain the house.

In January of 1997, Vera received the two-million-dollar check. A few weeks afterward, Eddy, Jim, and Jeff signed an agreement to forestall any legal disagreements after Vera's death. The Fadimans considered this a generous settlement to a man who was seeing their mother through the last years of her life. As part of the document, Eddy waived any rights he might have to overthrow the agreement.

Eddy signed the document largely out of pride, but the more he thought about it, the more upset he became. As he saw it, he had not married Vera for her money, but that did not mean that he would accept being treated wrongly. He believed he deserved as large a slice of the fortune as her sons. "It isn't fair," he said to Vera. "You don't need it," she said, throwing his words back at him.

Usually, when Eddy got angry, he exploded in a terrifying spasm of rage, and then just as suddenly as it began, his fury ebbed. But now a frigid fury enveloped him.

Eddy did not care how Vera tried to placate him; he was not a servant to be sent off with a tip. They were pawning him off with a cheap brass trinket because they thought he would not know the difference. They had destroyed his love for his wife. He might kiss her good-bye and tell her he loved her, but the words meant nothing. When he looked at Vera, he no longer saw the woman he thought he had married, but a deceiver like all the others. "I always thought women were angels," he said. "I didn't know they were little snakes who crawl up on you and eat you alive."

This was the man who would be there when Vera returned after her ladies' luncheon. Eddy had turned away from her over money, and his disavowal would have made any woman wonder if he had truly loved her at all, or if it had been merely a scheme to win access to her fortune. With the love gone, or at least roundly deflated, all that was left standing angrily before her was a bold, thwarted mercenary. It was devastating to Vera, but she was a woman who for nearly eight decades had prepared a public face to meet the day, and she gave little evidence of her own pain.

The fact that Vera could barely see out of her left eye did not bother her most of the time, but of course it affected her driving. Looking ahead, she could see the Colony Hotel and the business area where she would be meeting her friends. She would have been there in a minute, if not for the vehicle in front of her, a delivery truck from Green's Drug Store.

There were often slow-moving vehicles on the road, usually rubbernecking tourists looking at the mansions, and even though there was a broken double line, few drivers were tempted to pass. But Vera's friends were waiting for her. As she sped up to pass the truck, the driver turned left into a driveway. Swerving to avoid the delivery vehicle, Vera crashed into one of the few walls along a road lined with shrubs. She was cut out of the twisted wreckage and flown by helicopter across the Intracoastal Waterway to Good Samaritan Hospital.

. . .

When Vera's son James arrived at Good Samaritan Hospital, he went in to see his mother alone. Her wounds would heal, but she believed her beauty was ruined and her marriage was dead too. "I want the pills, Jimmy," she said. "I'd rather commit suicide than live as a crippled old lady."

Jim had long ago discussed death and decline with his mother. He had no philosophical or religious reason to deny her the pills; indeed, just the opposite. But he was tasked with looking over the family fortune, and he felt he could not foster an act that would bring him millions of dollars. And so he spurned her request. It hardly mattered, for within hours Vera was gone.

Eddy had not inherited the fortune he thought he deserved, but he was a wealthy man and he lived like one. He had a white Rolls-Royce, a red Ferrari, a splendid home, a firm stomach, and insatiable appetites. He was often out prowling the byways in search of pleasure. He had been married to a woman three decades his senior, and now he slept with women decades his junior.

Eddy had agreed to be the civilian chaplain for the Palm Beach chapter of the Fraternal Order of Police, and at the monthly meeting, he said the prayers before dinner. It was a motley group including some who considered it a cheap insurance policy in case they got in trouble with the police; none stranger than the Lebanese American chaplain mumbling the prayers.

One evening Eddy drove to Boca Raton in his red Ferrari to a party with Meaghan Karland,* a witty and provocative woman around town. Meaghan had known Eddy platonically for years, and she was startled when, during dinner, he took her hand and started moving it toward his groin. "Oh please," she begged, as Eddy pushed her hand against his crotch.

"Well, what do you think?" Eddy asked.

---

* *This is a pseudonym.*

"Well, it's certainly hard," the woman said, not knowing what answer was expected of her.

"Let me show you," Eddy said, upzipping his pants and reaching down for the .38 Smith & Wesson pistol that he was carrying in a crotch holder.

A few weeks later Eddy drove to Meaghan's home for a party. Afterward, early in the morning, he drove to Bradley's Saloon, where a Yellow Cab driven by Todd Ostivich was double-parked waiting for customers in the space Eddy wanted for his Rolls-Royce.

"Get the fuck out of the way," the cabbie remembers Eddy saying. "I want to park here." Eddy raised his middle finger at the cabbie, a gesture understood even in the most rarified precincts of Palm Beach.

Eddy got out of his car to tell the man to move on. The cabbie was convinced that he had as much right to the spot as Eddy, and the two men attacked each other with withering barrages of abuse.

"I'm going to kick your ass," the cabbie said to the dandylike figure confronting him.

"Fuck you, suck my dick!" Eddy replied.

"You've got no balls," Ostivich yelled.

"I've got more balls than you!" Eddy yelled.

"Well, show me!" the driver retorted.

Eddy unzipped his pants, and for a moment it appeared that he had taken the cabbie literally. But then he reached in and showed the man his pistol resting in its crotch holder. The cabbie had a gun in his car, but he had no time to reach for his weapon, and the frightened man drove away and approached a police officer to tell his story.

Sergeant Diana Burfield drove in her police car to Bradley's along with the cabbie, who identified Eddy at the bar. The officer unzipped Eddy's jeans, pulled out his loaded pistol and ammunition, and took him to be booked at the county jail on a felony charge for aggravated assault.

The Shiny Sheet headlined: "CIVILIAN CHAPLAIN ARRESTED AFTER DISPUTE WITH CABBIE." The following

Sunday, the editorial cartoon showed various men carrying their pistols in the approved manner. The detective bore his in a shoulder holster; the private investigator wore his behind his shirt; and the Palm Beach man carried his weapon in a crotch holder.

Eddy lost his position as chaplain, and pled guilty to a misdemeanor for assault and carrying a concealed weapon. He was given twelve months' probation. Many in the town shunned him, and Eddy decided to leave. He left his daughter with the maid to continue at her private school, and flew out of Palm Beach. He wandered the towns and cities of Asia searching for young women, and then moving on. Every few months, he showed up in Palm Beach.

On one of his visits, I ran into Eddy at a party. He pulled out a photo of a thin Thai girl with a boyish figure and a sad smile. He said that he was living with her deep in the jungle in a house he had built on leased land. He tried to make it sound irresistibly romantic. But it was both indescribably sad and chilling—in order to finally control the relationship, Eddy Louis had become his own sexual Kurtz, living with this childlike woman in Thailand. He had gone from one jungle to another.

8

Triumph of the Nouveau

Vera had been fatally injured almost in front of Elephant Walk, but Barbara Wainscott had hardly known the deceased, and she paid no attention to the story in the Shiny Sheet. Palm Beach's socialites have no interest in tales of death and disease, although that is an omnipresent reality, given the aging population. There is no hospital, no funeral home, no cemetery, and the few doctors are primarily plastic surgeons or dermatologists.

Barbara was about to have her fiftieth birthday, and it was a time for her own melancholy reflections on life and how she had ended up in this house in Palm Beach living with a man three and a half decades her senior, shepherding him through the social wilderness of Palm Beach. She could hardly believe that it was ten years ago when she had first met David, just after she had passed her fortieth birthday. She had been putting on parties and events for Blackstone, a new company run by Peter G. Peterson and Stephen A. Schwarzman. Barbara considered herself a poorly paid adjunct to what the men in the company thought was the real world. She was a middle-aged single woman brilliantly educated to be the wife of a wealthy man, but without such a man in sight.

So when her friends from Palm Beach called to ask her to go on a blind date with a rich Philadelphia lawyer, she did not play the reluctant maiden. They told her that he had just ended a long-term relationship, and would soon be plucked up. Barbara looked David up in *Who's Who* and saw that he was seventy-five years old. Her date was old enough to have been her father's elderly mentor.

David picked Barbara up at her East Side apartment with a car and driver. He wore a tailored suit with a silk handkerchief in his vest pocket, a dandyish touch. Barbara felt the whole look was spoiled by the dreadful, clunky watch he wore. David turned out to be an inventive, intriguing conversationalist with a quick and ready wit, but he was short and bald, and as they walked together along Madison Avenue, they were a Mutt and Jeff of a couple.

Barbara was a shiksa princess who represented everything David desired: a full-blown, classy woman who could open doors that until now had been closed to him. They soon became lovers, spending most of their free time with each other.

At times, David appeared to be generous, but whatever he paid, it was usually the least acceptable amount. He was a stingy man, no less so because few recognized that quality in him. Long ago, he had understood that the best way to disguise his penuriousness was to produce the illusion of generosity in the least expensive ways: tipping extravagantly, giving to charities in which his largese was publicly acknowledged, and making lavish gifts to those whose associations he valued. All this he did, but the stinginess remained, along with an inability to trust anyone with his deepest intimacies, and a compulsion to view each encounter as an exchange in which he either benefited or suffered.

After several months, David made it clear that he wanted Barbara to guide him to the social heights. He told her that he would pay whatever he had to pay to get where he wanted to go. He had his law firm put Barbara on a monthly retainer to do public relations in order to raise his status in Palm Beach.

Barbara painted a thin coat of romance over the arrangement, but she understood perfectly well that underneath lay a business agreement. Barbara fancied herself something of a romantic, but she did not love David in the way that she had once used the term.

She had a certain affection for the man, but it was hard to be passionate about someone who asked you to accept a position similar to that of an employee. He was hardly expecting the ardor of adolescent love. Even more a realist than his new younger lover, he was purchasing a certain service at a reasonable price.

Barbara approached it all with gritty realism. She had missed Prince Charming's call, and he was unlikely to call back. Barbara looked upon David the way she would a neglected house that she was contemplating renovating. For years, Barbara had been creating events to advance the lives and fortunes of others. Now she would be doing so to advance both David and herself. Barbara was a social artist, and David was staking her to an immense canvas.

Barbara learned that David had been married to a woman from a prominent Pennsylvania German Jewish family. After separating from his wife, David lived alone in what had once been a house for servants behind the grand house that served as offices of his boutique Philadelphia law firm, Berger & Montague. He had commissioned a well-known architect to gut the building, and told him to design a residence where no woman would want to spend more than a night. The architect had created rooms of cold white marble and mirrors that had all the ambience of a men's locker room.

What troubled Barbara most was not her morally ambiguous position, but that David had lied to her and told her he was divorced, when he was only separated. It also troubled her to have to deal with his two middle-aged sons, Jonathan and Daniel, whom she felt had done so little with so much. She was convinced that they looked at her with jaundiced, suspicious eyes. David was so distant from his sons' upbringing that Jonathan could not conjure up a single childhood memory of his father.

David had stayed separated from his wife, never formalizing the divorce, because he did not want to be pressured into marrying again. He was drawn to Barbara because she was a wellborn WASP, but that was also the very aspect of her that he found most unsettling, even unacceptable. As he grew older, he distanced himself from the Jewish world in public, yet grew ever closer to it in private. Three times a day, unbeknownst to almost anyone, behind a closed door, he donned a prayer shawl and said prayers in Hebrew. He was like one of the *conversos* of Spain, practicing his faith in secret.

As a Jew, David was part of a tradition that went back to the earliest years of the island. In the first part of the twentieth century, the Lehmanns, Warburgs, and Seligmans were among a number of prestigious New York German Jewish families who wintered in Palm Beach. In their public contact, they were as proper as the Windsors. They may not have been members of the Christian Everglades Club, but they were largely accepted into the exclusive society.

All that changed in 1944 when a Jewish entrepreneur, A. M. Sonnabend, purchased a major group of properties from the estate of Henry L. Doherty for $2.4 million. There was a hotel complex including the original Flagler mansion, and an attached twelve-story addition that together made up the Whitehall Hotel; the imposing Biltmore Hotel; a modest beach club called the Sun and Surf; and a moribund golf course and country club in the North End.

Sonnabend spoke the language of the Palm Beach elite. The Boston businessman had gone to Harvard. He had been an aviator in World War I, and was a champion squash player. But the town fathers feared that Sonnabend would not abide by the gentleman's agreement that kept the island a Christian community. An emergency meeting of the elite gentry of the town met at *their* club, the Everglades, in an atmosphere of near-hysteria. "We must at any cost keep those people out of this community," they agreed. "We must not allow the town to become a second Miami Beach."

The broker Claude D. Reese, who had put the deal together, was from one of the old frontier families. Threatened with losing his commission, Reese came up with a proposal. He knew that Sonnabend had not put up much money yet; if ten people in the room came up with forty thousand dollars each, they could take over the deal and send the Jewish businessman packing. But true to their WASP heritage, not one defender of Christian Palm Beach was willing to put up a nickel. The following year at the beginning of the postwar era, Sonnabend reportedly sold the Biltmore Hotel for more money than he had paid for all the properties.

The remaining properties became what the committee of the "select 100" had feared: a Jewish ghetto within the precincts of the island. These new arrivals were not the sophisticated German Jewish gentry from New York coming down on their private railroad cars. These were striving, successful provincial businesspeople like the Bergers from Pennsylvania and before that from some obscure European background; proud to be in such an exalted place, and delighted to return home and brag about it. They stayed at *their* Whitehall Hotel. They drove over to *their* Sun and Surf Beach Club, and up to *their* Palm Beach Country Club. They risked suffering no rebuke or rejection, as long as they did not venture off that one straight road.

Most of his adult life, David Berger had wanted to move beyond that one road. As Barbara set out to advance David, she was almost despairing at how inept and misguided he had been. David had tried to move up socially by renting a one-bedroom apartment at Breakers Row, part of the Breakers Hotel complex. Until the mid-sixties, Jews could not even stay at the hotel. In early 1965, the Anti-Defamation League of B'nai B'rith sent out twelve letters requesting reservations: six with Jewish-sounding names, and six with WASP names. When the responses arrived, there was room for all the apparent Christians, none for any of the supposed Jews, and plenty of room for a lawsuit.

Rather than furthering their public embarrassment, the management agreed to see that there was no discrimination. Before long, the old halls were full of Jewish families. When the hotel built extraordinarily expensive rental apartments, a largely Jewish clientele paid what to almost everyone else seemed willfully exorbitant. David belonged to the Breakers Club, which was not a true club but an adjunct to all the commercial activities of the hotel. Although David did not like to see it as such, it was almost as Jewish as the Palm Beach Country Club.

As a highly regarded attorney and a leading Democratic fund-raiser, David almost certainly would have sailed through the onerous application process at the Palm Beach Country Club. But he had no interest in joining the Jewish club, for that would have ended any chance of his being accepted at the B&T or the Everglades.

Many members of the Palm Beach Country Club snub those they consider unworthy of entering the sacred portals of their club in a manner that replicates and even exaggerates the way the restricted clubs treat *them.* Candidates for membership go through an even more rigorous vetting process than at the Everglades and B&T. Their backgrounds are seriously checked out, and they have to have made significant contributions to charity, especially to Jewish institutions and to Israel.

There are Jewish billionaires and others with great fortunes building thirty- or forty-million-dollar mansions that sometimes put the homes of the old WASP aristocracy literally in their shadows. The old WASP elite see these new arrivals as superior to them only in wealth. They refuse to recognize that the most sophisticated, cultured, philanthropic people to arrive on the island in the past quarter century are largely Jewish.

Across in West Palm Beach, a major cultural edifice, the Kravis Center, had risen. Not only is Raymond F. Kravis, the building's namesake, Jewish, but so doubtlessly are most of the donors whose names are emblazoned on the marble wall outside the major theater. Nearby stands the Norton Art Museum, which has been built into a world-class museum overwhelmingly with Jewish money. Every few days in the Shiny Sheet there is the story of a Jewish philanthropist giving millions of dollars to a hospital, university, or other organization. There are other major contributions that by choice go unheralded and largely unnoticed.

Many of the wealthiest Jews outdo the WASPs in their haughtiness, creating a hierarchy within the Palm Beach Country Club based largely on wealth, and looking with disdain at their coreligionists inside Palm Beach but outside the club. There are so many wealthy Jews arriving in Palm Beach that there are far more outside the Palm Beach Country Club than inside.

"You guys have a lot in common," one member of the club said, introducing a fellow member to Dick Nernberg, a friend who is not. "Dick here flies his own jet."

"Why would I want to fly my own plane?" the man said dismissively. He had already decided that this new arrival was unworthy of his interest. "*I've* got two *big* jets and *pilots* to fly them."

A man is defined by his toys. A man only plays with other men who have the same toys. That is only reasonable, because when you are not playing with your toys, you are talking about them, and one does not want to squander time trying to explain things to those incapable of understanding.

People sort themselves out into the group in which they belong based largely on how much money they have. If they go into the wrong group, they are elbowed until they get into the right one. At the Palm Beach Country Club, there are four or five distinct levels. Other than sitting in the same dining room and playing on the same golf course, those at each level rarely have much social contact. If one wants to put together a committee for a charity and invite someone in the bottom tier to link up with someone at the top, the committee fails before it begins.

Those with the misfortune of not being wealthy enough to join the club look enviously at their social betters and their glittering evenings. Yet joy proves elusive, even for the country club members, because there is always someone richer or better socially connected. Joy is driving out of your 25,000-square-foot mansion in your Bentley and tooling up to the entrance of Mar-a-Lago for your tenth ball of the season, the valet parkers salivating at the chance to take your car and the prospect of a twenty-dollar tip. Joy is having a wife wearing a diamond necklace once owned by the Aga Khan, or so it is said. Joy is having a wife younger and thinner than any of the other wives at your table. Joy is subtly announcing during dinner that your hedge fund scored 33 percent last year, while that of the arrogant son of a bitch across the table with the fat wife scored only 17 percent. And joy is heading home early and stiffing that smart-ass valet parker.

. . .

THERE WAS ONE EXCLUSIVE CLUB within the club whose members were exalted above everyone else. They were the blessed folks investing with their fellow club member Bernard Madoff in Bernard L. Madoff Investment Securities.

In a country club in which money defined status, Bernie was an unlikely king. He was an unprepossessing fellow hardly distinguishable from half of the other pudgy, aging, successful businessmen and entrepreneurs who dominated the golf course and the clubhouse. His biography was similar to that of at least half the men. He grew up in a modest, lower-middle-class, sometimes struggling family in Queens. He attended Hofstra, a school for those without the money or grades to go away to college. He graduated in 1960 with a degree in political science. The Wall Street firms might have hired him as a menial drudge but not as a broker, and he started his little brokerage firm that very year.

Bernie was ambitious in a way that no child of wealth could ever understand. He began on the edge because he had no choice, and he turned the edge into his center. The edge in those years was the fledgling, over-the-counter NASDAQ exchange, a hustler's enclave of penny stocks, hopelessly obscure tech ventures, and gambits that rose mightily riding on nothing but hype before falling, never to arise again. Madoff was the kind of hustler who bedeviled the establishment. His competitors accused him of "cherry picking" the best stocks, paying brokerage houses to send their orders his way and then running his mini-exchange buying and selling the stocks. Bernie's rebuttal was irresistible. He was only saving customers money. In the end, he helped to build the obscure NASDAQ exchange into a formidable competitor to the New York Stock Exchange. He was the chairman of NASDAQ in 1990, not as an honorific but because his early use of computers and other new forms of trading helped to revolutionize the financial industry.

While Bernie continued that lucrative business, he also began one of the earliest and largest hedge funds. His clients did not think that Bernard L. Madoff Investment Securities was a hedge fund, and technically they were right. It wasn't set up as a separate custodial fund but as a brokerage account. The benighted Bernie said that he purchased a list of the biggest, best-known stocks. He told his clients that he put a "collar" around the stocks. He locked them into puts and calls, betting both that the stocks would go up and down. He was sure that by shrewdly manipulating these calls, he was able to profit from whatever happened to the stock.

Unlike some hedge funds, Bernie did not hide what he was doing or the investments he made. Each month his clients received neat printouts of the stocks in which they were invested and the steady amounts they had earned. The wonder of it was that it didn't matter what happened to the stock market, how turbulent the financial waters—when you sailed with Bernie you sailed above the most violent seas.

Those who gave their money to Bernie dubbed their investments the "Jewish T-bill," and this ethnic treasury bill delivered a steady 10 to 15 percent a year, while the losers outside the sacred circle were getting only 3 or 4 percent in their miserably mundane version. Bernie's investors walked around as if they had bested the vicissitudes of fortune that bedeviled their less fortunate contemporaries. They were not gluttonous investors risking their fortunes on hedge funds and other speculative schemes that one year might deliver massive returns and the next plunge to nothing, all gained on a steady diet of Pepto-Bismol. Bernie's investors had the blessings of certitude. The only thing sweeter than good news is good news that brings bad news to others. It was doubly sweet because good old Bernie would not let just anyone in and seemed to take as much pleasure in turning down potential investors as he did in accepting their fortunes.

Madoff's Palm Beach investors did not think of themselves as greedy, even if they had invested all their money with him. A glutton can have good table manners, and theirs was a tailored greed. They fancied that they had mastered the secret of eternal wealth.

Bernie and his wife, Ruth, bought their home in the North End not five minutes from the club in 1994, and two years later joined the Palm Beach Country Club. Bernie was successful enough that he could have built himself a 30,000-square-foot home on the ocean, but in the context of Jewish Palm Beach, the man was not a showoff. His home was not a showpiece as the term was defined at the club, and although he had a yacht named Bull and homes in New York and the Riviera, and a private plane, in the circles in which he traveled, that was no more unusual than having your own golf clubs. If he had had the least desire, he could have been celebrated in the Shiny Sheet for his philanthropy. He could have become part of the publicity machine of which so many of his friends were a part, but he chose to step back from purchased public adulation. He enjoyed his golf game and fishing, and his wife and sons, who worked with him in the business. It was an enviable life.

The Palm Beach Country Club did not have the stern prohibition against discussing business that was so fundamental to life at the Everglades or the B&T, and many business deals were made on the links or in the locker room. But Bernie was a king you did not touch. Madoff kept his distance from the unseemly business of soliciting new clients.

Within the country club itself, the man to see if you wanted to place your fortune with Bernard L. Madoff Investment Securities was Robert M. Jaffe. In looking at the dandified Jaffe as he gave the keys to his MG roadster to the Latino valet and strutted into the country club, one could not help but reflect that in most animal species from lions to peacocks it is the male of the species who is the resplendent sex. Jaffe was a dandy from the bottom of his Italian sandals, through the tips of his manicured fingers, to the top of his dyed-black pompadour. He had an aging gigolo's looks, his hair sleek and shiny, a face if not lifted by the miracle of plastic surgery nonetheless looking not youthful but the caricature of youth. People trade in life on whatever their best assets are, and Jaffe's was his stunning appearance, an attribute that he traded on long and well.

Jaffe grew up in unassuming circumstances in Brookline, Massachusetts, and attended Suffolk University, a school hardly carrying the cachet of Boston's many world-class institutions of higher learning. Like Bernie, in high school Jaffe had been a lifeguard, an enviable platform from which to meet young women. During summers in the mid-Sixties, while in college, he worked for the fancy men's clothier Louis Boston, where the elite came to shop and schmooze.

Jaffe entered Suffolk's MBA program, but dropped out after the first year, just before he was scheduled to marry Ellen. For the socially ambitious Jaffe, Ellen was the catch of catches. Her father, Carl Shapiro, was a women's clothing manufacturer who in 1971 sold Kay Windsor for a reported $20 tc 30 million. He was generous to his daughter and his new son-in-law, and Jaffe began to live a rich life that fit him like a Gucci loafer.

Jaffe became a broker, the perfect vocation for a charming dilettante of no special attribute or ambition. Despite his stunning personal presentation, he reminded some people of Fredo in *The Godfather.* Jaffe was not smart but he was shrewd, and in his world that was enough. He might have been a better judge of clothes than he was of stocks, and that seems to have been fine with him. "The clothing I wear is more—dare I say—cutting edge," he told the *Daily News Record.* "It's a few years ahead of the pack. Once you've got filet mignon, you don't want to go back." And prime beef tastes especially good when you aren't paying for it, and with Ellen's generous allowance from her father, the Jaffes lived a luxurious life.

Jaffe's sense of taste was deep when it came to clothes and cars, but not so profound when it came to his clients. In the Seventies and early Eighties, one of his main clients was Gennaro Angiulo, then reputedly the head of the Boston mob, along with the don's brothers.

The broker could bid fond adieu to sleazy clients when in late 1989 Jaffe joined Cohmad Securities, a small firm that happened to be on the same floor with Bernard L. Madoff Investment Securities in Manhattan. All Jaffe had to do now was to bring investors to Madoff, a job he did with acumen unlike anything in his life. "Bernie would not solicit for business," recalls Jaffe. "People went to him." Or they went to Jaffe, who admits that he took one or two points for his trouble, a commission that he did not advertise. It was as if he thought people of a certain wealth and position should understand that in the real world, nobody did anything for nothing, and Robert Jaffe lived in the real world.

Jaffe didn't have to sell. He didn't have to promote. He only had to allow his clients the extreme privilege of giving their money to

Madoff and to see it rise with the regularity of a metronome. It was a lovely business. You might play eighteen holes of golf with another member and by the time you were back in the clubhouse, he was ready to write a check for five million dollars. That wasn't bad for an afternoon's outing, an eighty on the links, and fifty or a hundred thousand dollars in your pocket.

The Shiny Sheet called Jaffe "the toast of Palm Beach society . . . sought after by the wealthy and influential . . . chairman of the multi-million-dollar Palm HealthCare Foundation." His wife, Ellen, was equally charitable and was on the board of the Kravis Center.

The Jaffes were a power couple and if they thought you were on their exalted level—a space no wider than the observation deck on the Empire State Building—they treated you with grace, dignity, and warmth; but if you were part of unwashed humanity you were mercilessly snubbed, especially by Ellen. There were few in the world, even in Palm Beach, on her level, and if you did not realize it, she had the means to let you know. It did not endear her to others, but as long she had the money and the power, that was a matter of no apparent interest or concern to her.

Jaffe had another attribute in getting investors to give money to Madoff. In the years since his marriage to Ellen, his father-in-law had become as revered and honored as anyone in the country club. And like everything else, that led back to Madoff. Carl Shapiro had met Bernie when the investment guru was in his early twenties, opening his brokerage firm, and had been not only his first major client but his most successful. "He was twenty-two years old, a smart young guy," Shapiro recalls. "A friend asked me to meet him, maybe throw him a little business. I had plenty of irons in the fire, so I declined. But my friend insisted." At that point Shapiro made many arbitrage sales. "In those days, it took three weeks to complete a sale," Shapiro said. "This kid stood in front of me and said 'I can do it in three days.' And he did." That was impressive enough for Shapiro to hand the young man a $100,000 check. "And he did very well with it. That was the beginning."

Carl had three daughters and no sons, and Bernie was the son he always wanted, a virtual son who returned his life and loyalty a thousand fold. Thanks largely to Bernie, Carl's nest egg from his sale of Kay Windsor metamorphosed into likely over a billion dollars, and Shapiro had the largess to become an amazingly charitable man.

In 2004, Shapiro pledged $25 million to Brandeis University, the largest single donation in the university's history, adding to the $35 million that he and his wife had already contributed. By 2006, he had given $20.7 million to Beth Israel Deaconess Medical Center in Boston. That same year he donated $8 million to Hebrew SeniorLife in Dedham and $15 million to the Museum of Fine Arts in Boston. In South Florida, he was a Medici of the arts, giving massive contributions to both the Kravis Center for the Performing Arts and the Norton Museum of Art, helping to turn them into world class organizations.

Shapiro wanted his name on the hospital or the school that he supported, his generosity publicly celebrated. The humanitarian may have been overly concerned with personal publicity, but another Palm Beach Jewish philanthropist, Sydelle Meyer, says that Shapiro's public recognition played an important social role. "It's not such a terrible thing if the benefactor's name is publicized," Meyer insists. "It motivates other people to think about giving. We all like recognition in this world one way or another. And if people see other people's names, they say, 'Oh, isn't that nice, and can't I be there too?'"

That was the multiplier effect of Shapiro's philanthropy. He set a standard for his fellow Palm Beach Country Club members that resonated from one end of Palm Beach to the other. A certain portion of this mega-wealthy set was full of self pride and wildly competitive in their pursuit of money and status, and they took their competitiveness into the philanthropic world. As for Carl Shapiro, he was a man who paid his debts, and he knew how much his munificence was the result of the incomparable investment astuteness of his dear friend Bernie Madoff.

Unlike Carl Shapiro and Robert Jaffe, Bernie did not like social publicity, and his and his wife's name and picture were never in the Shiny Sheet. One of the few places other than the country club where he hung out sometimes was the little restaurant at Green's Drug Store. The counter and tables hosted everyone from billionaires to bartenders, socialites to cops, and was the most democratic setting on the island. It could have been transported to the Smithsonian as a classic Fifties restaurant. One of its appeals to Bernie may have been that it reminded him of his youth.

In this hustler's world, Bernie had learned that the greatest hustle is when you don't appear to be hustling at all. One day when he was at Green's there was a broker working the room who was not as fortunate as Bernie. Her name was Laura Goldman. She had been in the business for two decades working for several major firms, and here she was schmoozing these old Jewish guys over their cheese omelets, seeing if she could find a live one among the dead fish.

Bernie was famous in the financial world, and when Goldman spotted the celebrated investor, she hurried up to him and made her spiel, saying how her clients would likely want to invest with him. Bernie did not like to get caught selling, but if he could pluck off a few million in a half hour, he was sometimes willing, and so he sat down with Goldman.

Goldman was not someone who listened only to the words. She listened between the words, and she began not with credulity born of avarice but with skepticism. And the more Bernie talked the more skeptical she became. She knew all about the games of puts and calls, yet Bernie was very vague, pushing her away from any details. She kept prodding, looking for weakness and contradiction.

"Why do you have this one cheap accountant?" she asked. "And why do you charge such a small commission, especially when you're doing so well?"

"Jews don't like to buy retail," Bernie said. "I make up for the lower fees with the additional volume of investments that my fee structure attracts."

Not only did Goldman not invest her clients' money in Bernard L. Madoff Investment Securities, but she left that day strongly suspicious that there was something missing. She was not the only one with doubts. In May 2001, the *MAR Hedge Fund Report* puzzled over why others who have used the same strategy "are known to have nowhere near the same degree of success." That same month *Barron's* wrote an equally dubious article noting that "some on Wall Street remain skeptical about how Madoff achieves such stunning double-digit returns using options alone." The piece quoted a former Madoff investor: "Anybody who's a seasoned hedge-fund investor knows the split-strike conversion is not the whole story. To take it at face value is a bit naive." The subtle suggestion in both these pieces was not that the respected Bernie Madoff was a scam artist but that he was using other investment techniques to pull off his consistently high returns.

Goldman was an aggressive, in-your-face person. She took the two articles and mailed them to members of the country club and others invested with Madoff. She thought she was doing them a great service, although surely she would not have minded if they turned their investments over to her. What was striking was the furor of the response. She was the worst of all things, an anti-Semitic Jew, a Jew attacking a Jew who has made good, a Jew jealous at Bernie's success and wanting to pull down a man of generosity, goodness, and limitless financial acumen.

HAVING REJECTED THE Palm Beach Country Club, David Berger would have been a natural for Mar-a-Lago. If membership would have advanced his social position, he would have slapped down the $100,000 admission fee immediately. But in the society into which he was seeking entrée, joining would have signaled that he was hopelessly nouveau.

Trump had purchased the club in 1985 for eight million dollars, plus three million for the furnishings. By the early nineties, everything was falling apart, including his marriage to Ivana Trump. He had about nine hundred million dollars in personal debt, as well as three to four billion dollars in corporate debt, which led to three business bankruptcies though Trump never declared personal bankruptcy. He had not paid the mortgage on Mar-a-Lago for about two years, and sought to subdivide the seventeen-acre property into lots for eight other homes. The previous potential buyer of

Mar-a-Lago had received permission to divide the property, but the Landmarks Preservation Commission turned the New York mogul down cold. That left Trump with an incredibly expensive salmon-colored elephant costing him not only his unpaid mortgage, but also about two million dollars a year in upkeep.

In 1992, as he was trying to decide if he should sue the town, Trump had dinner with Paul Rampell, a local trust estate attorney. The Princeton graduate had grown up in a section in the North End of the island that was largely Jewish, and he had an astute understanding of the social dynamics of Palm Beach. When Rampell suggested that Trump consider turning Mar-a-Lago into a private club, the real estate mogul immediately rejected the idea.

A few days later, Trump called the attorney to talk some more. "I'll tell you another reason why the club isn't a good idea," Trump said, arguing as much with himself as the Jewish attorney. "The memberships will never sell."

"You don't understand the demographics of the island," Rampell replied forcefully. "The town of Palm Beach is probably about half Christian and about half Jewish. There are five clubs right now. Four of those clubs are restricted. No Jews. No African Americans. And there are about four or five thousand members. There's only one club where Jewish residents can go, and that's the Palm Beach Country Club. It only has three hundred membership slots. They're all full, and it's very expensive. So you've got an island with a lot of Jewish residents who have no club to go to."

"Well, maybe," Trump said, ending the conversation but buying into the idea.

Trump could get no recognized attorney to take on his case to win permission for a club. So reluctantly, but with a large retainer in his pocket, Rampell agreed to represent Trump, even though he says it cost him half his practice.

When it comes to politics, Palm Beach is like the former Soviet Union. The truths that matter are whispered, and even then only among those who share one's views. Everyone conversant with Trump's plan knew that the club would be largely Jewish, but no one said so publicly. And everyone knew that in the crucial vote in the town council, the three Christians would almost certainly vote no, the two Jews would vote yes, and Trump would be turned down. But nobody said that either.

Trump was the new Palm Beach; a loud, assertive, energetic force that overwhelmed the well-tended garden of entitlement. The WASP elite could fume and fuss over their vodka martinis at the B&T, but there was nothing they could do about Trump. He was the future. He was the herald of a gaudy gilded age of power and privilege that would sweep over the genteel old world of the island. He said what he had to say and did what he had to do, to get what he wanted to get. He had no problem suing the town for fifty million dollars for turning down his previous plan, all the while having his minions present his new plan for a club at the town council meetings. He could be civil and endlessly polite when such conduct served his purposes, but behind his courteous manner was an implied threat. He and the world he represented were not to be stopped by the meek, conciliatory leaders of the island.

In the end, the town council voted four to one in favor of the club. Mar-a-Lago became largely a Jewish club, though nobody called it that. It changed the social dynamic in a way nothing had in the hundred-year history of the island. Mar-a-Lago was anathema to much of the gentile gentry, some of whom refused to set foot in a place that they thought rightfully was theirs. And there were Jews like David Berger who wanted no part of it either; at Mar-a-Lago, they would have had intimate contact with their religious brethren, and in doing so be identified by their faith.

There is nothing the old elite hates so much and fears so profoundly as Donald Trump's club. The Everglades Club and B&T had been the enclave of the social elite. Those who sought to enter the sanctified portals slavishly copied the manners and mores of the members—but that is no longer true.

Mar-a-Lago is a pure plutocracy open to anybody who has the $100,000 membership fee, the $5,000 annual dues ($125,000 and $10,000 in 2008), and enough money to ring up hefty bills each month. The overwhelmingly Jewish club represents the most important social development in Palm Beach in decades. It broke the back of the old gentile establishment, and turned the island into a community where Jews could feel themselves no longer members of a gilded ghetto, but full participants in the most privileged activities on the island.

There are many Mar-a-Lago members who match those at the restricted clubs in grace and culture, but a vociferous minority sets the tone. Not only do they not intend to copy the WASP elite, they are largely unaware how far removed their behavior is from what once was considered civilized. Unlike previous generations of nouveau, they do not mimic the behavior of their social betters, but bring up their children with the same studied lack of what once were called manners. They are so insensitive to the world beyond them that they are unaware of the scenes they make and the disarray they often leave in their wake.

Most of these nouveau are Jewish, and no one is more embarrassed by their conduct than other Jewish islanders who call them "New Yorkers." The term is not geographically accurate, since most New York Jews do not qualify, and a good number of "New Yorkers" are not even from New York; but that is the term that is used. Jews from Pittsburgh and Toronto cringe at the behavior of their fellow Jews, but no one spoke more forcefully or more angrily than other Jews from New York City who hate to be associated with such gaudy guests. They had blown into Palm Beach on the high tide of money, and do whatever pleases them.

One day two "New Yorkers" came strutting into the luncheonette at Green's Pharmacy as if it were a theater and they the stars of the drama, and sat down at the counter. It is one of the few downscale places to eat on the island, and for locals, one of the most popular.

Nanci Hewitt knew that if she did not serve the men immediately, they would start kvetching loudly, and Nanci turned from other customers to take their orders. When the waitress set the hamburger special before the men, one of them looked down on it as if observing a crime. "There aren't enough French fries!" he screamed, his voice reverberating through the luncheonette. "You've cheated us!"

As Nanci walked back to the two men, almost anyone would

have recognized that she was furious, but to them her momentary pique was of no matter. By now everyone in the little restaurant had stopped eating. Nanci leaned over the counter and with her index finger no more than half an inch over the plate began loudly counting French fries.

"One . . . two . . . three . . . four . . . five . . . six," Nanci counted, her finger moving across the plate. "Seven . . . eight . . . nine . . . ten . . . eleven. . . . Eleven!!! There's one too *fucking* many!!!" She plucked a fry off the plate and threw it on the floor. If this had truly been a theater, Nanci would have received a standing ovation.

9

King of the New Yorkers

The Great Donald may have been the son of a wealthy real estate developer, but the Protestant mogul is the uncrowned king of the "New Yorkers." If the more difficult of the Mar-a-Lago members aspire to be like anyone, it is not one of the pallid WASPs next door at the B&T, but the Donald himself. Many of them call to see if he is flying in on his jet for the weekend, and if he is, they make reservations for brunch or dinner. If he is elsewhere, the club is often half-empty.

Trump is not some prissy, reclusive mogul like the late John D. Rockefeller, but a man of the people who on special occasions greets guests at the door like Uncle Ho at Uncle Ho's all-you-can-eat Chinese buffet. He has the social skills of a populist politician, calling members by their names as his butler walks behind him whispering them to him, backslapping and joshing as he glad-hands his way through those having lunch on the veranda.

The Donald is not only about money, he *is* money; to the nouveau, the one sure sign of human value. And like many of his fellow New Yorkers, the Donald believes that wealth does not require one to be laced into a cultural straitjacket. It means you can do what you want to do, when you want to do it. When Trump feels like playing the democrat, he is a man of the people, and when he wants to be alone, he sends off signals clear to all but the most foolhardy.

When he is angry at a member of his staff, he is perfectly capable of berating him in front of club members. And when he is hungry, he does not want the gussied-up cuisine on the Mar-a-Lago menu. At such moments, Tony Senecal, his butler, carries a silver platter full of cheeseburgers and French fries as big as small bananas to Donald's suite, and returns a few minutes later with a volcano of vanilla ice cream erupting in chocolate sauce.

The butler is the soul of Mar-a-Lago. Tony loves the estate with passionate, detailed concern and he is the true guardian of its past and its spirit. Tony has seen the movie *Remains of the Day* at least twenty-seven times, and would like nothing more than to be the American version of the classic butler played by Anthony Hopkins, but he will never quite make it. It is not only that he is too witty, too opinionated, and too lively, but unlike the Hopkins character, seventy-six-year-old Tony has had a richer life than most of the people he serves. He was a young man when he came to work for Marjorie Merriweather Post as a footman in 1959, and in the off-season he also worked as a teacher, restaurant proprietor, country club manager, and a radio talk show host. He had been on top of his world, and at the bottom, bankrupt. He had two children and one divorce.

Working for Mrs. Post, Tony saw a world of order, propriety, and organic concern that he found exquisite. Her father had not begun his life as a wealthy man, and she could easily be called nouveau, but she had a sense of manners and grace that largely died with her and her generation. She not only knew her servants' names, but their wives' and children's names and everything about them, and they generally stayed with her forever. She watched over them, almost as much as they watched out for her. When they retired they received what they thought were pensions, but when she died the monthly checks died too.

At eleven a.m. on the days of her frequent formal dinners for thirty-six, Tony helped set the table with priceless silver and magnificent china, and he stood behind that one chair all during the evenings. The servants were a collegial group who helped each other, and saw that when their colleague did well, they did well too.

It was unlike what it has become, each employee out for himself, no loyalty to anything but their own advance. "If you made a mistake in front of Mrs. Post in the morning, you would hear about it by noon, but never from her," Tony recalls. "It would come down the chain. These people sort of took you in and made you the best that you could be. There was no 'Well, if he falls, he falls.' They wanted to make sure you never failed."

Mrs. Post died in 1973, and Tony returned twenty years later to become Trump's butler. During the first year he helped oversee the restoration of the estate and the preparation to turn Mar-a-Lago into a club. One day Trump was making a tour of the facilities with Tony and Frank Moffet, the steward who oversaw the kitchen. When they walked into the kitchen, Trump noticed a big safe.

"What the hell's in it?" Trump asked.

"Well, the gold and silver," the steward said.

"Does anybody have the combination?"

The steward opened the wall safe and it was full of a treasure that because Post's heirs had not claimed it was now Trump's property.

Just before the club opened, Tony learned that he was going to be the concierge, a lucrative, prestigious position. He was serving breakfast to Trump when his employer brought up the new job. "Well, you don't sound too happy about it," Trump said, amazed at Tony's reaction.

"Of course I'm not happy about it."

"What the hell do you want to do?" an incredulous Trump replied.

"Well, I figured until I was too feeble to carry a tray that I would stay your butler."

"Are you serious?" asked the man who thought he had heard everything.

"Of course," Tony replied, as if how could there be any question.

Trump got up and hit Tony on the arm with a comradely swipe of his fist. "Well, then, goddamn it, the butler you'll be."

Tony would have stayed living in Mar-a-Lago until he could work no longer, but Trump could make good money renting out his room, and after a few years he asked his butler to live elsewhere.

TRUMP MAY BE A self-created caricature, but no one understands the psychology of the new gilded age as well as he does, and no one is both as emulated and as despised in Palm Beach. He hired and fired chefs until he had a formidable menu and an alert, personable staff. When Donald opened a great golden ballroom in 2005, it soon became the most desirable venue for charity events on the island, bringing streams of people onto the island most evenings during the season.

Palm Beach residents had always assumed that when they drove to the B&T or the Everglades for dinner, they were entering the most desirable venue in town, but at Mar-a-Lago, the entertainment is more exciting, the scene more energized. To the dying WASP breed next door, it is unthinkable that a group of pathetic parvenus should have taken over the greatest estate on the island and turned it into such a place.

Nothing more irritates members of the B&T than that Trump purchased beachfront land first offered to their club, and built a beach club there that dwarfs and diminishes everything next door. The two-story cabanas at Mar-a-Lago are gorgeous, whereas the old beachfront wooden cabanas at the B&T could sit comfortably next to the Bates Motel in *Psycho*. At Trump's club, the members lie on lounges next to the Olympic-size pool where white-coated waiters serve them piña coladas and shrimp salads; while next door, the B&T members stand in a cafeteria line for lunch.

One day in the late nineties, the black hip-hop artist Puff Daddy walked across the beach from Mar-a-Lago to the B&T with a white woman who was not his wife, and took up residence in a mini cabana on the beach. Puff Daddy began performing coitus on his willing partner. In possible deference to the conservative sentiment of the club, he employed only the missionary position. When a security guard approached and suggested that he stop, the rapper raged that the official had ruined his "concentration."

When the rap artist returned to the safety of Mar-a-Lago, he told Trump how rude the WASPs at the B&T had been. Trump was the Wizard of Publicity, sitting behind his little machine sending out vast clouds of bright, dark, malevolent sandstorms, hail, mist—it did not matter how it looked, as long as it made him more famous. He was picking up the phone to call a gossip columnist, when Senecal says that he gently suggested that perhaps Mr. Trump should wait a few minutes to learn just what had happened. In the end, when Trump heard in detail about this *From Here to Eternity* moment on the beach, he realized that it was not to his benefit to have a story out there about his weekend guest having sex within a few feet of children and non-consenting adults. The story got into the newspapers only because a member of the B&T conversant with public relations called a gossip columnist to tweak Donald and his déclassé Mar-a-Lago. When the story made *Time*, the rapper's spokesperson said that it could not have been Puff Daddy but must have been an imposter.

The final dénouement was a bitter drink for the gentry at the B&T to choke down. Estée Lauder was one of the great names of modern American merchandising, and a social fixture in Palm Beach for years, but she was one of "them." In the wake of the founder's death in 2004, her company signed a licensing agreement with Puff Daddy, now metamorphosed as Sean Combs, for what became the company's best-selling perfume line. The initial fragrance was *Unforgiveable*, a sentiment with which the gentlemen and ladies at the B&T would surely have agreed.

Even the most passionate enemies of Trump's club had never envisioned that the day would come when a man of color would fornicate on the beach in front of the B&T, or that millions of Americans would wear his perfume. These well-brought-up scions of wealth were bewildered, even shattered, by the incomprehensible changes. They heard the sounds of Tony Bennett and Wayne Newton wafting through the night air from the enormous Mar-a-Lago ballroom. They read about the celebrated pros playing tennis with Donald at the annual pro-am on the Mar-a-Lago courts. They saw Donald sailing in his yacht along the coast in front of the club as if to taunt them. They observed young beauties parading down the beach in the thongs and bikinis outlawed at the B&T.

One day a woman arrived at the Mar-a-Lago Olympic-size pool, took off her wrap, and strutted around the pool nude. She was a member's lover, but this day, she was decidedly by herself. No one was more surprised and upset than Steve Greenwald, an attorney who had retired while still in his forties after a heart attack. As he lay back on his chaise, Steve pretended to read the *Palm Beach Post*, but his eyes kept darting back to the woman who was prancing around the pool, ignoring the entreaties of one couple to cover herself. She appeared to be in her late thirties, and had a body that could have been built by Boeing.

The woman jumped into the heated water and swam back and forth, most of the time on her back. "Why don't you take off your trunks and come join me, Big Boy," the woman said. "You're kind of cute."

"I'm married," Steve sputtered, although even if he had been a confirmed bachelor, he would have stayed put.

"You'd better do something about this," Steve half whispered to one of the waiters.

The woman finally got out of the pool, lay down on a chaise, and ordered a hot dog. When the white-coated waiter brought the dish, she doused it in mustard as if trying to put out a fire. She devoured the food in three bites, leaving her face swathed in yellow like a mudpack.

After about forty-five minutes of frontal nudity, Bernd Lembcke, the German-born manager, arrived. No matter what Lembcke saw or heard, he had the same courtier's demeanor that hovered on the border of servility. By now, the chaises were full of members, and Lembcke went up to each one and greeted him or her with small talk, arranging it so that the last person he greeted was the nude woman. He stood before the nudist, looking uninterestedly at her breasts. Within a few minutes, she donned a beach wrap and sauntered away just as casually as she had arrived, and the members returned to their shrimp salads garnished with the gossip of the day.

. . .

Trump's greatest triumph in Palm Beach is not Mar-a-Lago but the creation of Palm Beach International Golf Club. There was no land for another golf course in Palm Beach and scarcely any in West Palm Beach. Only Trump could envision 214 acres of wretched scrub land south of Palm Beach International Airport, next to the Palm Beach County Detention Center, as a world-class golf course. And only Trump could figure a way to acquire the land at a bargain price while mitigating one of his most pesky problems.

When Marjorie Merriweather Post owned Mar-a-Lago, there was a tacit agreement that planes flying in and out of the airport would not pass directly over her estate. That agreement was long gone and PBIA was now a major facility with hundreds of planes every day during the season. On a Friday afternoon, playing tennis at Mar-a-Lago was like standing on the subway platform in Times Square. That was the time of day that often one heard a roaring, ominous sound in the sky above. That one of the noisiest planes in the air arriving for the weekend was Trump's own Boeing 727 did not prevent the real estate magnate from raging against this outrageous incursion.

Lawsuits were Trump's Kalashnikov, a cheap and effective weapon to kill his opponents. In June 1995 he ordered his attorneys to sue Palm Beach County for a whopping seventy-five million dollars for noise and air pollution and "visual intrusion." The following year he settled the suit overwhelmingly in his terms. The county promised to avoid flying over Mar-a-Lago and agreed to lease him the scrub land for $438,000 in annual rent for a minimum of thirty years. Upon that land he built his golf course, and charged those who wanted to play $300,000 memberships separate from Mar-a-Lago and $10,000 a year dues. The 2007–2008 member handbook lists 276 members willing to have their names and phone numbers listed. Those members alone likely netted Trump over $80,000,000 plus close to $3 million in annual dues.

I am not a golfer, but one day I drove out with a friend and his son-in-law in his Bentley to walk around the course while they played eighteen holes. The Bentley is the Volkswagen, the people's car, of Trump International, and the circular driveway was lined with valet-parked Bentleys. The clubhouse looks as if it had been built by a sultan who had seen too many Indiana Jones movies. There are massive kneeling bronze gladiators who had never had a golf club in their hands. The entire place is fastidiously rendered in similar taste.

While my friend and his son-in-law warmed up hitting balls at the driving range, I started talking to the caddy, a garrulous, entertaining man who had been hauling golf bags for years. Like his associates, he did not work for the club but was paid directly by each golfer. He had seen it all, and in some measure he had seen too much. It was beyond him why so many of the members were so intensely dissatisfied. Nothing pleased them. They fought over tee times. They complained about the food. The hot water wasn't hot enough or it was too hot, and the cold water was lukewarm. They whined about the pathetic, meandering foursome in front of them, and raged about the belligerent, threatening foursome behind.

The course itself is incomparable, with mini mountains and lakes, and all sorts of obstacles fascinating to a golfer. If not for the concrete spire of the county jail rising above everything, one could easily be playing at a top club in Nantucket or Santa Barbara. The caddy said that Trump was a compulsive perfectionist who every time he played golf on the course found something else to be improved and new work for his employees.

When we reached the seventeenth hole, I exclaimed how exquisite it was, a verdant oasis with a pond full of swans. That was when the caddy told me the story of what had happened there in 2004. These swans, like most animals and indeed like humans, are proprietary. If they feel their nesting area is threatened, they hiss and raise their wings. Apparently, a rare black swan did so to Cyril Wagner, a guest from New York. With one mighty swing of his titanium driver, Wagner killed the rare bird. He claimed self-defense—just him and the bird fighting for their lives—and was sentenced to thirty hours of community service.

As we walked back to the clubhouse, the caddy told me a story of an accident far more serious that had largely been covered up February 2007, club member Irving Stein was driving a golf cart that hit a caddy, Tyler Buchanan, knocking the man down and causing serious injuries. Stein drove on and apparently initially refused to pay the caddy's medical bills. It was a frightening occurrence, for Buchanan and for the other caddies, since they have no insurance or benefits, and in April 2008, Buchanan filed a suit against Stein.

For the caddy with whom I had been talking, it was all disconcerting and inexplicable. These club members that he saw every day had what he considered everything, but nothing was ever good enough. Even swans and caddies were not safe.

10

"Nice *Nothing*!"

There was something overwhelmingly nouveau about David Berger, from his two Mercedes-Benz 560Sls, the white car for day, the gold one for evening, to the books on his shelves, including *The Very Rich—a History of Wealth* and *True Greed.* Barbara had convinced David to give enough money to charity so that he now had a public image of generosity, but as much as she had tried to educate him into spending his fortune, Barbara saw David as philosophically cheap. She had to pry money out of him; and she could only do so by making him believe that he had spent it of his own volition.

There is no more crucial act in Palm Beach than buying the right house on the right street. It is important to have the proper Realtor who will champion one's social advance. Just before Barbara began living with David, he had moved from a one-bedroom to a penthouse apartment at overwhelmingly Jewish Breakers Row. That was a step up, but to Barbara, it was still ghetto living.

When David and Barbara received an invitation for dinner at Marylou Whitney's home on Jungle Road, David was ecstatic. He had never had such a prestigious invitation in Palm Beach, and he was almost childlike in his excitement.

Until the last few years, Marylou and her husband, Cornelius Vanderbilt "Sonny" Whitney, had stayed each season with the Gillets. Although Marylou never spent more than a few weeks on the island, she had an almost unequaled prestige there.

"When the Whitneys get here, it's like the Duke and Duchess of Windsor arriving," a Palm Beach socialite told *Town & Country*.

Like her close friend Brownie, Marylou had arrived in New York City from the provinces right after World War II. The Kansas City native was just as pretty as Brownie, and ten times as shrewd. Marylou hired her own theatrical press agent, Teddy Howard, who shepherded the sensational-looking petite blonde around town, introducing her as a cattle heiress. One evening she rode a horse up to El Boracho, hitched it outside as if the restaurant were a Montana saloon, and walked inside.

Marylou married Frank Hosford, heir to the John Deere agricultural equipment fortune. Hosford dissipated his fortune in drunken excess, and they divorced, leaving Marylou a single mother with four small children. On a blind date, Marylou met fifty-seven-year-old Whitney, almost twice Marylou's age. This dark, moody, complicated son of privilege was nicknamed Sonny. Rarely has a moniker been so misapplied. This difficult, unpredictable man called his book of autobiographical sketches *High Peaks*, and that was how he lived—high peaks and deep depressions.

Whitney was a tall, well-built man of courtly manners and a diffident, almost deferential demeanor. When he was younger, he had been only a few yards short of handsome, but as he aged, his chin receded unattractively.

When Marylou first came to New York, she had not dated far older men, but her prospects had changed. She was a single mother approaching middle age. To marry one of the wealthiest men in America, even one who was cantankerous and almost twice her age, was an enviable attainment.

In January 1958, Marylou and Sonny flew into Carson City, Nevada, to take their vows. Marylou had wanted a vastly wealthy husband, and she had gotten a real one this time, albeit a man twenty-six years her senior with psychological difficulties that had bedeviled his previous wives. The day after their wedding, Sonny's daughter Gail Whitney eloped with Richard Cowell, a young man Marylou had dated in New York.

Marylou was such a socially unacceptable match that for a decade Sonny was cast out of the *Social Register*. In the end, Marylou was not so much a social queen as a social superstar who loved to stand in the spotlight glare of publicity while Sonny stood in her shadows. At times, said a family friend, she employed "at least five press agents" to trumpet her praises in the society pages.

In her years with Sonny, Marylou turned herself into almost as much a Whitney and Vanderbilt as was Sonny himself. Marylou spoke in nasal tonalities, as if a surgeon had implanted corks in her nostrils. Hers had become an old-fashioned patrician accent rarely heard west of the Mississippi, or even on the West Side of Manhattan.

Marylou was a geishalike wife just over half her husband's age. Sonny was an aging man-boy with an overweening, blinding ego. She was devoted to his pleasure, from spectacular sex to home-cooked meals, and all of it delivered with the most refined flattery.

Marylou created an elaborate, exaggerated fantasy for her husband. Only a man with the crippling conceit that sometimes comes with inherited wealth would have thought it all true. Sonny had been a crack polo player as a young man, and he still fancied himself an athlete and sportsman. He challenged his young wife to footraces, and he always won. He was an avid angler, particularly on the private lakes that were part of his 55,000-acre preserve in the Adirondacks. No matter how many times the couple cast their poles into the cool blue water, he always caught the bigger fish. "You know you have to let a man do everything first," Marylou once said. "Men have to have their egos built up."

Sonny adored sitting in the kitchen watching as his ravishing wife prepared yet another gourmet specialty. "He loved for me to pop hot croissants or cookies in his mouth," Marylou says. "He was like a beautiful bird opening his mouth to be fed."

Marylou had brought Sonny moments of happiness, but he still had the same manic-depressive mood swings, the darkness descending on him like a full eclipse of the sun at high noon. She continued the same shrewd approach that she had applied from the evening she met him. "If he was morose, I'd say, 'I'm so sorry, it must be awful.' I'd cry and say, 'Oh, I feel awful too.' And he would be completely back to normal. That was the only way to handle it, to say, 'It's my fault.'"

Sonny was not only moody but also extremely jealous and suspicious. He still fancied himself something of a playboy, flirting outrageously with any attractive woman who came near. But woe to any man who dared to talk too much, to laugh too loud, or to dance too long with his wife. Sonny did not care who it was. One evening he berated Henry Kissinger as he had raged against scores of others. "I know you're a friend of mine," he said in a steely voice of contained fury. "But I just want you to know one thing. This is my girl, and I own her."

Like many of his contemporaries in Palm Beach, Sonny thought that by marrying a much younger woman, her youth would spill over to him, and he would cheat the gods of grayness and decline. But instead, every time he saw his vital young bride dancing with a man half his age, he felt even older. Increasingly, he admitted, "the frightening spectre of old age came to haunt me. All the more in my case, as I am married to a younger lady."

Sonny behaved with a crude possessiveness that would have crushed a weaker woman. But Marylou saw herself as a person who paid her debts. She accepted her husband's behavior because she was overwhelmingly thankful to him for the world of luxury and exclusion that was now hers.

In 1984, eighty-five-year-old Sonny suffered a serious aneurysm and sunk into a state of increasing dementia. From then on, he was in a wheelchair overseen by omnipresent nurses as much as by his wife. Sonny had always loved the bracing frigid weather of the far north, but now he cringed at even a breath of cold air. Nor did he like to go to the Adirondack camp that had always been his favorite retreat but now only reminded him of his disability. So the couple began spending more time each winter in Palm Beach.

Eles Gillet loved Marylou's company, but she found it exhausting having her as a houseguest. Marylou always had a glass of champagne in her small, manicured hands, although she drank little more than a sip. Late at night, she had the chauffeur drive her in a convertible up and down South Ocean Boulevard holding a champagne flute, past the estates, past Mar-a-Lago and the Bath and Tennis, past the great open beaches, with the moon hanging up there like stage lighting.

Marylou would arrive back in the house at four in the morning with her chauffeur. She would set her glass on the piano as the chauffeur played for hours before everyone greeted the dawn by finally heading to bed.

Eles was doubly happy when one day, Marylou said, "I've had so much fun here, I want to buy a house." That was cue enough to her husband, Warry Gillet, who that very afternoon showed Marylou two houses, including one a few streets away on Jungle Road that she bought without much ado or negotiating, as aristocrats weren't supposed to haggle or bargain.

Marylou's new home had only three bedrooms, but there were spectacularly large rooms for entertaining, and that would be the setting for several splendid parties. She brought with her seventeen gowns, one for every formal occasion during the monthlong visit.

When Marylou drove into Palm Beach, she was stepping on a stage. "I feel like this is a Cinderella world," she told the Shiny Sheet. "I go to all these balls and everyone looks beautiful. The music is fantastic and the food is glorious and everyone is drinking champagne. It's like a movie set or something."

Since Sonny was no longer in any shape to be out at social events, Marylou attended the major charity balls with an escort, usually James "Jimmy" Barker. Although technically Jimmy was a "walker," the term hardly defined him. Jimmy was a gay Kentuckian of impeccable stock who owned a house on the island and ran a Worth Avenue art gallery. The septuagenarian bon vivant was such a devoté of Staffordshire Cavalier King Charles spaniels that he not only had a hundred or so porcelain dogs in his sitting room, but as many as sixteen of them running live through his house.

Barker was an endlessly solicitous escort, faultlessly amusing and full of light patter. At the 1992 Red Cross Ball, he held Marylou's evening bag as she walked beside him in her pink strapless Scaasi, her hair adorned with a shimmering tiara.

"Jimmy, I guess I'm as bad at social climbing as anybody," Marylou confided. "And I'm still climbing, J., but you know what, there's nothing at the top."

"Marylou, if you get to the top, there'll be somebody there," Jimmy replied, laughing.

"Jimmy, you mean you don't think I've gotten there already?"

For years, Marylou watched over the sadly diminished figure of her husband. She sat in his lap in his wheelchair, and hugged him like a teenager in love, but it was an exhausting, thankless regimen that had no ending and no relief. "When is it going to be my time?" she asked Parker Ladd, a gay publishing executive and lover of dress designer Arnold Scaasi. "Be patient," he told her.

When ninety-three-year-old Sonny died in December 1992, Marylou did not don widow's weeds and mourn for months. She celebrated his life, and then quickly moved on. Neglecting his own children in death as he had in life, he had willed his wife his entire inheritance of over one hundred million dollars. The probating of the will took time, and there was a possibility that his grandchildren would file a suit trying to overturn the will. Marylou faced the unthinkable: a cash flow problem. She had a solution that was equally unthinkable: to sell her Palm Beach home. As Marylou recalls, "My oldest son said, 'You don't need it anymore. You had it to take care of Sonny, and you have so many other places. Why don't you think of selling?' "

Most sixty-six-year-old widows might have sold their remote Adirondacks camp, instead of an elegant Palm Beach home where a single woman of certain age would feel safe and wanted. If the glamorous widow had decided to spend more time in Palm Beach, she could have quickly become the acknowledged social queen of the island, but she did not want that. She had lived passively for too long watching over Sonny, and now she wanted to live adventurously. Friends such as Jimmy Barker told her that she was making a mistake, but she did not listen.

Scarcely a month after Sonny's death, she set out to sell Elephant Walk, and to do so with Warry as her agent. She started out, not with boring open houses and ads in the Shiny Sheet, but by giving a party to which she invited a few potential buyers, including David Berger and Barbara Wainscott.

"It's so nice of Marylou to invite us," David said in enthusiastic anticipation as they drove over to the Whitney home on Jungle Road.

"Nice *nothing*!" Barbara replied. "She's trying to sell the house. It's in her name, and the will is going to take forever. She's inviting everybody who has enough money to buy the house, and a few for window dressing. She wants to sell it furnished."

"I just might buy it," David mused.

"You'll *never* buy it," Barbara retorted, in both a realistic appraisal and an attempt to goad him into spending money that he did not want to spend.

Marylou spent no more than six weeks at Elephant Walk each year, and though the residential quarters were relatively modest, it was a fitting home for a couple who would be entertaining on a grand scale.

Marylou had spent her life pleasing men, and she knew precisely how to give a stylish dinner party that would appeal to David. That evening, he saw the life he wanted. The house had the social patina that David so profoundly desired. Like most major homes on the island, it had a name affixed to it, Elephant Walk, giving the cachet of a nobleman's ancient estate.

The next day, David returned to meet with his hostess. Over champagne and caviar, he bought "the Whitney estate" from Marylou for $2.8 million. In a time of little real estate appreciation, David paid nine hundred thousand dollars more than Marylou had paid six years earlier. It was a difference so profound that it amounted to yet another of David's many social gratuities. Then David bought the furnishings for four hundred thousand dollars and hired Marylou's entire staff, in an act as close as he could come to buying her position and ambience.

It often took a year or more to sell a house in Palm Beach. Marylou had done it in a wink at a fabulous premium. Given all that, it might have seemed that the heiress could have sprung for a bash honoring the new owners. Instead, in March of 1994, Barbara and David invited Marylou back to her former house for their first major Palm Beach party. She could hardly turn them down, and some of Marylou's closest friends arrived to spend an evening with David and Barbara. Marylou then invited the new owners to visit her at the Whitney summer camp in the Adirondacks, an invitation Barbara made sure others were well aware of.

11

Half of Everything

"All I'm asking for, Fred, is what any other European woman would have in her marriage," Rose Keller said, speaking in German into her husband's ear. "Half of *everything.* I deserve that." It was two o'clock in the morning, and thirty-year-old Rose had just awakened her sixty-four-year-old husband, Fred Keller, in the master bedroom of their 8,000-square-foot home to drone her message into his ear. It was a scenario repeated several times a week.

Rose thought of herself as doubly foreign, both German-born and alien to the social dramas of the island. She did not have the sense of history or psychological insight to realize that she was far closer to the lives of the women she read about in the *Palm Beach Daily News* than she possibly could have imagined. Many of these women pictured in the Shiny Sheet had married far older men, for reasons that were at least partially mercenary. Many of them had gone through the same struggles that Rose was having now. They had been much like her at one time, and they had applied plastic surgery not only to their faces but to their pasts, snipping away at the unseemly and unattractive, exercising the mean and the low. There was no reason why Rose could not do the same.

. . .

Henry Flagler, who founded the island, had also taken a much younger wife. Flagler was the son of an itinerant upstate New York minister. After Flagler and his partner John D. Rockefeller built Standard Oil into a monolith, the industrial baron embarked on the second act of his life, creating the basis for modern Florida by building railways, ship lines, and hotels.

Flagler had initially come to Jacksonville during the winter of 1878 with his tubercular first wife, Mary Flagler. Except for the narrow northern tier, Florida was then a largely uninhabited region, as wild as the remote areas of the West. South Florida was inhabited by former slaves, white renegades, frontiersmen, and those who sought only to hide.

Flagler's wife died three years later, and he married her nursemaid, Ida Alice Shourds. It was a marriage appalling to his son, and an insult to the haute world to which Flagler's money gave him entrée. Ida Alice was eighteen years his junior, of lower class status, in every respect a socially embarrassing match.

Flagler's wife changed in a matter of months from a modest servant to a wife of endless extravagance. Her husband worried that Ida Alice was going mad. Flagler was unused to problems he could not solve, but this was a conundrum.

In January 1891, sixty-one-year-old Flagler met twenty-three-year-old Mary Lily Kenan on a Caribbean cruise on a friend's yacht. Mary Lily hailed from Wilmington, North Carolina. Born after the Civil War in 1867, Lily had the gracious, eyelash-fluttering femininity of the antebellum Southern Belle, tempered with the tough spirit of survival of Reconstruction.

After the cruise, Flagler sent a train pulling his private railroad car, the Arcadia, to North Carolina to bring back Mary Lily and his other new friends to St. Augustine, Florida. This was a royal passage in a luxurious rail car that deposited the passengers at a rail siding at the magnificent Spanish-Renaissance-style hotel built by Flagler. At a ball that evening at the Ponce de Leon, Mary Lily danced with Flagler. He was over twice her age, and by the reckoning of his time, an old man. Yet he still cut a fine figure.

Flagler had several mistresses, as well as his intimate friendship with Mary Lily. He vested a million and a half dollars on Mary Lily in Standard Oil stocks. He was also generous to Mrs. C. W. Foote, whose estranged husband presented papers and affidavits documenting that Flagler had maintained his wife in a New York City apartment from December 1896 to June 1897. Mary Lily had sacrificed her opportunity to find an appropriate match to settle for the morally untenable but lucrative role as mistress to an unfaithful lover and married man.

There was no masking Ida Alice's debilitating mental illness, and Flagler was not about to have an insane wife dogging his steps. He had his wife committed to an asylum in Pleasantville, New York, where she spent the rest of her life.

Flagler wanted to marry Mary Lily, but the law was quite specific: A man could not divorce his wife simply because she was insane. Yet Flagler convinced the Florida legislature to pass a law so that he could divorce his institutionalized wife.

Mary Lily married seventy-one-year-old Flagler on August 24, 1901, ten days after the divorce became final. Flagler had aged dramatically and his thirty-four-year-old bride was not the youthful, buoyant belle of a decade ago. His son Harry described her accurately as "rather plain of face, but had red hair of an attractive hue and a beautiful figure."

For his bride, Flagler built a 55-room, 60,000-square-foot marble palace next to the Royal Poinciana Hotel that Mary Lily dubbed Whitehall. Here, the couple ruled as the sovereigns of the island. Eighty-three-year-old Flagler died in 1913, leaving forty-five-year-old Mary Lily the wealthiest woman in America. Worth over a hundred million dollars, the widow closed down Whitehall, moved to New York, and traveled restlessly on her private train car.

The wife of her youthful beau, Robert Bingham, had died at the same time as Flagler, and three years later, the former sweethearts decided to marry. Four and a half years younger than Mary Lily, the handsome Bingham was a trophy husband, pure and simple. Before marrying her, he signed a prenuptial agreement. Seven months after their November 1916 wedding, Mary Lily signed a codicil to her will, giving her husband five million dollars. Two months later, she was dead. Bingham took part of his money and purchased the *Louisville Courier*, starting one of the great newspaper dynasties of the twentieth century.

There were whispers that Bingham had murdered his wife, but the most authoritative researchers believe that she likely died of syphilis given to her by Flagler, though possibly by Bingham.

ROSE HAD MET FRED Keller through an ad in a German newspaper in the fall of 1991. Rose lied to Fred and said she had graduated from high school, when she had left one year short of graduation. At twenty-three, she had known that her most precious asset, her looks, was already diminishing. She called herself a model, but that was more an aspiration than reality.

Rose had lived for a while with a German Polish man in Bangkok, and then she had moved back to her hometown of Dorlar, near Düsseldorf in northwestern Germany. She was the oldest of six children. Her parents were divorced. She could not abide her father, and had nothing to do with him. Her mother ran a little dress shop, and Rose had accompanied her to Milan on a buying trip, where she had met a man who promised to help her with her modeling career. However, she had felt uneasy with him, and she had returned to Germany uncertain of what to do with her life.

Rose had sent a picture and a letter to Fred, and he had done the same. The bearded man seemed ancient, but she had been impressed by her talks with him on the phone. He spoke a courtly, old-fashioned German that he had learned from his immigrant parents, and could switch seamlessly from an almost fatherly role to that of a potential lover. He invited her to go on a worldwide trip with him. That gave her no exit if she could not abide him, and she turned that offer down. Instead, she accepted an airline ticket for a weeklong visit, and arrived at Miami International Airport in March 1992 with a hundred dollars in her purse. She was, in her estimation, "young, beautiful, the whole world in front of me, and a brain in my head too, even though I didn't have a diploma hanging on my wall."

Rose was impressed with her Palm Beach millionaire. Fred had all the accoutrements of wealth, including a spacious residence in the center of Palm Beach, a pool, a guesthouse, a maid, a yacht, and a car and driver. A true aficionado of wealth would have realized that almost everything was a little off, from the mismatched furniture and knockoff china to the inexpensive prints on the wall, even the cheap décor of the yacht. But Rose noticed none of these subtleties and found life with her millionaire magical.

The couple hit it off so well that it was unthinkable for Rose to leave. Fred had been diagnosed with chronic lymphocytic leukemia. They flew to Houston, Texas, to the M. D. Anderson Cancer Center. Rose drove Fred to doctors' appointments, waited patiently in the outer offices, and heard the good news that Fred might live far longer than the two or three years he thought he had left. Fred did not seem like a sick man, and Rose felt that with his close-cropped gray beard, he looked like the actor Sean Connery. He may have been in his late fifties, but he was in superb physical condition, enhanced by his almost daily tennis games, his rigorous diet that included a tuna fish sandwich for lunch each day, a moderate dinner, no smoking, and almost no drinking.

Fred often appeared unassuming, but he had a ruthless core. He had made his fortune in commercial real estate and he had done so by giving no man any quarter. He felt that he was the perfect example of the master race, a man who had risen out of dust and disdain to build a fortune.

In these first weeks together, they talked often about their pasts. Rose did not have much to tell, but Fred had a trove of epic tales. Fred told Rose that he had been born in the United States in the thirties, when his father, Ludwig, had spent a few years in the United States, probably as a secret agent of the German American Bund before returning to join the Waffen SS as an officer and fighting in many of the bloodiest battles on the Eastern Front. Fred told Rose that, after graduating from high school, he had joined the army and became a Ranger. He said that he fought in some of the bloodiest battles in Korea, winning two Purple Hearts and a Silver Star, distinguishing himself in hand-to-hand combat.

. . .

Rose hated it when people called her "a mail-order bride." She had chosen Fred. She loved him, and was always loyal to him. It was something that people never understood. From the day she arrived in Miami, they were with each other twenty-four hours a day. Although she had been in Florida only two months when they decided to marry, she felt it was as if they had known each other all their lives and as if their marriage was preordained.

Fred cared for Rose in his way, but business was business. Before he married her, he wanted a prenuptial agreement. He was an expert on such matters, having signed prenuptials with all but his first wife, when he had no assets to protect. With the help of an attorney, he poured all of his legal savvy and shrewdness into the document. It was fifteen pages of different ways of saying no. No community property. No alimony. No pension sharing. No payment of debts. It did not matter how long the couple was married or how many children they had, Rose would get nothing. At his whim, he could toss her out and she would have no recourse. As he saw it, he wasn't thoughtless. In case the couple divorced, Fred agreed to give his ex-wife whatever amount was necessary so that she was not "likely to become a public charge."

Keller did everything to make the document legally impregnable. The mistake most men make is to lie about their assets; in a divorce, that is the first thing the opposing attorney goes after. Fred listed his net worth accurately at $17,395,522. He had the prenuptial translated into German, and he gave Rose the Yellow Pages so she could hire her own lawyer to look over the document.

For Rose, the prenuptial offered a shattering insight into the man she was about to marry. However, she thought Fred would eventually change his mind, and that no husband who loved his wife would stand by such a document. So she signed it on July 2, 1992, and the following month, married Fred in a private ceremony.

Fred's sons were not impressed by their father's latest wife. Eric had been silently seething since he had learned from his brother

Paul that the chauffeur had said that upon Rose's arrival at Miami International, she had greeted Fred with the words "I love you" and called her "a real pro." As if all this weren't bad enough, now Fred and his bride had flown to Texas to have his twenty-year-old vasectomy reversed so they could try to have a baby. Fred was not home when Eric called in June 1993, but Eric had been drinking, and was so revved up that he left his diatribe on the answering machine.

"How's that cunt marry a sixty-year-old man out of love?" he fumed in words recorded on the machine. "And then demand to have children? What kind of fool is he? How would you feel if I was twenty-five, and dated some sixty-one-year-old dried-up bitch just for money? Now how would that feel? Rose gets children and alimony and two-thirds of your estate . . . What would you think about that? Rethink, my man."

Many times Fred had told his sons the story of how he had stood looking across at the island vowing that one day he would live there, and Eric recalled that in his harangue: "Is this what you thought of when you sat on that bench across from Palm Beach across the Intracoastal Waterway, 'I want to live there.' Was it just power, money, and sex? Or did you take us kids from our mother for a particular reason, such as love? Do you know what love is? Do you know what respect is? Or do you just know what leverage is? Who's leveraging who with your new scrotum?"

ERIC WAS OUTRAGED, HURT, and jealous too, for his father was creating a family—something Eric had yearned for all his life, but he and his brothers were not part of it. Rose had become pregnant and Fred looked forward to their baby, vowing to be the kind of father he had not been to his three previous children. When a baby boy was born on February 15, 1995, the child was not only named after his father, Fred "Fredchen" Keller, but Fred sought to forge this son into an ideal version of himself.

Fredchen had to speak German, and not only did the boy speak German as his first language, but he had a slight accent when he first spoke English. Fred did not want the child to go to a preschool where his son might squander his time playing games with self-indulgent children, so instead he spent his time with his father.

Fred was a strict disciplinarian with pedagogical techniques that had no room for childish weakness or laxity. If Fredchen did not drink his glass of milk or finish his meal, he had to stand in the corner. He did not allow Fredchen to watch the silly children's programming on television. And when he was with his son, he was always teaching him something, exploring a science problem, testing him with vocabulary flash cards, or teaching him a bit of history. He almost never hugged or kissed the boy, or told him he loved him. That was womanly stuff. He and Fredchen had serious business to pursue.

Rose was a far more emotive, nurturing parent; she saw herself as working in tandem with Fred. As in most marriages, Rose was the primary caregiver, spending far more time with the little boy than her husband. She also convinced Fred to bring over from Germany two of Rose's brothers, Wolfgang and Klaus, and a few years later, her sister Angelika "Angie" arrived. Rose set them up in a house in Palm Beach with their own car. Rose's mother, Brigitte, was a frequent visitor, and Fred paid for the young men's college education. Fred's intention was that, upon graduation, Wolfgang would go to work for Keller Trust, where he would manage the business and build it up until young Fredchen was ready to take over what was rightfully his.

The rest of the Keils treated Fred as the patriarch and noble patron. By any measure, Fred's largesse to the Keils was one of the most generous acts of his life. In the evenings, they got together for dinner and had long, laughing conversations in German.

Despite her young age, Rose was the *mater familias* of the Keil family, the benefactor and mentor who had orchestrated this incredible change in their fortunes. She was closer to her brother Wolfgang than to any of her siblings. He was devoted to her, and in awe of what she had accomplished. Fred had a special liking for Wolfgang too. Rose's sister Angie also went to work for the real estate trust company as a bookkeeper.

Rose realized that her elderly new husband was not part of the Palm Beach scene that she desired to explore. Fred wanted to please his young wife, and arranged to take her to the Boys Club Ball at the Breakers. The event was for charity, but he insisted upon a less expensive junior ticket for Rose and himself. Even so, he thought the Palm Beach social circuit was too expensive and boring, and that was the end of the Kellers' experience with it.

Rose, however, was enamored with the glittery social world on this island, and like so many of her predecessors, after her elderly husband passed on, she might well have become a Palm Beach matron, celebrated for her style and wealth. Yet despite what Rose wanted, Fred was not going to join the Beach Club or the Breakers either, squandering tens of thousands of dollars to spend time around people he did not like.

The closest Rose and Fred got to rubbing shoulders with the elite of the island was their walks along Worth Avenue, in those years still one of the most formal shopping streets in America. Even on the hottest days, many of the women wore designer dresses and heels, accompanied by men in sports coats and perfectly pressed trousers. Rose liked to dress up, though not quite to the standards of Worth Avenue, but Fred sauntered past Tiffany's and Gucci in his inevitable shorts, T-shirt, and sneakers. He felt that he was treated with snobbish disdain by shop girls who lived in the outer reaches of West Palm Beach.

As Rose grew comfortable in her role as the wife of a millionaire, she affected an imperious, dismissive manner toward her inferiors, and that meant most of the world. "Rose ended up becoming one vicious bitch," asserts Jeff Diamond, who worked for Fred as a leasing agent. Rose treated waiters as if they were in bondage. She considered herself far superior to the women who would have been her natural friends, and she lived largely among Fred and her German family. She was overpoweringly influenced by her husband, who was the one American with whom she had daily contact, her guide to the world and its ways. He was father figure, husband, mentor, and critic.

Rose had her own infrequently visited desk at Keller Trust.

When she did stop by the office, she saw that to Fred, business was war. He used the law as a bludgeon. He had sued hundreds of people, and he almost always won. "Lawsuits are Fred's weapon of choice," said his attorney, Bennett Cohn. If it cost ten thousand dollars to win a thousand-dollar judgment, that was money well spent for the sheer pleasure of it.

Fred preferred triple net leases where he could pass on increased costs such as higher taxes, insurance, or utilities. It was a sweet device to raise the cost of the lease dramatically by shuttling all kinds of expenses onto the tenant, sometimes buckling a small business under the increased costs. Nobody cheated Fred, and if a tenant fell behind a month or two in his rent, he tossed them out.

Fred's leukemia seemed to be controlled, and for the first time in his life, his situation seemed ideal. Real estate in South Florida was exploding, and he was buying warehouses and strip malls, his net worth rising by the tens of millions of dollars.

Fred purchased a major estate for his little family on the Intracoastal Waterway in the North End, at almost the precise spot where he had once looked across from West Palm Beach, vowing one day to live on the island. He was not about to waste money hiring an interior decorator, so he furnished the sprawling mansion with things he already had. He squeezed a pool table into a room so small that there was hardly room to play a game, and left the library half-empty.

Fred had helped create Rose in his own image, but while he was detached, she was emotive; and while he had everything he wanted, she had nothing that was solely hers. After the birth of their son, he started giving her 10 percent of new properties and having her cosign loans with the bank. What she did not know was that each time he "gave" her 10 percent of a property, Fred was actually the beneficiary of the gift. There was a seemingly innocuous little phrase in the prenuptial about each partner being "responsible for one-half of any obligations jointly incurred" to which neither Rose nor her lawyer had paid any attention. It meant that when she was given 10 percent of a property, she also received half the debt.

By controlling the amount of debt used to finance a property,

Fred could completely determine the value of his wife's separate property. If he wanted to give her nothing, the debt needed to be 20 percent of the value of the property. If he wanted to take money away from her, he could opt for more debt. Then if she and Fred divorced and the prenuptial held, she would owe her ex-husband millions of dollars. Fred thought it was the height of cunning, kept just within the boundaries of legality.

These should have been glorious years for Fred, but Rose's hectoring was relentless. She was not satisfied with what she considered a mere sliver of Fred's fortune. Nor was it sufficient that Fred said that he had rewritten his will to give his fifth wife all of his assets when he died. She did not want to be dependent on largesse that could be withdrawn. She was driving Fred to despair with her ceaseless badgering. She had a bad temper, and popped off for no reason at any time. And night after night she nagged him to give her half of his assets.

"I'm a German wife," she cried in the middle of the night, collapsing next to him in tears. "A German wife! Don't you understand?"

"But what about my sons, Rose, my sons?" Fred asked, though he had no intention of giving the ungrateful older offspring anything either.

Rose knew her husband well enough to realize that he was emotionally impenetrable, and disdainful toward most people, including all women. She had not an inkling of the legal predicament in which he had placed her, but she felt unsteady. As he refused to compromise, it became an obsession that had no limits.

What she did not know was that if he divorced her, he would strip her of all her pretensions, and leave her worse than when she had arrived. The nagging never stopped. Always before in his relationships, Fred had unassailable emotional boundaries that no women had ever violated, but Rose had wormed her way within.

Fred was playing tennis with Rose's brother Klaus one afternoon at the end of March 1999. While most men his age played two sets of doubles with their contemporaries, Fred sometimes played five sets of singles against opponents often half his age.

When he was walking to the other side of the court, he felt so dizzy that he thought he would collapse. He dismissed it as nothing and finished the game. Then he told Klaus that he did not feel right, and his brother-in-law drove him to the emergency room at Good Samaritan Hospital in West Palm Beach. When he was lifted upon a table for an EKG, his heart started thumping two hundred beats a minute and the medical team scurried around trying to save him. "That was the first time I felt close to death," Fred recalled. "I felt so quiet, and so peaceful."

Fred had the heart of a young man, and the doctors kept him in the hospital several days trying to figure out what had gone wrong. It did not seem to have been a heart attack, and they were not sure what had caused it. As Fred lay there, he thought he had a better answer than the doctors. Rose and her pitiless pestering had caused his near death. She had come to the hospital and had been wondrously solicitous and caring, but he knew she would soon be back to her familiar self.

As soon as he got out of the hospital, Fred drove to the office and asked his secretary to bring him all of the land trust documents. He took each one, and where the documents listed the ownership 90 percent Fred Keller and 10 percent Rose Keller, he changed it to fifty-fifty and signed his initials. Then he called Rose and told her, "I changed all the properties to fifty-fifty. You can go into the office and check it out."

Fred thought he would be able to sleep through the night again, with sleep that was doubly blessed. Since he had not signed a crucial second document, nothing had changed. "I misled her, no question about that," Fred admits. "My purpose was not to convey it to her, but to placate her, so hopefully things would be okay on the home front. I thought it would placate her, but it did not."

Fred had thought by pretending to give Rose Keller half his extensive business properties, he would buy some peace. Instead, he had created a wife who thought herself a woman of independent means worth over twenty million dollars. Rose fancied herself not only her husband's financial equal, but his superior in her youthfulness, health, energy, and ambition. Fred had created a monster, a wife in his own image, who gave him no quarter and considered herself the dominant partner.

Rose and Fred could hardly look at each other any longer without bile and rage rising within them. In July of 2000, after eight years of marriage, Rose filed for divorce, and set off a three-year-long legal and emotional struggle of enormous magnitude. Like almost everything else in Palm Beach, this drama was overwhelmingly about money. On one side stood Rose, who thought that for starters she was entitled to one-half of what at the end of the litigation was a seventy-million-dollar fortune. On the other side stood Fred, who thought that his estranged wife was entitled to less than nothing, and in fact owed him about ten million dollars.

12

The World Turned Upside Down

David Berger was delighted that he was not a member of Mar-a-Lago and had no part of observing the antics that went on there. Now that he lived at Elephant Walk and had Barbara on his arm, he was convinced that he would soon be walking into the great houses as a welcome guest. He envisioned himself as the first Jewish member of the Everglades and the B&T. The closest to the WASP world Berger had ever gotten was reading about it in the *Palm Beach Daily News.* For decades, he had opened the Shiny Sheet in the morning to read of places in Palm Beach he had not been and people he did not know.

Barbara could see that David was obsessed with getting his picture in the Shiny Sheet. Even if he had been unconcerned, she knew that the paper was one of the keys to her and David's ascent. People got up in the morning and read the daily as a social stock market, tracing the rise and fall of an ever-changing group of high-profile characters. The society stories were mere snippets of words surrounded by what the paper called "peeps," diminutive photos of couples shot at events that may have taken place a week or even a month or two previously. These pages looked more like a high school yearbook than a daily newspaper.

Shannon Donnelly, the society editor of the Shiny Sheet, was the daughter of an Irish cop in Newport, Rhode Island. The reporter had nothing in common with Palm Beach society. Nor when she arrived on the island did she have any understanding of the patois of privilege. Unlike previous society editors, Shannon was rarely invited to sup at the tables of those about whom she was writing. Like her ex-husband, a bartender at Café L'Europe, Shannon was treated as an amiable servant of the well-to-do.

Shannon had the respect for the upper class that cops have in rich resort towns, where what is a crime for a poor man is merely an indiscretion for a gentleman. She also had a savage wit, but when it raised its wicked head in her copy, she immediately yanked it back. She understood that her job was to celebrate this world, and to chronicle the golden fantasy of Palm Beach that the *Daily News* had been extolling for a hundred years.

When Shannon stood next to these matrons in their designer dresses, the ladies fluttered around her, giving her the bons mots that they hoped would find their way into her column. It took a while for Shannon to learn that these ladies were not her friends, but acquaintances who wanted to use her as she wanted to use them. The one person in this world she considered truly a friend was Barbara. They were of the same generation. Shannon was a divorced mother bringing up a son; Barbara was a divorcée living with a man who was not her husband. Barbara had her own weight problems. The two women became the best of friends, chatting for hours on the phone, with Barbara sometimes staying overnight where they could sit around half the night in their pajamas talking.

Although Shannon was loath to see it this way, it was useful to her career to be around Barbara. Her older friend had much to teach her. Beyond that, Shannon covered parties the way a movie critic reviewed movies, and there were as many clunkers in Palm Beach as bombs in Hollywood. Barbara gave spectacular parties, models of taste and decorum, and Shannon went home and wrote about them in detail.

Barbara had befriended Shannon in part because of what the reporter could do for her. She flattered Shannon and gave her gifts. One of the first things Barbara did when she moved into Elephant Walk was to invite Shannon to think of the house as hers, where she could come and go as she liked. Shannon told her associates how she swam nude in the protected pool, and it became common knowledge in Palm Beach that the two women were friends. No one wanted to offend Shannon, and that meant that no one wanted to offend her new friend and her escort, whose pictures had started appearing regularly in the pages of the Shiny Sheet. Barbara was always aware of the subtlest detail, standing behind David so he looked taller.

New arrivals to Palm Beach announced their presence by attending charity balls. Barbara had David buy tickets to the most exclusive WASP events, including the annual hospital and Red Cross balls. David would have bought two tickets to the balls and risked being shuttled into some obscure back table at the Breakers seated next to a rubbernecking dentist from Pittsburgh and his gabby wife. But Barbara told him that he had to buy whole tables, and so he did.

When Barbara walked into the Red Cross Ball, the Cancer Ball, or the Heart Ball at the Breakers Ballroom with her aged Jewish lover on her arm, she was aware of what she was doing. Even that was not statement enough. She needed to fill those tables, so she included Jewish couples and society reporters like Shannon who previously had been invited only for the cocktail hour. "I knew it was a step wrong socially, but a step right for David Berger," she reflects. "It was obvious he needed help. I had them as my guests, and it changed everything."

It was a coup of major proportions when thanks to his contribution, David was named corporate chairman of the 1996 annual Red Cross Ball at the Breakers' Venetian Ballroom. The ball was the ultimate symbol of the old Palm Beach. On this evening, the most publicly reticent ladies and gentlemen from the Everglades and the B&T arrived at the golden ballroom in their floor-length gowns, tiaras, and tailored white tie and tails, and celebrated not so much the Red Cross but themselves.

Barbara's close friend Eles Gillet was there, looking stunning in a purple gown. Marylou Whitney attended too, in white with a tiara crowning her blond hair. Brownie McLean was a fixture at the event as well. Many of these women were adorned with priceless diamonds, not so much symbols of romantic devotion, as the shrewd investments of the ultrawealthy, a means to pass on wealth without paying inheritance taxes, and an unfailing hedge against inflation.

As the guests arrived that January evening, they were anticipating yet another flawlessly presented event with a contingent of ambassadors flown down from Washington, invoking a prewar European diplomatic world; handsome marine escorts; and a hail-fellow-well-met sentiment wrapped up in red, white, and blue patriotism.

Chairwoman Betty Scripps danced the opening Viennese waltz with the debonair Hungarian ambassador, leaving her eighty-six-year-old husband at their table. That was a matter of much discussion until the Spanish singer Julio Iglesias got up to earn his $125,000 fee. Scripps had hired the international star to give a truly international flavor to the event.

Julio did not seem to grasp that he was appearing before a generally elderly, conservative audience that believed English the natural language of song, and the cha-cha-cha the most exotic and daring of dances. Julio gyrated his hips in a frenzy of mock copulation. The guests were not sure if he was singing Spanish-accented English or English-accented Spanish, or perhaps some bizarre third language, but they could not make out a word.

"Here we are in Palm Beach when just a few days ago we were playing for people whose eyes looked like this," he said, gesturing with his fingers like angled chopsticks. There were shudders and gasps at his brazen audacity. The ladies in the room did not know that the singer had just returned from an Asian tour; they thought he was critiquing them for their eye lifts.

"It doesn't matter what language I sing in," Iglesias said accurately, since no one had any idea what language it was. "I just want you all to go home later and make love. Maybe some babies will be made tonight."

Given the age of most of the ball-goers, that was an unlikely aspiration, and they heard his words not as the tired routine of a performer, but as a vulgar insult. One of the few to take it philosophically was Mary Underwood, who, as Shannon listened attentively, turned to the gay couple sitting next to her. "So, which one will it be?" she asked innocently.

As corporate chairman of the ball, David had nothing to do with hiring the Spanish singer, and for him the evening was an unrelieved triumph. His name and picture were prominently displayed in the book given to the attendees, an advertisement seemingly of his acceptance in the rarified circles of the island.

David had lived most of his life dealing with complicated, often groundbreaking legal and political issues. No way did he find fascinating the banalities and obvious truisms that passed as conversation at many of the events on the island. But it was unthinkable not to attend the most prestigious balls and parties. The pleasure was in knowing that you were there, not the evening itself, nor the conversation that ran the full Palm Beach spectrum from what gown did you wear yesterday, to what gown will you wear tomorrow.

Barbara knew that although Palm Beach pretended that it was about class, it was about money. When two women met for the first time, they chattered benignly while sizing each other up—shoes Gucci, dress Galanos, handbag Lieber, teeth capped, hair coiffed, accent understated, homes Park Avenue and Everglades Road—so that within five minutes they had precisely pegged each other.

Barbara was particularly brutal in her judgments. She had her own vision of how life should be lived. She felt that many of these people she was meeting had no individual taste at all. They had catered lives, not only the repasts at their dinner parties, but the clothes selected for them by vendeuses on Worth Avenue, the artwork on their walls selected by consultants, and pictures in the Shiny Sheet placed there by public relations hacks kept on monthly retainers. Barbara was trying to ingratiate herself with many people whom she privately disdained.

The Gillets were the couple whose company Barbara and David enjoyed the most. As the two couples arrived at Café L'Europe or Club Colette, they referred to themselves as the "four bears." The two "big bears" were Barbara and Warry, and they looked a race apart from their diminutive companions. Barbara was so big that she dominated any place where she stood. As for Warry, he was well over six feet tall, weighed close to three hundred pounds and looked like a gigantic teddy bear. Like his wife, he drank as if he had just opened the last bottle, and ate his meals the same way.

David was a brilliant, sophisticated man, but he knew little about the WASP world of wealth to which Barbara was his guide. She began his education by teaching him to spend money, especially on her. "He was not the kind of man who gave gifts," she reflects. "I encouraged him to buy me jewelry. He did not celebrate birthdays and anniversaries. I said, 'I do.' I said, 'You're going to get gifts and you're going to give gifts.' I said, 'David, what would you like to give me for Christmas?' I said, 'David, isn't this a lovely pair of ear clips in the Christie's catalog? Wouldn't that be a lovely Christmas present?' And he said, 'Wah, wah, wah, you can spend up to so much.' "

David fancied himself a spiffy dresser, but Barbara taught him that he was not even close to looking like the gentleman he aspired to be. Even in Palm Beach, many men stopped buying clothes at a certain age; one could tell the decade they had arrived in Florida by whichever forlorn, dated style they wore. Barbara thought of David as "very off the rack," a characteristic not only of his clothes, but of the man himself. She took him to a Savile Row tailor for his suits, and to Turnbull and Asser in London for his custom-made shirts. Every year they went back, and if David's size had changed even a quarter of an inch, he either ordered new clothes or had them remade.

David soon dressed as well as any man in Palm Beach, but Barbara was less successful in remaking the rest of him. David was a member of the private Club Colette where he distinguished himself by secretly bringing a flask and surreptitiously mixing his own drinks. No untoward act goes unnoticed in Palm Beach, and David's apparent manifestation of cheapness was duly noted in the virtual book of miscreants. No one realized that he was only doing this during Passover, and the flask was full of kosher wine.

If David had been a WASP, his living with a woman other than his wife and his raft of minor vulgarities would have been ignored, and he might well have won admittance to both the B&T and Everglades. But as a socially aspiring Jew, David was held to a far higher standard, and he did not quite pass muster. In the locker room at the Everglades and B&T, there was a manly patois full of joshing, but it was the most subtle parts of the WASP lingo, and at the Breakers and elsewhere, David did not come close to capturing it. He had his manly talk too, but to ears used to the WASP argot, he seemed crude and disrespectful, and those were taken as his true colors.

A man did not brag about having sex with his wife, but he might well brag about having sex with his mistress. Barbara had no idea that David loved boasting about the particulars of their love life. He liked to tell one acquaintance how much he liked to nestle his head between her ample breasts after lovemaking. At the Ritz-Carlton in Palm Beach, during a dinner honoring Prime Minister Margaret Thatcher, David turned toward Barbara and engaged in an animated, whispered discussion. Then he turned to the late James Sheeran, the publisher of *Palm Beach Society.* "I told her I wanted to get a room and go upstairs and fuck, but she said with Maggie here, we can't," he bragged, though Barbara asserts that he never asked her such a thing.

There had been few thank-you notes or even calls after the dinner dance for Prince Edward or for most of the events at Elephant Walk, and Barbara was appalled. She thought that she had a flawless sense of protocol. In a way she did, but that very strength blinded her from what was truly happening. Barbara was right that these people were rude, but they were calculatedly rude. In their boorish way, they were telling the couple that they were fortunate that they had even deigned to attend, and that Barbara and David were not even close to being accepted.

David was well preserved, but he was in his eighties, and on the most profound levels of human intercourse, Barbara could hardly confide in him. She was spending most of her time with people far older, so her few contemporaries tried to get her out; off to a crazy, casual party, or down to Delray Beach a half hour south for dinner at a hip new restaurant. Then she returned to the uncertainties of life with an old man who would not marry her, and whom she was not even sure she wanted to marry.

Barbara kept to herself. She woke up late. She started to gain weight; not a few pounds, but a surge so dramatic that it was like watching a balloon blowing up. She had back problems and could not exercise easily, and that made holding her weight down more difficult. But in this compulsively svelte world, obesity was a curse.

Only David, Shannon, and sometimes Dan Ponton saw Barbara wearing her bathrobe all day long, wandering around disoriented. At times she was shockingly different from the elegant woman who stood in the doorway greeting her guests. Society was the great stage of Barbara's life, where she played only leading roles. Everything else was a dressing room, where behind the closed door, it did not matter how you looked, acted, or dressed.

A few days after the dinner dance for Prince Edward, David asked Barbara, "Why aren't we ever invited to stay overnight at any of the Windsor palaces in England?"

"Because we're not married," Barbara answered curtly.

A few days later, after a decade of living together, David asked Barbara to marry him. She was convinced it had nothing to do with his desire for overnight accommodations at Buckingham Palace. She thought it was because David was afraid he might lose her. She was going to be fifty. She felt the future shutting down around her, and David could see that she was becoming anxious. He always knew when it was time to cut a deal and make a settlement.

David began his marriage with a lie. He presented to his fiancée a prenuptial agreement in which he professed to be worth fifty million dollars, a fib of such magnitude that it invalidated the document before it began. It was common for men like David to hide their wealth, and Barbara had no idea that his estate was seven or eight times that.

Soon after David asked Barbara to marry him, the couple announced their engagement and flew off on their annual trip to London. On the day before their dinner at Buckingham Palace, she had lunch with Prince Philip's secretary. "Prince Philip says, 'Get married in New Zealand,'" the private secretary said. "You'll avoid all the relatives, and he and Edward will stand up for you." The couple was planning to be in New Zealand for the annual meeting of the Duke of Edinburgh's Award World Fellowship in November 1997, but Barbara had never thought of being married there.

"Is that a real offer?" Barbara asked, sensing immediately how extraordinary this gesture was.

"I'm relaying a real offer from His Royal Highness," the official said with precision. David had given hundreds of thousands of dollars to Philip's foundation, but so had several others, and this was a surprising proposal.

"I'll take this offer," Barbara replied definitively.

There would be room for only sixteen people at the retreat, including two private secretaries, two protection officers, and the two princes. It meant that Barbara's own father and his wife could not be invited, but that was a piddling price to pay if it meant that David's two sons would not be coming either.

Barbara was overwhelmed by the idea that Prince Philip and Prince Edward would be attending her wedding, and she fairly skipped around London. The city was full of Palm Beach people attending Ascot, and she had all kinds of people to tell.

At a reception at Buckingham Palace hosted by Prince Philip and Prince Edward, Marylou Whitney and John Hendrickson were among the sixty or so guests. Like her late husband, Marylou loved the bracing cold weather of the far north. In 1994, the widow flew up to Alaska, where she was the sponsor of a dogsled team. One evening she was invited to dinner with Governor and Mrs. Walter Hickel, and his twenty-nine-year-old aide John Hendrickson. Hendrickson had escorted older women before, and was a man of easy charm. He said afterward that he thought Marylou was fifty-two or fifty-three, when she was in fact sixty-eight, old enough to be his grandmother. But that did not stop either of them, and their romance began.

During the palace cocktail party, thirty-one-year-old John took seventy-year-old Marylou aside to one end of the great room and took a dime-sized thirteen-carat diamond ring framed in exquisite sapphires out of his pocket. “Yes, yes, yes,” Marylou answered when John popped the obvious question.

Barbara was excited to hear Marylou’s news and she congratulated the former owner of Elephant Walk and her fiancé, but she knew that for once she had something that Marylou did not have and could not have. She and David would marry in the presence of the Duke of Edinburgh and Prince Edward. It was something that none of those who spurned David in Palm Beach could have replicated or even contemplated. The world had turned upside down, or right side up as Barbara saw it, and now everything would be different for both Barbara and for her new husband. Or so Barbara thought.

13

Outside the Guarded Gates

After a decade with a beau who did not intend to make her his wife, Barbara married David in a civil ceremony in November 1997. She could never let on to anyone all that she had gone through for this moment of triumph. In doing so, she believed that she had so solidified her and David's position at the height of society that no one could dislodge them.

Barbara planned every moment of her wedding day, and as she was the most exacting of perfectionists it had gone faultlessly. She stood wearing an azure blue Alfred Fiandaca dress at the remote Huka Lodge in the jungles of New Zealand. Often when David upset her, she made him pay by buying her something exquisitely tasteful and exquisitely expensive. She wore her twenty-four-carat fancy yellow engagement ring plus three items that David had given her as acts of penance: a string of South Sea pearls, pearl and diamond ear clips, and a diamond brooch. She also wore an art deco diamond and platinum bracelet that had belonged to her great-grandmother. She held a bouquet of flowers in her hand, and smiled with the beneficent manner of a monarch who had traveled to the far ends of the empire to accept a token of gratitude from her loyal subjects.

The primary guests who had arrived at the remote retreat for the wedding ceremony were the Duke of Edinburgh and his son,

Prince Edward. The debonair duke looked as if black tie dress had been created in his honor, and he was in what for him was an exuberant mood. Prince Edward was in a jovial mood too. He had flown in by helicopter so late that he was not even formally dressed, but wore a blue suit and blue tie. It was a perfect day, though at times the groom seemed almost superfluous, allowed only because of arcane custom.

When Barbara returned to Palm Beach later that year, her laugh was sharper, her wit edgier, and her disdain for the gauche wannabes who trundled along Worth Avenue proudly touting their bags more obvious. She was of a generation of wellborn women who did not consider living with a man a marital test-drive but a moral disgrace. And now that the title Mrs. was affixed to her name, she no longer had to suffer the catty whispers of ladies who considered her a kept mistress unworthy of the company of God-fearing married women, even if they were on their third or fourth husbands.

It was not just the fact that she was married, but the way it had happened that made it so precious, and Barbara took delight in telling her social intimates of the wedding. She was as deferential and as protocol-conscious in talking about the Windsors as she was in their presence, and this obsequiousness made her seem far more intimate with them than people who gossiped about them as their royal buddies.

Barbara had numerous opportunities to display her friendship with the Windsors. Practically every season, one royal snowbird arrived, accepted tributes to the Duke of Edinburgh Award from the assembled gentry, and flew out again, leaving them bowing on the tarmac. No Windsor was more in evidence than Prince Edward. In the *Mail on Sunday*'s investigation of the prince, the British paper dubbed him "Expenses Edward." As an ambassador of the Duke of Edinburgh Award, the prince was ever ready to visit places such as Palm Beach, Jamaica, and Monaco, where the program was small but the golf was good, and avoid places like the Ivory Coast, Benin, and Uganda, where the program was large but the eighteen holes were in the road.

A prince cannot spend all his time raising money for charity when he heads a failing film production company, and in March 1999, Edward arrived in Palm Beach once again as part of a lecture series under the auspices of the Northern Trust Bank, his fee a reported two hundred thousand dollars. In America, even the humblest of proffered canapés has a price tag attached somewhere, and in signing the contract, Edward agreed to wear a kilt at some of the events and enter heralded by a brace of bagpipers. In the Palm Beach extravaganza before seven hundred at the Ritz-Carlton Hotel, he spoke in front of a backdrop of the royal coat of arms. The dinner menu juxtaposed the royal coat of arms with the Northern Trust logo.

Just before his speech, Edward and his entourage stopped at Barbara's house on Jungle Road for a visit with the Bergers and their guests. Yet another diamond in Barbara's social tiara was the fact that Prince Philip had named the new Mrs. Berger the head of the North American program of the Duke of Edinburgh Award World Fellowship. Her closeness to the British royal family was in full evidence. In a town obsessed with royalty, Barbara had achieved even further social imprimatur.

Thanks in part to Barbara's friendship with Shannon Donnelly, the society editor peppered the pages with photos of the newly married Bergers. The couple was not only regularly pictured, but celebrated. That impressed most readers of the small paper, few of whom had the traditional upper-class abhorrence of publicity.

Another way for Barbara to judge her and David's elevated status was by noting their seating at the premier events of the season. The cognoscenti pored over the table settings the way Kremlinologists evaluated the placement of the Soviet leadership in Red Square during the May Day parade. It was better by far to stay home from the Red Cross Ball than to accept a table in the outer reaches.

The annual benefactors' dinner for the Society of the Four Arts was another reliable gauge of social position. The Four Arts membership included most members of the WASP aristocracy, but there were a number of Jews to create the illusion of inclusivity, and even before David met Barbara, he had become a member of the premier cultural institution on the island.

The dinner was held at the B&T, the most exclusive and exclusionary club on the island, a private precinct where the members believe that they are among their peers in the American elite. There never seems to be anyone in the club who is socially awkward. There are no gauche guests in the dining room chowing down, no inebriated poseurs in the bar, no swaggering braggarts, and no women wearing tacky resort clothing.

To protect their sanctuary of entitlement, the B&T treats manners not as the physical manifestation of class but as a series of legislated maxims. There is a wary watchfulness within the club, as if some new member or guest might explode with behavior so foul that the stench would never go away.

It was almost unthinkable even to contemplate, but some of their daughters, granddaughters, nieces, and their déclassé friends had tattoos, pierced ears, rings on the navels, or other unseemly embellishments. The ever-observant staff keep a drawer full of Band-Aids at the front desk, ready to pounce on crude interlopers who are told in no uncertain terms that Club Rules state that "members and guests are required to cover tattoos" and "the display of 'body piercing' other than earrings in the ears, is not permitted." On occasion a young guest enters the dining room so swathed in bandages that she looks as if she has just left intensive care.

The club rule book states the melancholy truth that "exercise can generate more than normal perspiration." When a lady goes out on the clay tennis courts wearing her white or ivory tennis outfit with up to one inch of trim color, her white tennis shoes, her white hat or visor or natural straw hat, and plays with decorum, she might still end up sweating like her Latino gardener. The club implores a member to maintain her clothing accordingly and practice proper hygiene, but it is best to avoid the courts in the heat and to limit exercise to a few sedate minutes on the stationary bike in the fitness center, just enough to put a slight flush on one's cheeks, but no unseemly signs of perspiration.

If a member brings a guest whose cell phone goes off in the dining room, she risks being denied club privileges for a month or two. On the beach, the board has deputized the staff "to remind inappropriately dressed swimmers and their guests" that "modest beach attire would be appreciated." There must be not even a hint of sexuality among gentlemen and ladies, and a swimsuit that on a forty-year-old would have gone without notice, becomes wildly inappropriate on a buxom twenty-year-old. Maids and nannies are allowed to swim with their charges in the mornings, but at the stroke of noon, they must dress in servant's garb so that they cannot possibly be mistaken for a member or guest.

Lunch is served cafeteria style in a setting reminiscent of junior high school. At the end of the line, an obsequious retainer takes one's tray to a table either outside or to a large room with a vaguely nautical motif that reminds some guests of an Omaha seafood restaurant.

On Sunday afternoons when it is too cold for swimming or sunbathing, some of the older ladies of the club sit on the veranda wearing leather shoes as stylish as combat boots, long skirts, wool sweaters, and kerchiefs. They look as if they are about to head out for a hike in the Scottish highlands with Queen Elizabeth, and as they sit, they scan everyone and everything for improprieties that only they are capable of noting.

THERE ARE MANY MEMBERS of the B&T who do not consider themselves prejudiced at all but they would not think of risking their status by objecting to club rules. Just as next door at Mar-a-Lago, where the tone is set by a vulgar, vociferous minority, so the rules at the B&T are enforced by a coterie who consider themselves model ladies and gentlemen, and the protectors of civilization itself.

One of the places B&T members might occasionally find themselves seated next to Jews is at a charity event. At one such dinner, a member of the B&T elite found himself seated next to Larry Gold. The WASP gentleman was an avid tennis player and so was

Gold, and the two men had a spirited conversation about many aspects of the game. Gold was delighted that his beloved sport had brought him such commonality with this man that it had broken through all the ethnic stereotypes.

"Let me ask you a question, Larry," the man said, well into the dinner. "Why do you Jews slice the ball so much?"

"It's because of our delicatessen training," Gold replied, without missing a beat, moving his right hand up and down as if cutting salami.

Few of the B&T members have achieved wealth on their own. Many of them consider that a mark of superiority to the glittery new arrivals who have ingots of gold, while they hold on to a few antique coins. They disdain the new money class, rationalizing that they are above grubbing for money. The ladies and gentlemen of the B&T wield wicked fish knives, dance foxtrots to die for, and mistake manners for culture. They are so inbred that they have not a glimmer of how insulated and isolated they have become.

In the salons of the gentile elite, there has been a long decline into intellectual and spiritual decadence. Dinner at the B&T is a scene not unlike that described by Stendhal in *The Red and the Black* in the splendorous mansion of the Marquis De La Mole just before the French Revolution: "In the marquis's dining room, provided that you did not make jokes about God, or priests, or the king, or those holding government posts, or artists patronized by the court, or all the established ideas and institutions . . . and provided, above all, that you never discussed politics . . . you were free to talk about anything you liked . . . Any idea with a scrap of vitality seemed gross coarseness. Despite polished manners, complete courtesy, and a desire to please, boredom could be seen on every face."

These WASPs are overwhelmingly Republican, almost as much a given as Christian faith. To many of them, politics is not a body of ideas based on certain premises about one's feelings about human nature and how people should live in society. Politics is threadbare gauze over the imperative to hold on to one's often diminishing wealth. They support candidates who vow never to raise taxes, and spend time with accountants who specialize in tax avoiding and elaborate estate planning. All of this is considered class patriotism, a way to protect what is theirs. They look across the Intracoastal Waterway at the seething ghettos and the Latino hordes, and thank their blessed God that they are living in their secure island sanctuary.

The B&T stands firmly behind its restrictive policy, considering it a mark not of prejudice but of liberty and good taste. As a token of its cosmopolitanism, the club has no objection to Jewish guests at private parties.

David had belonged to the Society of the Four Arts even before he met Barbara. She had pushed him to become a major donor, and that was why the couple was attending a Four Arts dinner at the B&T for the first time. Barbara was placed at the best table next to Fitz Eugene Dixon Jr., chairman of the Four Arts (and president of the B&T). Barbara considered this placement an extraordinary public acknowledgment of her status.

The chairman was the perfect example of the old Palm Beach gentleman. The heir to a Philadelphia streetcar fortune, he sometimes wore the emerald ring that his grandfather gave to his grandmother before he helped her onto a lifeboat and remained aboard the sinking *Titanic*. A Harvard graduate, Dixon had worked for a number of years as a teacher at Episcopal Academy in Philadelphia before going into business. Over the years, he had owned part of the 76ers, the Flyers, and the Eagles—every major sports team in Philadelphia except the Phillies. He was also a noted philanthropist, contributing to innumerable charities and institutions.

When Dixon was at Harvard in the early forties, Jews were not members of the elite clubs. If he saw them at all, it was only in class, where they were largely a studious lot, shooting their hands up to answer questions as if they thought they had won the lottery. In Philadelphia, he was willing to do business with them if the deal was right, but he was not about to invite the David Bergers of the city into his club, and God knows not into his house.

Barbara had a manner that announced she belonged nowhere but at head tables, and she was a witty, charming, if self-conscious, dinner companion. As Barbara sat chattering with Dixon, he surprised her by turning to a painfully difficult subject. His daughter had married a Jew. "He's not going to be able to come to the B&T," Dixon said with double authority, both as a father and as president of the club. "We just don't allow Jews, and we aren't starting now."

What Barbara did not know was that Dixon had brought the matter up to the board of the B&T. They could have been his brothers, elderly gentlemen who had gone to Princeton, Yale, and Harvard, where they had been members of Porcellian, Skull and Bones, and the other elite Ivy League clubs. Dixon listened to their counsel, but he was a martinet who ruled the B&T like a Prussian general. The board usually did little but affirm his actions. Dixon said that it was time to relax the rules a little and to allow a certain kind of well-mannered Jew to come as guests. That would not lead to a deluge of them taking over, and they certainly could not be members, but times were changing.

The other board members knew that this was not about changing times but Dixon's new son-in-law. To a man, they said the club should stay just as it was, and as far as they were concerned, just as it always would be. Even today, a decade later, Ellin Dixon is a member of the club, but her husband is not, and though he has sometimes entered the precincts with his family, he is not accorded the rights that his wife assumes as her natural due.

As Barbara listened to Dixon's impassioned account of life with a Jewish son-in-law, she realized that he was not only talking about his own family, he was offering up a parable. Dixon was telling her that David might come to dinners like this, but he would never be allowed at the B&T on a normal day, even as a guest. This evening was as far as he would ever get. He would never be welcome in the private enclaves of the gentile elite. And if he was not welcome, neither was Barbara.

Barbara thought about Dixon's comments many times in the months and years to come, but she tried to go on as if she never heard his words. She and David were regularly featured in the

Shiny Sheet, where people like Dixon were hardly ever pictured. To the old guard, the society pages of the *Daily News* had become a rogue's gallery of grand pretenders and hustling schemers.

Still, the Shiny Sheet was a crucial element in Barbara's social strategy, and her prominence was due largely to her friendship with Shannon. Barbara had rarely had a pure motive in her life, and she surely did not have one with Shannon. The society editor was her friend, but she was also an incredibly useful device to get her favorable publicity. She gave Shannon gifts, talked girl talk with her for hours, and shared a savagely cynical take on Palm Beach that neither graced Shannon's columns nor Barbara's public utterances on the social scene.

One morning Barbara went to the door and found her latest gift to Shannon sitting there accompanied by a letter saying that she could not accept it because it would make her feel beholden to David. Barbara says that there was no antecedent to Shannon's dramatic gesture, and it was a brutal slap in the face. "I've never in my whole life been cut dead by anybody, and by somebody to whom I'd been more than kind," Barbara says.

Shannon has a fierce, retributive temper, but she usually does not get angry unless she thinks she has good reason. "Barbara called me and bawled me out because David's and her photo was not in my story," Shannon recalls. "There was a space problem. I had their names in the story and when I mentioned somebody, their photos often weren't run. I thought she was my friend, but she was ordering me around, and from then on I never ran their pictures again."

Barbara denies she ever made such a call, instead suggesting that perhaps it was David who confronted Shannon. "I would not be surprised that David said something," reflects Barbara.

Whatever the truth, the result was indisputable. From then on, Barbara and David's picture almost never ran in the daily, and if one did not know them, it would seem that they had abruptly departed from Palm Beach. It was a devastating result, especially for David, who thought that having your picture in the Palm Beach paper was the sine qua non of acceptance. Barbara knew better. She realized that the problem was not merely the Shiny Sheet, but that she and her husband had run into a wall that no matter her connections, his money, and all their considerable effort and planning, they could ultimately never climb.

14

The Shiny Sheet

Shannon had never had a friend like Barbara, and she never had one like her again. This was a measure not of Shannon's inadequacies, but of the nature of her job, the social world that was her habitat, and her painfully deep awareness of her role in life. She had been burned, and she was not about to put her scarred hand back where she might suffer further pain and disfigurement.

Barbara had taught her many things, the most important being that she could trust no one, and that even the warmest and seemingly most genuine of friendships was a calculated device. "I have no friends," Shannon says. "If I leave my job as society editor, I will have no one except my son." Those were not maudlin or self-pitying words. This was a woman who stared straight on at the realities of her life without flinching. In a town where almost everyone reinvented herself, choosing a new, elaborate costume, Shannon wore the same clothes she had always worn.

Shannon was the most powerful journalist in Palm Beach, and she had begun to realize it. This was a tiny island and a tiny paper with a winter weekday circulation of around 7,000, but her imprimatur was a formidable honor. She was treated with gingerly deference, calculated bonhomie, subtle flattery, flirtatious wooing, ingratiating joshing—anything to get her attention and goodwill so that one would find one's name in her column and one's picture beside it.

Her predecessors had been white-gloved ladies who fancied themselves the arbiters of what they considered *their* world, or gay gentlemen who took inordinate pleasure in describing elegant parties and balls. Shannon was different. In her childhood and youth, she had traveled places that almost no one in society had ventured, or if they had, would never have talked about it.

Shannon was the daughter of a Newport cop who had been Jackie Kennedy's caddy when the young woman came to Newport in the summer to be with her mother and her new husband. Her father drank too much, and when she stood on a street corner waiting for him to pick her up at a given hour, he might not be there on time or he might never be there at all. He left much of the parenting to his wife, who believed that goodness could be beaten into a child. When Shannon was entering her teens, her mother divorced her father and married a rich man, but life did not get any better, at least for Shannon. And so on a frigid January morning in 1969, fifteen-year-old Shannon stuck her thumb out on Route 24, and hitchhiked to Providence. And she never returned home.

Shannon was a natural actress with a gift of mimicry. Lying about her age, she got a job as a waitress and a room in a boardinghouse. She ended up two years later working as a nanny for a doctor and his wife in Manhattan. Even though she did not have a high school diploma, she decided that she wanted to go to college. Her SAT scores were so good that she was admitted to Cazenovia College in upstate New York.

Shannon's parents gave her neither money nor encouragement for her education, and she had to work to pay her way at the small women's college. Every afternoon she hitchhiked the nineteen miles to Syracuse to work as a cocktail waitress at Uncle Sam's on Erie Boulevard. She wore a tiny black skirt, a tight white sweater, and a bowtie around her neck, an outfit that not only guaranteed good tips but quick rides to and from Cazenovia. She was sexy, witty, and wild, with a gift for the quick riposte that could shrivel a male ego. She had many flings that ended the moment anybody tried to get too close to her.

At the end of her sophomore year, Shannon transferred to Randolph Macon College in Virginia. She got on her bicycle every afternoon to ride out to a country club, where she waited tables until midnight. Her roommates and friends had fathers who were oil company executives, neurosurgeons, and network journalists; when they went to a country club, it was to play.

In Palm Beach, a single woman hardly accepts a canapé from a single man unless she has some sense of his financial wherewithal, and if he is an impecunious sort, she turns her head away and moves on. By those rules, Shannon would never have spoken a word to her first husband, Peter Charles Barrett. Peter had neither much of a past nor much of a future, but he had a gift of wit, and enough blarney to take him farther than a subway token. Peter looked like a handsome Irish tenor, and though he was eighteen years her senior, twenty-four-year-old Shannon fell in love and married him.

Peter's one great moment in life had come years before when he played a quarter for the New York Giants before hurting his knee and ending his professional football career before it began. Everyone has a second dream, and at forty-four, Peter's was to move down to Florida where he could play golf during the day and tend bar at night. Peter liked to drink so much that bartending was more like prep for his after-hours avocation than a job.

Peter got hired as a bartender at Café L'Europe, the premier restaurant in Palm Beach. Shannon needed a job too, and she became a proofreader at the West Palm Beach regional daily, the *Palm Beach Post*. She was so good at adding commas and subtracting typos that after three months she was offered a position at their sister publication across the Intracoastal Waterway, the *Palm Beach Daily News*, the oldest newspaper in South Florida.

Shannon had no social connections with the Palm Beach world, and no interest in its intricacies. As copy editor she was the scullery maid of the office, cleaning up copy, writing captions as the writers filed their stories and the photographers dumped their pictures on her crowded desk. After several months, the society editor needed some help. Instead of squandering another modest salary on a socially acceptable recruit, Shannon was sent out to cover the least desirable events.

Shannon covered the events that nobody wanted to cover, and in Palm Beach that often meant Jewish events. The Jewish philanthropies did not have aging socialites who demanded coverage with an imperious "we." They had professional development officers who called well in advance, made polite requests, and studiously followed up. Knowing no better, Shannon brightly showed up at their gatherings to cover them.

One day when Shannon was still newly covering social occasions, she ran into publisher Agnes Ash at the Publix supermarket. "Every single picture in the paper today is Jewish," Ash said, standing beside her reporter, thumbing through the six-page daily. "Look at this. It looks like the *Jerusalem Post*. There's just too much."

Agnes does not remember that incident, but she does recall another one involving Bob and Arlette Gordon, who probably would have been among those pictured. When the Gordons arrived from Boston to buy a house in late 1973, they asked the Realtor a profound philosophical question: "Which side is the better side, the lake side or the ocean side?" The Realtor replied, "The lake is better. The old families live on the lake. When they have to sell one house or the other, they sell the ocean house." And so later that day, the Gordons bought a mansion on North Lake Way, thus becoming one of the first Jewish couples in that part of town.

Much of the Gordon family money came from rental property in the slums of Boston, a commercial sector that they shared with the Astors, but tainted money to many in the Jewish elite of the island. Despite their innumerable gifts to charity, they were not members of the Palm Beach Country Club. They were clubless and clueless, and sought to make their social mark through publicity.

Agnes recalls the Gordons' appearances in the paper becoming a problem, and she thinks she may have told Shannon to stop printing their pictures so often. That led to a call from Bob Gordon, who asked the publisher if it was true. "Yes, it's true," she told him. "You can't be on every page because we have to cover the general population. You're at every party."

That was the way the machine the paper had created worked. If you went to a charity event, and made a contribution beyond the price of the ticket, you could almost guarantee your picture in the Shiny Sheet. The Gordons were only playing the game, and they continued playing it night after night, season after season, year after year, always stopping to be photographed.

Shannon had never cared about the nuances of class and status, and she had the ignominy of a husband who was a bartender in the very restaurant where many of the people she wrote about dined. "I was still so unsophisticated," Shannon says, cringing at the memory. "People who invited me to these parties, I would think, 'Oh my God, they were so wonderful to invite me.' It was interesting to watch how these people lived. And I thought, 'Well, this is just an aberration. People don't really live like this.' Then I realized that everyone in this town lives like that pretty much."

In the early eighties, the *Palm Beach Daily News* looked like most small-town newspapers across America, albeit one with an overwhelmingly wealthy readership. There were news stories including some from the rest of the state. There was a plant column, an astrology column, a sports column, and so on. And there was the society section where photos illustrated the stories.

Within a few years of Shannon's arrival, however, the paper had transformed itself into one of the most peculiar dailies in America. The paper no longer in any way covered events outside Palm Beach. People whose only source of written news was the Shiny Sheet woke up to the front-page headline: "EGGS OVER UNEASY: CAVIAR PRICES JUMP AS SUPPLY DWINDLES" or "MORE THAN 80 TO PLAY WHEN CROQUET INVITATIONAL BEGINS MONDAY." There were often front-page stories about the latest major charitable donation. The rich mix of advertisers that had long been one reason for a local person to read the paper was largely gone, replaced overwhelmingly by real estate advertising. Some days the Shiny Sheet looked like a real estate brochure.

Most importantly, publisher Agnes had grasped the obsession with social publicity, and instead of photos illustrating stories, the stories had become little more than frames to feature endless rows of social mug shots. The "peeps" were the de facto social register of the island, a matter of life and death. And who was the final arbiter but Shannon, the daughter of a cop.

In 1982 Shannon gave birth to her son, Ian, and she had a whole range of new burdens. Eventually her marriage came to an end, and Shannon left Palm Beach for what she thought was good in the spring of 1985. For half a dozen years she lived in Newport and worked as city editor of the *Herald News* in Fall River, Massachusetts, covering murder and mayhem the way she had previously covered ladies' teas and cotillions. Six years later, she was invited back by the new Shiny Sheet publisher and her close friend, Joyce Reingold, to take over as society editor.

The wealthiest strata travel to the island by private plane or at least first class. If flying tourist, they scurry past the passengers in the front cabin as if in a police lineup, hoping that acquaintances will not see them sitting ignominiously in steerage. On Thanksgiving 1992, Shannon packed up her clunker of an old car to the gills, set up her ten-year-old son in the back surrounded by pillows, watching a mini TV attached to the cigarette lighter, and headed south, hoping for the best.

When Shannon unpacked her black evening gown and headed out to cover social events, she was the poorest person at the ball. By 2007, when she had gotten several raises, she was making $47,210 a year, living in a humbly furnished ground-floor one-bedroom apartment a few blocks from her office. And she was interviewing the likes of hedge fund managers making a hundred million dollars a year, living in forty-million-dollar homes. And the black dress she was wearing was not a ten-thousand-dollar Scaasi that she might not wear again for a season or two, but the same black knockoff she would probably don the next evening about ten minutes after feeding her kid.

Despite all that stood against her, Shannon had a deeply honed savvy that elevated her to an unprecedented place not only in society journalism but in the life of the island. Shannon had arrived back at a watershed moment in the history of the island which elevated her role even further. "When I was at the paper before, I would call and ask, 'Can I send a photographer?' They'd say, 'Oh, my God, no. We wouldn't dream of having our picture in the paper.' Now they're calling me, 'Hey, come here, send a photographer to my house, come to my party, stop by.'" For the most part, the new people were the ones obsessed with publicity.

Shannon anointed and took away. She defined the parameters of the social world, those who were elevated to its heights, and those who fell into the darkness of obscurity. In her episodic, often cryptic way, she not only chronicled the emergence of the new Palm Beach, but by her calculated choices of subjects, was one of its primary creators.

In November 2001, Shannon married for the second time, a sixty-six-year old former marine whom she had known for more than a decade. There was a rehearsal dinner, a civil ceremony performed by Mayor Lesly Smith, and a reception at Club Colette. Almost everyone in Palm Beach sought Shannon's favor, and she was overwhelmed by gifts. Gossip is the only food that Palm Beachers gorge on, and there was an undertone of whispering that if you wanted to be covered in the Shiny Sheet, you'd better pay up, and a wedding gift was the easiest way of all.

There was no hard evidence that Shannon was accepting favors, and she passionately denied every last allegation. Shannon was hardly a newlywed when her husband moved back to Newport and was rarely heard of again.

AT THE TOP OF the milieu that Shannon covered was a new breed of billionaire and near-billionaire who set themselves apart and above the old elite. For the most part, they did not join the clubs, and they held themselves separate from the community. The gods of irony or unintended consequence had played a cosmic joke, giving them money beyond human imagination, money so grand that there were no pleasures expensive enough to be beyond them; yet in having everything, they risked caring for nothing.

They came to Palm Beach because that is where you came if you had great wealth, and there they created a new aesthetics of wealth where everything had to be bigger, and more grandiose. Size mattered, and if that meant they had to bulldoze some of the finest, most unique homes of the past, that was a small price to be paid. Their idea of freedom was to do whatever they wanted to do on their property, and to prevent their obnoxious neighbors from developing their land in a noisy and spectacular fashion.

One such mogul is Sydell Miller. Her story is not unlike that of Estée Lauder, who had begun her business concocting cosmetics in her kitchen. In her hometown of Cleveland, Miller had gone into the neighborhood beauty parlor for a perm, where she met the man who became her husband and partner in Matrix Essentials Inc., a beauty products company that brought the widow to the Forbes 400.

Estée had lived in a 13,000-square-foot oceanfront home where her son Leonard and his family now spend time in the winter. That home had once been the ultimate of Palm Beach living, but in terms of the gilded new money, it is hardly big enough. This group seeks huge houses.

In the mid-nineties, there were still good empty lots dotting the island, and Miller began by buying a major oceanfront lot in the estate section for $4.9 million. The roughly two-acre property was ample size for a major residence, but it was not big enough for Sydell's vision. So two years later, she purchased the 16,200-square-foot house next door from Ralph and Alice Muller. The discriminating ten-year-old home had eighteen-foot ceilings and two wine tasting rooms, one for red wine and the other for white. The first thing Sydell did was to tear the home down so she could appropriate the two acres of land.

This was not the first time the Mullers' prized home had been destroyed. The publishing heiress Betty Scripps had purchased their previous home to demolish it to make room for her garden. When the Mullers' real estate agent told the couple that their beloved house was once again to be pulped, he reported that "they laughed—they thought it was funny."

It was a perverse example of economist Joseph Schumpeter's "creative destruction" of capitalism, taking a good solid wallop out of somebody's dream house so somebody else can have her dream. As the bulldozers ripped through the luxurious ceilings and tore away the marble bathrooms, it was all to make way for Sydell's reverie.

A ten-bedroom, nineteen-bathroom, 84,626-square-foot monolith rose out of the clearing, shadowing everything around it. The house is beyond what once was considered human scale. It is so monumental that the mind can barely accept that this is a *home* looming above the skyline, not a railroad station or state library. The colossal structure stands behind a barrier of high shrubs and walls that could have hidden a prison. The lady of the house, who had once been a salesperson, traveling from beauty shop to beauty shop, is now living by herself in a home so large that it takes an hour to walk through all its rooms.

A house like this needs a company of workers, constantly repairing, mowing, polishing, refurbishing. The water required to run it is overwhelming, over a million gallons a month. It takes two hundred thousand gallons to maintain the Har-Tru tennis courts, and tens of thousands more to feed the nozzles that every day automatically hose the salt off the 128 windows, not to mention the watering of the two-acre lawn.

In addition to professional security twenty-four hours a day, there is a staff of maids, cooks, and gardeners, a small army. It is in essence a minor principality all to serve the needs of one aging woman.

Less than half a mile from Sydell's monolith stood "Four Winds," the historic 1937 home built for financier E. F. Hutton by Maurice Fatio, who, next to Mizner, was the most celebrated early Palm Beach architect. The Bermuda-style mansion was a sterling example of Fatio's style, and one of the last remaining of his houses.

The house was purchased in 2003 by Barbara Wainscott's former boss Steven A. Schwarzman, who is to this era what Hutton was to the twenties. Schwarzman is an emperor of the virtual age, a financier whose Blackstone Group stands at the forefront of infinitely complicated leveraged deals that make him one of the wealthiest men in the world. It was almost inevitable that he would have his own place on the island.

Schwarzman wanted to expand the house by adding a second story, but it was a complicated, subtle task to renovate these exquisite aging mansions. The restoration work had to be done with nuance and respect. Only a few architects have the sensitivity to do so.

There was another way to do it, and that was simply to tear the structure down and re-create it on a massive scale. As soon as Schwarzman received permission for his second story, the bulldozers arrived and razed the historic home to the ground.

When those concerned with the preservation of their island rose up in anger and dismay, Schwarzman said that he was only following the rules. The various permissions he had received were ambiguous, vague, and contradictory, and Schwarzman is a man used to doing all that the law allows. "My intent has been to maintain the Four Winds and comply with the law in a way consistent with community standards," the financier told an investigative panel.

Architect Gene Pandula, the chairman of the Landmarks Preservation Committee, said, "My own philosophy is not to freeze buildings in time, and look at what has been, but to look at what can be." As the architect looked out on the empty space where once the exquisite house had stood, he had ample opportunity "to look at what can be."

The Shiny Sheet captured the reality in a powerful editorial: "Knocking a building to the ground and rebuilding it in the approximate image of what it once was isn't preservation—it's Disney World."

From one end of the island to the other, the process ground on. Great mansions were going up by the score, overshadowing what once had been deemed great homes. In the North End, a village within the village, bungalows were coming down and aspiring mansions going up, nudging hard up against their more modest neighbors. In the score or so of midtown condominiums, units that had been purchased for a few hundred thousand dollars were being bought now for millions, almost always with cash, and almost always gutted and redone, so no touch of the older owner stayed. And whatever remnants of the middle class remained largely took their profits, packed up their belongings, and moved on.

By 2008 the market in homes ten million dollars or less had largely shriveled up into a hard nervous nut, but the high end soared. These megamansions, leviathans of the earth, grabbed up the most precious oceanfront, and destroyed everything in their wake, their buyers impervious to the vicissitudes of the stock market that bedeviled mere mortals.

No one is more understanding of the trend to megamansions than Dan Swanson, who is building the most expensive spec homes in history. Swanson calls his company Addison Development. In his office he displays one of the few oversized red leather-bound copies of Addison Mizner's autobiography, but whereas the great Palm Beach architect was building fantasies largely for women, Swanson is constructing business deals in which the man is usually the primary player.

"Maybe it was more a woman's thing then, but today, though women really want to be involved, the guys are really paying attention," Swanson reflects. "Not only are these gorgeous homes, but they're a hell of an investment. There's a whole mind-set if you buy the best diamond, it's not going down in value. If you buy the best of things, normally they're free at the end of the day. That's how the rich stay rich and get richer. In 1993, I sold a 33,000-square-foot house for thirty-five million dollars. Eleven months later, the owner turned down sixty-five million dollars. I felt like an idiot. It's like the old saying, pigs get slaughtered."

These are usually the buyers' third or fourth homes, and they view them as pleasant additions to their financial portfolio. The scent of almost certain profit has brought new people to the island, at least a dozen of whom are searching for homes in the $100 million price range. Swanson is currently building four spec homes, one of which has already been sold. There is almost no land left in the most desirable locations, and Swanson is building one of his homes on the lake side just south of Eddy Louis's home. It has an unenviable view of an island in the Intracoastal Waterway and behind that the spire of several West Palm Beach condominiums. The house is a shell. Swanson is willing to sell the mansion now for sixty-five million dollars or eighty million when it is finished.

15

Winter Dreams

When things were bad, Eric Purcell's rule was to get out and move on. He was under indictment for aggravated battery and false imprisonment for allegedly attacking his Argentinean girlfriend in their Miami apartment. He could not flee the country for good, but at least attend a wedding in Aruba with his mother, Monique van Vooren. Eric flew first to San Juan, where he met his celebrity mother flying in from New York, and the two of them flew on together to the hundred-acre St. James Club on a private bay on the Caribbean island. New York socialite Denise Rich hosted the glittery event.

Denise invited her friend Meaghan Karland, who she saw a lot of in New York until Meaghan moved down to Palm Beach, where she lived in a house in the North End with her husband and two children. She was a sophisticated woman of mixed Arab and European background who mingled well in the café societies of New York and London. She had gained weight and fought depression living with a husband who paid her little attention and was often gone. Her mother was staying with her, but she rarely got away from the endless chores of mothering her two young children. The wedding celebration was a return to what her life once had been, if only for three days.

Meaghan was having a drink when a friend introduced her to

Eric. "The reason I like you is you don't wear secretary jewelry," Eric said as his entry speech, looking at her huge diamond-and-ruby-encrusted bangles.

"What the hell are you talking about!" replied the abrupt Meaghan.

"Come on, you're not wearing gold chains with little hearts, all that cheap stuff that tries to be something it's not."

Meaghan took Eric's comments as a compliment. Only later did she think that he had picked her out as somebody with money and cut to the chase even before the game had begun. She had not come to Aruba for a tawdry holiday affair before heading home to her clueless husband, but it had been so long, and Eric was so smooth. He was a master in the bedroom. Women did not forget their encounters with him. "I didn't want to be with my husband any longer," Meaghan says. "I had never had an affair in my life, and it just happened. I must have been blind, but he was paying attention to me. I didn't have men looking at me for sex, but he was."

Meaghan had been back in Palm Beach a few days when Eric called. He told her he was in trouble. He had to get out of Miami, and asked if he could stay in her guesthouse. She was in love, or what seemed like love, and she said yes. Eric had almost no wardrobe, and surely nothing appropriate for Palm Beach. Meaghan went out and filled his closet with fine suits, Italian shoes, sports jackets, and pants. He told her nobody in his life had ever done anything like that for him. That was one thing Eric told her that was the truth.

Except for the nasty business of the criminal charges, Eric began enjoying himself more than he had in years. That was when Eric started playing tennis at the Breakers. Eric did not have the exalted social ambitions of David Berger; he just wanted to survive and to give the illusion that he was a man of substance. Eric understood luxury goods, vintage wines, and fine hotels, and had everything a wealthy man should have except for money. As he strolled down Worth Avenue, he rarely bought anything, but he walked with such a peacock's strut that no one ever seemed to notice.

Eric traveled two hours south to Miami occasionally to keep

his elevator advertising business afloat, but most of the time, he stayed with Meaghan. She was overwhelmingly generous to Eric, loaning or giving him by her estimate over $120,000. "Not only does she know what I'm facing, she's putting out money too," Eric recalls. "I have to go to court because of the child support. So she puts up money to help me for that. And I'm living at her house. She's in love with me, and I'm great with her kids. I'm basically the camp counselor."

Eric knew that he would probably have gone to jail for back child support if Meaghan had not written out a check to the court. And she wrote another check for five thousand dollars to Eric's lawyer. He did not mind living in Meaghan's guesthouse, but it got dicey at times when her husband came home from business trips. He pretended that nothing untoward was happening, but eventually he was bound to say something, and even if he didn't, her mother was roaming the perimeters. "You know, it would be a better idea if you get a little single," Meaghan told Eric one day, and he moved over to a tiny apartment in West Palm Beach.

That was even better because Meaghan was still funding him, yet he now had the kind of wiggle room he desired. He could comfortably go out with other women as well, including Martha Reed, an elderly matron with a red sports car and invitations to exclusive dinner parties, and to events out at the polo grounds in Wellington. There was still plenty of time for tennis with Eddy Louis, and several others. I had many conversations with Eric, but I knew almost nothing about his background. I thought he was just another spoiled rich man measuring out his life in cocktail parties, dinner invitations, and afternoon tennis matches. He was a consummate actor, and he played a wealthy gentleman far better than most wealthy gentlemen played the role.

The unfortunate criminal matter had been going on for months, nothing but an endless stream of continuances and meaningless hearings. Every time Eric walked into the courtroom, he had his trump card at his side. "Meaghan's always with me," he says. "And when I come into court with Meaghan, she comes in with the two kids, you know, dressed with jewelry, and I come in a suit. No one is going to prosecute me on this charge, especially when we tell the judge I'm living in Palm Beach with Meaghan."

After close to two years, Eric grew tired of his life in Palm Beach. He was an actor, after all, and it was time to move back to New York and start auditioning. That did not mean that he had ended things forever with Meaghan and the others, but for now he had other interests.

In June 1997, Eric arrived back in Manhattan. He had hardly unpacked when his lawyer called to tell him there was a new judge, and the case was going to trial in Florida. A few days later he flew to Miami, and when he walked into the courtroom in his fancy suit, he no longer had Meaghan and her two kids as his props. It was just Eric and his lawyer, facing a female prosecutor, a female judge, and a heavily Latino jury.

"So I come walking in the door like, 'What's going on? Oh, there's a trial,'" Eric recalls. "I say, 'Oh, let's have fun with this.' I'm like, 'This is theater.' Well, it's going to be my word against hers, there were no witnesses."

The jury found Eric guilty on all charges, and the deputies took him away to jail. As soon as she heard about the verdict, Meaghan drove down with bail money. In the weeks before the sentencing, a number of people wrote letters calling for probation. In August, the judge sentenced Eric to forty months in prison. When the sheriff deputies came to take him to jail, they thought he was a duded-up lawyer. Eric had to tell them he was the one they wanted.

Once the guards delivered Eric to the enormous 3,098-bed Metro West Detention Center, Eric became just another prisoner in a gymnasium-size room with rows of bunk beds. There were almost no upscale white men in this room; he quickly cased the large room, looking for the prisoner who ran things. It took him no more than twenty minutes to spot the man, an African American who had killed two employees in a jewelry heist gone bad.

As soon as Eric learned that the murderer played chess, Eric walked up to him and asked him for a game. Eric had made the most important friend in the room. It was the summer that the improbable Florida Marlins won the World Series, and for Eric it was a good time. "I'm enjoying it," Eric says. "I'm having this experience. I'm in the moment. And in many ways, I'm happy. I'm laughing, I'm having fun with these guys, I'm playing cards, I'm watching television. I don't have to worry about the rent or this or that. I have sports. We go outside for rec. I'm weight lifting."

It livened things up when Meaghan came to visit, and when he was lonely, he called her collect. Then everything changed when Meaghan told him her incredible scheme. "Terry Von Pantz has died," Meaghan said. Von Pantz was the widow of Eric's paternal grandfather. McConnell Sr. had divided his will in three, giving a third to Eric's father, who had blown everything; a third to Eric's uncle, Neil McConnell; and the interest on a third to his widow. Neil McConnell had died previously, and the estate now passed to the next generation of grandchildren. "Listen, you've got to get out of there," Meaghan implored, "because there's millions at stake here, and you are a grandson."

Eric would get nowhere without money to pay his new lawyer, and money to pay Medina. "His mother was crying to me, and his stepfather wouldn't give him anything," says Meaghan. "He wanted fifty-five thousand dollars to pay his lawyer. I had my diamond ring, which was appraised for sixty-nine thousand, and he made me give it to some pawnbroker down in Plantation."

Eric could not let anyone in the judicial system know that his contrition had nothing to do with remorse, and everything with his one chance to catch the golden ring and to live as a true Palm Beach millionaire, not simply an impecunious middle-aged man playing one. "Your Honor, I see the past and the present very clear now," Eric wrote Judge Ellen Leesfield in late November 1997. "I promise only that one day—should you hear my name again, you will say—well, I'll be damned. He did amount to something, and I gave him a chance at a time in his life that was critical. Your Honor please, I have learned. I have grown. In a way, I have been gifted."

In February 1998, after Eric agreed to pay thirty-five thousand dollars toward full restitution and waived his right to an appeal, Judge Leesfield granted Eric a furlough to raise more money from a list of friends that included his college girlfriend Deborah Dean, his socialite companion Martha Reed, and his tennis friend Eddy Louis.

Meaghan drove down to Miami to pick up Eric, and bring him back to Palm Beach. The couple stopped at Meaghan's friend's house to borrow a tuxedo, and then sped on to Mar-a-Lago for a major charity event attended by Donald Trump. Eric had never looked better in his life, and though his hair was only about an inch long, he cut a formidable figure.

After staying with Meaghan a few days, Eric flew up to New York to live with his mother and to work as a stockbroker earning about $300 a week. He asked his friends for money, but they turned him down, and he was desperate to come up with the $120,000 in total restitution ordered by the court. He managed to pull together $20,000, and after he agreed to pay $20,000 more, Judge Leesfield mitigated his sentence to the seven months served, and he was a free man.

The Van Pantz estate was worth $80,000,000, to be divided among nine acknowledged grandchildren. If Eric could prove paternity, he would be the tenth grandchild, and walk away with $8 million. There was no DNA evidence, so his lawyers negotiated an undisclosed settlement sealed with a pledge of confidentiality. Afterward, Eric purchased a condominium in Ibis Isle on the southern part of the island for $485,000, a 1993 Bentley Brooklands, and part ownership in a gym. And he began to live the life that he had always played at living. There were many young women, many late nights, and many tennis games.

One of Eric's new friends was Dr. G. Heath King, a psychoanalyst practicing in Boca Raton. King had trained in Germany and taught interdisciplinary studies at Yale University before moving down to Florida. He was an immensely literate man and after talking extensively to Eric, King suggested that he might find it worthwhile reading F. Scott Fitzgerald's classic short story "Winter Dreams." The analyst felt that there was an extraordinary affinity between Eric and Dexter Green, the main character. Eric not only read the tale once, but again and again, as if in these pages he had found some meaning, some understanding that he had found nowhere else.

"Winter Dreams" is the story of a poor boy, Dexter Green, who falls in love with a rich girl. She is very much like the Debbie Dean of Eric's youthful imagination. Dexter marries someone else, but the memory of Judy Jones and what could have been burns his soul. Years later he learns that Jones has married too. She is unhappy and has lost her beauty, and none of her magic remains. Dexter sees her plain and whole, and in that moment the solace of melancholy is gone. There is nothing left for him except a terrifying, chilling aloneness.

"He wanted to care, and he could not care," Fitzgerald writes. "Even the grief he could have borne was left behind in the country of illusion, of youth, of the richness of life, where his winter dreams had flourished."

In late October 2006 Eric showed up at the hip Asian restaurant Echo, where a woman that he was seeing, Maria Pita, was having a late dinner. Pita accused Eric of possibly having an inappropriate relationship with a sixteen-year-old. Eric said that was ridiculous and when the woman said that she was going to call the teenager's father, Eric became infuriated. Witnessed by one waiter, he reached over and grabbed her around the neck. He had reason to fear that another assault conviction would send him away again, and when Pita said she was going to call the police, she says that he squeezed her neck even harder.

When the woman did, indeed, call the police, Eric said that he may have raised his hand, but he had not touched her; he had merely told her that if she did not stop making the accusations he would "spit in her face." In the end, the complainant refused to press charges, and except for an item in the *Palm Beach Post*'s gossip column, he suffered no harm.

Meaghan, who had put on even more weight, did not fit into Eric's world. She had fallen on hard times after her divorce, and was living in a rental house on a dirt road in Wellington, fifteen miles west of Palm Beach. Eric saw how she was living, but he paid her back none of the money that Meaghan says she loaned him, and which he says was a pure gift. For a while, she was desperate. She says that she asked Eric for five thousand dollars; he said that he would be wiling to give her five hundred, which she accepted.

My wife and I liked Meaghan, and one night we took her to dinner at Trevini on Worth Avenue. After dinner, we were already in bed when she called, saying that the police had stopped her on South County Road. There was one squad car in front of her, and another behind. She was driving a used Audi that she had recently purchased. The car was dusty and had temporary plates, and she did not have her insurance papers with her. The officers said she could not drive. We dressed, and when we arrived, I drove her car across the southern bridge, followed by my wife in our car. Once into West Palm Beach, Meaghan got in her car and drove back to Wellington.

Several nights later, I got a phone call from Eric. He said that the previous evening he had been so drunk that he did not know where he was. The police had stopped his Bentley, driven the car home, and tucked him into bed. The police say they have no record of either one of these incidents.

16

The Dance of Wealth

The men who once came to Palm Beach generally had such a sense of fulfillment in their careers that they were happy playing golf and tennis, and left the intricacies of social life to their wives. The men who now came to Palm Beach have often made killings, not livings. They seem not to have the profound sense of accomplishment of many of their predecessors, and a number of them seek it by entering what had largely been a woman's social world and muscling their way into prominence.

One of the first men to do this was Simon C. Fireman, who made his fortune in plastic pool toys. Fireman had been shamed by his 1996 conviction for illegal campaign contributions to Senator Robert Dole, for which the Jewish multimillionaire received a million-dollar fine and six months under house arrest. That was a humiliating fate for a seventy-one-year-old businessman who fancied himself a public servant and philanthropist.

Fireman was neither stylish nor learned, nor did he have any other gift to set him apart except for his wealth and his willingness to part with a portion of it. Whenever I spoke with him, he exhibited a dual personality. He either displayed an arrogant grandiosity or an extremely ingratiating humility. He proclaimed his own good works, and insisted that he be celebrated for his philanthropy.

Shortly after his conviction, Fireman came to Florida and began a bold campaign to restore his reputation. Fireman was not going to make it into the Everglades or the B&T, and unlike men such as David Berger, he had no illusion that he ever would. He was far too controversial to pass muster with the Palm Beach Country Club either. But he thought that publicity celebrating his largesse could elevate him into the social heights.

Fireman understood that at charity balls, a public relations representative stood at the door signaling to the Shiny Sheet photographer the couples who had given enough money to merit being photographed. The next day, Shannon Donnelly went through the pictures, choosing the anointed. It seemed unfair to those members of the old WASP elite who mistook cheapness for frugality and figured it was enough to pay for a ticket. But to the nouveau like Fireman, it was a wondrously fair device to get your picture in the paper.

At the 2000 Cancer Ball, Fireman came bounding up to the podium to announce a surprise one-million-dollar gift. "That's right—$1 million, right out of the blue," Shannon wrote. "Maybe the can-can dancers did it. Ball chairwoman Alicia Blodgett was at first stunned, then grateful. Then the whole place burst into applause." Fireman had invented the headline-grabbing act of standing up and announcing a spontaneous, huge contribution. For Shannon and the Shiny Sheet, it was exciting news, taking the game to a place it had never been.

When Fireman began his social ascent, the International Red Cross Ball was the most prestigious event of the season, and was protected from the vulgar hordes by an icy wall of manners and mores that intimidated even the most intrepid of the wannabes. For two decades, Sue Whitmore ran the ball like a private party, underwriting much of it herself, inviting the elite of the island, and welcoming the guests at the entrance to the Breakers Ballroom.

Whitmore had come to Florida for the first time in her parents' private railroad car in 1914, when she was only six months old. Her wealth came from her great-grandfather Dr. Joseph Lawrence, who had been the co-inventor of Listerine, an astringent concoction that was peddled with wild success as a cure for "chronic halitosis."

At the annual ball, the rotund Whitmore dressed in voluminous gowns that looked like circus tents. The matriarch wore her diamond and ruby tiara as she was led into the ballroom on the arms of two U.S. Marines. Everyone applauded Whitmore and competed for the honor of her company, and no one blurted out that the whole thing had become exceedingly tedious and redundant.

In the years since Whitmore's death in 1993, the chairmanship had been passed on to a number of members of the old elite, until Diana Ecclestone took over in 2001. Ecclestone had been what in the hoary prefeminist days was called a secretary, and had since evolved into an executive assistant. She had become the third wife of a far older, wealthy developer, and in the traditional way, was using charity work as her means of advance. She was hardly more a figure of the old establishment than was Fireman. She was in some ways a mercurial, difficult woman, but she had turned the ball from a social occasion that threw off some money, to a charitable function in which the bottom line counted.

In January 2004, Ecclestone was chairing the event for the fourth year in a row. For Fireman, it was not enough merely to have his own table at the forty-seventh annual ball. He had to make a move so dramatic that Shannon would have little choice but to make it the lead of her story.

Early in the long evening at the Breakers, Fireman had one of his minions walk up to Ecclestone to ask her to come over to his table. She was busy resolving table mix-ups, so Fireman had to walk over to her.

"Young lady, do you know who I am?" he asked, as if there could be any doubt. "I'm going to give a million dollars this evening, and I want my friend Dick Robinson to announce it." Instead of being grateful for a gift that would have almost doubled the amount raised, Ecclestone told Fireman that she could not publicly thank him. She had other donors who expected to have their contributions celebrated this evening, and was not about to upstage their gifts.

Ecclestone may have had her sound reasons, but Fireman was rightfully upset that his huge gift was rebuffed, even if she suggested that they plan to announce his contribution at another event. As far as Fireman was concerned, there was only one event worthy enough to publicly celebrate his largesse, and that was the International Red Cross Ball.

Although Ecclestone had once again run a successful evening, she was in dispute with the Red Cross over other matters, and was fired. She learned about her dismissal secondhand, deepening her bitterness at the organization's ingratitude.

The Red Cross turned to spurned donor Fireman to ask him to run the celebrated function. After pledging $750,000, Fireman was named the chairman of the 2005 ball. It was a moment of overwhelming satisfaction to go in less than a decade from a convicted felon to the chairmanship of the highest status ball in Palm Beach, the first man ever single-handedly to steer the historic event.

Even in the beginning of his chairmanship, Fireman had problems that his predecessors had not had. What set the Red Cross Ball apart from other charity events was not only the white tie–tiara ultraformality, but the slew of ambassadors Trump flew down in his private plane from Washington. However, Trump now said that he was not doing it any longer. He had his shrewd reason for the turndown: He had a brand-new ballroom at Mar-a-Lago. What could be better for business than to host the Red Cross Ball? His plane became available the moment the Red Cross moved the event to his new facility, in which everything except the waiters was gilded gold.

Revenge is best when served piping hot, and Ecclestone became a crucial figure behind the International Centre for Missing and Exploited Children's first annual gala. Ecclestone and her associates decided to have the ball in the Breakers Ballroom the same evening as the Red Cross Ball at Mar-a-Lago. She was not a grande dame like Sue Whitmore, but she was decidedly preferred to an interloper like Fireman, who was not even the right faith, and most of the old elite and those who aspired to their company bought tickets to the new event.

Fireman had to come up with a new crowd enamored of the idea of spending an evening at legendary Mar-a-Lago. In his first decade in Palm Beach, he had stepped on so many toes that it was like a ritual dance, but the biggest toe he stepped on and the one that stayed eternally stubbed was Shannon's. "The enemy I had was Shannon Donnelly because Ecclestone was her close friend," Fireman said.

Shannon saw Fireman as the worst aspect of the crude new money, and she set herself against him. She promoted those who gave most generously to charity, and Fireman had gamed the system. She had no choice but to write about him, but she did not like it. He was going to feel the merciless sting of her wit, and she was going to try to stop his ascent.

"I took the executive director of the Red Cross chapter to lunch and I said, 'Don't get involved with this man. You're making a mistake,'" Shannon says. "He didn't listen to me. It was obvious to everybody pretty much what this man was. And everybody's kissing his ass because all these charity people care about is getting the money so they can get a big bonus. And I knew what this man was, and I felt terrible that the Red Cross suffered. They took a real black eye because of him. They'll never recover from it."

In writing about the January 2005 ball, Shannon embedded her zingers in a standard journalistic account of the evening. She wrote that "the crowd was made up mostly of out-of-towners fleeing the cold Northern climes," which to the cognoscenti meant that the ballroom was full of hapless outsiders. "Fireman took the microphone for a speech that started out graciously, but soon turned too long and not a little catty," she continued.

If Fireman had walked away after that evening, he could have felt a measure of accomplishment. Instead he decided to chair the ball for a second year. The Red Cross announced that Fireman had promised that the Forty-ninth International Red Cross Ball would net at least one million dollars, and if it did not, he would make up the difference. To Fireman it was a goal, not a promise. He was a man given to acts of instant largesse, but he did not enjoy being played the chump. He was not about to write out endless checks to a Red Cross that did not truly appreciate his efforts. It was hard to get people to come out again, especially when the social cachet was threadbare, but he did it, and if he drew guests from obscurity, at least he filled the tables.

My wife and I were there that evening as guests of Chris Ruddy, who runs *Newsmax*, the conservative news site and magazine. Neither Chris nor I, nor most of the men, were in white tie. Nor did I see many tiaras either. During the cocktail hour, I talked to a police chief from northern Florida and other out-of-towners who seemed partially in awe, partially bewildered.

Most ambassadors in Washington had neither the time nor the interest to fly down to Palm Beach for three days of endless parties. Those who did were generally those from obscure, tiny nations who welcomed the chance to march into the grand ballroom to be fêted.

And so the ambassadors entered to a blare of show tunes, some of them so weighted down with medals that they looked as if they might keel over. Bulgaria. Costa Rica. Grenada. Liechtenstein. Lithuania. Slovenia. Sweden. When Fireman made his grand entrance, announced like the Sun King, there was only a smattering of applause.

Fireman was tired, and had had several drinks. He listened to the endless bouquets of praise spoken from the podium by his associate, Sumner Kaye. After Frankie Avalon finished singing, the guests began leaving. It was not yet eleven and the evening should have been in full sway. Fireman rose to seize a sixteenth minute of fame by directing the Michael Rose Orchestra. As he bounded up on stage, he slipped and fell off, hitting his head on the marble floor.

I jumped up and, along with Trump and a few others, stood over the crumpled body of Fireman lying with his head in a small pool of blood. There were many Red Cross employees in the ballroom, and during the evening, speakers had gone on endlessly about the healing hands of the organization. I thought there must be somebody to come forward to take care of the poor man, but for a while nobody did. The crowd did not seem terribly interested either, filing out to the valet parkers, paying no attention to the distressed chairman. Finally, several waiters lifted Fireman up and half carried him to an ambulance, which took him to Good Samaritan Hospital, where he was treated for a nose broken in three places.

For Shannon, it was a wondrous opportunity to ridicule Fireman. "There's a lesson in timing here," the society editor wrote after describing the accident. "Had this been the Animal Rescue League Ball, those first responders might well have been two beagles and a golden retriever." Then she went on to pick apart the entire evening. "The color guard—bearing the American flag—marched from the ballroom without music," she wrote. "There was no Marines' Hymn, no Sousa, nothing but the undercurrent of conversation. This was more than a breach of protocol. It was a disservice to the members of the military, and a slight to one of the main missions of the Red Cross."

Fireman did not pay up the money to net the Red Cross a million dollars from the forty-ninth annual ball, as the organization insisted the chairman had promised. In her account of the Fiftieth International Red Cross Ball, which was not chaired by Fireman, Shannon managed to tweak him again, calling the 2007 ball a "return to dignity and elegance," as if Fireman's guests had shown up in tank tops and cutoff jeans.

But Shannon had other, more important news to cover and lives to celebrate. Marvin and Edie Schur were one of the most admired couples in the Palm Beach Country Club. The Schurs lived in a great house on the Intracoastal Waterway. The businessman was largely retired, though he dabbled in philanthropy and had served on the board of the company that ran the two major hospitals in West Palm Beach. He and Edie had been married for fifty-one years, and were pillars of Jewish life in Palm Beach. Edie was a prestigious asset to her husband, and had been named Palm Beach Atlantic College's "Woman of Distinction" for her fundraising and charity work.

Seventy-two-year-old Schur may not have had a shiksa trophy wife, but he had a Chinese mistress, and that was a toy that none of his friends possessed. Thirty-nine-year-old Dora Chong had been his lover for a decade. For Schur's purposes, one of the wonderful things about the island was how insulated it was from everything beyond. Schur's mistress lived first in a lovely apartment in the Trump Plaza in West Palm Beach, and then in a house in the El Cid section on the Intracoastal Waterway, across from the Schurs' home.

Dora gave birth to Marvin's son, Matthew Henry Schur. His father was not very interested in the child and rarely spent much time with him, but agreed to send him to preschool at the Academy of the Palm Beaches, where many of the leading Palm Beach families sent their children. The little boy used Schur's last name, and either this never got back to Edie Schur, or else she chose to ignore her husband's second family.

One day in April 2002, a hysterical Chong called her lover, saying that she could not find Matthew. The two-year-old had been sleeping in his bedroom when she had left to drive over the bridge to Worth Avenue to shop. She had purchased a suitcase for four hundred dollars, and when she got back, the boy was nowhere to be seen. Schur told Chong to look in the pool, and there she found Matthew's drowned body. Chong called Schur back and told him what had happened. He went to Good Samaritan Hospital, where an ambulance had taken the body and where he had served on the board. Schur wanted to know if there was some way to keep this quiet, but he was told this was impossible.

Marvin had not made tens of millions of dollars as a commodities trader by making slow decisions. He picked up the phone and told his wife that he had a mistress and a son, and the son had just drowned. Schur attended the funeral, and the day before the police came to arrest Dora and take her to county jail, she says that he called to tell her their affair was at an end and he was getting on with his life.

Chong was tried for aggravated manslaughter, and she was given ten years' probation for a crime in which a poor woman likely would have spent months in prison. Even that was too onerous for Chong, who fled the country.

The Schurs hung their heads for about a year, and then reestablished themselves in the cultural elite. Edie was much admired by the women in the Jewish community. They understood her decision to stay with her husband of five decades. To divorce him would have left Edie to live a lonely existence, an unwanted accessory to the social life of the island.

If the women of the club importuned their husbands to shun Marvin, they would be punishing Edie, and that they did not want to do. So instead they embraced the Schurs, inviting them to the most exclusive of parties, greeting them effusively at the club. It is doubtful that Schur had the sensitivity to realize that he was still part of the establishment only due to his wife's loyalty and honored position.

Shannon soon was featuring the Schurs more than ever in the Shiny Sheet. Marvin and Edie at a private party with Senator Hillary Clinton. Marvin surprising Edie by flying a group of friends to Paris for her birthday. Marvin and Edie at Club Colette for a Planned Parenthood benefit.

The Schurs continued as honored members of the Palm Beach Country Club. It had by far the most onerous, complicated admission processions of any of the clubs in Palm Beach. Marvin's misconduct did not change in any way the members' pride that their club had only the most morally exemplary of members, and everything was done to keep it that way. Widows were not appreciated in the club. Once due obeisance had been paid to the memory of the deceased, what was left was a potential predator. Thus, the country club was a version of Noah's Ark, with wives eternally bonded to their husbands.

The incident with the Schurs had been profoundly troubling, particularly to women in the club. That was why it was so gratifying when, that same year, two long-term members, Leonard and Sandy Heine Jr., sponsored a charming, vivacious couple from Pittsburgh, Reid and Abby Ruttenberg. The Ruttenbergs were a popular new addition, though there was a little discussion when fifty-nine-year-old Abby Ruttenberg was seen in overlong, intimate discussions with seventy-nine-year-old Leonard Heine. But the members assumed that this was merely a little innocent flirtation.

In January 2004, Abby Ruttenberg called 911 to say that Leonard Heine was lying not breathing in the bedroom of her home. When the police arrived and found him dead, the officers asked her what had happened. "He's a friend of my husband, and had come to look at improvements in our rented house," she told the police.

Officer Michele Pagan observantly noticed that Heine was not dressed in the usual wardrobe for discussions of home improvements.

"Why is he undressed from the waist down?" the officer asked.

"I took off his shorts because 911 advised me to loosen his clothing."

Abby Ruttenberg later admitted that "she and Heine Jr. were in the bedroom kissing and fondling when he collapsed." For the members of the country club, here was a sickening moral conundrum. Unlike the Schur incident, where the women of the club perceived Edie as the aggrieved victim, in this instance, Abby Ruttenberg was considered by some a temptress who had lured poor Heine to his death. From that day on, both Ruttenbergs were shunned at the club. Many members would not play golf with them. They would not eat with them. Shannon did not write about the couple. But the Ruttenbergs kept coming back year after year, and nothing could be done about it.

One woman summed it up concisely: "If we threw everyone out for adultery, we wouldn't have any members."

17

Palaces of Privilege

Women ruled Palm Beach's social life, but male wealth and power were the high cards, often slapped down with such force that they trumped everything else. When Shannon had written about relatively young and very attractive Angela Koch at the 1997 dinner dance honoring Prince Edward, the thirty-eight-year-old wife of William Koch had only been on the island for several months. Her fifty-six-year-old husband, however, had long been one of its major players.

Koch was an overlarge figure, and his six-foot-four-inch height was the least of it. He had a PhD from MIT in chemical engineering, where he had played varsity basketball. He had his own successful energy trading company. Intellect aside, he had all the sensitivities, passions, distractions, and self-indulgent whims of a teenager.

Koch sold his shares in the Wichita-based family business, Koch Industries, in 1983 for $470 million. He decided soon afterward that his two brothers, Charles and David, had cheated him out of his fair share of the largest or second-largest privately held company in America. And he set out on a two-decades-long lawsuit against his two brothers. When the *Boston Globe* reported that he also sued his "invalid mother," who died during the epic battle, Koch's lawyers demanded a retraction, insisting that she was not an invalid. The brutal dispute involved savage recriminations, investigators posing as journalists, and allegations of corruption. Koch and his fraternal twin brother, David, did not talk to each other, although they ended up living within a mile of each other in Palm Beach.

Koch came to national prominence as the skipper of an America's Cup–winning yacht in 1992. It was a triumph as much for the technological savvy of his MIT team as old-fashioned sailing ability. And the aftermath was a triumph for his accountants, who turned one of the organizations in the racing syndicate into a tax-exempt foundation so their boss could save millions of dollars in tax write-offs.

A single man of Koch's stature—now a billionaire twice over—did not go out looking for the ladies; the ladies came looking for him. In 1992, he recalled that he was having dinner with some friends when one of the women at the party, Catherine de Castelbajac, started kissing him passionately. "I must admit I did not resist," Koch reflected, as if he was not strong enough to avoid the clutches of this Delilah. Catherine was a sensuous woman who, when she was not in his arms, sent him scores of faxes that burned the wires. "Your X-rated Protestant princess," she signed one. In another missive, she called him "the greatest lover this side of the Rockies."

Several years later, when Koch was suffering from a leg injury, the couple was at a fancy event in London. Instead of watching out for him, he claimed that Catherine strutted around the room in a sexy, revealing dress. That rankled him so much that he ended the affair and asked her to vacate the luxury $2.5-million Boston condominium where he had installed her. When she refused, saying that he had promised to support her, he took the case to Boston Housing Court, a venue unused to gentlemen who frequent the Forbes 400. When the jury ruled in his favor on November 28, 1995, Koch told the *Boston Globe* that he wanted her gone in a month, not a particularly harsh demand. "I want to have a Christmas party there," he said, sounding more Scrooge-like than he intended.

While Koch was going through this unseemly ending with his long-term lover, he flew down to New Orleans for a blind date with Angela Browder Gauntt, a gorgeous blond divorcée living with her two children. After presenting Angela with an America's Cup scarf, he took her to dinner at the exclusive Commander's Palace.

Koch saw Angela only a couple of times in the next nine months, in part probably because he had another romantic crisis on his hands. Another former girlfriend, Marie Beard, was pregnant with his daughter, of whom he later took custody. In the end, Angela says that after only five dates, Koch asked her to marry him. That may have been the height of romanticism, but the prenuptial was the depths of realism.

Here was the emotional dichotomy of the man, the flamboyant, daring, generous romantic ready to fly into marriage on little more than a whim, whose instincts were quickly contained and controlled by a legion of advisers. The forty-four-page document was a shield to protect him from any assault. Koch's fiancée agreed to forego any rights to his estate. In exchange, in a divorce she would receive "one percent (1%) of the value of Bill's net worth, multiplied by the number of full years and pro-rated monthly for a year of less than 12 months" minus "cash or property paid, transferred and conveyed by Bill to Angela" but not including jewelry, cash, or property up to one hundred thousand dollars in value, and any living expenses. If they had any children, not only were the child support payments spelled out, but also his visiting rights. The prenuptial even had a literary clause that envisioned a day far in the future when Koch's former wife might be a grandmother: "Bill is permitted to provide information to any biographer, but he shall make no negative comments therein about Angela, her children, or children's children."

In Palm Beach, a prenuptial is as much a part of marriage as a wedding ring. The richer the man, the bigger the ring, the longer the document, and the more cynical its view of the dark possibilities within the human psyche. The Koch prenuptial was conceived by his attorneys as a realistic and savvy attempt to protect their client's wealth. But its lawyerly pessimism was so extreme that it would set any woman on edge, and made it less likely that love would stay alive.

After three and a half years of marriage and two children, Angela and William were staying at their summer home in Osterville, Massachusetts, when one evening in July 2000 Angela called 911, alleging that her husband had punched her in the stomach as she stood with their one-year-old daughter, Robin, in her arms. When the police arrived, she told them that Koch had also threatened "to beat his whole family to death with his belt."

The police arrested Koch and charged him with domestic assault and battery, as well as threatened murder. In November, Angela amended her statement to the police and said that her husband had not threatened to beat the family to death. Instead, in a conversation over dinner that evening, Koch had said how his father had beaten him with a belt, and mused that perhaps corporal punishment should be used today.

Although he denied the charges, Koch's initial response was not a belligerent verbal attack on his wife, but a conciliatory statement to the press. "Every marriage has its problems, and my marriage to Angela is no exception," he said. "I love my wife and have every confidence that with the help of competent professionals, we will be able to work out our problems and enjoy a long and happy marriage," he said.

This was a marriage overwhelmed by the excesses of wealth. Angela's lawyer, Jeffrey Fisher, tried to obtain documents to portray Koch as a deeply troubled man who had a pattern of abuse to women. He sought to open up records of Koch's previous divorce, which Angela believed would show "prior incident of domestic violence." Koch's spokesperson Brad Goldstein replied in outraged rebuttal, calling the charge false and "absolutely scurrilous."

In court filings, Angela presented a portrait of a husband who after drinking, might well have lost control and struck his wife. He was one of the world's greatest wine collectors. "The husband enjoys drinking these rare wines, frequently to excess," Angela alleged in court documents. Her lawyer charged in court that Koch had "an alcohol abuse problem, and he recently completed a thirty-day, inpatient program."

Koch replied by saying that it was not he who had an alcohol problem, but his estranged wife, and it involved even her children. He said that there needed to be nannies present when Angela was with the children "to preclude the wife from giving any alcohol beverages or medications that are not designed for children's use, to the minor children." Although Koch said that to protect their children he did not want to go into Angela's alcoholic problems, if pushed, he was prepared with a salvo of detail.

The prenuptial theoretically set out the parameters of the divorce in every detail, and yet Angela said that Koch had "private investigators flying all around the country interviewing anyone that has ever known [Angela]." Angela was temporarily staying in the Palm Beach home. The staff in the house chose sides, and as she saw it, inevitably their loyalty was to the master of the house and the controller of the wealth.

The prenuptial covered almost all the details of the divorce, and within a few months, everything was settled. The assault case was dropped after Angela refused to testify against her husband, leaving the district attorney with a lack of evidence. Her attorney said she backed away from testifying because "the resolution of the criminal charges is consistent with Angela's desire for the best interests of her two small children." Angela walked away with sixteen million dollars and $21,800 a month in child support payments for their children. That money allowed Angela to buy an 8,986-square-foot mansion for $5.3 million near her ex-husband's home. There she lived with her own staff, eventually including Shannon Donnelly's son, Ian.

During her first months as a divorcée, Angela dated Palm Beach Police Chief Frank Croft. The forty-six-year-old retiring chief had been born with nothing but desire. He came to South Florida because he liked to surf, and he had ended up a patrolman on the island. He had a flatboat that he sailed through the Everglades pursuing snook and bonefish.

Initially attractive to Angela, the relationship with the chief did not last. On her first New Year's Eve as a single woman, she showed up alone at a party wearing an outfit that Robert Janjigian of the Shiny Sheet wrote "caused some jaws to drop, others to rattle off how fab she looked. Her lacy black Sweet Pea top and embroidered Le Jealous denims from Eye of The Needle were the talk of the tony black-tie-clad assemblage." In 2007, forty-nine-year-old Angela married fifty-one-year-old Doug Stockham, a retiring, laid-back commercial real estate developer from Alabama, a man unlike Koch or other powerful, outgoing men of the island.

In the wake of the divorce, Koch began a relationship with a woman who was in some ways a daring step outside the expected. Bridget Rooney was from the Pittsburgh Rooneys, who owned the Pittsburgh Steelers and were one of the leading Catholic families in Palm Beach. Bridget had been coming to the island for most of her life. In 1991, she and two of her friends arrived at the Kennedy estate on Good Friday evening. They went out to a nightclub with three of the young Kennedys, including William Kennedy Smith. Later that evening, Smith went out again with his uncle Senator Ted Kennedy, and was accused of raping a woman he brought back to their estate. Rooney received her own full measure of notoriety when in 1996 she gave birth to a son fathered by movie star Kevin Costner.

Rooney had a lean, graceful body and dark-haired Irish good looks, and the couple was a public item in Palm Beach by December 2001. In May 2002, William and Bridget gave a dual birthday bash celebrating his sixty-second birthday and her thirty-ninth. At Koch's level of affluence, one did not simply give a dinner but a theme party developed by a professional planner with every detail scripted. This evening was a 1970s costume party on his terrace overlooking the massive sweep of lawn to the Intracoastal Waterway. The dance floor was full of disco wannabes and women in bouffant hairdos that looked like radar antennae. The party planner set up a tent where an elaborate gourmet dinner was served, including potatoes stuffed with caviar, greens enhanced with walnuts and gorgonzola, and lamb neatly wrapped up in phyllo and garnished with potatoes. After dessert, the Boogie Wonderband blasted off on a professional stage with first-rate light and sound equipment.

This was an event worthy of Shannon's presence. Although she appeared to be just another boogieing partygoer, she carefully recorded a list of all the notables in attendance, including Koch's once estranged brother David.

Also on the premises was Jeffrey Epstein, an intense, mysterious bachelor from New York, who in 1990 had purchased a mansion on the Intracoastal Waterway in the estate section. Unbeknownst to his neighbors, the wealthy financier was using several of his aides as pimps, soliciting high school students, including one purportedly fourteen years old, to give him massages. Once in his private quarters, the teenagers learned that "massage" had a special meaning here. The teenagers were often asked to undress and provide a variety of services.

The parents of a fifteen-year-old victim came to see Police Chief Michael Reiter. Reiter authorized a secret surveillance or the multimillionaire could have gone on amusing himself. As it was, he was indicted and immediately hired several of the top defense attorneys in America, including Alan Dershowitz and Kenneth Starr, who had gone from attacking President Bill Clinton for lying about having sex with a young woman to defending a man who had sex with children.

In 2008 Epstein negotiated a plea that sent him to the Palm Beach County Jail for eighteen months, for a crime that would have sent a poor man to a state prison for a far longer term. "The slow, dissatisfying resolution of the case sends a message to the public that there's a different system of justice for the wealthy who hire high-powered lawyers," the *Palm Beach Post* editorialized.

KOCH'S 35,000-SQUARE-FOOT RESIDENCE WAS in an area on the island where the homes ran the whole width of the island from the South Country Road on the ocean west to the Intracoastal Waterway. No one had created a more splendid expanse of garden than Koch's, with its wondrous lush plantings and Botero sculptures.

One evening, I attended a large cocktail party there. Many hosts on the island are so worried about their décor that they do not serve red wine, so I was happily surprised when the waiter brought an ample glass of pinot noir. Almost never did I enter a mansion where the owner had created a home in his own style, as opposed to that of an impersonal interior decorator. I found that so strange. These people had great fortunes and had incomparable places to live. I could not understand why they rarely imposed something of themselves and their own aesthetic values, no matter how ill-formed, upon their dwellings. However, Koch's home was different.

As I wandered looking at his art collection, I was astounded. Koch said once that he used his collection as his "fantasy world." It was a beautiful, passionate, erotic, heroic world. I stood in front of Winslow Homer's 1873 painting *Three Boys in a Dory*, which evokes the most idyllic moments in a boy's summer. There was a Renoir; not a buxomly fresh-faced maiden, but *Ice Skating in the Bois de Boulogne*. There was a reclining nude by Modigliani that Koch had a hard time looking at during his divorce. "I liked looking at it when I was happily married, right before I would go to bed with my wife," he told Jan Sjostrom of the Shiny Sheet in December 2000, right after his divorce was finalized. "You can't tell what she's feeling. Is she pensive? Is she happy? Bored? Is she looking to get out of there? In a way, this painting combines the sensuality of women and the elegance of their bodies with the mystery of their souls."

When Bill was a boy, Koch's father had sent him out west to work as a ranch hand, and he developed an appreciation for the historic West. His art includes Frederic Remington and Charles M. Russell. In addition, he has collected some of the greatest artifacts of the Old West, not only Jesse James's gun but also that of Robert Ford, who shot him to death; General Custer's rifle; and Sitting Bull's pistol.

In every room, cold-eyed men silently watched the partygoers. They were not the ten-dollar-an-hour rent-a-cops who stand outside the jewelry stores on Worth Avenue, but professional security people. Only a few men in Palm Beach had such elaborate, serious protection. It was as much a mark of wealth and exclusivity as flying a Boeing 727.

I walked down into the basement, where a room housed models of all the America's Cup winners. They evoked the epic history of the sea, as well as the struggle of men to journey on the boundless oceans.

Next to the room with the ships was Koch's wine cellar, where his rarest eighteenth-century bottles were locked away behind bars as if they were precious jewels, which in a way they were. Only about half of his 35,000 bottles were stored here.

Beyond the wine cellar in one direction was a gym large enough for a commercial enterprise, and the only bowling alley on the island. In the other direction was a gigantic Western bar that looked as if Koch had shipped it here from Deadwood City, or at least from a Hollywood movie lot. Beyond that was a perfect replica of Lord Nelson's stateroom. The make-believe lanterns swayed back and forth on the ceiling so that the vulnerable might get seasick if they stayed too long.

When I came upstairs, I looked again at Koch's art. No matter how great the individual pieces, most art in Palm Beach is decorative, fundamentally an assertion of class and taste. Perhaps it was self-indulgent, but there was something magnificently different about the vision.

In 2004, Koch had loaned much of his collection to the Boston Museum of Fine Arts, and paid for a major part of the show. The title of the show was "Things I Love," and that's precisely what it was, as if Koch was loaning part of himself.

The leading culture reporters in Boston criticized Koch and his collection in an unusually personal, vindictive way. The museum had placed two of the America's Cup racing yachts outside on the lawn. That they ridiculed as a pathetic gimmick to draw in the unwashed masses. The *Boston Globe*'s Cate McQuaid criticized even the name of the show, calling it "narcissistically titled." The critic condemned the exhibit itself as a "big sycophantic bouquet." At the *Boston Herald*, Keith Powers savaged the "unrepentantly lowbrow" exhibition from Koch's "monumentally egomaniacal collection."

I decided that I should at least say hello to Koch. The host stood as one guest after another took turns making a few moments of small talk and moving on. With his thick swatch of white hair and his generally benign demeanor, sixty-eight-year-old Koch looked more like a kindly grandfather than the father of one adult son from his first marriage and the four young children who play together in the house on given weekends.

I seized my moment and went forward to say hello. I learned long ago that most people are more introverted than extroverted, and half the extroverts are cured introverts. Koch was pleasant, but he was hardly expansive.

"I can't tell you how moved I was by your collection," I said.

"I'm glad," Koch said, seemingly genuine enough in his response.

"I can't believe it," I sputtered onward. "I mean, every other house on this island has the sensibility of either women or decorators. How did you do it? This is a man's place. It's the only man's place on the whole island."

"I was between marriages," Koch said.

IF MONEY IS THE measure of all things, then the greatest estate on the island is a gargantuan 81,738-square-foot property in the North End that in 2008, Trump sold for $95 million to Dmitry Rybolovlev, a Russian fertilizer billionaire. It is reportedly the highest price ever for a residential property in the United States.

The Russian was making a currency play, having announced he had no intention of living in the mansion but had purchased it as an investment. Those close to the deal said that Rybolovlev was planning to tear down the titanic house and build three or four homes in its place, most likely walking away with a $50- or $75-million profit. That was a sweet, enviable piece of work, and no one condemned destroying the incredible mansion as immoral and profligate. Profit was god, and this was a blood sacrifice to the golden calf.

A few weeks after the sale, I walked up the beach past a number of megamansions that from a distance looked like faux Mizners topped off with a quasi-Oriental grandiosity. The homes are blocked off on the oceanfront by concrete floodwalls that keep the ocean waters at bay and intruders outside. Then there stood a property three times as wide with a broad expanse of impeccably kept lawn running down to the beach sands.

On the lawn stood a colossal, cream-colored structure that on the ocean side was elliptical and looked like a football stadium. A series of tall, oval-shaped windows ran the length of the humongous edifice. As I walked around the building, I was sure some sentry or guard would confront me. But no one ever bothered me, and there was an eerie quiet about the place, an emptiness that went beyond the vacant rooms.

The only man who had ever lived in the house, and almost certainly would ever live there, was Abraham D. Gosman. The building was overwhelmingly his architectural vision. The previous owner of the property, Leslie Wexner of the Limited Stores, had demolished the historic Wrightsman estate that stood on this property, giving Gosman an enormous six-and-a-half-acre plot on which to build. His dream was not a great home for there were only three bedrooms in the humongous 61,744-square-foot main building. Everything focused on two incredible rooms, a ballroom larger than that found in many hotels and a glass-enclosed 4,100-square-foot veranda that housed full-grown trees. Here in these two rooms, Abe could invite guests who would be endlessly awed.

Abe festooned the walls with copies of the masterworks of art from Rembrandt to Goya, having the copyists paint to a precise size to fit the space available on the wall, and to provide a neat symmetry. And then he invited all kinds of people, from Mario Cuomo to Luciano Pavarotti. Abe was worth $500 or $600 million but he had a lifestyle beyond any of the billionaires on the island. None of them had their name on a pavilion at the Kravis Center in exchange for their contributions. None of them had dinner parties for 400 on their estates. And none of them had his 131-foot yacht *Octopussy*, the fastest luxury boat in the world, roaring through the ocean at sixty-one miles an hour.

Gosman had grown up a poor kid in Manchester, New Hampshire, with a knack for making a buck. He went from selling fake alligator skins to building an empire of nursing homes, shopping centers, hotels, banks, whatever he could buy cheap and sell high. He had no great vision except for making a buck, and if he wanted to take over your business, he was one tough customer. He had an instinct for what was happening, whether it be nursing homes or intrastate banks, and he was often in and out before other players even figured out the game. In 1986, he sold his Mediplex Group of nursing homes and rehabilitation centers for two hundred million dollars. Four years later, he bought it back for the bargain basement price of fifty million. Four years later, he sold Mediplex once again, for more than three hundred million dollars. No wonder he thought that whatever he touched turned to gold.

In 1990, Abe pensioned off his first wife, Betty, after a twelve-day trial for thirty-five million dollars and their Boston suburban home. He had taken up with Lin Castre, a real estate agent in Palm Beach nineteen years his junior, and he soon was suffering the perennial problem of a trophy girlfriend, a constant nagging over money. He eventually settled one million dollars on her in a palimony agreement and cursed her presence by getting her to agree to appear in the county only seven days a year. But he missed her and asked her back and in 1996 on the *Octopussy* he married her.

Abe was a little old man with a younger wife, a characteristic that is boilerplate for half the moguls on the island. At his estate, he mixed masterpieces of art with copies and he seemed neither to know the difference nor to care. He was not only remarkably devoid of taste, but of even knowing who had a modicum of taste, and seeking to elevate himself with that knowledge. He did not care because his business instincts had always been impeccable, and people loved to invest in Abe Gosman's companies because he was minting money. He could not lose and he got wilder and wilder, buying the Santa Anita racetrack and its assets for $458 million and rolling that into his company of health-care properties, and then adding five Texas golf courses to the gumbo. But his magic touch went bad. He had overextended, and it all started crumbling. There wasn't too much he could do about it, and as quickly he had risen, he fell even quicker. First, there was corporate bankruptcy, then personal bankruptcy.

Nothing meant as much to Abe as his palace in Palm Beach, and he tried to shelter that by making his wife the coowner. But it turned out that she was a bigamist. She had never gotten finally divorced from her previous husband, and so he lost even that. Trump bought the estate for $41.35 million in a 2004 auction, much of his art and furnishings went for next to nothing in another auction, and Gosman ended up living by himself in a leased property on the Intracoastal Waterway in West Palm Beach. He was no longer apparently even living with his wife, and I would see him sometimes having dinner alone with his dog at Trevini on Worth Avenue.

When I started the research for my book, I called Abe and asked for an interview. I told him I was interested in knowing what he had gone through, how he had gone through it, and what he had learned. Abe was proud to be a member of the Palm Beach Country Club, and he invited me to lunch one day. After I gave my car to the valet, I was told that he had been unable to make it and I should meet him in his apartment.

The Watermark condominium is ultraexpensive. It is a concrete fortress with security that makes it seem a spiffed-up version of the Palm Beach County Jail. I took the elevator up to Gosman's rental apartment, where his secretary showed me into the living room. Abe had decorated it as if he had pulled out a few pieces of little value from his Palm Beach home and placed them randomly on the cold marble. Abe shuffled into the room and introduced himself almost shyly, and said he was working on a business deal and would have to reschedule.

I called Abe the next day and he told me he was going away and to try him in a week. When I called he said something else had come up, and I should contact him again in about a month. This went on for over a year. I finally became more insistent, saying that if we were going to do this, we would have to do it soon. Two more times I drove over to his apartment and two more times he cancelled.

Finally, I was finishing the writing of this book, and I figured I would give it one last shot. I called and pressed him and he said to come over the following Sunday afternoon at three. I was visiting a friend in Boca and on the drive back, I called him to confirm but nobody answered. A few minutes later, Abe called back and said that some friends had shown up and we would do it the following morning, but I should call beforehand. I did and nobody answered. I had had it by this time, but that afternoon he called and told me to come the following afternoon at five o'clock.

As I drove over to West Palm Beach, I kept thinking about Arthur Miller's *Death of a Salesman.* I have seen the classic American play many times, and each time I see it, I see it differently. The tragedy takes place during the last days of Willy Loman, that boastful braggart who has made his last sale. He has filled his bold, strong sons, Biff and Happy, with his dishonest palaver and they are empty vessels, albeit in different ways.

The first time I saw the play, I was a fire-breathing young liberal, and I saw it as a parable on capitalism that makes salesmen of us all. Poor Willy was nothing more than a cog in a gigantic machine. As I grew older, I saw it more as a psychological family drama, how emotional dishonesty distorts and destroys. In recent years, I have come to view it as a profoundly conservative play. "Pop! I'm a dime a dozen, and so are you," Willy's son Biff tells his father. "You were never anything but a hardworking drummer who landed in the ash can like all the rest of them!" The perverse egalitarianism of America has convinced Willy that he can be anything, but he cannot. He is just a drummer.

Living in Palm Beach I see something else in the play now. *Death of a Salesman* takes place in a lower-middle-class milieu, but Willy's life could have been different. Willy could have been peddling a different product. Willy could have had a better territory. Willy could have been selling in a different era. Willy could have ended up in a great mansion on the ocean, and he still would be Willy. Willy would still be selling himself, selling a product he did not believe in.

Abe's secretary showed me into his office, where the seventy-nine-year-old businessman sat behind a great desk far too big for the room. He was a tiny man and he looked even smaller. He spent much time on the phone each day trying to make new deals. "After three decades here it's God's waiting room," he said. "We were all younger. I've lost a lot of friends in the last ten years. People just die. The Rudins. Friedman. Whatcha-ma-call-it. Julie Cohen. Davidson. And on and on and on."

People say they like Abe, and why not. He gave great parties. He invited people on his yacht. He was charitable.

We started talking about some of the people he knew, and focused on Bob Gordon, who was an old friend. "His father was not well liked," Abe said. "Bob thought he would come here and became part of the country club and never was."

Abe was silent for a moment. "Tell me how you want to frame this whole thing," he said finally.

I had told him this at least twenty times, but I did it again.

"I'm not going to talk now," Abe said. "Let me jot some things down. I wanted to get a feeling with where you were going."

"And what about the sale for ninety-five million?"

"I don't want to talk about that. It's aggravating."

When I left that day, Abe went back on the phone trying to make a deal. I knew he would never jot anything down. I knew he would never talk about what had happened. I knew that when I called him in a few days, he would not answer the phone, and I would never see or talk to him again.

As I drove away, I started thinking about *Death of a Salesman* again. I remembered the funeral scene after Willy has committed suicide. He thought that salesmen would come from all over to his funeral, drummers from Maine and Boston, Hartford and Providence. But standing at his graveside were only his wife, his two sons, and his only friend, Charley, a friend Willy did not even like because he was successful.

"Nobody dast blame this man," Charley says. "You don't understand: Willy was a salesman. And for a salesman, there is no rock bottom to the life. He don't put a bolt to a nut, he don't tell you the law or give you medicine. He's a man way out there in the blue, riding on a smile and shoeshine. And when they start not smiling back—that's an earthquake. And then you get yourself a couple of spots on your hat, and you're finished. Nobody dast blame this man. A salesman is got to dream, boy. It comes with the territory."

Barbara Wainscott re-created David Berger's image in their quest for social acceptance at the height of Palm Beach society. *(Courtesy Barbara Wainscott)*

Henry Flagler, the founder of Palm Beach, with his wife Mary Kenan Flagler in a rare casual moment. (© *Flagler Museum Archives. Not to be reproduced without permission.)*

The brilliant architect Addison Mizner was the most extravagant of all Palm Beach characters. *(Courtesy Historical Society of Palm Beach County)*

Afternoon tea in the Cocoanut Grove at the Royal Poinciana Hotel was a formal affair. *(© Flagler Museum Archives. Not to be reproduced without permission.)*

The Royal Poinciana Hotel was the biggest hotel in the world. *(© Flagler Museum Archives. Not to be reproduced without permission.)*

Eric Purcell cut a striking
figure in Palm Beach.
(Courtesy Eric Purcell)

When Eddy and Vera Louis went out socially, she did not look to be in her eighties, thirty-two years older than her husband. *(© Mort Kaye)*

Fred and Rose Keller posed for a formal portrait, symbolizing their supposedly happy marriage. *(© Mort Kaye)*

Shannon Donnelly, society editor of the *Palm Beach Daily News*, is by far the most powerful journalist in Palm Beach. *(© Mort Kaye)*

Mildred "Brownie" McLean and John "Jock" McLean II were the ultimate in Palm Beach sophistication. *(Courtesy Mildred McLean)*

Tony Senecal wants to be Donald Trump's butler for the rest of his life.
(Courtesy Tony Senecal)

Nanci Hewitt, a waitress at Green's Drug Store, is popular with everyone from billionaires to construction workers. *(© Laurence Leamer)*

More than anyone on the island, Bruce Sutka evokes the irascible, daring image of Addison Mizner. *(Courtesy Bruce Sutka)*

Simon C. Fireman and wife Norma making their social ascent.
(© Mort Kaye)

Marylou Whitney reinvented herself as the grandest of the grande dames. (© *Mort Kaye)*

In her prime, no one cut a more glamorous figure than Eles Gillet. (© *Mort Kaye)*

Dan Ponton made his living running Club Colette. *(© Lucien Capehart Photography)*

Billionaire William Koch is one of the richest, most powerful men in Palm Beach. *(© Mort Kaye)*

James "Jimmy" Barker at his most stylish during the years he ran his own art gallery. *(Courtesy James Barker)*

Helder "Sonny" Peixoto (left) had not even gone out for a date with Amity Kozak (far left) and he was already possessive of her. *(Courtesy Ashley Swain)*

Stanley M. Rumbough, Jr., and his wife Janna are among the elite couples of the island. *(© Mort Kaye)*

The Coconuts get together for a formal photo before their celebrated New Year's Eve party. *(© Lucien Capehart Photography)*

For fifteen years, James "Jimmy" Barker (left) provided a loving home for the mildly mentally disabled James "Jimmy" Heyman (right). *(Courtesy James Barker)*

18

Spinning and Spinning and Spinning

Fredchen Keller was far too young to think about the wages of wealth. He was a thin, bespectacled five-year-old child who looked like a miniature blond version of Daniel Radcliffe in *Harry Potter*. He was a highly intelligent boy, preternaturally sensitive to all that was going on around him, especially concerning his estranged parents, Fred and Rose.

Early on in the divorce proceedings, Rose's advocate Martin Haines presented evidence that four decades before, Fred had kidnapped his three sons from his former wife Blanch and hid them from her for years. Haines argued successfully that because of this, Fred should be allowed only supervised visits with Fredchen.

Rose used her son as a vehicle of her wrath. She had so poisoned young Fred's attitude toward his father that his love was tainted with fear. Fredchen had heard the stories about what his father had done, and was so afraid that Fred would spirit him away from his mother that he was most comfortable when the supervisor was within view. "Papa will steal me," he told one supervisor who wanted to go into the other room to make a phone call. When Fredchen went on Fred's boat with his father and his half brother Eric, he refused to eat the sandwiches Eric had prepared because he feared they were poisoned.

Fred did not demean Rose in front of Fredchen, in part because the supervisor would have duly noted his remarks. He realized that Rose was a good mother, and an essential part of his son's life.

Fredchen had learned to be two different people. In front of his father he played the little scholar, answering the vocabulary cards that Fred flashed by him as they sat with the supervisor eating dinner at Toojay's, a local delicatessen; listening as his father attempted to explain the Keller Trust financial statements; or snuggling up next to Fred as they watched yet another program on the Discovery Channel. And then it came time to go to Mama, and in the first minutes with Rose he was manic, a crazed little boy, running and yelling until finally he calmed down and became the little Fredchen his mother knew.

One day in July 2001, Rose brought little Fred to the courthouse and sat him outside the courtroom to be watched over by her brother Wolfgang, who was scheduled to testify that day. Rose's excuse was that she had no babysitter, but she wanted her son to witness what Fred was doing to her. It was potentially so hurtful to the little boy that later in the day the judge admonished Rose.

When Fred arrived outside the courtroom, Fredchen looked first at his father, then at his mother. Then he began spinning around and around in endless circles. Fred walked up to his son and asked, "How you doing?" And Fredchen just kept spinning. "Fredchen, how you doing?" Fred asked again. "Speak to me." Fredchen kept spinning. And then Rose stood up and tried to get him to stop, but Fredchen kept spinning and spinning and spinning. The situation was only resolved when Fred and Rose entered the courtroom, but in another sense it was not resolved at all.

Rose had two truths that wrestled with each other in her brain. There was a hopeful, nurturing earth mother and a manipulative overlord. In 2001 when Fred grew grievously ill, falling into a coma and almost dying of leukemia, Rose was there at his bedside at Good Samaritan Hospital nursing him with loving concern. For Fred it was a horrendously difficult time; despite Rose's presence, no longer was he supported by the constant succoring love of family, and he knew that once he recovered, the other Rose would again emerge.

As Fred slowly recuperated and walked the ward, he saw that in an adjoining room lay his son Paul dying of cancer. They had not talked for more than ten years and Paul had been the architect of the most savage testimony against Fred, but that was another day, and in what proved to be the last months of Paul's life, the father and son came together in sickness as they had never come together in health.

THERE WERE TO BE three phases to the divorce: a trial to determine the validity of the prenuptial, a second trial to decide the custody and visitation rights for Fredchen, and a third trial to determine the financial settlement. Much to the distress of Rose, at the end of the first trial, the judge ruled that the prenuptial was largely valid, a devastating beginning for her case.

In the second phase, Rose's attorney sought to severely limit Fred's contact with his son. As part of his strategy, Haines decided that he would put Fred on trial, exposing what he considered his deceits and duplicities, leaving him denuded and despised. This went far beyond mere legal strategy. He was attempting to turn the modest family court into a high tribunal that rendered spiritual and moral justice.

The attorneys flew up to Washington, D.C., to take the deposition of Fred's adopted son, Brian Bohlander. Brian was a purported witness to a dark past, his psychic scars from the kidnapping painfully visible. Fred despised Brian and considered him a pathetic character bemired in the muck of the past. He was a recovering alcoholic who had not had a drink for eight years. He had never married or even had a long-term relationship. He made a meager living working on home improvement projects. Brian blamed Fred for his troubles, not only for tearing him away from his mother, but for abusing him so horrendously that he had never fully risen from those assaults. It was this conduct, Brian said, that had brought social services into the house and Brian into the loving arms of a foster mother, Mrs. Lois Yost. Brian told his foster mother stories about his past that led Mrs. Yost and a social worker to write letters that located his mother.

"Brian was more than a little disturbed," Mrs. Yost recalls. "He didn't like to talk about it, but I remember him telling me the stories, some of it was like torture, holding his head down in some kind of container of water. And he had been burned between the toes, and that was one of the stories too."

Back in Florida, Fred's son Paul also testified. He had his own stories of abuse, including an especially vivid recollection of fifth grade when, for stealing some colored markers, he suffered "a bare butt whipping by Fred, using Grandpa's three-inch leather razor strap, one lashing for each of the stolen pens." Fred dismissed these tales as lies told by a son who would do anything to hurt him.

Paul had also written a manuscript that was made part of the court record. He called the unpublished book *Isthmus*, in the sense of "the sole remaining connection between legend and truth." Out of the pain of his estrangement from Fred, he had sought to write the truthful story of his father, and in doing so, to free himself.

Paul discovered that the stories Fred had told him about his grandfather serving as an officer in the Waffen-SS in World War II were not true. Ludwig Bohlander had arrived on Long Island as an immigrant in the early thirties, where he had lived and worked as a carpenter, never returning to live in Germany. Also untrue were Fred's stories about his heroic war service in Korea. Fred had entered the army after the war was over, his most notable duty peeling potatoes. Fred said that he had invented these stories to please his Neo-Nazi wife; he had been telling these tales long before he met Rose, who had no deep political beliefs.

The most important testimony in the second part of the trial came from Dr. Stephen R. Alexander. His wife was a judge in the same courthouse, and the soft-spoken psychologist was something of a fixture in the legal scene of South Florida. He had been hired by the court to evaluate both Rose and Fred. Alexander was practically the only person to give important testimony who was not financially or emotionally tied to one side or the other. His evaluations were unsettling portraits of two disturbed individuals with deathlike grips on each other's emotional innards.

The psychologist portrayed Fred as a man of profound isolation. The underlying dynamic of his life was "an inability to develop or maintain a truly empathetic relationship with another person. His orientation toward the world is essentially narcissistic, so he views people, places, and things in terms of how that person, place, or thing benefits or diminishes him. Mr. Keller is capable of controlling himself whenever he thinks it is in his best interests to do so. However, Mr. Keller is prone toward hostile reactions whenever a threat to his narcissistic self-image is seen, such as a perceived challenge to his authority, control, dominance, or sense of superiority."

Alexander's portrait of Rose was even more disturbing, a psychological horror film in which Fred had created a clone in his image. "Ms. Keller probably was a naive and optimistic young woman when she met her husband, and more likely than not she was the doting, attentive, and admiring wife in the early stages of the marriage," Alexander concluded. "She apparently proved to be a quick study, for she has obviously learned to be self-servingly manipulative to get her way. She developed her narcissism by emulation as part of her histrionic attachment to her husband. In short, she learned from observing him and by his direct instruction in business matters to always place your own interests first, and to do whatever is necessary to protect those interests. She believes she is better off without him. She believes she has set in place everything necessary to ensure she gets what she wants."

The divorce was so drawn out and so emotionally brutal that Judge Kroll commented, "You know and I know that nothing will end this case except for death."

In their epic battle, Fred and Rose traded the most savage charges and tried to force-feed Fredchen their love and affection. Fredchen was seen by various therapists, whose opinions generally favored the side that paid for their expertise. No one asked was it even healthy for the boy to be shuttled between so many therapists.

Through all this, Fredchen developed a caginess that became one of his tools of survival. No one could authoritatively say just what the divorce was costing the sensitive little boy.

Alexander concluded that Fred should see his son, but that for the immediate future, the visits should continue to be supervised. Yet contrary to the psychologist's tempered judgment and her lawyer's strong admonitions, Rose decided that Fred should be allowed unsupervised visits with their son. If Rose's stories about Fred were true, it was wrong to allow this. But to *this* Rose, it was all a glorious charade in which the endless divorce was little more than a device to teach her husband a lesson. And so before the second trial took place, the parties agreed that Fred should have almost equal access to Fredchen as his mother. The little boy continued shuttling back and forth.

As Fred saw it, he had triumphed in the first two acts of this divorce, and was convinced he would triumph in the third and most important act as well. The problem of having lied to Rose that he had signed 50 percent of his properties over to her was little more than a meaningless aside. "My intention was to placate her," Fred says. "I wouldn't have put her out on the street. I would not have had my son live with her in a dump. I would have provided."

On October 30, 2003 Judge Kroll ruled on the third part of the divorce. She released a decision that gave Rose half of everything, and made her an immensely wealthy woman. When the verdict was released, Rose happened to be at Haines's offices, where she visited so frequently that the lawyer had given her a separate office. She was doing his paralegal's hair, and when she heard the decision, she started crying and kept doing the hair. She was now Fred's equal in the only arena that truly mattered, and she fancied that once they divided the properties, they might well get back together now and live peaceably with Fredchen.

Fred did not cry. He showed no emotion. He had learned that Judge Kroll had made a mistake: She had forgotten to issue the divorce. If Rose drove off the bridge on the way back to her home and drowned, none of this would be valid; the couple would still be married, and Fred would own everything. Haines realized this as well, and immediately filed a brief to have the judge fix her mistake.

AT EIGHT A.M. ON the morning of November 10, 2003, Rose and her thirty-one-year-old brother, Wolfgang, left the mansion on the far north end of the island in a red minivan. The siblings were accompanied by Michael Easton, a massage therapist who had once worked for both Kellers.

It had been only ten days since Judge Kroll's decision, and today the thirty-four-year-old Rose and sixty-nine-year-old Fred would begin the process of dividing up the properties of Keller Trust. Rose wanted her brother with her, and not simply because he had worked for Fred for nine months before Fred fired him when Rose set out to seek a divorce. Wolfgang had become his sister's primary emotional support. He was stolid and provincial, but he was unflinchingly loyal to his sister.

As the same time that Rose left her home, Fred walked out of his condominium at Winthrop House, on the corner of Worth Avenue and the ocean that he had purchased after Rose left him, and got into the backseat of his 1999 Cadillac. As he set down his Gatorade and briefcase, the businessman murmured a greeting to Roy Bourgault, his driver. Fred was dressed in what for him bordered on formal wear, a pair of long pants and a shirt with a collar.

As Fred saw it, he had done everything for Rose and her family, and they had turned on him. He alleged that she and her brother Wolfgang had broken into his offices and stolen documents. She said that she had a perfect right to examine what was half hers.

When his estranged wife had come into the building to look at files, she had driven some of the employees to tears. He told his business subordinates that Rose had threatened to kill not only him, but all of them. Just three days ago, he had sent a fax to the Riviera Beach police near Keller Trust, alerting them to this supposed danger. An officer had given him a call and promised to look into the matter. And now this morning he was being asked to rip asunder his life's work, to tear it in two and give half to a woman who demeaned and defamed him, a woman who deserved nothing but his eternal enmity.

Rose arrived at the offices a few minutes before the man who was still legally her husband, and waited outside until Fred arrived before entering. The offices of Keller Trust could have been the premises of a seedy Boca Raton boiler room selling penny stocks. There were chartreuse carpets, wooden pine paneling, and cheap knockoff office furniture, much of which had been accumulated from commercial real estate clients late on their payments. Bourgault trailed off to go to his desk while Keller and his three guests walked into Keller's large private office. Keller asked Easton to leave so that confidential matters could be discussed. As the masseuse departed, Rose shut the door behind him.

About five minutes later, a series of shots rang out from inside the room. When the police and paramedics arrived, they found Fred in an outer office sitting on the ground with his back propped up against a wall. He had been shot in the face, and was holding paper towels to his bloody left cheek. They then came upon Wolfgang lying nearby with three bullet wounds in his body. A gun lay near him. Finally, they reached the inner office, where Rose rested in a pool of blood, shot in the head. Even before they reached her, they knew that she was gone.

The paramedics strapped Fred on a backboard and transported him to St. Mary's Hospital in an ambulance. He was immediately taken into the trauma room, a compacted space with only enough room for an X-ray machine between the two beds. Fred had been there scarcely five minutes before the nurses wheeled Wolfgang in and placed him on the other bed. Fred painfully turned his head toward the other bed, and breathing heavily, exclaimed, "Get the police, that's the man who shot me."

A few minutes later, Wolfgang realized who was in the bed next to him. "Get the police," he said. "That's the man who shot me."

19

A Bird of a Different Feather

Cathleen McFarlane-Ross stood in the intimate, romantic living room of her Mizner house at the western end of Worth Avenue beneath her full-length portrait as a beautiful, ebullient blonde in an exquisite gown. Water lapped up close to the windowsills, and out beyond the Intracoastal Waterway, the spires of West Palm Beach rose up like a picket fence.

Cathleen turned and looked out on a room that had taken on the appearance of an aviary. Several white swanlike bonnets sailed gracefully from the living room to the patio. A couple of robin-red panamas flew across the dining room in search of canapés and chardonnay. Then without warning, a dark hawklike pillbox swooped down on the spiced shrimp and stuffed mushrooms.

These ladies in their extravagant hats were there for the annual tea of the Ladies' Auxiliary of the Lord's Place. The Lord's Place began in 1979 as a soup kitchen in West Palm Beach. The charity feeds the hungry, shelters the homeless, and succors those on whom society has turned its back.

While the ladies were kibitzing merrily, a photographer from the Shiny Sheet entered the room and lifted his camera up. The ladies fluttered in front of his lens. As soon as the man packed up his camera, several women flew out the front door, having taken care of the important business, and unwilling to squander this sunny afternoon listening to morbid tales of the homeless.

Many of those remaining were there primarily to have an opportunity to see one of the most exquisite homes on the island. When Cathleen purchased the decrepit mansion, it had been broken up into four long uninhabited apartments. As she began restoring the Mizner mansion, staircases appeared out of the void, and when a plaster ceiling came smashing down, it revealed an astonishing frescoed ceiling.

That afternoon Cathleen cracked one joke after another as she moved through the sixty or so ladies. She was the epitome of a grande dame; strong willed, larger than life. She appeared the master of this womanly domain. What none of the guests grasped was that this extravagant performance was exactly that—a performance. She was saddened at the travesty the auxiliary had become, and how far it had journeyed from the ideals it had once espoused. It depressed and sickened her, for this profound unconcern mirrored what she considered a growing inauthenticity about so much of life in Palm Beach.

Cathleen was one of the earliest volunteers. In the early eighties for three years once a week she drove a scruffy, non-air-conditioned van to pick up day-old food from Publix and stale donuts from Dunkin' Donuts, and then out to the migrant labor camps in the western part of the county. She came upon waterless shanties not that much different from those lived in by Florida frontiersmen over a century before. She saw unimaginable human need.

Cathleen decided that the Lord's Place should have a fund-raiser on the island, and it should be something unique that resonated with her own experiences driving that van every week. In April 1984, Cathleen chaired a dinnerless dance at the Beach Club, a cheaper and less prestigious setting than the Breakers. The guests were served only champagne and dessert. That was unusual enough, but what truly set the event apart was that everyone donated their services, including the orchestra, the waiters, the bakers, the cooks, the grocery store, the club staff, even the valet parkers. They ran for each car, hustling for yet another donation into their tip jar that would all go to the Lord's Place.

In the years since, the auxiliary had lost its way. Cathleen was not sure just how it had happened. The dinnerless dance had been a phenomenon. But after a few years, the orchestra wanted to be paid, the waiters needed to make a living, the valet parkers were not going to be denied either, and slowly the annual dinner dance turned into just another evening on the ever-lengthening social calendar. As for the auxiliary, at first a number of Cathleen's friends were involved who volunteered along with her. But after a while, most of the ladies who showed up for the teas had no true interest in the Lord's Place.

The annual tea party had become so disconnected from the cause it presumably served that after 2006, Cathleen had given up not only offering her home but having anything to do with the auxiliary that she had founded. She had a good excuse for not going to the December 2007 event at the home of Rena and Vic Damone; that very evening she and her fourth husband, Walter Ross, were giving their "Seven-Year Itch" dinner dance at the Everglades. If she had gone, she would have found it a good example of why she had walked away from the auxiliary.

Rena Rowan Damone, wife of singer Vic Damone, had offered her elegant home in the estate section for the tea. Rena was a socialite of some standing, and it would not do to have anything less than a first-class event. She spent what she said was five thousand dollars on caterers, valet parkers, and security.

The development officers at the Lord's Place would have been far happier if their benefactress had simply written them a check, but when they arrived on the island with their begging bowls, they took whatever was tossed their way. No more than forty or so guests, the majority of them women, wandered among stations set around the pool and in various rooms for quesadillas, wine and champagne, massive blocks of cheese, and an enormous table laden with desserts. Since prepared foods could not legally be donated to the clients at the Lord's Place, most of the mountains of uneaten food would not go to those who would have appreciated it the most. A Lord's Place representative gave a spirited and overlong speech about the organization's efforts, her voice echoing across the swimming pool, and when she finally finished, the guests began departing, not wanting to be late for their next event. A number of the guests were in black tie, many of them going to Cathleen's dinner dance.

At the dot of seven, the guests started arriving at the Everglades Club, a parade of Rolls-Royces, Bentleys, BMWs, and Mercedeses slowly moving down Worth Avenue. Unlike most of the Mizner buildings in Palm Beach, which have either been torn down or so mercilessly renovated that the spiritual essence has been squeezed out of them, the Everglades has been fastidiously, even reverentially preserved. It is here that the genius of Mizner resonates most profoundly, not simply as an architect, but as a set designer creating fantasies that dare its inhabitants to don wardrobes, language, and styles commensurate with the magical world of his conception.

The guests entered the club through two enormous old wood doors leading into a labyrinthlike passage. After several twists and turns, the formally attired couples waited in a long, serpentine line to greet the host and hostess.

Unlike in most receiving lines, Cathleen McFarlane-Ross and Walter Ross did not welcome their guests to their "Seven-Year Itch" party with a perfunctory salutation before quickly moving them on, but had active conversations with almost everyone. As she stood there exuberantly greeting the guests, Cathleen was the personification of a lady born to this life. She was a perennial optimist who thought practically anything in life was possible, but even she found her life journey improbable. Her father, James Cox, was a big, boisterous Irishman who made his living setting up Singer sewing machine stores around the Midwest. Of her eight older siblings, Cathleen was closest to her oldest sister. Edna Margaret Cox had run off to join a chorus line, and as Margie Hart

M4A-30785

4BQFS9000NR5

Thank you for your order! We hope that it arrived quickly and ask that you review your purchase below:

Title	MADNESS UNDER THE ROYAL PALMS: L
Condition	Good
Location	Aisle 48 Section 5 Shelf 8 Item 209
Description	This item shows signs of wear from consistent use, but it remains in good condition and works perfectly. All pages and cover are intact , but may hav aesthetic issues such as small tears, bends, scratches, and scuffs. Spine may also show signs of wear. Pages may include some notes and highlighting. May include "From the library of" labels. Satisfaction Guaranteed.
ASIN	1401310117
Employee	1226

If anything is incorrect, please contact us immediately at orders@jensononline.com and we will make it right. Thank you again for your purchase and please leave feedback online!

became a burlesque queen. She is sometimes credited as the first burlesque star to perform nude.

When seventeen-year-old Cathleen arrived in New York in 1947, Margie had already left both the city and her profession. She was living in Los Angeles, where she married John Ferraro, the city council president. Unlike most of the women who arrived in New York in the immediate postwar era and eventually made it to Palm Beach, Cathleen was not part of the café society world. She kept to herself, her work, and her girlfriends, and rarely dated. Like her sister, she was a sensational redhead with a provocative body. "I was probably the only girl who danced, traveled in a road show, worked in a nightclub in New York, and was still a virgin," Cathleen says. "I was a virgin until I got married the first time. I've made up for it since."

On a trip back to Kansas City, where her mother had gone to live after the death of Cathleen's father, she met an old high school flame, and a crush turned into love. He had already been married, and they said their vows in a civil ceremony. She became pregnant and when she lost the child, they adopted a five-day-old baby whom they named Melissa.* Her husband went off to fight in Korea, and Cathleen made a life for herself in Los Angeles. The couple annulled their marriage soon after he returned from Asia, and she went into business with Margie. The two sisters renovated homes and sold them at big profits. They also had dress stores and other business enterprises.

At the 1960 Democratic convention in Los Angeles that nominated John F. Kennedy, Cathleen met fifty-year-old Rep. James C. Healey, an Irish American widower with four children. She calls marrying the Bronx congressman "the dumbest thing I ever did." A few years afterward, Healey had a stroke, and she was left caring for an invalid and his four children. When the politician recovered, he celebrated his newfound health by drinking twenty-four beers at a time and womanizing at roughly the same rate. In the end, he divorced Cathleen to marry another woman.

---

* *This is a pseudonym.*

As soon as Healey left, Cathleen went back to Manhattan as an interior decorator. When a friend tried to set her up with a businessman named Norris McFarlane, she almost said no. But it was St. Patrick's Day 1970, and she decided what the hell. After her annual lunch with her girlfriends to watch the parade, there was no harm in having a drink with McFarlane at the Plaza Hotel, where he held court at a table at the Oak Room. Fifty-seven-year-old McFarlane was seventeen years Cathleen's senior, but he had been an athlete at the University of Pennsylvania and was not only good-looking but in great shape. His company was the biggest producer of ferrochrome in the United States, a crucial item in the production of cars.

"What do you do?" Cathleen asked, the American hello.

"I'm a metallurgist," he said.

"Oh, that's wonderful!" Cathleen exclaimed. "We're meant for each other."

"Why's that?" McFarlane asked.

"I'm a gold digger," laughed Cathleen.

Cathleen was unwilling to marry again, and an older man at that, and it took her five years to agree to become Mrs. Cathleen McFarlane. She gave up her own business, and for the first time in her life lived in luxury. The couple had a great estate outside Buffalo, where McFarlane's company had a plant. They had an apartment in New York City, another one in Southern France, a home in Charleston, two apartments in Fort Lauderdale, and a plane to fly them wherever they chose to go. Cathleen had dreamed of living in Palm Beach, and Norris added to the collection of homes by buying a luxury apartment on the island and spending the season there. "You know, I thought we were old and rich, but goddamn, we're young and poor," he told Cathleen one evening returning from a dinner dance.

McFarlane was a reticent, taciturn man not given to socializing. He enjoyed a couple of drinks in the evening more than lengthy conversation. He flew across America in his plane visiting his various plants, and generally spent only the weekends in Palm Beach.

The couple joined the Everglades. Catholics had once been almost as outré as Jews in Palm Beach, and to gain acceptance, most of them had become mock WASPs, cloaking whatever ethnicity they had in buttoned-up mannerisms. Not Cathleen. Off-color was her favorite hue, and she took pleasure in turning faces crimson by the simple expedient of a joke that could have been spoken onstage at Minsky's Burlesque. In an era when it was almost unthinkable, she brought Jewish guests through the doors of the Everglades Club, almost daring the management to send her a letter of complaint.

One morning in August 1994 in their estate outside Buffalo, eighty-one-year-old Norris just up and died. Cathleen knew that she would miss her husband profoundly, but she did not know in how many ways and in what profundity. "You're married to a guy who's dynamite," she says. "I had always been on my own and able to handle everything, but I had just sort of relaxed and let Daddy Warbucks take care of me, which he did so beautifully."

For a number of years she dated a Palm Beach lawyer with whom she at times argued in public. She was stuck in a Palm Beach widow's melancholy condition in which a man is always better than no man, although she was beginning to have her doubts. She set out in a systematic way to meet a man, not a boy-toy, not a gay pretender, but a man of her age and class and interests.

That was how Walter Ross flew into Palm Beach for a blind date. Every evening that Walter suggested, Cathleen said she was busy. She was hardly the coy maiden; more the overbooked matron. They settled on dinner at Café L'Europe, and Walter arrived from his Houston home. He was a Scottish gentleman with a brogue that had not been broken in all his years in Texas. He had a wry wit that matched neatly against Cathleen's broad humor. He had headed one of the largest property equity companies in America. Both of his wives had died of cancer, and those struggles had marked him.

In their wedding reception at the Everglades, Cathleen gave a talk that will forever after go down in club annals as one of the more unforgettable moments. She said that after her blind date with Walter, she had only accepted his invitation to fly to his Houston home because he had sent her a first-class ticket.

Cathleen recalled how, on the first evening of her visit, Walter had prepared a bedroom for her, but she had marched down the hall to his bedroom, jumped in bed with him, and had never left. She did not go into the details, but there were nonetheless more gasps than giggles.

Walter greeted his guests dressed in a plaid kilt that he wore with perfect aplomb, unlike several of the other younger guests, who looked like men in drag. Once past the hosts, the couples moved down a few stairs to the outdoor Marble Patio for drinks and hors d'oeuvres. Cathleen had invited a wide cross section of the elite of the island, and most of those present were either Everglades members or often frequented the club.

The patio, surrounded by the walls of Mizner's masterwork, was a superb setting for conversation with at least a modicum of the originality of the surroundings. Yet what passed as conversation was for the most part, mundane and obvious social patter, exchanges of such tedium and obviousness that they lasted no more than half a dozen sentences before the speaker moved on to repeat his trite politesse on someone else, and to be greeted in kind. Most of these guests had been trained to think that a monotone of banalities constituted manners, and wit and passionate dialogue the marks of a vulgar arriviste.

There was nothing more difficult in Palm Beach than to host a memorable evening, and not have one's event end up just another cog in the social machine. There were 150 major charity events for the 2007–2008 season, including balls, dinners, luncheons, fashion shows, or other large events, and probably another hundred charity cocktail parties and smaller events. There were perhaps fifty private events the magnitude of Cathleen and Walter's gigantic celebration, and several thousand dinner parties either catered or served by a professional staff. If a socially active person stayed home more than a couple of nights, it was as if she had been ostracized. It had reached the point where some people not only did not expect an event to be memorable, but would have found it unnecessarily enervating if it had been.

This particular evening had cost over two hundred thousand

dollars, shared in part by another couple. Cathleen had done her best to create an event to be savored in the memories of the three hundred guests. When it came time for dinner, the guests moved up the steps through an arcade into the Orange Room. The room with its retractable roof was not part of the original building. It was the scene of the largest events at the club, from the annual New Year's Eve party to private weddings and spectacular parties such as this was. The guests slowly worked their way around the tables that ran from the edge of the dance floor to beyond the farthest reaches of the room, looking for their tables.

Cathleen and Walter were both comfortable public figures, and they introduced the evening with panache and grace. That Cathleen did not traipse imprudently into off-color humor disappointed those who would have laughed loudest and then savagely berated her for weeks for her social insolence. This evening she merely expressed her love for her husband, and he did the same; then the two danced as the orchestra played "Just in Time."

At precisely ten o'clock, several of the couples got up from their tables and began walking to the exits. Before long, almost the entire room was emptying out. It was like the bell had gone off for the next class. A few guests who had flown in from Canada stood dumbstruck at this lemminglike march to the valet parkers. It was Friday evening, the night was in its infancy, and the celebration should have been beginning, not ending.

One of the immutable rules at the Everglades Club is that tipping is not allowed. The staff is presumably sufficiently remunerated that gratuities are not needed, and are an unnecessary intrusion on the social life of ladies and gentlemen.

A long line of couples waited for their cars, including General and Mrs. Alexander Haig. The former White House chief of staff was wearing hearing aids and in other ways was showing his age. No one would have faulted him for asking for some minor preference, but he was a longtime club member and waited like everyone else. Far behind him stood a rotund New York businessman who had purchased a Mizner estate and renovated it in such a manner that it had the spiritual essence of a Marriott Hotel. He pushed his way out of line, flipped his car stub to one of the Latino parkers, and after stuffing bills in the parker's hand, was off with his equally rotund wife in their Rolls-Royce while others waited. The husband of an aged woman who had made a fortune making wedding dresses also gave the parker a tip and drove off in their Rolls-Royce. Others guests shifted nervously, some of them pulling out bills.

Even half a dozen years ago, such a scene would have been unthinkable, but now it was common. It was not just manners that were breaking down, but a profound social code that had governed Palm Beach for a hundred years. The Everglades board tried to admit only those who would adhere to all of the clubs rules and mandates, but at times it seemed that things were breaking down in Palm Beach almost as much within the clubs as outside.

When the valet parker brought Cathleen's Rolls, Walter did not even consider tipping. The couple's home was a few hundred yards down Worth Avenue. Cathleen and Walter went to bed almost the minute they arrived. They got up early in the morning and swam nude in their heated pool, and then spent much of the day together in an endless series of social events and charity meetings.

As had been her tradition for three decades, Cathleen went to the Orange Room of the Everglades for Christmas Eve dinner. Walter sat beside her as did her daughter, Melissa, who was the overwhelming anxiety of Cathleen's life. Her alcoholic daughter had been in and out of rehab much of her adult life. When she was sober, Melissa was a boon companion, not only Cathleen's daughter but also a charming friend. Cathleen still felt about Melissa like a young mother. Cathleen might be at a fancy dinner, but there was still part of her thinking and worrying about Melissa. The drinking was trouble enough, but then Melissa had been stricken with cancer and almost died, and with all the painkillers, there was yet another series of problems. The phone rang constantly from doctors, pharmacists, and various professionals, and if she was not fielding one problem, she was fielding another. Cathleen had been to all the meetings,

AA and Al-Anon, group therapists, consultants, quacks, doctors, and pseudo-doctors. The problem was not that Melissa liked liquor. The problem was, as Melissa said, that she loved it.

Her mother's endless solicitiousness irritated her daughter, who acted as if she could never be an adult until her mother left her alone. But how could Melissa be a true adult when she drank as she did and was financially dependent on Cathleen, and showed no signs of giving up either addiction?

The other guest at Christmas dinner was her Filipino maid, whom Cathleen had nicknamed "Grumpy" because she smiled all the time. Grumpy was doubtless the only servant seated with members. Every Sunday, Cathleen let Grumpy invite her Filipino friends to the house for a party, and for hours, music and laughter reverberated through the mansion.

It should have been the most joyous and celebratory of evenings, but for Cathleen, something was just not right. The room was so crowded with revelers, compressed with the same faces, and there was such a sense of self-conscious joy, it was as if the spirit was being force-fed. Everywhere she went these days, even to the most elaborate and brilliantly presented of charity balls, she could not wait to leave, to finish her dinner and to go home with Walter on her arm.

Cathleen invited Melissa, her Alcoholics Anonymous sponsor, and her favorite priest, Father Bill, for New Year's dinner at her home. When Melissa returned to the table after going to the bathroom, her sponsor exclaimed, "You're drunk." She had downed a fifth of vodka in no more than five minutes, and Cathleen had to take her to the emergency room at Good Samaritan Hospital to have her stomach pumped.

Melissa blamed Cathleen for forcing her to come to Palm Beach for dinner, when if she had stayed near her home, she would not have started drinking. And so it went.

When Cathleen looked back on her years in Palm Beach, nothing meant more to her than her work founding the Palm Beach Auxiliary to the Lord's Place. Cathleen was not sure if she wanted to attend the "private reception honoring Rena & Vic Damone for their ongoing support of The Lord's Place Palm Beach Auxiliary hosted by Mr. and Mrs. John Castle" at the historic former home of the Kennedys on North Ocean Boulevard. The ladies' auxiliary was honoring the Damones, largely for hosting the auxiliary tea party four months before the evening of Cathleen and Walter's party at the Everglades.

Cathleen cringed at these ladies' events. It was $150 a ticket for the 6–8 p.m. cocktail party, and she thought perhaps she would just send a donation and be done with it, but in the end she and Walter drove north in the new Rolls-Royce her husband had given her as an anniversary gift.

The guests were mainly matrons dressed in designer décor and holding designer purses. In the main rooms, they mingled, ate fancy appetizers, drank wine and mixed drinks, and socialized. The Castles had placed staff in the two diminutive, unrestored rooms where Robert and John F. Kennedy had slept. This unpretentious décor harkened back to an era that was gone.

Diana Stanley, the new executive director of the Lord's Place, worked the room. In her black dress, she looked like a no-nonsense nurse who specialized in tough love. She had brought along as speaker a formerly homeless woman who was living with her three children in an apartment provided by the nonprofit. Holly had dressed in her best clothes. She looked as if she might have shopped at Wal-Mart or JCPenney. My wife and I talked to Holly, but in all the time that I was watching, nobody else in the room said a word to her.

After about an hour, Diana Stanley quieted the room. She vowed that she would not rest until everyone, including these ladies here today, understood and felt the challenge of homelessness.

"We have been so blessed by your support and donations," Diana said, looking at the Damones. "So we give thanks for all that you do. And of course, we can never talk about the auxiliary unless we honor our founder, and that would be Cathleen McFarlane-Ross, who had a vision."

Then Diana turned to the woman beside her. "I'm here with Holly. She's from our family campus and she's one of our favorite people. And she's going to tell you a little of her story about how her life has been touched by the Lord's Place. First tell us a little about your family."

"Okay, I'm a mother of three, I graduated the program in December. I was in a rush to finish and get with my family, and my mother was kind enough to let us . . ." Holly went on in a stream of largely unconnected words. Diana understood the endless travail of homelessness, and she coaxed Holly's story out of her, and the optimism that she felt in her new apartment. "I'm staying at the Lord's Place as long as it takes," she concluded, articulating each word.

Diana thanked Holly and then said what she had come here to say. "When we gather together in a beautiful cocktail event like this, sometimes we don't always stop and pause to think about why we're here," she said in a preacher's voice. "I guess it's what I'd like us all to do tonight. We've been graced with this beautiful home, and less than three miles away we have families living in cars, families living in fields, children that are two and four like my little Rosa and my little Michelle whom I've just met, children that have no home, but have been blessed enough to connect with the Lord's Place."

As soon as Diana finished her remarks, almost everyone moved toward the door, on to the next event.

20

Pierced by Sorrows

David was a big drinker. He usually started dinner with three martinis, and then he and Barbara shared at least one bottle of wine. In December 1999, Barbara noticed David leaving his second martini half touched on the dinner table. In the lives of most people, that would have been hardly worth noticing, but Barbara knew how much her husband was a man of habit, and sensed that something was wrong.

"How do you feel?" she asked.

"Not great," replied David, who had never been sick in his adult life.

"I want you to go to Brigham and Women's Hospital in Boston for a checkup," Barbara said, more a command than a request. "We'll take the dog and get a corner suite at the Ritz. And I want you not to tell the boys, because it may be nothing."

Barbara feared that if David's sons knew, they would push their father to seek medical treatment in Philadelphia, where they would have more control. The couple flew up to Boston, and after checking in at the Ritz-Carlton Boston, David began his tests. It took only a few hours for the specialists to confirm that David had both Alzheimer's and stomach cancer so advanced that without treatment, he would die in a few weeks. He was operated on, losing about half his stomach, and afterward began chemotherapy that burned away whatever cancer remained.

When David first became sick and his death seemed imminent, Barbara realized that she had not paid enough attention to her financial condition. In their prenuptial agreement, David had legally promised to create a trust in his wife's name, add her as a coowner to his apartment in Manhattan, and transfer one of his Mercedes to her name, but he had done none of this. Once David's condition improved, Barbara confronted him. He said he had merely let matters slide, and quickly ordered his attorneys to make things right. A trust owned the Palm Beach house, and Barbara insisted that he buy a house for her on the island where she could live after he died. He authorized her to spend up to a million dollars, and she bought a house in the North End.

For the long seven weeks that they were in Boston, Barbara spent much of her little free time shopping at the luxury stores along Newbury Street. "I want you to spend whatever you want on whatever you want," David had told her several years before. "You know why I'm saying this?"

Barbara did not say anything, but she thought, "David's sons are going to screw me when David dies. So If I want things, I'd better get them now."

Barbara took David's remarks as his way of telling her that his sons would do whatever they could to see that she did not cut deeply into their inheritance. And she took her husband at his word. Barbara loved exquisite things, and she bought whatever struck her expensive fancy, including couture clothes especially fit for her large figure; shoes handmade for her outsized feet; hats uniquely designed for her big head; handbags, scarves, artwork, and home furnishings.

When the couple returned to Palm Beach, they knew that their lives would never be the same again. Many women would have handed their husband over to a nurse as they hurried out of the house for lunch and an afternoon of bridge, but Barbara did not do that. There were nurses, but she was the primary caregiver.

Barbara learned to set up the IV-like device with nutrient packets that fed to a tube in David's stomach. It took several hours to feed him, and at night, she lay restlessly next to her sleeping husband, waiting for the alarm to go off, signaling that it was time for a new nutrient packet.

Those who only knew Barbara from her social life in Palm Beach would not have predicted her behavior. "I loved him and I wanted to preserve his dignity," she says. "By doing this myself I felt there wouldn't be people who could say he's got a hole in his stomach."

As much as she performed as a caregiver, Barbara's larger role was to try to keep David's life as unchanged as possible. The couple flew to London on private planes, taking their medical equipment with them to their suite at Claridge's. They continued to go to the races at Ascot, and to stay with Prince Edward at his country estate.

Barbara watched as David fought tenaciously to forestall the dying of the light. He had been a superb trial lawyer with a dramatic sense of theater; now he knew that he had to play a new role. With the onset of Alzheimer's, he could no longer be his loquacious self. He learned to be quiet and to rely upon a few stock phrases, and to those who did not know him, he seemed a quiet old gentleman in pristine health.

In June of 2003, the Bergers were staying with Prince Edward and his wife, Sophie, Countess of Wessex, in their country estate. David had come down to breakfast first, and was sitting with the prince and a couple of other guests. As Barbara appeared, she could tell that the guests were indulging in their favorite sport, taking turns complimenting the prince. "Isn't the food at Bagshot Park delicious!" one of the guests exclaimed. David looked at the food and then at his acquaintance. "It tastes like shit," he said.

Barbara apologized for the wildly inappropriate comment, and as the chauffeured car drove them back to Claridge's, she knew that she would no longer be able to take David out socially. In their two-bedroom suite, he went into one of the bathrooms and fell against the closed door. He could not get up, and his body blocked

Barbara from pushing open the door. A worker had to crawl out on the ledge and work his way over to the bathroom, where he entered through the window and propped David up enough to open the door.

David suffered no permanent damage from his fall, but that was about the only good news, and Barbara and David began living full-time in Palm Beach. Except for David hitting tennis balls with a pro at the Breakers, they rarely left the house. For Barbara, the summer months were excruciatingly boring. No one she knew was in town, and her life was what it would be until David died, devoting herself to a husband who soon would not even recognize her.

In July of 2003, Barbara flew up to Boston to have her gall bladder taken out at Brigham Hospital. She left David in the competent hands of a team of nurses. While Barbara was focusing on her recovery, she received a call from her lawyer. "I've gotten a communiqué from David's lawyers," he said. "It's a list of supposedly everything you've bought in the last three years. I'm sending it to you overnight. I don't know what it's about, but it's not good."

Barbara was startled that the attorneys could have gotten hold of such information, but David's son Daniel worked at his father's law firm and she assumed he was behind this. The accuracy of the list impressed Barbara. She found only one mistake, an item for $225 from Victoria's Secret. That was not her kind of store, but the rest was accurate except for the handkerchiefs she had bought at Au Trousseau, where an antique French batiste handkerchief cost as much as two hundred dollars. The handkerchiefs were listed as furniture.

"This can't be right," the lawyer said on the phone. "What did you buy at Hermès on Newbury Street for $12,500?"

"I bought a pocketbook," Barbara replied, growing uncomfortable with this quasi-inquisition.

"How many?"

"One."

"How could you spend so much?" asked the incredulous attorney, whose wife boasted of buying knockoff designer purses from pushcarts on Madison Avenue.

"It's red ostrich," Barbara said, as if that should settle the matter.

When she got off the phone, Barbara knew she was in trouble if even her own attorney did not empathize with her. She had him fly down to Palm Beach to talk to David, but he was so far gone that it did no good.

In January of 2004, Barbara received formal notification that she was being divorced. Unbeknownst to her, David had signed his power of attorney over to his sons, and this was the result. Barbara's husband apparently had no idea what he had done. "David, do you want to divorce?" Barbara asked imploringly.

"No. Of course not. I love you."

Barbara had been prepared to succor her husband for the rest of his life, and she could have fought to hold on to her marriage. But if David had taught her anything, it was that in life you watch out for yourself, and she had studied at his feet long and well. Her relationship with David had started as a business relationship and it ended as one. She set out to try to take away as much money as she could from their marriage.

David had lied about his assets in the prenuptial, and she was convinced any judge would throw it out of court. Then she would face a brutal, onerous divorce in which the opposing lawyers would portray her as a wildly profligate woman squandering millions of dollars without conscience or concern. And there would be all kinds of allegations that while shamelessly squandering David's money, she was not taking proper care of her husband. The theme would have resonated with most middle-class Americans, but if she could have gotten a true jury of her peers—women married to fabulously wealthy older men—they probably would have judged her conduct and her expenses as nothing more than normal.

David's lawyers offered her a generous cash payment, and Barbara decided to accept. The negotiations took place rapidly. Barbara felt the overwhelming desire of David's sons to get her out of the house as soon as possible. In exchange for a settlement that would allow her to live a life of wealth on her own, the lawyers presented her with an agreement that contained many onerous clauses. The worst of it was that she had to agree never to see David again nor to contact him in any way.

The agreement was to be signed and millions of dollars transferred to her name on March 8, 2004, Barbara's fifty-seventh birthday. The evening before, Barbara went into David's bedroom just before he went to sleep at 6:45 p.m. to say good night for the last time. She was full of a mounting sense of horror and rage and perhaps a modicum of guilt. She knew that with Alzheimer's patients, it is crucial to keep everything in their lives the same, not even moving a chair a few feet or buying a new dresser.

When Barbara got up the next morning and left the house at around 7:30, David's door was shut. She drove over to her lawyer's office. At shortly before eleven, she and her attorneys arrived at the offices of David's attorney, where David was shuttered away in another room to sign the final agreement. Much of the furniture in the Jungle Road house was Barbara's, and while the final documents were being signed, movers were taking away the furnishings and moving them to Barbara's house in the North End.

David's sons flew him to Philadelphia immediately after the signing. When he was returned to the house a week later, Barbara was gone. The furniture was gone. The nurses his ex-wife had hired were gone. This man who had come to Palm Beach so long ago with dreams of rising to the heights of society was now living in a house among people he did not know in a world he barely comprehended.

David's new caretaker was waiting for him. "Son of a bitch," he kept saying as he saw how different things were. "Son of a bitch. Son of a bitch."

The caretaker had been told that Barbara was an evil woman who kept David drugged, and abused him by locking him up in his bedroom. It took her a long while to decide that this was not true. It was partially the way David acted sometimes, thinking that the caretaker was Barbara, and it was partially the way his sons treated him, or more accurately did not treat him. They rarely came to visit, and the caretaker concluded that their primary concern was David's fortune.

The caretaker kept David busy. He loved music and she took him to every musical performance in the area. He loved to walk and she took him along Worth Avenue and out to the malls. He loved tennis and every morning at 8:30, she brought him over to the Breakers to hit with one of the pros for a half hour. She led him to the center of the court where his competitiveness took over. The pro hit the ball and he hit it back twenty or thirty times before missing. And wherever they went and whatever they did, David never saw Barbara again.

PALM BEACH IS FULL of people pierced by sorrows brought on by the pursuit of money. It sets wives against husbands, children against stepmothers, the young against the old, and the healthy against the infirm.

When the widow of a man who had owned an extremely lucrative business in Manhattan was dying, her children did not arrive to be there for her last moments, but the lawyers flew in with their briefcases in hand, ready to begin the distribution of her fortune. The supposed benefactors of another aged woman shipped her off to a nursing home in Poland, while they cavorted in Palm Beach with what remained of her fortune.

Almost everywhere, the mindless pursuit of money tore apart the most fragile emotional sutures of family and friends. There is no better example than Eles Gillet. Barbara and David had seen Eles and Warry often when David was healthy, but now Barbara saw her old friend only occasionally.

Unlike Brownie, Cathleen, and Marylou, Eles had been born to privilege. Eles had grown up in enclaves of advantage, and had never had her dainty hands soiled with the mundane travails of quotidian life. When she was a child, her parents traveled extensively, shuttling their two daughters into the arms of a black nanny who was more their mother than their biological mother was. When her parents were home, Eles and her sister were brought out in their dainty dresses to christen the latest ship launched by Ingalls Shipbuilding Corp., a subsidiary of Ingalls Iron Works, a company built, in the words of her grandfather, from "a one-horse ship—one Negro and one mule" into the biggest steelworks in the South.

In 1938, her grandparents built their six-bedroom house on Via Del Lago in the estate section. The family patriarch, Robert Ingersoll Ingalls Sr., was a man of deep Presbyterian faith. In 1948 when his only son and namesake, Robert Jr., divorced his wife to marry a widow with two children, his father severed his son from the family company he was serving as president.

Eles was twelve years old when her parents divorced. She was shuttled out of Pelican Hall and moved to her father's yacht, docked at the end of Worth Avenue. As a preteen, she was especially vulnerable to the adult games of duplicity, and there is no neat tabulation of the damage rendered.

Eles grew into a gorgeous upper-class Southern belle, but she was as remote from the world as the concubines in the emperor's palace in imperial China. The result was a creature of ultrafemininity, unready for life in the workaday world, but brilliantly prepared to be a hostess par excellence, and both a protector and a symbol of upper-class traditional values. She was a lovely, strong-willed, highly opinionated, ultraconservative woman.

When I had lunch with Eles every few months, it was like going on a formal date. I would drive over to Pelican Hall and park my car in the sweeping driveway, to be shown inside either by her social secretary or maid. Within a few minutes, this tiny, impeccably dressed woman would walk down the stairs, and after air kisses, off we would go to one of the best restaurants on the island.

Innumerable people told me that she would be an impossible interview. We both would have a couple of glasses of chardonnay, but she was articulate and witty, with her own savage take on the pretenders invading her island. When she opened her mouth, she sometimes spoke language so foul that it would have wilted a rose. I will not be quoting her most lurid remarks, because in print they look so unrelentingly ugly, but it was different being with her. As she spewed out her profanity, she made charming what would have sounded vile coming from almost anyone else.

Researching my book, I was often with people professing their endless virtue, promoting their philanthropic endeavors, boasting of their concerns with the plight of the world, when I saw often it was only about them, to promote themselves, to enhance their social status. Eles had none of that pretense. Her children had never consumed her energy or emotions. Her husbands were there only to please her; her friends were there to amuse her.

One time over lunch at Café L'Europe, Eles was livid over the five-hundred-dollar hair coloring she had received at Salon Margrit, the beauty parlor across the street where she and many of her friends went most days. It had been the owner's birthday, and all these people kept coming in wishing Margrit a happy birthday. It was an outrageous assault on Eles's appointment.

If Cathleen did not like you, she turned her back. If Brownie did not like you, she pretended she did not know you. If Eles did not like you, she told you to your face in the most brutal, searing terms. If she could not reach you, she left a message on your answering machine that when you got home would burn your ears.

Eles had been brought up to marry well, and she did so, to Samuel Boykin Jr., a wealthy young man with impeccable social connections. They had two children and had what outsiders called blessed lives. The couple did not see happiness as the by-product of a life well lived, but as its central focus, and when they did not feel pleasure, they reached out and grasped for it.

During the season, Eles spent much of her time in her boat docked at the pier at the end of Worth Avenue. "I was in Palm Beach and my husband was up in Birmingham. He had a girlfriend in Chicago, so I got a boyfriend down here," Eles recalls with relish. "Tit for tat. And my boyfriend down here was Warry Gillet."

F. Warrington "Warry" Gillet Jr. had three children with his wife, Eleanor Tydings. The daughter of former U.S. senator Millard E. Tydings and sister of former U.S. senator Joseph D. Tydings, Eleanor bore the name of one of Maryland's most famous families. Warry feared that his closest friend had had an affair with his wife. Thus Eles and her second husband not only shared childhoods of great privilege, but first marriages that ended in sexual betrayal that left them incapable of a complete commitment to another human being. There was always something hanging back, a wariness that never left them.

Eles had many times Warry's money, but both had been brought up in protective luxury and were as fitted to each other as two pieces of a puzzle. Warry's father was one of the great aces of World War I, and his son and namesake was lesser in most ways except for his manners and grace. Warry could have been Rhett Butler's grandson. Tall and handsome, Warry had been brought up in an old Maryland family. He had been living in a condominium in West Palm Beach when he met Eles. Although he had income each year from his father's trust, he was not wealthy in the sense that Eles was, but he had an incredible collection of Gillet family treasures, including a priceless Chippendale dining table, a treasure of bronzes, antique silver, a grandfather clock, and eighteenth-century sideboards.

Warry had matchless taste, and considered it his role in life to indulge that taste to the full measure. He had clothes perfectly tailored to his six-foot-two-inch frame. He wore impeccable hunting pants and shot with the finest of guns. He was a talented chef who, in their summer house in Maine, loved to cook, often shooing the servants out of the kitchen so he could prepare his succulent barbecue.

Warry was also a connoisseur of wine. Every time the couple traveled to London, they stopped at Berry Bros. & Rudd, Britain's oldest and most celebrated wine and spirit merchant. They were such good customers that the proprietors put on six-hour-long wine tasting luncheons for the wealthy visitors from America, who shipped home cases of the finest vintages to add yet another dimension to what for years was one of the finest wine cellars in Palm Beach.

Their grandfathers had been founding members of the Everglades Club, and as Eles and Warry sat down to dinner in the Orange Court, they were the perfect examples of the local elite. Eles brilliantly complemented her husband, and was as much the creator of their lifestyle as Warry. One of the first things she did was to buy back the 9,425-square-foot mansion in the estate section that was one of her childhood homes. She then hired Sister Parish, the esteemed interior decorator who had redone the Family Dining Room and the Yellow Oval Room in the White House during the Kennedy administration. The result was a richly traditional old English décor that might have been from a Georgia plantation home. The furnishings were mainly family heirlooms from both the Ingalls and Gillets, including Warry's nineteenth-century bronzes on the walls.

Eles was dressed by Arnold Scaasi, who created formal wardrobes for many of the island's most prominent women. The dress designer had learned long ago that in his business, discretion was the only moral absolute. As he fitted his newest customer, he had the distinct impression that her husband was educating Eles in spending *her* money, and spend it she did, on, among other things, a score of Scaasi dresses, each one between ten and twenty thousand dollars.

Eles was not only a perfectionist but also a miniaturist, and she planned her elaborate dinner parties months in advance. If there was to be a hunt dinner featuring some of the game her husband shot, it would not do simply to serve it on any fine china. There must be pheasant service plates and table settings that created the illusion of grasses. If salmon was the main course, then the tables should be outside, covered with conch shells and sea grass leaves, and there must be a shell motif on the finger bowls and dessert plates. And of course, just beforehand, her personal floral arranger created his own unique arrangements to underscore the evening's theme.

In 1982 when Dan Ponton opened private Club Colette, Eles, Warry, and another couple were his first guests dining there a week before the opening. He has vibrant memories of Eles that evening. "She was the chicest woman of all," Dan says. "She was the most glamorous, the richest, and the most socially powerful of the pack."

In the late seventies and eighties, there were no more than half a dozen major charity balls each season, and Eles chaired or served on committees for most of them. "I did cancer three times," she says.

These balls were overwhelmingly venues of social display, in which charity was little more than a means. Like other chairs, Eles sought corporate and personal sponsors to underwrite the events, who then took generous tax write-offs. There were always elaborate dinners and cocktail parties before the events, in which the hostesses sought to upstage each other. They took tax write-offs too.

Eles did not think of herself as especially charitable, a parsimonious trait that she shared with many of her WASP neighbors. If they gave, they liked to give to things like heart disease or cancer that might personally benefit them, or perhaps the arts, but nothing controversial like AIDS, or notably unpleasant like the homeless, and surely nothing that taxed their trust funds. She would never have involved herself in anything so outré as the Lord's Place with its unseemly annual dinner dance at the Beach Club in the North End, the Siberia of the island.

Eles's wealth had not shielded her from the melancholy realities of family life, only exacerbated them. When the children from their first marriages were jammed into their second, there was an unwieldy, painful joining with sharp edges everywhere. Obsessions with money and inheritance became as much features of childhood as puberty.

Eles had particular difficulties with two of the boys. Her husband's namesake was endless trouble. She had tried in her way to mother F. Warrington Gillet III, but as he grew into adolescence, Warry III increasingly viewed her with wary distance. She did not see the pain in young Warry's eyes, how he felt that he belonged nowhere, not with his mother's rich new husband, or with his own father in Palm Beach, but shuttled off to prep school, ignored and largely forgotten.

Young Warry was his father's son, outrageously handsome and charismatic, and able to get what he wanted with little more than a charming quip. His father looked at his namesake and saw a spoiled scion of wealth, an image that he could have observed in the mirror. One year he decided that Warry III could not "sit on his ass." The young man needed a lesson in World 101. Warry insisted that his son work as a day laborer in Palm Beach, an experience that taught young Warry primarily that he did not want to be a day laborer.

Warry III had an acting role in 1981 when, wearing a hockey mask, he played the pathological killer Jason in *Friday the 13th, Part 2.* That was the beginning and end of his film career. He returned to New York, where he cut a wide bachelor swath through watering holes both elegant and inelegant. One of Young Warry's friends, Ernie Garrett, recalls Warry's father advising his son: "You don't marry a good-looking woman and then be hurting for money. You marry for money, son, and you can have good-looking women all your life." That was one of the many fatherly axioms young Warry did not follow.

In 1997, Warry III's Swedish model bride gave birth to F. Warrington Gillet IV. The following year, the FBI arrested the former actor for his role in a stock swindle. He then developed a plan to place photography studios in malls where young women would have model portfolios taken and buy cosmetics. Young Warry talked several of his mother's friends, including Marylou Whitney, into getting involved, but the investors lost everything; yet another embarrassment for Eles and Warry.

Eles's own son, Robert Ingalls Boykin, was troubled too. In 1983, the twenty-six-year-old had been so infuriated at American Airlines for losing his eight pieces of luggage that he called Palm Beach International Airport from his mother's house, threatening to blow it up. "We are gonna blow those [expletive deleted] Jews up," he said. When the phone company supervisor called the Gillet residence, the man who answered the phone laughed and called the matter "no big deal" before hanging up. Thanks to his lawyers, Boykin was able to slither out of charges that might well have sent another man to prison.

Robert inherited wealth, but what he needed was to forge his own sense of manhood, outside the walled city of privilege. His positions included an executive post at Bluebonnet Savings Bank of Dallas, a virtual sinecure, when what he needed was something he had truly won himself. He inherited social graces and manners that made him attractive to the daughters of wealth, one of whom he married, when what he needed was to meet with the new and the untried. He drank; so did his mother and stepfather, but booze grabbed on to him. He tried drugs too, and that was worse. But he was rich, not a junkie on a poor block in West Palm Beach, and everyone protected him and figured it would get better.

21

Goblets of Revenge

If a poor man eats two Big Macs and a couple orders of large fries all washed down with a large Coke, he is a pig. If a rich man eats a dozen Chesapeake Bay oysters, rondelle of salmon with juniper berry sauce, and chocolate truffle marquise accompanied by a worthy bottle of Haut-Brion Blanc, he is a gourmet. Warry loved food and drink, and as he enjoyed the finest wines and the richest foods, he gained weight, until his handsome form was lost in his bulk. He went on radical diets, often talking personally to diet guru Dr. Robert C. Atkins, but he always returned to the fancy food and the vintage wines, and back came the weight. Eventually he reached an obese 280 pounds.

On the morning of May 13, 2002, seventy-one-year-old Warry drove over to the Ultima Health Club in West Palm Beach for a workout, and returned in time for lunch. Part of his daily ritual was to have his first stiff drink at noontime. He was quite particular about this. He took one cube of Swanson's beef broth and another of Campbell's beef broth, and put them in a blender. Into this, he poured lemon juice, a squirt of Worcestershire sauce, a strong jolt of Tabasco, and lots of vodka. Then he turned on the blender and left it on until he had a frothy blend. He poured the mixture into big glass goblets, and garnished the drinks with cherries. One of these drinks was enough for anybody, and too much for many.

After lunch with Eles and a visiting priest, Warry went upstairs to his bedroom, and as he did each afternoon, took a long nap. When he had not come down by six o'clock, Eles went upstairs to wake him, and found that her husband of twenty-seven years had died in his sleep.

The family flew down to Palm Beach, and the next day Warry III says that his stepmother took him aside in her bedroom. "You're not going to get anything," she told him. "You've been cut out."

The Gillets had befriended George and Frayda Lindemann, who had taken the role that Barbara and David had once played with the socially prominent couple. The Lindemanns had several factors that hobbled their acceptance in the island's elite, including not only their Jewish faith, but the fact that their son had served time in prison for executing a Thoroughbred horse in an insurance scheme. The Lindemanns offered their private plane to fly the family and friends up to Maryland for the burial. Afterward, they flew back home, and that evening Eles went for dinner at the B&T.

There was a dispute over who was to pay for the funeral. Warry's will stated that "all funeral expenses be paid as soon as practical," and it would seem indisputable that the services should have been paid by his estate. In any event, Warry III claims that he and his sister were billed $27,000 to pay for the expenses, including $12,000 for the funeral home, $2,300 for C'est Si Bon! for the catering, and $528 for a casket spray. In the end, Warry's estate paid for his funeral, but Eles says that Warry III owes her money over the event, and that is why her late husband lies buried in the cemetery at St. John's Episcopal Church in Glyndon, Maryland, without a headstone. Then Eles went ahead and sold the adjoining plots so Warry's son and daughter would not be buried next to him.

The unmarked grave was only one measure of the emotionally brutal conflict. Eles was worth tens of millions of dollars. With Eles so wealthy, it would have seemed right for a father to leave at least half his relatively small estate to his son and daughter. But in 1993, Warry wrote a will that gave everything to Eles, and on the same day signed a quitclaim relinquishing his right to a share of their Palm Beach home. The codicil signed eight years later in 2001 only made that commitment stronger. Eles asserts that her husband thought that his two children had received plenty from their grandfather's trust after Warry died; young Warry and Susan received about two hundred thousand dollars apiece from the assets of the trust.

For Warry III and his sister, the will was a brutal rebuke. Yes, it was about money, but not only about money. It was as if their father had taken a torch to the proud heritage of the Gillet line by deeding Eles even the most precious family heirlooms. Susan called Eles and asked if she might have the Gillet silver. Susan thought she was making a legitimate request. Eles considered Susan a greedy, unpleasant heir making unseemly demands on a grieving widow.

"The silver is well protected in a closet with a special lock," Susan told her stepmother.

"And that's where it's staying. The way you're treating me, you're not getting anything."

That was not strictly true. Eles sent Warry III and Susan a few boxes of their father's belongings. Susan opened one package to find an old cookbook and legal documents dealing with her parents' divorce. Young Warry received such memorabilia as one of his father's old license plates, some old shoes, and a belt emblazoned with a nude woman.

Warry III learned from a friend that his stepmother had donated his father's elegant suits, Louis Vuitton luggage, and other possessions to the Church Mouse, a Palm Beach thrift store. The friend purchased a couple of items and gave them to Warry III as a gift. In New York, a prominent tailor told him that he had a number of his father's suits still on his premises. "I went over there and she got wind of it and ordered all the clothes chopped up," Warry III said.

Warry III heard from friends in Palm Beach that Eles had taken up with one of his father's closest friends, Andy Avello, a Cuban American clothing buyer for Versace two decades Eles's junior.

Avello eventually moved into Pelican Hall, where Eles referred to him as her "good friend."

The more Warry III thought about his father's death and his actions, the more convinced he was that the malevolent figure of his stepmother stood behind it all, and that he must strike boldly back at her. "She hurt us badly, so what's the next thing?" Warry III says. "Of course you're going to talk to a reporter and say, 'I don't think my dad had lunch on the thirteenth and dropped dead. And I don't think he meant to disown his whole family. And now Eles has gone out and is porking Andy Avello.' Of course somebody tells Richard Johnson [editor of the *New York Post*'s Page Six gossip column], whom I've known forever, and that was the beginning of six articles that railed her."

Shannon rushed to Eles's defense in the method approved by the most esteemed of national media: Spread the story in detail and nuance, while condemning the whole sordid business from a pedestal high above the tabloids. "Eles Gillet's friends are coming to her defense after recent news reports depicted her in an unflattering light," Shannon began her much-read weekly column in January 2004. "A New York newspaper reported that Gillet, the widow of F. Warrington 'Big Warry' Gillet, was 'fleeing' Palm Beach for all kinds of reasons—she was omitted from the *Vanity Fair* spread, her stepson kicked up a fuss over his inheritance, and she's running off to South America with her tie salesman beau because his horizontal rumba is 'the best sex ever.' Yikes!"

Warry III made the firm suggestion that his father may have been poisoned with the oleander plant, and the body quickly buried without an autopsy. His was a scenario as richly detailed and compelling as it was unlikely. There was no evidence that Eles knew anything about the poison or had any reason to kill her husband. Warry III hired a detective and filed a suit to have his father's body exhumed, saying that there was reason to believe that Eles was "responsible for the untimely death." He said that his stepmother had argued with her husband in the weeks before his death, turned down an autopsy, controlled her late husband's entire fortune, and had taken up with a younger man.

Some of that may have been true, but the only thing definitely murdered was several reputations. Young Warry's own mother, appalled by all the publicity, got him to back off, and he moved on with plans to parlay his suspicions into a Palm Beach movie, *Bloody Social*, which he describes as "the story of a wealthy tobacco heiress who kills her husband and then runs off and marries her Italian stallion and comes back to town."

The movie never quite happened, and as the years went by, Warry III's anger at his stepmother was matched by his hatred for his father. "All of his children and grandchildren look at him in disgust because he's disinherited everyone," Warry III says. "People have distaste for him. They loathe his name and call him a buffoon and an idiot."

Eles continued to socialize almost every night and to have elegant dinner parties. Her "good friend" was a heavy drinker and needed a liver transplant. Eles had never waited in a line in her life. She went out and helped to raise a million dollars, dispersed in such a way that Andy got his transplant.

As a heavy drinker himself, Andy was one of the few people who could talk a modicum of sense to Eles's alcoholic son, Robert. He was even more handsome than Warry III, and had a sweetness of disposition unlike anyone else in the family. His wife had left him and his alcohol-sodden life and taken their children with her. And that had made him even more despondent. He had a condominium in Palm Beach, and the police had grown too familiar with the 911 calls alerting them to a drunken relic lying huddled somewhere.

In 2005, Andy died on a trip to France. By then he was no longer staying at Eles's house. He had been an anchor to her life in the three years since Warry died. That was a mild misfortune compared to the following year when her forty-nine-year-old son killed himself by jumping off the roof of his five-story condominium in South Palm Beach. Robert had been so unhappy, his life such a litany of despair, that Eles rationalized that her son had found the one ending that gave him peace.

Eles was not one to mope around, leaving her demons easy

entrée into her soul. She headed back out into the frenetic social whirl of the island. Wherever she went, though, nothing was the same. It had always been her island, but who were all these people?

Eles always went to the annual Preservation Foundation's dinner dance. The organization was devoted to holding on to what was best in Palm Beach, and its members included whatever was left of the old social elite and those who hoped to be among them. In the years just before Mar-a-Lago became a club, the event had been held at the estate, but Trump felt that his generosity had been treated with disdain and he turned them away. Since then it was as if Trump had called in his New York shamans to put a curse on the event. Something always seemed to go wrong. Eles was a witness to the carnage. One year the golden paint on some of the chairs had not dried and a number of the ladies left with unwanted souvenirs on their designer-dressed posteriors.

On Eles's latest foray to the annual ball, there was an Indian theme in the Venetian Ballroom at the Breakers. The room had been transformed into a Raja's Palace vividly described by Shannon with its "dupioni silk in burnished oranges, reds and yellow, round tables centered with tall trumpet vases filled with kumquats, baby lemons, limes, grapes and oranges, and rectangular tables centered with enormous elephant topiaries draped in ceremonial robes." It all looked Indian enough, but there was a small problem with the life-size baby elephants on the tables. "I couldn't see anybody and neither could anyone else," Eles recalls. "I had a damn leg in my face. Those who had an asshole in their face were really upset."

At the Everglades, it was hardly better. She had once known everybody, and now she walked in and it was like somebody else's club. She had the feeling that the Everglades was being taken over by Midwesterners, a strange species that as far as Eles was concerned could have come from Albania. The club had begun admitting many new members whose only obvious virtue was a lack of obvious vices. There was no reason to blackball such potential members, but there was equally no reason to choose to sit next to them at dinner.

At least they were not Jewish. Jews were now admitted even to the Sailfish Club and the Beach Club in the North End, and God knows where it would all end. "Everything the Jews get into, they take over," Eles reflects. "And people don't want them to take over the last two things that we have. Those are our clubs."

Eles was suffering such back pain that she had little interest in contemplating the further decline of her Palm Beach world. If anything, she had too many doctors and too much advice, and no matter where she went or what she did, the pain did not go away. In the evenings, she went to the Everglades, the B&T, restaurants, or dinner parties, and sometimes she had to go home early. Sometimes she just did not show up.

Eles always had a man on her arm; since Andy had left, it had generally been Peter Rock. Peter had been on the island so long and had escorted so many women that few people even knew that the man had a wife in New York working as a decorator. He was by definition more walker than lover, and he was perfectly happy with that appellation. He was a large, boisterous fellow with a showy, overflowing personality that enlivened whatever watering spot in which he happened to land. He liked to drink, and had immortalized himself as one of Brownie's troops on a trip to Morocco on Royal Air Maroc by falling asleep in the aisle. He was a big man, and no one or nothing could lift him. King Hassan II ordained that he never be allowed in the kingdom again. Brownie's teacup poodle ran up and down the aisle as well, but the king was so enchanted with the dog that he gave him a passport.

Rock was too busy going out to bemoan the sad fact that he would never see Marrakech again. He and Eles and most of their friends had an inordinate interest in grapes, as long as they were fermented and of a decent vintage. Eles had a dilemma when she had Peter and her other friends over for dinner. There were bottles of wine in Warry's cellar worth as much as twenty-five thousand dollars. She knew it was gauche to tell her guests that they were drinking incredibly expensive bottles of wine, but she could not abide sitting there watching them slurping it down like *vin ordinaire*. By the time the evening was late, she could have served them

Two Buck Chuck, and they would have raved knowingly about the bouquet.

In March 2006, after a dinner at Eles's honoring Marylou Whitney and her new husband, John Hendrickson, Peter headed home to his condominium at the Palm Beach Towers. As he drove into the parking lot, he rammed his Red Chrysler into a Ford SUV, which in turn hit a Honda. When the police arrived, Peter was still sitting behind the wheel with his seat belt on and the motor running. He could hardly walk and smelled of liquor, and after taking a blood sample, Fire Rescue took him to Good Samaritan Hospital. In the morning, Peter woke up and realized he was lying in a bed with all kinds of tubes and wires attached to him. He knew that when the test came back, there might be a dispute whether it was blood or burgundy, and indeed it proved to be more than three times the permissible alcohol level.

Peter tore the paraphernalia off his arms and legs, put his clothes on, and ran out. When he called Eles, she came over immediately and went with him to see a criminal defense attorney. Eles wrote out a five-thousand-dollar check for a retainer, and the attorney set out to make sure that Peter did not go to prison.

When Eles called later that day, wanting Peter to escort her to a party that evening, he reminded her that the attorney said that if was caught again, he would surely go to prison. If she wanted him to go out with her, she would have to have a driver. Eles was not going to stay home, so she hired a chauffeur who took them to dinner parties, gallery openings, cocktail parties, and other events.

Peter was a party animal, but he found the narrow elite circles of Eles's world tedious beyond measure. After a while, no drink was big enough to deaden the boredom of it all. He started making excuses and going out with a friend on his boat. Nobody had ever dumped Eles, but in his unseemly way, that was precisely what Rock was doing.

I know Peter, and when Eles told me she was going to sue him for the lawyer's money and the chauffeurs' charges, I said no good would come of it for anyone. I told her that the *Palm Beach Post* keeps track of suits and as soon as she filed, it would find its way into Jose Lambiet's Page Two gossip column. The more I talked to her, the more I thought that instead of dissuading her, I had given her another reason to go ahead.

The moment Eles's attorney filed the suit, a story about it appeared in Lambiet's column: "According to paperwork filed in a West Palm court, the multimillionaire Gillet says she lent Rock $5,500 to pay for his legal bills. What's more, she wants another $3,300 for allowing him to use her chauffeured car for nearly 16 months while he was banned from driving himself. Steel and shipping heiress Gillet actually described Rock as her walker—using Palm Beach parlance to refer to him as the kind of oft-hired escort who squires rich unmarried or widowed women. 'It's worse for a female to go to a party unaccompanied,' she said when asked about the practice. 'Now that he has another keeper, he needs to pay me back.'"

Eles did not care how she looked. She cared about vengeance, and she got it once in the pages of the *Palm Beach Post*, and a second time when the story ran in Peter's hometown newspaper the *New York Post*. Eles liked fine food and vintage wine, but nothing tasted quite as refreshing as an overflowing goblet of revenge.

22

Dirty Energy

In those trying months before Barbara Wainscott and David Berger's divorce, practically the only place David and Barbara felt comfortable had been Club Colette. Dan Ponton was not only a genial host at his private dinner club, but he was endlessly solicitous to the needs of his members.

Palm Beach is a place where a sixty-year-old man is considered middle-aged, and a man in his twenties is viewed as a childish intruder. It was almost unthinkable, then, that at the age of twenty-three, Dan could have been the impresario of an exclusive private club. From day one, the revived Club Colette worked brilliantly, largely because almost no one thought of it as Danny's club. Everyone considered it Aldo Gucci's place, and Dan little more than a lackey and errand boy to the man who was not only Dan's landlord but the celebrated moniker of Italian fashion. And Dan was shrewd enough to realize that was not a putdown, but a blessing.

Since his parents' arrival in the United States from Argentina when he was six, Dan had spent much time in Palm Beach, where his mother ran a women's clothing store on Worth Avenue. His father owned various restaurants, and by the time Dan had reached thirteen, he was working as a busboy. His father spent more time with his mistresses than in the kitchen, and when the couple divorced, Dan's mother opened a boutique in the very building on Peruvian Avenue that also included the private Club Colette. Dan was fully Americanized and spoke without an accent. While attending college, Dan was already running a bar in Nantucket, and had the shrewdly congenial manner of a salon owner or maitre d'.

When Dan graduated and returned to Palm Beach, Club Colette was closed and Gucci was looking for a new tenant. Gucci had turned the carriage trade into a vehicle for the mass elite and was Europeanizing American dress. He was the persona of Italian sophistication, a flamboyant, gregarious, womanizing bon vivant; the very model of what many on the island wanted to be.

At a dinner honoring the board of directors for the newly opened club, Gucci got up to speak before a room full of members. "I want you to know that I have absolute confidence in Daniel Ponton," Gucci said. "He's one of my favorite people. He's nice, and you know I don't sleep with men."

It was a superb device to quash the rumors of a sexual relationship between a wildly heterosexual Italian and a wildly homosexual Argentinean American. Dan's mother had been overwhelmingly hurt by the divorce, and her only son felt alienated from his own father. In Gucci, he found a second father and a mentor. Gucci was in a lawsuit against his own son, Paolo Gucci, and that made Gucci and his young acolyte even closer.

Whenever Gucci was in town, he hung out at Club Colette, and when he was there, just as with Trump at Mar-a-Lago, the members wanted to be there too, by osmosis imbibing the gloss of European class. Gucci was so important to the image of the club that potential members often arrived for their meetings with Dan with their arms full of Gucci bags fresh from Worth Avenue, hoping that would be an unimpeachable recommendation.

But Gucci had evaded over seven million dollars in American taxes, and in 1986 he was sentenced to a year in prison. Everything was closing down on the man, and he sold the building to Dan on the most enviable of terms.

Here, then, was this young man not yet thirty, owning the premier private club in the premier elite resort town in America. Club

Colette is basically nothing but a restaurant, but that is like saying a Gucci slipper is nothing but a few strips of leather. Dan understood that he was selling not dinners and fine wine but exclusivity. He made his living by being what some would consider a merciless snob. That was not the role he played when he drove down to the gay world of South Beach, but when he returned, he was once again the young Palm Beach gentleman overseeing the exclusive club.

Dan convinced a list of eminent islanders that it was a marvelous entitlement to be allowed to pay a $7,500 nonrefundable membership fee plus $1,500 annual dues to enter a dark nightclublike room and buy some of the most expensive dinners in town. During the day when he walked around the club in his shorts and T-shirt, he often looked more like a busboy than the owner.

Ponton had a shrewd sense of the social dynamics among both Christian and Jewish communities, and he fancied himself the impresario of the one place in town where the WASP and Jewish elites mixed—though most of them did not so much mix as sit side by side in a manner that reminded one of the cliques in a high school cafeteria. And there were probably more Jews than WASPS.

The Boston Jews fancied themselves a more intellectual, charitable lot than their New York brethren, and preferred to be among themselves rather than to attempt social intercourse with those they considered their inferiors. The New Yorkers knew that they were still kings of the world, and they generally preferred not to squander their evenings with Bostonians affecting Brahmin airs. The WASPs did not sort themselves out so much into geographically desirables and undesirables, but they too sorted themselves out, and although they pretended that it had to do with social graces, interests, or pursuits, it often had as much to do with money as anything else.

Dan made his living playing the professional snob. He could spot a false Hermès Kelly bag from twenty yards, hear a "dem" and "tose" from ten yards, smell a pretender's sweat from five yards, and when he touched a hand callused from work seeking to join his club, he jumped back in revulsion.

Let them try to enter, just let them try. "There are these people who join Mar-a-Lago," Dan says as if describing a particularly foul breed of humanity. "They buy a Bentley, get a house on the lake, have all their body parts reassigned, chair a B-grade charity ball twice, then run out of either money or stamina, or realize they're not getting anywhere and disappear.

"If you spent the first sixty-five of your years making money, that doesn't tell you that on your sixty-sixth birthday when you move to Palm Beach, you're going to know what's right. It isn't that way. If you're lucky enough that you're very socially aware, then it's possible you're prepared to show up here. You also rise to the level of your last interior decorator. When you go to someone's house that was designed by a seventy-five out of a hundred scale designer, then your house and anything that happened before in your life immediately is worthless."

That was all wondrously philosophical stuff, but Dan had a few members who were embarrassing to behold, and their presence was at times like a drop of vinegar in a glass of Lafite Rothschild 1949. He was offered fancy cars and bags of cash for membership, and said that he always turned them down. "People who walk in the door think they know what's going on," he reflects. "They say things like, 'Why is that one here and I'm not?' And some people say, 'Well, you should really be more careful of who you take as a member, because I saw XYZ there and if that person can get in, my friend should get in.' Well, okay, that's fine, but first of all, you don't know if that person sitting in the chair is actually a member."

Dan prided himself on serving meals as good as Café L'Europe or Jean Pierre, the two best restaurants on the island, but here was the paradox: The wealthier the members were, the most exalted their social placement, the thinner they tended to be and the less they ate. If he ever reached a membership only of the most privileged, he could have served a bunch of grapes each evening, one grape to a plate.

"People think that eating should be extraordinary, but then they take out all qualifiers that make it extraordinary," Dan points out. "If you use butter, don't use butter. If you use salt, don't use salt. If it has skin, take the skin off. If you have dessert, of course no dessert. So what you end up eating is the lowest possible common denominator. And if you do that and you come to the place for dinner three or four times a week, then you'd think that all we know how to do is blowfish and chicken."

Dan stood at that door barring the riffraff and the pretenders, but he felt he was part of an honorable tradition, and nothing had changed in a hundred years, nothing at all.

"If you take this dynamic and go back twenty-five years or fifty years or seventy-five years, the topography has changed, the residence size has changed, the amenities have changed, but the people are the same. The war is the war. It's not a war about religion. It's a war about establishment versus anti-establishment. 'I am a member of something, and I have been rich a long time. You haven't. Pooh-pooh on you.' "

For most of Palm Beach's history, there had been a dynamic struggle between the staid self-consciousness that Henry James had found so tedious and witless, and gaiety and daring that sought to enhance the original fantasy that had been created by those two master fabulists Flagler and Mizner. This has often been viewed as a struggle between youth and age, or sometimes immorality and virtue, but that is not what it is at all.

There are many people in Palm Beach whose names are rarely if ever mentioned in the Shiny Sheet, who live sincerely and passionately. But the banal, uptight world that Henry James chronicled is overwhelmingly seductive, and it is the dominant public mode. It is difficult not to be co-opted into the staid social life of the island. The new arrival is swept up in the initial excitement of it, the welcoming acquaintances in the charity world, the designer clothes that are the uniform of acceptance, the catered parties with the engraved menu and the priceless china, the mentions in the Shiny Sheet. There are never any cruel rejections; there is nothing but endless deference. It goes on night after night, year after year.

The fantasy has to be maintained and serviced. What passes as journalism about the island are largely tributes that pander to the pretensions of the wealthy. What passes as art in some of the galleries is often conventional and merely pretty; decorative pieces to complement one's furnishings. What passes as ideas in lectures and forums are occasionally little more than florid hortatory, asserting boldly that all is right with the world. What passes as glamorous social occasions are often tediously stilted parties where the most exciting moment in the evenings are the good-byes.

Enter Bruce Sutka. In contemporary Palm Beach, Sutka comes closest to the impish, daring originality of Mizner. For a number of years, he brought back something of that joyous unpredictability that had made Palm Beach in the early years seem like an endless party, not just an endless raft of social obligations.

When he arrived in Palm Beach in the early seventies, Sutka had long hair, a beard, and a lean frame; he looked like a professional hippie who could have been on stage in *Hair*. He can appear to be a flamboyant extrovert, but he is basically a cured introvert, ever ready to snap his head back into his shell.

Sutka grew up in an Amish community in Ohio. Although he had not been a member of that faith, he was far different from most people who came to Palm Beach. As a young man, he married Stephanie Wrightsman from one of the most prominent families in Palm Beach. The newlyweds were part of a set, some of whom fueled their late nights on cocaine and other diversions illicit and otherwise. Those were not Sutka's pleasures, and that was not why the marriage failed. He shared another secret pleasure with a number of the wealthy young men of the island: He was gay.

Sutka began in Palm Beach as a window designer who had aspirations of becoming an interior decorator. "But finally I realized that I was a stage designer and a person who liked to live out my own fantasy in front of a broad audience," he told the Shiny Sheet in 1979, in words that Mizner could have spoken. "Also, I don't think in small scale, only in large."

The shop windows along Worth Avenue are hardly the venue for anything but luxury merchandising, but in the seventies and early eighties, Sutka turned them into an ever-changing fantasy, often more intriguing than many of the paintings in the galleries. In those years, there were mainly local shopkeepers on the avenue, and there was a quirky, upscale boutique feel to the street. Sutka was so original, so inventive that he eventually was doing most of the windows on the three blocks.

Sutka was always looking for an edge, and he was not beyond clipping his art from the headlines. The infamous 1982 divorce trial between Roxanne and Peter Pulitzer brought out all kinds of kinky allegations and the worst sort of tabloid publicity to the celebrated island. It exposed the salacious underbelly of Palm Beach, where the favorite sport is not three-hour-long, eighteen-hole games of golf but quick games of adultery in which the score is certain.

There was testimony that Roxanne had a trumpet swathed in a black cloth on her bed during séances with her psychic. This became transposed in the *New York Post*'s headlines as "**PULITZER** SEX TRIAL SHOCKER: 'I SLEPT WITH A **TRUMPET**.'" Roxanne and the psychic sued for libel, but that did not prevent Sutka from creating a window featuring four female legs, a trumpet, a fur rug, and a champagne bottle. It was unclear whether this evoked a mythical attachment to a musical instrument, or some kind of bizarre sex act. "I want the people to identify with what is happening in the window, no matter how outrageous it may be," he said, though the ladies standing there trying to make sense of the weird couplings were unlikely to identify with the peculiar scene. "People have dreams and fantasies, and I fulfill them by creating them in my windows."

Sutka's great patron for his épater le bourgeois moments was Donald Bruce, who ran a specialty store and gave his window over to Sutka's most outré fantasies, including the trumpet montage. The shop owner had a droll nonchalance that most merchants on Worth Avenue did not have. Bruce sold everything, from $320 tins of caviar to polo shirts that would have been knockoffs of Ralph Lauren's signature shirt except for the fact that the logo showed the rear end of a horse.

Sutka's approach is to become more and more shocking until

the screams of dismay drown out the squeals of pleasure. One Christmas, he had Bruce's mechanical Santa Claus dressed up like a pied piper of wealth in gold lamé from head to foot, holding a gold cup, panhandling with a sign: "Support the Rich." That was hardly the vision of Santa Claus the gentry wanted to explain to their children and grandchildren as they strolled down the avenue, but since there were no picketing Episcopalians, Sutka escalated. Three years later, he twisted poor Santa around, bent the old man over, pulled his pants down, emblazoned a tattoo on his buttocks, and set him out in the window mechanically mooning passersby. That led to a threat by the Civic Association to shut Bruce down, intimidation that made the shop owner stand firm. All that holiday season, Santa kept on mooning.

The most savage joke of all was considered by many of those who saw it as a tribute to them and their fortunes. At the National Bank, Sutka began conventionally one year with a gingerbread house that would have brought a tear to Scrooge's dry eyes. The following year, Sutka put up another holiday house, but this one covered with dollars held together not with sugary white frosting but mortar made of coins. To Sutka, it was a visual representation of Palm Beach, but almost no one got it, particularly not the grande dames coming in to get their diamonds out of their safe-deposit boxes for the Christmas balls, nor the worthy gentlemen wiring thousands of dollars into other accounts.

In 1977, a youthful executive at the National Bank, Loy Anderson Jr., and a group of what passed as the jet set in Palm Beach decided to have a New Year's party, and asked Sutka to do the decorations. Their underwriter was Sally Fenelon Young, who was interested in promoting her pharmaceutical company. In her honor and to distinguish the New Year's event from the annual Red Cross Ball at the Breakers, the event was called the Young Friends of the Red Cross Ball.

Everyone wanted to go to an event in which mere attendance defined you as youthful. Friends and the friends of friends flew in from New York and elsewhere, and the event sold out that first year at the Flagler Museum, the enormous mansion Henry Flagler had built for his bride, Mary Kenan Flagler. For "An Evening of Paradise," Sutka placed birds of paradise bouquets and live goldfish on the tables, and splashed the rooms with strobe lighting. It was hardly inspired, but the event was roundly acclaimed, and became the place to be New Year's Eve.

As Sutka moved on to a career of event planning, his signature party became the annual Young Friends Ball. The event came into its own in 1981 when Sutka designed a New Year's ball with a circus theme. He brought in an elephant, llamas, and a camel, and tethered them odorously near to the Palm Beach Towers, a high-rise condominium where once the Royal Poinciana Hotel had stood. He rented circus costumes from Ringling Museum in Sarasota, and he flew down a group of ballet dancers from Atlanta to wear them. Sutka chose a garish spangled outfit, a clown's red rose, and an unruly mop of hair.

As the performers began feverishly putting on their elaborate outfits, Sutka was apprised that the leopard costume had a splendid head and gigantic paws, but the body was missing. The dancer who was to wear the costume stood before Sutka, dressed only in a black studded G-string. The impresario told him to put on his head and paws and go out among the formally dressed crowd. The leopard leaped upon a table and began dancing, shaking his G-string in the faces of a number of enchanted young Kennedys.

That was all fine, but the elephant almost stampeded when a rescue truck sped by, its siren blaring, and some of the guests decided that they were high-wire artists themselves, scurrying up a rope that had been used by a student aerialist group from Florida State University, the Flying High Troupe. Other guests were flying high themselves, stoned on grass and coke. There were over eight hundred guests jammed into the rooms by midnight, and hundreds more roaring in later. The windows in the old non-air-conditioned building were so steamed up, it was as if Flagler's ghost did not want anyone to see what bacchanalian revels were taking place in the home that he had envisioned as a royal palace.

The Coconuts held their celebrated event on New Year's too,

but who wanted to be with the old guard? "Choosing one of the two events is a little like deciding between marrying the woman you love or staying in the Everglades Club," Agnes Ash wrote in the Shiny Sheet. "Everyone wants to stay on the list, but all are reluctant to miss the mad scene at the Flagler."

Sutka thought he was being true to the traditions of Mary Kenan Flagler, who had given masked balls in these very rooms, and on occasion, felt he was communing with her spirit. "It wasn't like a voice from somebody speaking. It was from another dimension," Sutka said.

Mary Kenan Flagler was a devoté of elaborate costume parties, and would have appreciated the extravagant detail of these evenings, but in her era it was the guests who came in costumes. If her ghost had walked through the old Flagler mansion dressed as Marie Antoinette, she would have seemed just another character fitting in with ersatz human sacrifices, Greek statues with television sets as heads, perverse Rapunzels, specimens adorned in silver lamé, fifteen-foot-tall Alice in Wonderlands, Grace Jones look-alikes arriving on gigantic gorilla paws, and Peter Pans zooming down from the heavens on a wire at midnight.

After a number of years, the jaundiced islanders expected to be titillated with calculated decadence and outrage, folly and perversity, all to be observed in black tie and formal gown. At the 1990 "Fall of the Roman Empire" event, the haven of sanity in the midst of the madness was the VIP Emperor's Orgy Room protected by Roman Centurions who looked as if they had been dipped in silver lamé.

Ah, but it was a struggle each year to outdo himself. "Bruce will have to come up with something good next year to make up for this," one Young Friend commented to the Shiny Sheet after the ho-hum 1991 event in which Cupid came sailing through the room at midnight to smash into a gigantic wedding cake. Good, but not good enough.

When in doubt, drag queens are always the answer, and the following year Sutka flew down a whole troupe from New York City and dressed them as cavemen to people the prehistoric setting.

"What do you want us to do?" they asked, seeking some guidance. "Scandalize Palm Beach," Sutka said, and being literalists, they took him at his word.

The drag queens headed out among the elite of Palm Beach and the life-size dinosaurs. This was supposed to be Fred Flintstone's comic prehistoric world, but they performed skits that would have caused Mae West to blush and sang sweet little ditties that may have been meant as poetry, but sounded like pornography ("I have a little kitty, I have a wet, juicy kitty").

There was no hotter New Year's ticket than the Young Friends in 1995, which included movie stars George Hamilton and Don Johnson, and infamous arms dealer Adnan Khashoggi. The theme was "The Twilight Zone," and Sutka hired a number of strippers and male dancers to go with the drag queens. One of the drag queens stood at the entrance, gently paddling the guests as they arrived. This was greeted as a delightful bit of wildness until one discomfited man slugged the congenial drag queen, sending her running into the kitchen in tears. The drag queens reconnoitered and headed out into the party in full force, but they were upstaged by some of the other performers who had stripped naked and were performing certain acts that are usually done in private. "Oh my God," screamed the chairwoman, seeing her social status in Palm Beach burning away. "She's got his thing in her mouth on stage!! And my mother!!! My mother's here!!!"

Sutka hurried over and told the dancers to end their performance and put on some clothes. One of the revelers was so impressed with the activities on the stage that he wanted to give his son a gift. He offered one of the performers his Rolex watch if she would perform oral sex on his son. The woman left with a Rolex in her purse.

The clock had finally run out on Sutka's legendary New Year's Eve parties, and he never put on another event at the Flagler Museum.

Still, Sutka's company had become the leading party planner in Palm Beach. He caters entertainment, caters sociability, and caters wit. He might charge $25,000 to put on a dinner party for twenty-four on the balcony of a lakefront condominium, or $250,000 to put on a barbecue for 400 under a tent in an oceanfront mansion. Yet whatever the brilliance of some of his themes and settings, most people leave his events with barely a snapshot of memory. Sutka is like the art on the wall, or the Bentley or Rolls-Royce in the garage—merely one of the costs of doing social business.

"You know, you would think that this island would be just bubbling over with happiness and joy," Sutka says. "And it's not. There's this dirty energy. And a lot of people feel that. Dirty energy. They're avaricious and all the things that are bad human qualities just show up here for some reason."

23

Cowboys and Indians

When I arrived in Palm Beach, Phillip Beam and Terry Nun* were one of the very few openly gay couples on the island, and they were not only out, but out there. Phillip came from an aristocratic family and had a fey, supercilious manner that often disguised his wit and insight. Terry was from what he called "hillbilly trailer trash" and spoke with a languid Southern Appalachian accent.

They were astute businessmen who had made a fortune in a chain of fast-food restaurants. Now, while exploring other ventures, the two were flipping homes, buying one place after another, fixing them up, and moving on with a profit of many hundreds of thousands of dollars. They are wealthy men, and I saw it as a strange preoccupation, time and again fixing up what appeared to be homes but were really just marketing devices.

Phillip and Terry also gave parties like no one else on the island. The guests included any number of men as macho as Arnold Schwarzenegger, a prominent real estate agent about to leave his wife and two kids to join the chosen people, lawyers, businessmen, billionaires, and street punks—as widely varied a group as imaginable, except they were mostly gay men.

---

* *These are pseudonyms.*

Phillip and Terry gloried in having costume parties—a toga party one year, a Hawaiian party the next, and then a celebrated Western theme party where everyone came as either cowboys or Indians. Only in their masks could some people spend an evening unmasked. At the entrance was a basket of makeshift costumes, feathers, and bandannas, so those who came in standard party clothes would not seem merely pathetic voyeurs but full participants in the orgiastic fantasy.

Palm Beach's proper citizens have not always had the best of experiences with gay society. One evening Eles Gillet was arriving at the Everglades Club when she looked up in the window of a classic old house and saw a totally nude Christ on the cross. The elderly owner of the house is a member of the B&T who cruises around town in his Rolls. His living religious tableau was not appreciated. The gentleman in question arrived at one of Phillip and Terry's parties with a gorgeous Brazilian who looked like a mannequin who had just stepped out of a Worth Avenue window. The Brazilian was too well dressed to be hung on a cross. The man's English was barely good enough to sweetly convey that he was the gentleman's slave.

It is just barely thinkable to have a gay man in the B&T or the Everglades, but not a gay couple. Even at Mar-a-Lago, it had not seemed a sure thing until Phillip and Terry. When they wanted to join, they thought it imperative to go through a gay intermediary already a member to ask Trump if he was comfortable with his first gay couple. They heard back through their friend that Donald had said that they could pay their hundred thousand dollars as a couple and become members.

"I don't have any problem with it, but you don't want to yell fire in a crowded theater," he reportedly said. It was doubtless the first time that Justice Oliver Wendell Holmes's famous opinion had been used to tell a gay couple that they should not flaunt their sexuality. And so Phillip and Terry became the first openly gay couple not just in Mar-a-Lago, but almost certainly in any club on the island.

When the two had a child with a surrogate mother in California, their lifestyle totally changed. They stopped going out at night;

they ended their parties. I would see them along the ocean sidewalk with their nanny walking their baby in a Rolls-Royce of a carriage. They were dedicated parents. They were poster boys for gay marriage, exhibiting the very sort of lifestyle that conservatives might have applauded. But there were those appalled at this technological tinkering. Phillip and Terry had no idea how much they were the focal point of spirited debate and condemnation among the Old Guard.

Phillip and Terry are harbingers of a new island where gays are no longer primarily the servants of the wealthy, but the wealthy themselves. There are any number of immensely affluent gay couples moving to the island, living in a gay community that is another separate subset of the island. Along with the opening of Trump's club at Mar-a-Lago, the emergence of this gay community is the single most significant social change in Palm Beach in several decades.

The two men said that now that they had a child to protect, they did not want to be in my book. I understood and agreed to give them pseudonyms, but I was startled by the response of much of the gay community. Person after person turned me down, wanting nothing do with a book dealing in part with gay life on the island.

I had known the gay dress designer Arnold Scaasi and his partner, Parker Ladd, a retired publishing executive, for years before I decided to write this book, and they could hardly refuse my interview request. They have been coming to the island since 1967, when Scaasi had a trunk show at the Colony Hotel. For decades, he was the favorite dresser of elite Palm Beach ladies. A Scaasi ball gown might be worn only twice in a lifetime and cost upward of twenty thousand dollars, but women such as Eles Gillet had their closets full of Scaasis. Arnold has dressed most of the women in this book, including Marylou Whitney, Eles Gillet, Brownie McLean, and Pauline Pitt.

The diminutive designer became famous for provocative designs such as the apparently see-through black net pants that Barbra Streisand wore in 1969 to receive a best actress Oscar at the

Academy Awards. He has also dressed first ladies Laura and Barbara Bush, but he has made his living largely creating handmade unique dresses for immeasurably wealthy American ladies. He can disguise the un-disguisable, diminish the deplorable, and make princesses out of practically anyone.

During his heyday in the seventies and eighties, the most stunning part of the ambience at the most exclusive Palm Beach balls was not the food or the music, but a dance floor full of Scaasi creations often far more extraordinary than some of the women wearing them. He spoke wistfully of those years when gentlemen wore black tie to private parties, and ladies were far more ready to pay a prince's ransom for a Scaasi gown.

Arnold has a wit so acidic that it is a wonder it does not burn his tongue. He can be curtly dismissive of those vulgarians unworthy of wearing a Scaasi gown or too cheap to outlay the money, categories that in his mind are much the same. But in our interview, I was talking to a man I did not know. It was as if he was running for office in a district where the best way to win was to hold no opinions.

When I discussed Phillip's feeling that gays were eternal outsiders in Palm Beach, Arnold bristled. He was both appalled and dismissive. He did not like being pigeonholed either as Jewish (*Scaasi* is *Isaacs* spelled backward) or gay, neither of which he said had anything to do with his talent. He said he had never suffered discrimination and he could not understand why I was obsessed with such a foolish matter. "In my whole life anywhere in the world, Paris, London, New York, anywhere, I thought I was always accepted for myself," he said. "Okay?"

Arnold's partner of forty years sees matters differently. "Gays are never truly accepted," Ladd said sadly in a separate interview. "You're always an oddity, a freak." When he and Scaasi started coming to Palm Beach regularly beginning in the late sixties, the elite regarded them as a bizarre curiosity set upon the island to amuse and distract. Parker realized that and while being civil, was ceaselessly observant. "Many rich women from families of cars or asbestos or oils or things had middle-aged gay husbands who were discreet," Parker recalls.

When Arnold and Parker wanted gay society, they drove south to Fort Lauderdale or South Beach, where there was a frenetic nightlife. They do not have to do that any longer. A full, open, sophisticated gay life has come to the island. The couple had been regulars at the most uninhibited of Phillip and Terry's parties, but that was only a canapé to the main course of gay life on the island now.

What the gays in Palm Beach have produced is largely a society that replicates the straight world with the same preoccupations and the same narrow preconceptions and judgments. They play the same games with charity and go through the same struggles to get their Botoxed features in the Shiny Sheet. They are probably more promiscuous than their heterosexual brethren, or perhaps simply less devious in disguising it. They suffer far less onus hanging out in the back rooms at the gay stripper and go-go boy male sex club Cupids in West Palm Beach than married men do stuffing twenty-dollar bills into G-strings at Rachel's. And they probably are even more obsessed with creating the illusion of youthfulness than the straight society.

Gay men are as segregated by money as any other group in the island, and the megawealthy hang out with each other. They have extravagant parties at their mansions and fly off for long weekends together in the Caribbean. And like their heterosexual counterparts, they too have trophy wives. "Most gay trophy guys are more boring than straight trophy women," sniffs Parker. "They don't seem to have any hobbies or any intellectual pursuits. They're very subservient to the interest that the rich partner has."

MARK BRENTLINGER WAS THIRTY-NINE and his partner, Bryan McDonald, two years older—infants in Palm Beach terms—when they first came to Palm Beach in 2004. Brentlinger has an unassuming Midwestern demeanor that effectively disguises a brilliant businessman who along with his mother runs Midwestern Auto Group, foreign car dealerships in Columbus, Ohio. The plump investor has impeccable instincts, and almost everything he touches makes money. He is a scion of the Ohio establishment, and as a young man was married for ten years to an Eli Lilly heiress.

If Brentlinger had arrived on the island with his wife on his arm, the couple would have been welcomed into the B&T and the Everglades. Instead, long after his divorce, he arrived with McDonald, and the clubs did not beckon. His ripped lover is a classic trophy spouse who over the years has had seemingly every body part replaced, redone, built up, toned down, strengthened, or refined. Bryan is a muscular hunk. The couple divert themselves at Bice or Café L'Europe watching married men casting furtive glances McDonald's way.

The two initially sailed into the Palm Beach docks on their ice-class blue yacht with bulletproof glass and steel sides and professional security team. Mark and Bryan already knew Phillip and Terry, along with another gay couple in Palm Beach, and they had such a good time they never wanted to sail away. Mark was too old and too rich for the gay Catskills in South Beach. Palm Beach fit, and the couple locked into the vibrant gay community from day one. They became known as "the car boys," their blue boat one of the best party scenes on the island.

Soon after the couple arrived, I met them at one of Phillip and Terry's parties. Bryan is flamboyant, outgoing, and provocative, a type of gay man I have often known in my life, though not in Palm Beach. He is far from an intellectual, but has an engaging protectiveness toward his partner. Mark has a sincere, unpretentious, open manner that I think of as being the essence of the Midwest, and one of the reasons that both Mark and his state are often rudely underestimated.

Palm Beach is an education for almost anyone, and Mark and Bryan began their PhD course when in 2004 Mark purchased an old mansion on Jungle Road up from where David Berger was still living out the last years of his life. But the $8,800,000 home was in sad condition. Construction and reconstruction is one of the perennial curses of Palm Beach life. Mark and Bryan considered perfection only barely acceptable, and after two and a half years, most of their neighbors had had quite enough of the Ohio couple.

One of their few friends was their next-door neighbor, Donald Trump's ex-wife Ivana, living there in recent years with her own trophy boyfriend. But from one end of Jungle Road to the other, there was one common denominator. "There is so much money and ego on this street, it's surprising it hasn't blown up," Mark muses. "So, people have to pick a way of differentiating themselves because everybody's rich."

When the last truck finally left, in December 2007, Bryan and Mark decided to make amends to one angry couple across the road. The "car boys" delivered to their neighbors Pepe and Emilia Fanjul a two-thousand-dollar case of Cristal champagne. Two days before Christmas, one of Mark and Bryan's guests parked his Vespa on Jungle Road facing the wrong direction. This apparently so outraged the Cuban-American sugar mogul and his wife that they called the police. Then a servant delivered the case back to the offending couple with a curt note stating that it had not been given in the true sprit of Christmas. The true spirit of Christmas apparently is to park your Vespa in the correct direction on the street.

The Fanjuls are members of the B&T, where they do not have to worry about squandering their time among gay riffraff, but even here the "car boys" occasionally intruded. On his one visit to the club, Mark sat outside having dinner. He is largely deaf, but is such a superb lip-reader that many people do not realize his disability. His eyes moved from table to table, where members were raging about how such people could be allowed into the rarefied precincts.

Mark never returned, but Bryan was struck from stronger stuff. He came back to go swimming one afternoon in the pool wearing tight little trunks with fish on them and a tank top. He was provocative enough with his clothes on, but strutting around the pool in a swimsuit in his outrageous tan and sculptured body, it was as if a plague of gay sexuality had been unleashed. What Bryan was wearing was not a violation of the rule book, but damn the rule book, and his hostess for the occasion received a stern letter of reprimand.

In the same way that to be accepted Catholics had toned down their ethnicity, so gays who coveted invitations to the Everglades and the B&T mimicked the manners and mannerisms of the straight elite. Mark and Bryan were not going to copy anyone or be anything but what they were. Damn the cost and consequence. They joined Mar-a-Lago, where a whole contingent of wealthy gay couples now sat around the pool.

Mark and Bryan were not going to squander their years dancing the stilted social dance of the island. They were bemused by the thank-you notes they were constantly receiving after their parties from those with approved island manners. It was a pain dealing with a mailbox full of these things as stiff as cardboard, but the weirdest part was the notes themselves. "People take their pen and slash their name," Mark said as if describing the custom of an exotic lost tribe. "Do you know why they do that? You slash your name out on the card and then write a note. Why the hell do that? It's some old WASP rule."

Mark knew that when they were through slashing a line above their name on thank-you cards, it came down to money, and money was Mark's game. The ostentatious display of wealth is not merely a frivolous indulgence but a means of social intimidation and control, but how does one impress? The Windsors' friendships can be purchased for cash on the barrel head, and the streets are full of ersatz counts and princes, titles made up or bought or largely meaningless. Two of the leading socialites are beer princesses, wearing the tiaras of former Miss Rheingolds. Worth Avenue is full of luxury goods to set one apart and above, but most of it is either counterfeited or bought for a pittance at Off 5th and other outlet stores. Even before the wearer has worn her stunning new Versace to the Red Cross Ball, it has been copied in Shanghai and is on sale in America.

The endless Bentleys outside the Trump International Golf Course look as distinctive as a parking lot full of Hyundai Accents and Honda Civics. In Palm Beach the Everglades and B&T have lost much of their ultimate status and no longer define social success. And what is first class when the retired druggist next to you has traded in frequent flyer mileage for his seat?

Private jets are the best defining distinction left, not time sharing, not piddling planes, but jets big enough for a mogul and his entourage, and the general aviation building at Palm Beach International Airport is the new Everglades Club. Mark and Bryan travel in their own Bombardier Challenger 300, a midsize jet able to fly to Europe, and they are intimately familiar with the denizens of general aviation.

"In the gay world, it doesn't make any difference—WASP, Jew, social background," Mark says, choosing his words carefully. "But there is absolutely rank and prestige assigned to someone's perceived financial wherewithal. I don't know if I'm right or not, but I've heard people say that Bryan and I run around with sort of the A-crowd gay people."

James "Jimmy" Barker is eighty years old, and is an emissary from a world in Palm Beach that has almost disappeared. He lives in the middle of town in a modest, nondescript two-story wooden house built in 1936. A stroller could walk by a thousand times without even noticing the 5,600-square-foot home nestled back among far more imposing residences.

Jimmy and his longtime partner, Kenneth W. Douglas Jr., purchased the house in 1973 when he was running his eponymously named art gallery on Worth Avenue. The James Hunt Barker Galleries did not feature the marquee names of international art, but an eclectic collection largely of American artists. Jimmy was an unpretentious man who did not make searing intellectual commentaries on the art that he sold. He had a cocktail party every week where his friends in the room met his friends on the walls. It was the place to be, a congenial, happy crowd with the ubiquitous Jimmy introducing people and helping to pass drinks.

Many of the paintings in the gallery ended up on the walls of Jimmy's house. He had a large collection of paintings by his lifelong friend the late Channing Hare, including three portraits of Jimmy as a young man, elegantly stylish and lean, a *Town & Country* gentleman. There were valuable paintings as well by Eastman Johnson, the nineteenth-century portraitist whose subjects ranged from Abraham Lincoln to cranberry pickers and Indians. Jimmy was not an abstract man, so there was no abstract art in what was a treasure of nineteenth- and early-twentieth-century portraiture.

Some of the displayed china had been in the Andrew Jackson White House and there was silverware that was at least as old. The furnishings ranged from antiques to bric-a-brac, and included an armchair upholstered in silk and a brocade divan. There was a virtual kennel of over a hundred porcelain Staffordshire Cavalier King Charles spaniels. It had been Jimmy's mother's favorite dog, and it had become his as well. No interior decorator would have laid claim to such a hopeless mishmash of styles and tastes, but if one set aside conventional judgment, it worked brilliantly and was a stunning signature marking the life and artistic loves of James "Jimmy" Barker.

Jimmy grew up on a Kentucky tobacco farm run by his formidable divorced mother. The Barkers were either land poor or land rich, however one chose to see it. They had the lifestyle of the aristocracy without the money. He had not been brought up in a great antebellum mansion, but on a working farm. There was a cook in the kitchen, jackets mandatory for dinner, and public school during the day. He went to the University of Kentucky, not Princeton. He had the easy manners and confidence that come only with generations of wealth and are far more difficult to acquire than money. When he went to New York in the fifties, he hobnobbed with the Whitneys and other elite families. For him, life shone brightest among the wealthy.

Jimmy came down to Palm Beach in 1961 to be the assistant manager of the Palm Beach Art Gallery, then the only gallery on Worth Avenue. He spent the summers in another gallery on Nantucket, but he never truly left Palm Beach. By the time he had started his own gallery, he had already become what is often called a character. Palm Beach used to have any number of idiosyncratic individualists who survived and prospered in the rarefied hothouse of the island, where the broader world would have smothered them.

Jimmy loved Staffordshire Cavalier King Charles spaniels so

much that at one time he had sixteen of them, six beyond the liberal limit set by a dog-loving town council. Jimmy was so beloved that the elected officials were reluctant to punish him. One council member offered to help by taking one of the dogs. In the end, Jimmy whittled it down to only two spaniels, Holly Golightly and Annabel Lee.

Jimmy has a generous character, and years ago had taken into his house sixty-five-year-old James Heyman. The man was what people called slow, but if you took time with him, he was a pleasure to have around, and helpful too. Every morning Heyman ate a late breakfast of eggs and toast with his patron.

I had talked to a number of gay men of Jimmy's age, and the conversation was almost always difficult. I took one man to lunch who also lived most of his adult life in Palm Beach. He is one of the best-known walkers, and in the last years of his life is still deeply in the closet, imprisoned in an image that he finds necessary to project. On another occasion I had lunch with a man on his yacht. He had just moved to Palm Beach and appeared to be in his late fifties. He had been married twice, had several children, and for the first time in his life was acknowledging his homosexuality. He was leading a schizophrenic life, escorting ladies to the Everglades and also hanging out with the gay elite of the island, the latter more pleasurable than the former. He was trying to have it both ways, and he had not yet realized the impossibility. We ate lobster salad served by his chef, and drank a bottle of chilled chablis, but never once in our two hours together did we discuss what was the most important fact in his life.

I felt comfortable asking Jimmy about his sexuality. He was a wry, elfin figure of a man, far younger in spirit than his eight decades. The fact that he was gay seemed less a statement of his sexuality than a unique addition to his personality. It was as if he had tried all the categories in which humanity encased itself, and decided he would wear this one. When I asked him about being gay on the island, he acted as if was a strange question.

"Well, you know, most artists have a tendency to live in a way that the family people don't approve of," he laughed, his words rushing out of him in a torrent. "Living in resort areas like here and Nantucket and coming from a horsey family in Lexington, it's not something one thinks about. Most people dealing with the art world don't care. It's just not a question that I can answer for you, because I've never really paid any attention to it."

In some people I would have considered such an answer a pathetic evasion, but I did not feel that way with Jimmy. "The difference from your era is that there's an open gay world here now," I insisted.

"Is there?" he asked incredulously, as if I was suggesting his life had been less than open. "See, I don't know who they are. There is a thing of mending it together in all sorts of ways, but I don't really know what you mean when you say it's more open. I think it's more publicly used as something to cause people to pay attention. You know, any time you talk about sex, everybody sits up and takes an interest, but in polite circles, you don't spend a lot of time discussing it."

And that was the end of that discussion.

24

The Most Precious Asset

Rose Keller's death, Fred's arrest for her murder, and his plea of innocence were front-page news for days in the *Palm Beach Daily News.* The opinion of many men seemed to be that Rose had gotten what she deserved. No one wanted her dead, but it was unthinkable that this German gold digger should, after ten years of marriage, walk away with half of the wealth that her husband had taken a lifetime to accumulate. Others blamed Judge Kroll for her outrageous decision, and thought that if anyone should be sitting out in the Palm Beach County Detention Center, it should be the judge. When the first trial ended in a hung jury in 2005, with the majority for conviction, there were those who thought that Fred would end up beating the charge.

The court ruled that Rose's estate had a right to half of the Keller Trust properties; her will gave 70 percent of her estate to young Fred, and 30 percent to the Keils. And thus the great struggle was over Fred's 50 percent. How much of that fifty million dollars would go to Wolfgang in his wrongful injury suit? How much would go to Wolfgang and the other Keils in Rose's unlawful death suit? And how much would go to young Fred, either as the result of his suit against his father, or in his father's will? And how much would go to the lawyers?

By early 2007, these lawyers were involved with at least eleven civil cases pending in the Florida courts and still more to come, in what Judge Kroll described as "the messiest case the court has ever seen . . . Sadly the person who will lose the most at this point is the couple's only child, the most precious asset of this marriage."

Almost from the day he arrived in county jail, Fred began writing weekly letters to his son that were redacted by the boy's therapist and then read to young Fred. Fredchen listened to the letters, but he did not reply. This was in part because immediately after Rose's death, his aunt Angie informed the eight-year-old boy that Fred had murdered his mother. The following day, she brought the boy to the office of Dr. Nicholas S. Aradi, a marriage and family therapist who became in essence the Keil family counselor. Unbeknownst to Fred, he had been treating Rose during the divorce. He was also seeing Angie, who took custody of Fredchen, and would later see Wolfgang, in addition to the weekly session with young Fred.

In his sessions with the family therapist, Fredchen expressed a profoundly conflicted love for his father tainted with sadness, anger, and hate. He missed his mother in ways that he could not even begin to articulate, and he wanted his father to be punished for the terrible thing he had been told he had done, and yet he loved and needed his father. In wanting Fred hurt, he was hurting himself. He was torn apart, and the way to survive was not to feel. One way not to feel was not to see his father.

During Keller's second murder trial in January 2007, I often sat looking at Fred and wondering what lay behind that impassive, unemotional countenance. As far as I was concerned, he might win the verdict, but he had already lost in human terms. Like his brother Paul, Fred's second son, Eric, had died of cancer while Fred was in jail, and all he had left of immediate family was a young son who refused to see him and a stepson who hated him. And he had no one in the courtroom to offer him emotional support, no adult son, no daughters-in-law, no former lovers, no business colleagues, no subordinates, nobody. Occasionally two of Fred's tennis-playing acquaintances showed up separately. They twisted and turned in their seats, and usually were gone after no more than a half hour. It was as devastating testimony about Fred's life as anything presented in the courtroom.

Douglas Duncan, who had led his defense in 2005, stayed on for the second trial, bringing with him his partner, David Roth. Forensic experts and other minor witnesses appeared for both sides, but it came down largely to the testimony of Wolfgang and Fred, the only two living people who knew what happened in that office at Keller Trust on November 10, 2003.

Wolfgang sat in the witness chair, the lines on his pallid countenance far outstripping his age, deep-set small eyes overshadowed by his thick eyebrows. Rose's brother did not so much sit as slouch, as if the burden of holding himself up erect was too much for him. He was over six feet tall, but his posture was so bad that he seemed much shorter, and he had gained about thirty pounds since the shooting. He leaned back in apparent agony even to the most benign of questions, then answered in a thin voice barely audible without the microphone.

In words devoid of affect, Wolfgang described how on the morning of the shooting, Rose and he had sat behind a table with Fred across from them. As Wolfgang sat down, he took out his cell phone and placed it on the table. He said that Fred asked that they close the door, and the three of them began discussing splitting up the business. The discussions had hardly begun when Fred turned and walked back a few feet to where his briefcase was resting under a table.

As Wolfgang told his story, he largely controlled his emotions, until Assistant State Attorney Andrew Slater displayed a large photograph of Rose lying in a pool of blood. Then Wolfgang began to cry almost inaudibly, holding his right hand over his stomach.

"I thought he [Fred] was going to get some more papers from out of his bag," Wolfgang said. "The next thing I know I hear a bang and smell gun powder and I have excruciating pain in my chest. I look down and see him. The pain was going through my chest like a hot piece of iron, and I look up and he is coming forward with a gun in his hand."

As Wolfgang retold the story, his mother, Brigitte, and sister

Angie sat in the front row of the courtroom as far from the defense table as physically possible. Brigitte leaned forward in her seat as if trying to reach out to comfort her son in his agony.

"He was firing at Rose and I was screaming in shock," Wolfgang went on. "As soon as he shot me, Rose screamed and jumped out of her chair and tried to get out and he took a shot at her. I turned out of my chair. I tried to grab the gun. He held on to the gun, and I had my hand over his hand. I was hit, but I didn't pay attention. I just wanted to get the gun away from him. I grabbed the gun by the barrel and we were pulling and pushing. We bumped into some stuff and we ended up on the sofa. I was looking into his face and he had this mean look in his eyes. I was thinking, 'I'm going to die, I'm dying today, I can't believe it's happening.'"

"How long did it take you to struggle for the gun with the defendant on the couch?" the prosecutor asked.

"Just a few seconds," Wolfgang said, anguished. "I kind of pushed him on the sofa on his back. I twisted and pulled the gun at the same time, and now I had the gun. He slipped off the sofa. I got off the sofa and was standing and I pointed the gun at him, he tried to grab for it, and I took a shot at him. I was thinking that was the only way to survive, but I was in so much pain, I thought I was going to die that day. I looked over at my sister and saw her bleeding right out of her neck. I kneeled down next to her and I put the gun to the right of her and I tried to hold the blood in her with both my hands around her neck. I said 'Rose, Rose' but she didn't react anymore."

"What did you to do?" Slater asked.

"Almost to the left there's a desk where the secretary works, and I picked up the phone and called 911."

The jury had already heard the 911 tape, its words and emotions resonating with everything Wolfgang had just said. "Fred Keller shot me," he said moments after he was shot, his voice trembling with emotion, almost hyperventilating. A few minutes later he added, "He shot my sister too."

The testimony had been going on for an emotional eternity, and Judge Edward Garrison called a break. All through this overwhelmingly dramatic testimony, Fred sat looking at his yellow legal pad, making notes and showing not a glimmer of emotion, though his attorney Duncan kept clutching his hands together, looking as if he were about to explode with tension.

As soon as the jury stepped out into the jury room, Wolfgang walked with painful steps over to his mother and sister. Angie hugged her brother and rubbed his back. His mother came to his other side, and Wolfgang sobbed inconsolably. If agony is the one costume the truth always wears, Wolfgang seemed to have spoken the truth. If he had lied in this courtroom and in his 911 call, it was a lie of such proportion that he was a man of evil beyond even the magnitude of this crime.

After Wolfgang's testimony, I walked out of the courtroom and saw him sitting by himself in the corridor on a bench that looked out through immense picture windows on a panoramic view of the Palm Beach that had been the island of Wolfgang's dreams as much as it had been his sister's. I went over and talked to him for a while. Wolfgang was hardly more than a teenager when he arrived to go to college. He thought he was beginning what would be a life of affluence and privilege beyond anything he had ever seen or contemplated. Now it had come to this, his nights punctuated with nightmares, his days full of fears and paranoia. He worried that Fred might hire someone to kill him, to finish off the job he had begun, and he wanted Fred locked away forever. He wanted money too, lots of it, because that was all that was left. His pleasures had been emptied out like a reservoir drained of water. He was in his mid-thirties, but he was in some ways an old man, suffering from what he said was almost constant pain, his athletic pursuits finished, haunted by his sister's death.

THE SECOND CRUCIAL MOMENT in the trial came when Fred testified during the defense's two-day presentation of its case. Fred spoke softly in hardly more than a whisper, pressing hard on each syllable but barely audible, as if he were telling secrets that he wanted no one to hear. He wore a blue sports jacket, a light blue shirt, and gold-tinged glasses that reflected the afternoon sunlight. His lips were clenched so tightly it was as if he had only one thin lip. The downturned cast of his frown lines was not quite covered by his trim gray beard. He looked straight at the jury, but it seemed not a mark of character as much as something that his defense attorneys had told him he should do.

Fred spoke in a pained voice, as if to make every word a vehicle to pronounce the unfairness of his situation. Through the careful prodding of his attorney Duncan, Fred portrayed himself as a generous, caring man who, to please his wife, brought over her entire family to America and gave them lives of affluence and possibility.

Fred described Rose as a woman who, during the years of their marriage, had nothing to do with his business except spending its profits. She was so out of control that even after winning her extraordinary financial victory, she threatened to kill Fred and everyone in his office. That was the reason Fred had faxed the Riviera Beach police to alert them of this threat, and the reason he was carrying a gun in his briefcase when he had his meeting with Rose and Wolfgang.

As Fred recollected that fateful morning, his testimony of the casual discussion in the office with Rose and Wolfgang did not differ much from what Wolfgang had said. The main difference was that Fred said that he was nervous when Rose shut the door.

"At one point when you were discussing, did you see Wolfgang do something?" Duncan asked.

"He was sitting there and he had what I saw was a gun in his hand with a barrel on it pointing at me. I said, 'He's going to shoot me. He's going to shoot me.' Wolfgang would do anything for Rose. He had the ability, he had done target practice, and he would do something like that if Rose wanted."

(The supposed gun that Fred said he had seen was Wolfgang's cell phone. Even if Wolfgang had pulled the phone off his belt clip at that precise moment, it was almost unthinkable that he would have pointed the black instrument at Fred with the antenna like the barrel of a gun.)

"What did you do?" Duncan asked gently.

"I was cornered," Fred continued. "I was scared. I had never had a gun pointed at me my whole life. I couldn't get out. I didn't know if Rose had a gun or not. I turned around with my back to him so he would have to shoot me in the back. I went over to my briefcase and got the gun out and turned around and shot him. I fired one shot at him, not to kill him, to disable him from shooting me."

"After you shot Wolfgang, what happened?" Duncan continued his gentle questioning.

"He got up and charged me," Fred said as if his former brother-in-law had acted with mindless aggressiveness. "I thought I had to get away, he's charging me like he's going to knock me down. And I shot him again. I was concerned about dying. He's up on top of me and grabs the gun out of my hand and points it at me and I'm shoving the gun away from me so he can't shoot me. A shot gets fired and we end up on the sofa. I try to prevent him from shooting me in the head. He shot me behind the ear and I passed out.

"I regained consciousness and saw Rose lying there on the floor. I did not see Wolfgang. The door was opened. I cried for help, help, help and ran out and went to the front door and Wolfgang was sitting in a chair talking on the phone and a gun was on the desk, and I thought, 'I got to get out of here.' "

The jury began their deliberations late in the afternoon. When they reached their unanimous verdict after only five and a half hours, defense attorney Duncan knew what they were going to say. So did Fred, usually the perennial optimist. He stood between Duncan and Roth in a gray sports coat and open shirt and heard the verdict. Nearby stood half a dozen sheriff deputies.

Fred was found guilty of first-degree murder, attempted murder, and shooting in a building. It was not until a day later back in his cellblock that he realized the magnitude of what had happened, and for a few days collapsed into abject despair.

25

The Golden Ring

The networks and local and regional newspapers wanted to talk to Fred, but he turned everyone down. I spent a lot of time thinking of how I could approach him. In the end, I wrote him a letter to the county jail. "My book will likely be the main historical record of your life," I wrote. "It's something that one day your son will read to learn about his father, and it represents an opportunity for you to have a major say in how your life is presented."

Within a couple of days, Fred's civil lawyer Bennett Cohn called to tell me that Fred was considering talking to me. I knew that Keller was a controlling, litigious man, and when he asked me to sign a seemingly benign agreement, I turned him down. He backed off and agreed to talk without any conditions, except for my promise that one day I would give Fredchen copies of my interviews with his father.

Fred called from jail, but sometimes I went to see him in person. He was living in a pod with fifteen other older prisoners, his belongings relegated to a shoebox. The Palm Beach County Detention Center is a sparse, concrete shell, and has a reputation as a county jail harsher than many state prisons. Fred's defense attorney Roth has had some of the toughest criminals as his clients, and he says that in all his years of practice, he has never seen anyone handle life at the county jail as well as Fred did. The jail is as cold as a morgue, and I talked with him through thick glass scratched with evocations of eternal love ("Darlie & Dave"). He wore the standard blue prison issue garb. If we had been dressed alike, he would have seemed the confident, composed journalist, and I the nervous, uncertain convicted murderer trying to make my case.

After Fred got over his initial despair, his quiet rage only intensified, and in the next few weeks, he had something more important on his mind than talking to me. He had what he knew might be his one last great public forum. That was the sentencing hearing. There he could righteously condemn what he called "the criminal conviction system" led by arrogant men like Judge Garrison, who had not permitted Fred's lawyers to present a case that might have won. And there too he could condemn the Keils and the legal leeches feeding off what he considered Fredchen's money.

In April 2007 for his sentencing, the sheriff deputies brought Fred into the courtroom in shackles, wearing the prison garb that would be his uniform the rest of his life. For the first time in the trial, Fred had a relative in the courtroom, Brian Bohlander, his estranged adopted son. Brian had flown down from Washington to take rich satisfaction in seeing his stepfather sentenced to prison for the rest of his life.

The Keils spoke first as the victims publicly witnessing Fred's crime. Fred's hearing was bad and he hardly listened to their savaging of him. He did not care what they said. He had no intention of making the apologies or tepid avowals of innocence that were standard fare. He was about to be sentenced to an automatic two life terms. He could have gotten on the floor and begged, and nothing would have changed.

Unlike the soft-spoken persona he affected for his testimony during the trial, Fred spoke this morning with intensity, passion, and anger. "You talk about your love for Fred, all of you," Fred said, looking out at the Keils in the courtroom. "Yet what you want is twenty-five million dollars to have all of this go away. That is Fred's money. You think you have earned that? You are a hypocrite, Wolfgang. You grasp your chest like you did at the trial. I could have half a dozen witnesses testify how false it is. You know what happened. Terrible. Wolfgang, you will carry this burden accidentally shooting your sister and killing her, and you will further suffer for lying to your siblings and to your mom and to the court as to what happened that tragic morning."

Fred tried to move into an equally impassioned attack on the legal system, but Garrison cut him off before he had hardly begun. "Mr. Keller, I don't need to hear your opinions about the criminal justice system," the judge said, and Fred resumed his attack on the Keils.

"What happened that Monday morning was a spontaneous act that has caused our twelve-year-old son to be a virtual orphan, ostracized—and Angie, you and Wolfgang are responsible for this—ostracized from his dad, friends, and relatives, in total control. If you love him, stop this litigation for money. I gave him everything I have, let him have that, not you."

Garrison had had enough of Fred Keller, and when the judge sentenced him, he did not have him rise and stand with his lawyers, as was the common practice. Instead, he sentenced him to two life sentences, and a further fifteen years as Fred sat at the defendant's table. This happened so quickly and in such a desultory way that Wolfgang feared something had gone wrong and Fred had not been sentenced at all.

Janet Malcolm has famously written that a journalist "is a kind of confidence man, preying on people's vanity, ignorance, or loneliness, gaining their trust and betraying them without remorse." Although Malcolm's thesis has widely been accepted as the truth, I do not think that studied empathy is a code word for calculated deception. And sometimes it is the subject who is the confidence man preying on the vanity, ignorance, and gullibility of the reporter while "gaining their trust and betraying them without remorse."

From the moment I first talked to Fred, I hoped I would gain enough of his trust so that he would confess to me, while he hoped he could convince me of his innocence. As he saw it, I would then write a book vindicating him that his son would read one day. I did not believe in Fred's innocence and never led him to believe that I did, but because of young Fred, I considered that I was taking on a responsibility that transcended my role as a journalist.

Fred had nothing but time now to think about why things had gone so wrong, but our discussions were hardly in a setting conducive to philosophical dialogue. He called me several times a week. We generally spoke for an hour, sometimes with the sounds of bantering prisoners in the background. Each fifteen minutes the phone went dead and he had to call collect again.

Fred cursed the Keils for their brainwashing of his son. It never occurred to Fred that maybe young Fredchen had a mind of his own. He did not see that his obsession with money and a life of wealth had distorted him. He was a private person, but he had worn a badge saying "Palm Beach millionaire," and that had created his world, the women who approached him, and the men he called friends. He had hurt so many people in his life, but he did not grasp that either. He did not see that in the last years of his life he had an opportunity to make amends and the means to do so.

For three months I was Fred's analyst, priest, and friend. Keller was talking about things he had never talked about to anyone, and he told me that our sessions were therapeutic.

Except for his civil attorney Cohn and one tennis-playing acquaintance, there may have been no one who believed Fred was innocent. When I realized he was never going to admit his guilt, I attempted to get him to take some responsibly, if not for the crimes, then in his purported innocence, at least for his complicity in the tragedy.

"I'm trying to put myself in your shoes, Fred, and if I pulled out my gun and Rose died and Wolfgang was wounded, I would feel that I had done something wrong," I said insistently one morning. "I was the one with the gun. I was the one who made the mistake."

"I can understand you saying that, but you have to be part of what happened," Fred replied as if lecturing a child. "Rose losing an increasing sense of reality. You have to experience what's going on where everyone was on heightened alert. You have to experience that to have a mind-set where this stuff was terrible."

"I'm still surprised that you don't say, 'I screwed up, I had a right to be paranoid, but I screwed up. I had a right to be paranoid, but they didn't do it.'"

"That's the prosecutor's line! 'Mr. Keller, why didn't you run out the door? Mr. Keller, why didn't you holler?' I was scared. I reacted instinctively. I didn't think."

"I still would say, 'I messed up,'" I insisted, holding the phone mouthpiece back from my mouth. "'I'm guilty of something. I did something wrong.'"

"I did what I thought I had to do to protect my life," Fred replied as if I were incapable of understanding. "It's as simple as that. We all sit here and Monday-morning quarterback. It played out the way it did, right or wrong. I had no choice."

"Do you think young Fred will see it this way?" I asked.

"I know you're going to address all the issues and the court transcript is there. I've tried to give the explanation in court and hopefully I'm doing it with you. It's terrible. The worst thing any child can experience is the death of their parent. You feel all alone. It's sad. It's terrible."

"And then what about when you're taken physically to a prison farther away from young Fred?" That was a question that had long been on my mind.

"I hope I'm still here when the judge rules on my seeing Fred," he said. Then he stopped for a moment, choking up. "I wake up frequently at night thinking about things and making notes. And the thought occurred to me that I wrote down that really describes what I have here. 'As hope fades, despair takes its place.'"

"And Fred is the one piece of hope you have?" I queried.

"He's the one that keeps me going. Without him, what's left for me but to be warehoused in prison until I die?"

Fred planned an appeal, but in the immediate future, he focused on the one positive thing in his life, his son Fredchen. He and his attorney Cohn planned a vigorous legal attack that Fred believed would give him access to the boy so that Fred could tell him *his* story of his mother's death.

I suggested to Fred that it was not the best thing to tell an impressionable, vulnerable youth that his beloved uncle had accidentally murdered his mother, and that the family with whom he lived were liars and greedy interlopers trying to steal his money. I said that the noble thing might be to write a letter to his son to be given to him as an adult, saying that his father had loved him so much that he had gone to his grave not even trying to tell him his side of what happened.

"That's crazy," Fred said. "Young Fred's been ostracized and fed the company line and believes it. The harm psychologically would come later on if he's never had an opportunity to sit down with his dad and find out from his dad what happened. I want him to understand that the underlying reason for this is money."

Fredchen was the vehicle of his father's wrath. If Fred was motivated in part by love of his son, he was motivated even more by hatred of the Keils. He did not care about the cost to the vulnerable psyche of a twelve-year-old boy. Nor was he willing to minimize that by promising the court he would not tell the boy his story of his mother's death.

Circuit Court Judge Karen L. Martin asked Dr. Alexander, the psychologist who had interviewed Fred, Rose, and Fredchen during the divorce, to interview Fredchen again. That way she could have independent medical input into her decision as to whether Fred should see his son. In his new session with Fredchen, Dr. Alexander saw that young Fred's opinion of his father had not changed since the day of his mother's death. It was only deeper and more articulately and resolutely pronounced. He did not want to see his father. "He's still my dad, but there's no excuse for what he did." He did not want to read his letters. "He can write fifty billion, I just don't want to see them." He did not want to hear his name. "I don't want to communicate with him." He knew Fred had been convicted, and he wanted him away, gone, finished, out of his life forever.

Fredchen is an intelligent child whose opinions are deeply felt and well stated, and in his letter of opinion, Dr. Alexander did little but to agree with what young Fred had said and desired. And the judge in her decision did little but put legal substance to Dr. Alexander's opinions that Fred should be freed of the shadowy image of his father. There should never be any contact between Fredchen and the father, not even by letter. They were the words of a judge, but it was young Fred speaking out of the depths of his pain.

FRED HAD BEEN KEPT alive by his hope of seeing Fredchen, and now that he would never see the boy again, something died within him. I felt that once he was shipped to the prison that would be his final home, seventy-three-year-old Fred would not live more than a year. And I thought that now was the time to find something positive to come up out of the darkness of Fred's life. I wanted to see if I could somehow bring this man to some kind of moral closure, to help him end his life with a series of good acts that would live beyond him.

Fred was always complaining about what he called the criminal injustice system, and all the innocent men and women incarcerated in America's prisons. I suggested that he take ten million dollars of his money and start a foundation to help the falsely convicted, but he swatted that idea away with a curt dismissal.

Then I turned to his family. I had talked to his sons' widows and to his stepson, and knew what a modest amount of Fred's money would mean to them and to his grandchildren's educations. Fred bragged how he had sent a letter to his grandson Austin Keller, offering to pay for his college education. Fred was alienated from Austin's mother, and Fred said that the ungrateful wretch had not even replied. I had talked to family members about this and saw the letter in which Fred wrote about "relocating to Florida, going to college here and working for our company." The young man did not want to work for Keller's company. I suggested that Fred send the teenager tuition money for whatever school he chose to attend.

Fred was not interested. Everything for Fred was a matter of exchanges, even his grandson's education.

"Who else do you plan to give it to but young Fred?" I asked him.

"Well, I don't know what other family I have left."

"Come on, Fred, you've got three grandkids. You've got your two sons' widows and ex-wives. You've got your adopted son, Brian."

"I want to give everything to my son," Fred insisted.

"But why? I don't understand."

"Well, ah that's me," he said as if the answer should be self-evident. "That's me."

"These people have been problems for you, so forget it," I replied, growing irritated with him. "That's your attitude. They haven't come through and given you anything good, so you aren't going to give them anything good."

"I've never taken a step back, but I think I'm doing the right thing. If I'm erring because I choose to give everything to my son, that's my error."

Fred was not, however, giving everything to his son without an explicit trade-off. Young Fred was to be the engine of his father's wrath, casting away the Keils, and forcefully proclaiming Fred's innocence to a cynical, corrupt world.

On some profound, unspoken level, the boy must have understood what the trade-off would be. It was a terrible thing to say that you never want to see your father again, a father whom you once loved. It took courage for a boy to say that—not in a guilt-ridden, half-embarrassed way, but with resolve, and that one act is the most positive sign that Fredchen might end up a young man of character and purpose.

As I look back on the thirty or so hours I spent talking with Fred, I realize that my studied empathy was a faulty technique. I was projecting myself upon Fred and looking for things that were not in him. He was an evil man, and he was no less evil because he did not understood good and evil. What he wanted he called good, and those who kept him from what he wanted, he considered evil.

He was neither Adolf Hitler nor Jeffrey Dahmer, but he was a study in wickedness. His profound self-absorption and narcissism had metastasized into malevolence. Fred hoarded money because it constituted his only true sense of self-worth. To lose half his money was to lose half his being. When he went into his office that tragic morning, he probably exploded in narcissistic rage, willing to do whatever he had to do to keep himself whole.

Cutting Fred's money in half had cut him in half. His only salvation now was to hold on to as much of that money as was left, hold on to as much of himself, and hold on to it for his son.

Fred had nothing left to live for until he heard some extraordinary news that he hoped would give his tale a proper ending. Not for him a middling foundation. Not for him parceling out his money to ingrates who unfortunately bore his name. He would not have done that anyway, but now he would have his exquisite revenge. One of his lawyers suggested to him that if he should die while his case was being appealed, then his conviction would be thrown out, and the Keils' civil suits would shrink to almost nothing. It was sweet beyond belief. In death, Fred could have revenge that he could not have in life. He had something to live for now, or rather something to die for; so he stopped taking his pills.

In early June when Fred was taken down to the South Florida Reception Center on his way to a state prison, he was immediately transferred to the hospital. There in Miami, on August 23, 2007, he died. "It was a tragic thing to see," reflects his civil attorney Cohn, who was at his deathbed.

Fred had died thinking that in death he had delivered his enemies the Keils a blow fatal to their aspirations of feeding off great portions of his fortune. But it turned out his lawyer had given him misinformation. Criminal verdicts are negated in federal but not in state courts, and Fred's death changed nothing.

Fred wanted no priest or minister intoning what he considered meaningless words over his grave, and no memorial service. He wanted to be cremated and the ashes tossed to the winds. The body was brought up to a funeral home in Lake Worth, just south of Palm Beach, where Wolfgang insisted on seeing the remains. It was a mark of how complicated and conflicted Fredchen was about Fred that he also asked to see the body of a father he had not wanted to see in life. The body was cremated and the ashes secretly strewn somewhere.

Fredchen could not visit his father's grave even if he wanted to, but he drives out with his aunt Angie to the cemetery in West Palm Beach where his mother's body rests in a mausoleum. The boy usually sits on a fence in front of the marble vault and says that he talks to Rose. He trusts almost no one, and is afraid that his aunt Angie will die. "He holds everything in," says Angie. "He doesn't express his feelings. He still calls what happened 'a thing.' He doesn't talk about it. Always when it is brought up, he wants to change the subject. I don't think he has really grieved his mother's death. He tries not to think about it. That's what worries me, that he will eventually explode."

All that was left of Fred was his money. All that was left was an epic legal struggle involving about twenty highly paid attorneys whose fees will probably total over twenty million dollars. Fredchen was shielded from this, but one day the richest boy in Palm Beach will learn about the millions of dollars the lawyers earned, and the struggle of the Keils for a goodly portion of his inheritance, and he will learn lessons about life and humanity that most people never learn. He will learn about his father too, and the wages of wealth.

"Fred Keller spent his whole life accumulating a fortune that gave him freedom and control, but it became only a source of evil, greed, and sorrow for everybody who touched it," reflects Dr. Alexander. "It's the ring in Tolkien's trilogy. Everyone else wants it, but if you put the ring on, it destroys you."

26

Two Wild and Crazy Guys

I was going out to cocktail parties, dinners, and balls and often I saw Eric Purcell and Helder "Sonny" Peixoto. Eric and Sonny were inseparable, wildly appreciative of each other. They finished each other's jokes and routines. They shared liquor and food, and if at the end of the evening they ended up foiled in their search for women, they enjoyed each other's company so much that it hardly mattered. They reminded me of an upscale version of Georg and Yortuk Festrunk, the two wild and crazy guys played by Dan Aykroyd and Steve Martin on *Saturday Night Live*.

I was one of the few people on the island who knew about Eric's time in prison. Since then, he had put on some weight, and dressed in clothes artfully designed to disguise the poundage. For the first time in his life, he looked like what he was: a middle-aged Palm Beach millionaire out on the prowl.

Sonny was nearly twenty years younger than Eric, and had he lost thirty pounds, the Portuguese American bon vivant would have been darkly handsome, with the smooth looks of a matinee idol. Sonny was good with young women, but he was good with practically everyone. He remembered your name the first time he heard it, and after that unfailingly came up and gave a hearty hello, with maybe a slap on the back or a firm handshake that included grasping your arm with his second hand.

Fifty-three-year-old Eric had met thirty-four-year-old Sonny at a Halloween party at the Ann Norton Sculpture Gardens in West Palm Beach in October 2006. Eric had bought a ticket to the event, but Sonny never paid his way anywhere. He had such an authoritative manner that he could just walk into events with the most rigorous security and vetting. That was an ability that impressed, even awed Eric. Even more impressive were Sonny's business ventures, doubly notable since it was hard to understand why a megamillionaire enjoyed sneaking into events. The supposedly wildly successful Boston entrepreneur talked about his elaborate project to build a major development in Portugal. He often called Eric from what he said was his home in Delray Beach, just south of Palm Beach, to discuss their plans for the evening.

Each man had something that the other wanted, and that brought them close together. Sonny gave Eric youth, while Eric gave Sonny sophistication. They both liked pretty young women. Sonny knew where all the parties were and how to get into them, while Eric had a Bentley and a Palm Beach address. They headed out together to the Palm Beach party world almost every evening. To some of the events, they had even been invited.

Eric was used to conning people. He did not see a con as anything despicable, but just a shrewd and necessary way to maneuver through the endless shoals of life. After a few weeks listening to Sonny's tales, Eric realized that that was precisely what they were—tales. Sonny talked about his homes and his yacht, and most afternoons Eric drove over to West Palm Beach to pick up Sonny outside what he said was his local residence, a large house in the El Cid area, just across the Intracoastal Waterway from Palm Beach.

"Sonny, you know, I've been broke before, and you don't need to bullshit me," Eric said one day as they were driving across the middle bridge back into West Palm Beach. "I checked the records. You don't own that house."

"No, no, the company owns it," Sonny replied with casual confidence.

"Why don't you just drop all this? Because I don't need it. I still like you, Sonny. Just drop it."

For a while Sonny was silent, but from then on he did not run his numbers on Eric. Sonny told his friend that he had been a cop in Boston and things had gone bad.

The two men told each other about their secret lives. Stories that would have driven many people apart only brought them closer. Sonny could see how a woman could make you so mad that you flailed out at her, and how she might bludgeon you half to death with the legal system, taking your money and seven months of your life. And Eric could see that Sonny had been a tough cop beating up on the bad guys, until the system came down on him. He loved Sonny's stories of working the Latino hood, where they called Sonny the "El Diablo Blanca" and his black partner "El Diablo Negro." Anyway, Sonny was not just a cop. He had ambitions, and had even run twice for the city council in Cambridge. Eric could see how you could have a silly traffic accident and some old guy dies and you get blamed, and poof, there goes your career. It could happen to anybody.

The truth can be comprised of a mosaic of half-truths, and even when Sonny presented the most truthful story of his life to his compadre Eric, the details fell apart. He told Eric that he was a Boston cop, but he was a transit cop. There was nothing dishonorable about that, but it was more prestigious to say that he worked only aboveground. And he was a bad cop, not because he was overly tough and merciless to criminals, but because he was overly tough and merciless to anyone who irked him. He was a bad cop because he was bad tempered and swaggering, and used his badge as a license to do whatever he wanted. He had had at least five traffic accidents in which he was to blame, but he learned nothing.

One day in January 2003, Sonny was in uniform and was supposed to be on duty. Instead, he was roaring along in his own car at forty-five miles per hour in a thirty-mph zone when he barreled into seventy-nine-year-old John J. Todd's Buick, killing the World War II veteran and caretaker for his disabled wife. In exchange for five years' probation and giving up his driver's license for ten years, Sonny pled guilty to vehicular homicide and headed south to Palm

Beach County, where his brother Samuel Peixoto worked as a sheriff's deputy.

Sonny was living largely on a few hundred dollars a month that his mother sent him from Boston. He was not staying in the main house in West Palm Beach where Eric picked him up, but in a modest rental apartment in the rear. The Louis Vuitton suits and designer tuxedo he wore he had picked up used at the Goodwill Embassy Boutique. He had no car. He had no computer. Every afternoon he went over to the boutique Hotel Biba to use their free computer to check his e-mails and learn where the party scene was that evening. Each day a coterie of bartenders, waiters, photographers, and various hangers-on passed along information.

Eric loved to go out every evening, but he was not particularly outgoing; it was Sonny who pulled it off. They attended elaborate celebrations on yachts at the town dock. They went to private dinner parties at some of the greatest homes on the island. They walked into the most exclusive balls in their tuxedos. They sought a table in the ballroom at the Breakers where they could sit down to dinner, but if they could not find two vacant seats, they had a few free drinks and then sat at one of the bars before returning after dinner to dance the evening away.

At the March of Dimes Ball at the Breakers, Sonny and Eric not only found a table, but Sonny decided to bid on one auction item: a chance to have his name as a character in the next novel by best-selling Palm Beach author James Patterson. Sonny stood up and hung in as the bidding got higher and higher, finally winning at a formidable ten thousand dollars. When a March of Dimes representative tried to collect for the winning bid as well as for the three-hundred dollar ticket to the event, Sonny grew livid, and left belligerent messages on the woman's answering machine.

Only one other time did Eric and Sonny get caught. That was at a cocktail party at Neiman Marcus on Worth Avenue where most of the guests were far older and there were few attractive young women. Shannon was there at the department store that evening, and the society editor noticed Sonny. "Who the hell is that?" she asked one of the executives. "I don't know," the woman replied. "He just walked in off the street." When approached by security, they merely sidled out of the store and moved on to the next party.

Sonny was an inordinately charming man. No one except for his brother and Eric had any idea of the darkness of his past, and Eric did not consider it dark so much as intense, fascinating, manly, and unlucky. In Palm Beach, it usually took money to become part of the public society celebrated in the Shiny Sheet, but Sonny was a regular practically from the day he arrived, usually with Eric beside him. Sonny was the facilitator. He put people and events together. He was the party man. Everyone liked getting Sonny's calls, for there was always something happening somewhere, and he was the man who knew about it.

The two wild and crazy guys spent New Year's Eve at the Breakers and had their pictures in the Shiny Sheet. Success played on success. There was nothing rarer than a bachelor with even a hint of youth, and Eric and Sonny were increasingly on invitation lists.

Even if Sonny had not been invited to a party, he acted so effusively that he could have been one of the hosts. At one Palm Beach gathering, he went up to a dark-haired middle-aged man dressed in the proper island sports attire and started a conversation. The good-looking man he had instantly befriended was Dr. G. Heath King, a psychoanalyst whom Eric had already gotten to know.

To King, therapy is not merely a profession but a way of seeing, and it combined philosophy, history, and literature in an eclectic manner unique to him. He is perfectly capable of interjecting into the most banal of social chitchat an insight of such savage penetration that it shatters the demeanor of the most sophisticated partygoer. One of his intellectual mentors is the dark Danish philosopher Søren Kierkegaard, who said that if one can read the language, there is great meaning in something as small and subtle as the intonation of a voice or a mere handshake.

King had a Kierkegaardian moment with Sonny. The psychoanalyst sensed that beyond the extrovert's bluster was a needy man pathetically promiscuous in his attempts at creating friends. He was fleeing from some dark secret, and even in this artificial world, was marked by a special inauthenticity.

Sonny may not have read Kierkegaard, but he had a profound instinctive awareness of his impact on those immediately around him. He doubtless was both attracted to this man of obvious insight and frightened by him, and for both reasons sought to draw him near. He started e-mailing King to give him the one thing of value he could offer: invitations to parties to which Sonny himself might not even have been invited.

The psychoanalyst replied with the abrupt idiom of truth:

> Quite frankly, I suspect you of being a con man, a dissembler who failed in politics and now lurks the courtyards of Palm Beach.
>
> Heath

That was King's entire e-mail, devastating in its brevity and accuracy. Sonny replied in a semiliterate screed full of one lie after another about his past, from deceitfully declaring that he had full disability benefits to blaming the elderly man for the automobile accident in which he died. Sonny was not confrontational, but in King's words, "more muted and subdued, a whining, petulant plea to appease."

King was an immensely intelligent man, but he risked enraging Sonny if he got too close to the man's inner life. After a few exchanges, they both broke off with a conciliatory détente.

ERIC AND SONNY WERE friends the way men often are friends—joshing, irreverent buddies. They were both drinkers, and as they wended their way from party to party, Sonny mixed drinks as if there was a rule that one could not down two of the same beverages. By midnight he was slurring his words.

Late one evening, Eric was driving Sonny back to West Palm Beach in the Bentley. Eric could tell that his friend was about to throw up.

"You know, I'm not going to live very long," Sonny said with great seriousness.

"What are you talking about?" Eric replied, nonplussed at his friend's morbid musings.

"No, seriously," he said. "I like you. You're my best friend. But I'm not going to live very long."

Sonny was so drunk that the next day he could not remember just what he had said. "Did I say anything last night?" he asked Eric. "No, nothing," Eric said, and moved on quickly to another subject. Eric liked to keep things light.

SONNY MET THE WOMAN he had always been looking for when he crashed a bachelorette party at the Players Room at the International Polo Club in Wellington. Amity Kozak was breathtakingly gorgeous, and Sonny was smitten from the moment he saw her. He would have made up a story anyway, but in her honor he made up an even larger one. He told the woman that he was in the mortgage business and had his own sponsor's tent at the U.S. Open finals at the polo grounds the following Sunday. He invited Amity to join him.

The polo matches in Wellington twelve miles west of Palm Beach are part of the elaborate social schema of the island. Every Sunday during the season, the parade of Rolls, Mercedes, and BMWs makes the dismal trek west on Southern Boulevard to what was once farmland and is now a growing community centered around horses.

The games are occasions for afternoons of drinking and eating, with sporadic ganders at the competition itself. As on the island, there is an elaborate class system. The most prestigious place to watch is from the covered seats in the clubhouse. Then there are sponsor tents with catered food and drink, and on the other side of the field next to the parking lot, a line of tailgate parties, some of them little more than a few six-packs of beer, deviled eggs, salted nuts, and inebriated sportifs.

The following Sunday afternoon, Sonny was standing at the

center of his gregarious drinking buddies when Amity arrived with another stylish thirtyish woman, Ashley Swain, and her date. Ashley worked affixing permanent makeup, tattooing lipsticklike coloring and eye shadowing. The two women became friends when Amity had gone in to have her lips done and to set up a Botox appointment. It used to be that women were fifty before they thought seriously of plastic surgery and other cosmetic treatments, then it was forty, and now it is thirty, with even twentysomethings like Amity coming in for preventive maintenance.

Amity had never been to a polo match before, and she was impressed with Sonny and his friends. She did not notice that the sponsor's name on the tent was not Sonny's but a beverage company's. It was a hot day, and although Ashley's date was in a sports shirt, Sonny was dressed in the approved Palm Beach way. He wore a blue blazer with a silk handkerchief in his pocket, and a white sports shirt, his dark hair greased so it would not dry out in the merciless South Florida sun.

Amity found everything about the scene exciting. "Sonny says this is the best place," Amity whispered to Ashley.

"This is the shit box," Ashley replied dismissively.

"He's in the scene and I like to be in the scene," Amity said, rebuking her friend's negativity.

Ashley had been around a little longer than her newest best friend, and she felt that Amity could be pathetically naive. Ashley had seen too many men like Sonny. She thought him little but a pathetic poseur. "Sonny put himself with these needy people who have to have a crew to go anywhere," she says. "Palm Beach is full of these trust fund misfits leaning on the Sonnys of the world, who are there only to prey on them."

When Ashley asked another guest to take a photo of the two couples, Sonny put his arm around Amity in a manner more possessive than protective. His other hand grasped his drink. It was the couple's first date, and he cast a knowing, mocking look at the camera as if to say, This stunning woman is mine, not yours.

During the afternoon Sonny ran into King, and introduced Amity to the psychoanalyst. She sidled away from Sonny and hugged

King in a greeting exaggerated in its friendliness. The psychoanalyst had a penchant for beautiful women, but he could not separate beauty from character, and he felt that Amity was tormenting poor Sonny. She was dazzling, but she was treating the polo match as a singles bar. She was quickly going through the possibilities before making her choice. King had made the short list, but as friendly as Amity appeared, he backed off, sensing that the woman holding him was as dangerous in her own right as Sonny. And just as with Sonny, he was convinced that there was a dark history back somewhere that might rise out to bedevil her and those around her.

That night after midnight Sonny called King. "Look, Heath, I didn't know if you knew, but Amity is my girlfriend," he said, quietly persuasive and polite, not telling the psychoanalyst that he was in Amity's townhouse. "You're dating several girls. I'd appreciate it if you'd leave her alone."

There was anxiety hidden in Sonny's words, and King tried to calm him down. "Don't worry, Sonny, I'm not interested," King said. "She's yours." The psychoanalyst found it strange since he had made no play for Amity, but he was used to strangeness, and he thought little more of it.

The next morning, Amity called Ashley and whispered to her friend that Sonny was still in her apartment. "He's had a little incident in Boston," Amity told her friend. "He's in litigation and he doesn't have a driver's license or a car."

"Where does he live?" Ashley asked, all of her suspicions justified in one moment.

"He rents his house in El Cid to this family because he's trying to hide money until the lawsuit and his divorce is done."

The story made no sense to anyone except Amity. Neither she nor Sonny was anything like the images they projected onto a critical, suspicious world. Their days together were a ritualistic unfolding of that reality. If they had reached out for what was most profound about each other—their anguished insecurities—they might have found some commonality. That is not what they looked for, but the opposite; and Amity found only deeper and deeper levels of disillusion.

27

Everybody Hurts

The next time I saw Eric and Sonny was at Eric's annual Tropics Party at his ground-floor condominium at Ibis Isle, a small island that protrudes into the Intracoastal Waterway. There was a Caribbean band, tropical drinks, and a prowling crowd spilling out along the lawn.

At the highest social level in Palm Beach, there are almost always as many men as women, perfect symmetry at the dinner table. At gatherings like this, there are usually more women than men. They come over the bridge from West Palm Beach, Delray, or points inland, looking for treasure in the shape of a wealthy man. Amity could not make the party, but all kinds of other single women did.

On my way to the party, I picked up Eddy Louis at his house at the end of Regent Park. Eddy was no longer living in Thailand, but was roaming across Asia. We used Yahoo Messenger to talk to each other every few days. One time I would see him on the screen sitting on his bed in a small hotel room in the Philippines. Another time he would be in a mountainous village somewhere in China after having traveled there on the back of a motorcycle. His daughter was in a Catholic high school in West Palm Beach, and every two months or so, Eddy returned for a few days.

The sixty-four-year-old millionaire was precisely what many of these women were looking for. He was wearing tight jeans and a

T-shirt, his skin like mahogany. He had lost considerable weight, and he was an imposing specimen.

But Eddy, still emerging from his Kurtz world, reacted almost violently to some of the guests. They might look twenty to the untrained eye in the half-light of the party, but not to Eddy, who figured most of these women were closer to forty. "A bunch of fucking hookers, whores, hoping to score with a rich guy," he snarled. "All fucking wannabes."

As Louis continued his diatribe, Purcell came bursting into the circle looking almost boyish, a little plump, and effusive in his welcome. "You're a god, one of the gods, Eddy," he said, his voiced tinged with awe. "You're a legend. And you look fantastic."

As the three of us talked, Sonny was working the crowd as if he were the maestro of the evening. He had a good word to say to everyone, and moved seamlessly from one guest to another, one of the most desirable bachelors at the party.

AT THE END OF the season in late April, Eric gave a dinner party. My wife was in Europe visiting her family, and once again I drove south alone to Ibis Isle. The three other men were Sonny, the psychoanalyst King, and a local businessman. They were accompanied by their trophy girlfriends, all with the rich glaze of youthfulness that shone among these middle-aged men.

Eric's girlfriend of the moment was Natalie Kalinka Paavola, a twenty-nine-year-old blond Finnish American real estate agent. With the help of Eric's maid and her son, Natalie had cooked a gourmet Indian dinner. She was a circumspect, empathetic woman, but she was not wealthy, nor was she sophisticated. Although she was enjoying going out with Eric, it troubled her to be dating a man old enough to be her father.

The psychoanalyst was sitting with a striking twenty-eight-year-old blonde half his age. The woman spent much of the night talking of her fears of going blind while the analyst gently kneaded her back and soothed her model's body.

All of the men were solicitous of their dates, but no one as much as Sonny. He had worked his way through the parties for months until finally he had gotten what he wanted in twenty-nine-year-old Amity, who stood out, even in this evening's company. She had a classy quiet manner, and a sensual body that she was not trying to show off by dressing provocatively. She was a woman a man could have happily taken to almost any party.

Across from me, Sonny and Amity were having their own private dinner party. I have either a realistic or a jaundiced attitude toward romance, seeing it as the market economy at its purest, each person trading realistically for the best they can get. My theory faltered here, for I could not understand what Amity was doing with Sonny. I thought that even though, at the time, I knew nothing about his tortured past or impecunious present, and considered Sonny to be just another wealthy man.

Sonny acted with the confidence of wealth, and that was the most seductive thing about him. He and Amity whispered together as if nobody else in the room existed. In the middle of dinner, Amity became angry and ran out onto the patio. Sonny ran after her, shut the door behind them, and had a fervent conversation with her.

When they returned, Eric started to make fun of Amity. It had been a strangely stilted evening. As the host, he had to do something to have at least a few moments of engaging conversation. And this was his favorite form of discourse.

"Don't you think you two are spending too much time together, Sonny?" Eric asked. Sonny said nothing, and Eric raised the ante. "What do you *really* see in Amity?"

Sonny still said nothing, but Amity had had enough. "Well, look at me," she said, the trump card in her deck. "Look at me!"

King said little, all through the evening never once speaking to Amity. The psychoanalyst feared that any attention might provoke Sonny and that "anything could set him off, all that pent-up rage originating in his childhood."

AMITY HAD GROWN UP in Lawrenceville, Georgia, a small town thirty miles northeast of Atlanta. She was a church-going cheerleader when, at seventeen, her father announced that he was gay—a devastating, unacceptable admission in a fundamentalist community where homosexuality is considered wanton sin.

After graduating from high school in 1996, Amity left town and moved to Atlanta, where she ended up an exotic dancer at a "gentleman's club." Beauty was all Amity had, and although she was making untold amounts of money, she had traded her beauty cheaply. She did not like the work, and needed a drink or two before she got up on the bar, but she was addicted to it.

"Amity said she needed the attention," says Ashley. "It was a massive driving force. Everything she did was about getting all this attention, she didn't care who it was from." There were always men wanting her, watching her. Wherever she was, the cell phone was ringing, the text messages were popping up, men were seeking her, telling her how much they cared.

Amity projected an innocent quality that enhanced her beauty and the fascination that men felt for her. There was nothing innocent in the money and the favors she accepted, not only the twenty-dollar bills stuffed in her G-string, but thousands of dollars given to her by her pursuers.

Amity left the business for a while and lived with a wealthy man twice her age. He was worldly enough to teach her rudiments of sophistication, but beneath there was no culture, no education, no great wit, nothing but a little girl from a little town living in a big world. When she went off to the Caribbean with her older lover, she fell off a balcony under peculiar circumstances and was seriously injured, and the relationship ended.

When this man and others who dated her talk of Amity, it is with fond regret and devotion, but there is a strange lack of specificity in their accounts. As she left them one after another, there was nothing left to hold on to but gossamer and the scent of perfume.

Amity sold real estate for a few months in Belize, and tried to distance herself from her exotic dancer past, but it kept coming back to her. She had come to Florida four years before and worked for a time as a dancer at Rachel's, an upscale club in West Palm

Beach. After that, she had lived with a man in a townhouse in a small town outside Atlanta. He loved her, but she was used to the electric, dangerous excitement of her erotic dancing, and it was deadly dull to sit out there, especially in the evenings when her boyfriend drove into Atlanta, where he managed a gentleman's club.

And so she returned to Florida, where she had bought her own townhouse. Twice a month she flew to New York City for what she called "a date" with a man who paid her what she told Ashley was ten thousand dollars a month. When she went to work at the title company, she gave that up. And now she decided to take a male roommate to help pay her mortgage. Amity told Sonny that the man was gay, but he was not about to have some guy living in Amity's townhouse. He immediately wrote a check for the annual rental, and just as immediately, the check bounced.

Amity generally preferred jewelry to money. Her favorites were her "girls," the diamond earrings that she kept in the safe in her townhouse. She loved her girls, and wore them only for the most special of occasions. One evening Sonny gave her a fistful of jewelry, secondhand stuff unworthy to be worn with the girls. Even then, most of it was so dirty that she would have to have it cleaned before wearing the pieces.

Amity considered Palm Beach an exalted kingdom. Her dream was one day to be accepted there, and not as an attractive outsider. She needed the proper man, and she thought that she had found him in Sonny. Men were consumed with her, pressing forward, trying to touch her both physically and emotionally, and she danced away from them and their everlasting needs. There were scores of them, with their endless entreaties and gifts, and promises and bouquets of praise.

Sonny pressed forward even more insistently than the others. She so desperately wanted him to be what he said he was, and he was such a consummate performer that she did not push back away from him.

The couple had only known each other a few days when they drove up to Lawrenceville to attend a birthday party for Amity's younger brother, John. Her siblings knew nothing of the glittery world to which their sister aspired, but they did not like Sonny. He drank too much, and said little. Amity's mother, Pat, thought he "looked like a mobster." Amity did not care, and the couple left as quickly as they had arrived.

Their romance was like a film that had been sped up. Sonny insisted that Amity fly to Boston to meet his family. He had no money, so he borrowed five hundred dollars from Eric, the first time his friend loaned him anything, and four hundred dollars from another friend, and off the couple flew.

Sonny was telling Eric these baroque tales of sex with Amity; awesome, mindboggling epics. Amity told her friend Ashley a very different tale that had the sad specificity of truth. Amity did not see sex as pleasure but as the final payoff in the game between women and men. It was the dazzling prize that enhanced its value the more rarely it was offered. Amity had expected that this bull of a man with his wild sexual bantering and his endless avowals of love would devour her sexually. She had put it off as long as she could, but in the middle of one drunken night in their hotel room in Boston, she woke up from sleep and realized that he was on top of her. "She said he made no noises, and when he came he pulled out and he was finished and it was so weird," Ashley says. "She was expecting the opposite of this; he was going to be awesome, this animal. But he just rolled over and went to sleep."

Amity had had sex with Lotharios who lay next to her impotent, and runts who came all night, and one mattered to her no more than the other. Sex was so unimportant to her that she could easily have lived with Sonny's quick, tortured sexuality. That weekend she learned something else that was far more devastating. Sonny's sister took Amity aside and warned her about her brother in the most detailed, frightening terms, talking about his violent potential. Ashley had already been imploring Amity to end this crazed affair with this dangerous, duplicitous man, and as the plane flew south, she knew that she would have to move on.

Sonny projected an image of a party guy, a good-time, good-hearted guy, but he was a man of preternatural sensitivity. King, the Boca psychoanalyst, had gotten to know Sonny as well as anyone, other than Eric. The psychoanalyst sometimes stood back and observed Sonny at parties. He realized that Sonny was doing the same thing, playing the gregarious party animal when he was studiously observing everyone and everything.

Sonny understood how marginal his place was in Palm Beach. People were using him more than he was using them. They were amusing themselves while he was paying an emotional price, always playing the supplicant, the court jester, the tour guide. As long as he had Amity, he was no longer this pitiable hanger-on. As long as he had Amity, he had a possession that trumped them all. As long as he had Amity, he had something they all wanted, no matter how big their homes, how expensive their cars. He knew it and they knew it. He was so attuned to Amity that he realized she was going to try to leave him even before she realized it herself.

Everything was going wrong. He was negotiating a deal to buy a popular sandwich shop in West Palm Beach. He was about to close on that, and had no money. Sonny could talk his way almost anywhere and to anyone, and he had cosponsored a fund-raiser for West Palm Beach Mayor Lois Frankel. But that had recently led to an article in the *Palm Beach Post* about his past. "In 2004, he pleaded guilty to vehicular homicide in the death of a seventy-nine-year-old motorist while speeding on duty," the paper said. "He also was accused—but later cleared—of police brutality in the beatings of a suspect and a love rival. A colleague once called him 'dangerous' in a published report." The story was potentially devastating to his social life.

None of that mattered if he could hold on to Amity, and the more she tried to loosen his grip, the tighter he held on to her. Amity was used to men obsessed with her, but this was different. She had only been dating him six weeks, but it was overwhelming as nothing she had ever experienced. She had to get away from him; that was the only way to loosen his grip. She decided that she would fly to New York and once again be with the "date" she had given up. She had no idea how long she would stay away, but she would not return until Sonny had accepted that it was all over between them.

Amity always took care of herself, and since her plane was not until 4:30, she drove over to the Ultima Gym in West Palm Beach to work out. As she rode a stationary bike, her cell phone kept going off every few minutes, as time and again Sonny kept calling.

Eric had been in New York, and as soon as he got back that day at the end of May, he called Sonny to see what was happening. Since his friend had become involved with Amity, the two had not been going out much together, and Eric was anxious to reconnect. Sonny was in an exuberant mood. "Let's get together around eight o'clock," Sonny said. "I'm doing some yoga with Amity, then I'm going to do a little sexy time with her, but I'll be free this evening."

THE LAND ALONG THE western shore of the Intracoastal Waterway could have been an irresistibly inviting mix of restaurants, shops, and midsize buildings that would have matched up well with the community across the water, and made West Palm Beach and Palm Beach truly one community. Instead, developers have taken a stranglehold on the city government, and the skyline has been darkened by so many massive condominiums that at some places the small city looks more like Manhattan than South Florida. The buildings have gone up so quickly and in such profusion that with the real estate market collapse, many of them are half-empty.

A number of the condominium projects have become rental buildings. One of these is the Slade, and that is the building that Sonny wanted to see when he called real estate broker Jonathan Mann. Sonny arrived in the lobby around five p.m., not in island garb, but in a black short-sleeve shirt, matching black shorts, and running shoes. The two men chatted as they took the elevator up to the eleventh floor to see a penthouse apartment.

"Gee, this is nice," Sonny said as he made a cursory tour of the apartment. The two-bedroom apartment would have been perfect for a hip, thirty-four-year-old single fellow—if only Sonny had the money. It was not just the two pools and the health club, but the awesome view. In a similar apartment in Palm Beach, the ocean-front view is nothing but a line on the window. Here the whole expanse of Palm Beach is out there; the Flagler Museum, the Biltmore, the entire world that Sonny made his own each evening. It is an incomparable view, and Sonny unlocked the sliding door and walked out onto the balcony.

Party planner Bruce Sutka lives in a spacious apartment next to the Slade, and the impresario of parties and events happened to be looking out his window that afternoon. As Bruce stood there, Sonny fell through the afternoon sky and thudded against the concrete, the body twisted and contorted. It was so nightmarish a vision that for a time Bruce placed screens across the window and took an antidepressant.

Eric was having a hard time charging his cell phone. It was eight o'clock by the time he got it working, and saw that he had an incredible forty messages, many of them from Jonathan Mann. He called the real estate broker back, and when he heard that Sonny had committed suicide, he went over to the Slade. The body was gone, and all that was left was one police car and several officers.

Eric decided that it might be a good idea to go over to Sonny's apartment and see if he had left a suicide note. Eric and a photographer acquaintance drove south half a mile to the historic El Cid area. Eric had picked Sonny up many times, but he had never been to his place. He had not wanted to embarrass Sonny by seeing how modestly his friend lived. He knocked on the door of the main house, and after hearing the tragic news, the landlord led them to the back to the tiny apartment. When the landlord opened the door, the song "Everybody Hurts" by R.E.M. was playing.

Sonny may have had almost nothing, but the little he had, he kept neatly. There was no suicide note on the desk, and everything else looked in perfect order. The cover on the daybed was a little rumpled, and Eric realized that there was someone under the covers.

He figured it was probably Amity, so distraught that she had returned to mourn her lost lover and had fallen asleep. As he pulled back the quilt, he saw a head so bloodied and bludgeoned that if not for the nude female body to which it was attached, he would not have known that it was a human head.

28

Regrets Only

At the second annual Turquoise and Denim Ball at the Breakers to raise money for ovarian cancer research, Brownie had her own table, and was dressed in her inevitable black gown, for her the color of gaiety. No longer living in a ratty efficiency in West Palm Beach, Brownie had moved into a one-bedroom apartment in the massive Palm Beach Towers, a largely Jewish condominium on the very grounds where the Royal Poinciana Hotel had stood. One of the men who had been Brownie's escorts, the late Philip Rauch, gave her the apartment as a life estate.

In recent years, Brownie has learned that she cannot always romp with the most spirited and upscale of crews, and tonight she was stuck with a relatively motley group, though they never guessed that she had taken their measure. She found the whole idea of dressing little better than farmers—given the ball's Western-style dress code—terribly outré, and she was counting the minutes until she could politely leave.

A country music band was playing Hank Williams's "Your Cheatin' Heart," and scores of Palm Beachers were dancing to music that was as peculiar to them as Gregorian chants. Out on the dance floor, all eyes focused on one handsome couple in perfectly matched outfits. They danced, dipping and whirling, immersed in each other's arms, moving gracefully in a style unique to them. They looked like two movie stars from the thirties who had driven their roadster down to the Racquet Club in Palm Springs on a winter weekend and had duded themselves up in country-and-western garb.

At first I did not realize that it was Eric Purcell dancing with Jasmine Horowitz. Eric had met Jasmine a few months after his friend Sonny murdered Amity and committed suicide. Jasmine is as much the woman of Eric's fantasies as Amity had been Sonny's. Jasmine has the semi-emaciated look favored in haute circles and a five-million-dollar wardrobe fitted to the smallest nuances of her frame. She maintains her rail-thin body with astounding discipline. She does not drink, looks at dinner rolls as if they are an illegal drug, and eats only a few string beans or a couple pieces of cantaloupe before pronouncing herself full.

Jasmine has the figure of a teenager, the face of a matron in the full bloom of her beauty, and the hands of an old woman. She has an accent that is as difficult to define as her age. At times she says she is Swiss, though she looks vaguely Middle Eastern, and in other moments says that she is Polish, which is probably the case.

As a young divorcée she married Manfredo Horowitz, who was decades her senior. "I needed a man who would be a god, whom I would admire, and who would be my father image," Jasmine reflects. Manfredo had been one of the primary jewelry dealers in the world, the European representative of Harry Winston. He lived in Monte Carlo but traveled the world. He looked like an ugly Humphrey Bogart, if that is not redundant. He was so stunningly ugly that if he had been a woman he would have been shunned. But with men sexual aesthetics sometimes turn around, and women found Manfredo irresistible.

Manfredo had been married three times before, but when the aging diamond dealer married Jasmine in the mid-seventies, she was his sweet sparrow, his Pygmalion. To him a beautiful woman was the most spectacular of diamonds, and he polished her to perfection and placed her in settings where she shone brilliantly.

In 1994 the couple purchased a large house in the North End. It was here they came each winter, and it was here after the death of her octogenarian husband in November 2006 that Jasmine came alone.

Manfredo had been Jasmine's father, lover, and friend. Eric could be her lover in a way her elderly husband could not be, but he could not be her father, and he was not so much her friend as an ever solicitous manager, watching out for the myriad details of her life. She had lived in a social world where nuance was everything and she knew that Eric was charming and attentive but also that he was a man with a spotted past and a dubious present.

"But you see, now I'm a single lady in Palm Beach," Jasmine says. "People like to gossip about me. Right? And they gossip so much more if sometimes I appear in public with somebody who might really be controversial." Although Eric was Jasmine's escort to the great balls, she did not go with him to the Everglades or to certain parties among certain friends.

Jasmine wanted to worship a man like a god and Eric wanted to worship a woman like a goddess, and emotionally they warily moved around each other. Monique's emotional absence from her son had caused Eric to love her beyond all women with awestruck wonder, and it was that same love that he now pushed upon Jasmine.

Eric is not a man who likes to think about the past, but a shadow of yesterdays hangs over him. He had not even stayed in town for Amity's memorial service, and he shrugged in disregard when Sonny's brother Samuel shot and killed a man during a routine traffic stop and then, when he was likely to face charges of manslaughter, put his service revolver to his head and killed himself.

Eric had gotten a real estate license. He said that he had paid four thousand dollars to have his picture flashing every few minutes above the bar on a television screen for the season at the Italian restaurant Bice. It seemed less an advertisement for real estate as for Eric himself. He probably did not have the dogged determination to succeed in the mercilessly competitive world of high-end real estate, and was far more attuned to a role as paramour of a wealthy, glamorous widow. He stopped drinking and lost twenty pounds and became a perfect physical match for Jasmine.

Thanks to his Belgian mother, Eric was fluent in French and loved to chatter away with Jasmine in that language especially when others were listening. He took her to see Marianne "Mimi" Strong, an agent in New York, with thoughts of having Jasmine do a reality television series on her life, but the agent pooh-poohed the idea. He thought of helping her write her memoir of her life with Manfredo. He hovered around her, seeing in her a future that he saw nowhere else.

THE CANCER BALL IS one of the major events of the season. On the morning of the fiftieth annual gala, Eric and Jasmine got in an argument, and she arrived that evening with another of her standbys.

Events such as this are as much about self-aggrandizement as about charity. Each guest received a 124-page book with 65 full-page color portraits of the benefactors of the evening, starting with the Golden Anniversary Chairmen Patrick Park and Diana Ecclestone, followed by the Honorary Chairman/Chairman Emeritus/Platinum Benefactor Dame Celia Lipton Farris. Then there were the Ambassadors of Hope Mr. and Mrs. Simon C. Fireman, and the Leading Benefactors Mr. and Mrs. Robert G. Gordon. The Gordons had also purchased two other pages to display pictures of their trip to Europe and the Orient and photos of their grandchildren.

Fifty-four-year-old Park has been living in Palm Beach since the late nineties, but he remains one of the few social innocents in town. His weakness, and it is an enormous one, is that he is almost mindlessly generous and good. He is so far from being a showoff that the only speech he ever made in his life was at his daughter's wedding. He works in a family-owned company with his father, Raymond P. Park, and his brothers, Daniel and Kelly. In 1997 *Forbes* called Patrick's father a "classic entrepreneur" who had "built a billion-dollar fortune recycling yesterday's industrial wonders."

Patrick is a big, husky unprepossessing man, a good thirty

pounds overweight. Put a whistle around his neck and he could have been a high school football coach. He loves the beauty of Palm Beach, and he likes doing good big charitable things with the family money. "God has given us a lot," he says, though he is not a man to facilely evoke God's name. "And I feel that wherever we live, we should give to the community and do those things. You know, it would be terrible to move into an area where a charity is one of the biggest industries and not do anything."

Patrick knew that most people did not come to the Cancer Ball because they cared about the charity. They had paid a thousand dollars a ticket for a good time, and as chairman he intended to show them one with food and wine they would not forget.

The evening began with a tour de force of a cocktail buffet almost unprecedented even in the excessive world of Palm Beach charities. Wherever one looked either inside Mar-a-Lago or outside around the pool, there were food stations featuring one incredible delicacy after another: black mountains of caviar, shrimp as big as fists, a sushi boat that could have sailed the seven seas, and oysters, stone crab, and clams in endless assortment. There was such an array of desserts that it could have been a confectioner's convention.

Shannon and Robert Janjigian, from the Shiny Sheet, were both here this evening, as they were at almost all the major social events. The fashion editor noted that "the standouts were the high-drama dresses that glistened in the night" and took photos of ladies in their gowns by Oscar de la Renta, Caché, Giorgio Armani, and Vicky Tiel. When he was finished, he put his camera away and left the party, while Shannon stayed for the evening.

Outside around the pool was an ice sculpture of an enormous martini glass, the perfect symbol for the evening. The guests were eating and drinking with such abandon that they were reluctant to move on into the golden ballroom, but as soon as they did the waiters were there to pour them the first of several fine wines.

The wines that Park served at dinner were even better than those during the cocktail hour. Each was more exquisite than the last, including a 2005 Rocca Bernarda Pinot Grigio; a 2004 Zenato

Ripassa; a 2005 Louis Latour Puligny Montrachet, and a 2001 Lafite Rothschild Pauillac that sells in restaurants for as much as $1,200 a bottle.

Park was the impresario of the food as well and had come up with a unique idea. He would take a signature dish from the leading restaurants to be delivered to the ballroom at the precise moment it was needed. Dinner would start with a green and white vichyssoise from Jean-Pierre, followed by timbale of crabmeat with grilled shrimp from Café L'Europe, the two most celebrated restaurants on the island. Then Café Sapori would prove that West Palm Beach was no culinary slouch either with cavatelli all'aurora, a cheese pasta dish. The main course would be beef tenderloin, a specialty of Mar-a-Lago's chef. Park planned to top it off with a populist dessert, lemon coconut cake from Palm Beach's own Hamburger Heaven.

In the midst of this wine drinker's Oktoberfest, Mr. Las Vegas himself, Wayne Newton, walked out on the dance floor to perform. His pompadour looked as if he had been picked up and dunked head down in an enormous vat of black ink. He wore heels so elevated that they made it seem as if he might topple. His face was so well preserved that one was tempted to offer condolences. His voice had not been as well maintained as his hair, but he was a consummate performer ready to sing a set that would have people on their feet in any lounge from Atlantic City to Vegas. But he was facing one of the more difficult audiences in America.

Palm Beachers are democratic in their rudeness, treating the greatest and the most mediocre equally badly. Newton soldiered on while half the crowd continued talking. One of those listening was Shannon, who little more than a decade ago was not even invited to stay for dinner at the major social events. Now she not only was invited, but she was sitting at the head table alongside chairman Park and Newton who sang a song in her honor.

At 11:20 when dessert had not yet been served at our table and the bottomless glasses of wine had lost their appeal, my wife and I got up to leave, and walked out among the staggering elite of Palm Beach. Droves of people had already departed. As the guests got up, many of them realized that it would be a more difficult journey home than it was getting to Mar-a-Lago. One woman at the head table wandered back up the pathway held up by her husband like a drunken sailor returning from shore leave. Some of the men were so disheveled that their cummerbunds popped up around their midsections and become so twisted that they looked like tourniquets. It was *Animal House* meets *Cocoon*.

THE ANNUAL COCONUTS NEW Year's Eve party is the one event of the season where the hidden aristocracy of the island makes a quasi-public appearance, and is one of the oldest, most revered traditions in Palm Beach. The 2008 event took place not in the ballroom at the Whitehall mansion, where so long ago the Coconuts had cavorted, but at a new glassed pavilion at the Flagler Museum whose centerpiece is Flagler's private railway car running the whole course of the eastern side of the building. Some of the Coconuts had grandparents who had come down to the island in such cars. The twenty-five Coconuts had each contributed $5,000 to put on this evening. David Koch, one of the three Coconut billionaires, anonymously added $250,000 more to pay for fireworks. Each year people dropped on and off the guest list, but to keep the party a reasonable size there was a list of regulars, plus each Coconut could invite four other couples.

Most of the guests began filtering in at around quarter to eleven, many from private dinner parties and private clubs, and some from their homes. The room is a perfect setting for a brilliant party. The Earl Smith Orchestra played wonderfully danceable music. On each table there were party hats and noisemakers. The waiters moved gracefully through the crowd with champagne and chardonnay.

This evening began as a meeting of the tribal clan, a ritual of greeting. Most of these early arrivals knew each other, the twenty-five white-coated Coconuts greeting men in fitted black tie, and women mainly in black gowns.

Shannon stood at the wide entrance to the pavilion with a photographer directing him whose picture to take. Her son, Ian, and his girlfriend stood nearby. Shannon's son is the one deep, true love of her life, and Ian had agreed to come as long as he could leave these Palm Beachers no later than midnight. The Coconuts had invited the *Palm Beach Daily News* society editor because this was the one event where most of them not only tolerated publicity but solicited it. An invitation here was social imprimatur that lasted a season, and even some of the most media reclusive of the Coconuts and guests wanted their picture in the Shiny Sheet.

Brownie was a perennial, but she had turned down her invitation. She had visitors from out of town and had invited twenty-four people to her three tables in the Orange Room at the Everglades. Brownie would have invited Marylou but she was recovering from a stroke and was not in town. Brownie's was the biggest party in the building, an expensive, indeed extravagant evening, but it was a mark of Brownie's panache to live now as she had always lived. Cathleen and Walter also were at the Everglades with a small group. In all her years on the island, Cathleen had never once been invited to the Coconuts, the most telling evidence that she was still not completely accepted by the establishment. Eles had been invited to the Coconuts, as she always was, and she had planned to go after dinner at the Everglades, but she became so weak that she had to go home in the middle of dinner.

The evening at the Everglades was oversubscribed, in part because the B&T had canceled its New Year's Eve, a first in the history of the club. Next door Mar-a-Lago was rocking with bands and midnight fireworks. Some of those B&T members who came to the Everglades were roundly upset by the proceedings. The decorum that was supposedly the mark of the club was being roundly abused. Some members and guests pulled out cameras and cell phones and, violating one of the basic club tenets, took pictures and called friends as if they were standing in Times Square at midnight.

Jasmine arrived at the Flagler Museum with an escort other than Eric, and late in the evening met him at Club Colette, where they danced as if they had spent the whole evening in each other's arms. There the couple saw Dan Ponton, for whom this was the most extraordinary New Year's Eve of his life, and the proprietor of Club Colette was as much a celebrant as anyone. It had been no more than a year and a half ago when he started getting irritable and thought that he must have been working too hard too long. When his tennis game fell apart, the forty-seven-year-old club owner checked that off to age. He had problems with his walk that he tried to pretend was nothing. And when his vision began to fail him, he figured age was a bitch and he'd better get glasses. He went to see several eye specialists who could find nothing wrong. One of them sent him to have an MRI and that procedure discovered that he had a brain tumor, a benign meningioma as big as a fist growing on the frontal lobe of his brain.

Dan was further diagnosed and operated on at Brigham and Women's Hospital in Boston in December 2006. Dr. Arthur Day opened up Dan's skull and operated on him for an astounding seventeen hours before finally sewing him back up. It had happened so quickly that he had hardly contemplated the risk, but in the weeks of recuperation he fully reflected upon the incredible good fortune, and this evening was yet another occasion for celebration.

Also at Club Colette that evening was Barbara Wainscott and her escort. How many evenings she had spent in this room with David, and how long ago it seemed when she had fêted Prince Edward at Elephant Walk for their mutual birthdays and envisioned herself and David at the heights of Palm Beach society. She had had a surgical procedure to lose weight and she looked stunning. She had unfettered pride, a dubious virtue in a single woman of a certain age in Palm Beach, and she was usually alone. She might be here this evening, but she was no longer a major part of the social scene. She came out when the royals were in town, but she preferred largely to stay at home.

For Barbara this evening had a special poignancy, for David had died in February after three years alone in the house on Jungle Road. Barbara's name was not mentioned in the *New York Times* obituary, although the article named his previous ex-wife, in all probability a studied omission, not an oversight.

When David died, he was buried in a cemetery in the small town in Pennsylvania from whence he came. Above his grave there is a tombstone, and on the tombstone is engraving. At the top there is the Star of David that in Palm Beach David sought to keep away from his name. Below there is writing:

DAVID BERGER

BELOVED
SON, HUSBAND, BROTHER
FATHER, FATHER-IN-LAW
GRANDFATHER, UNCLE, FRIEND
WAR HERO, POLITICAL REFORMER,
THE PEOPLE'S LAWYER
SEPT. 1, 1912
FEB. 22, 2007

David was born on September 6, 1912.

THE BEST PARTY, OR at least the party where people had the most fun, was at Mark Brentlinger and Bryan McDonald's open house at their newly renovated home. In a dig at the ultraexclusivity of the island (and the precise opposite of the Coconuts' mandate), the invitations read: "Guests of guests may bring guests." At the stroke of midnight, the muscular bartenders ripped off their shirts, and the new year began.

There were not enough of the old aristocrats to fill the pavilion at the Flagler Museum, and the Coconuts had invited many new people, but as the guests poured in, several of the old-timers told me afterward that they had been filled with a sense of disquiet. They did not know these people, and these people did not know them. There were few couples of stunning appearance, few classic gowns or daring décolletage, and a surfeit of sheer pedestrian ordinariness. And there was a terrible self-consciousness, a killer of delight and spontaneity, and the guests mingled with all the stylized formality of a corporate cocktail party.

The whole model of an American aristocrat is to act unselfconsciously with certainty and grace, but there was a wariness that affected the entire evening and almost everyone. Where once there was glee, there was at best mere conviviality. Where once there was joy, there was social calculation. Where once one knew a couple were a lady and a gentleman by their mere presence, here one knew nothing.

There were hundreds of people, perhaps five hundred in all, overwhelming the white-coated Coconuts and the old world of Palm Beach. Lost in the crowd, the Coconuts looked like scraps of paper tossing on an undulating black sea. What was the point of this evening if one had to greet new people? And why were there so many of them?

When my wife and I arrived, Dick Cowell, a third-generation Palm Beacher whose son is a Coconut, invited us to sit at his table, warning us that we'd better take our places before everything filled up. We sat down but did not stay very long. There would be fireworks at midnight, and almost no one sat at the elaborately set-out tables, picked up the hats and noisemakers, or danced to the music, but moved immediately out onto the patio to wait for the fireworks.

At precisely midnight, the celebrated Gruccis set off a gigantic display of pyrotechnics from two rafts on the Intracoastal Waterway. Looking up into the skies were people like Cowell, who had seen the famous fireworks in Monte Carlo on the evening of Prince Rainier's wedding in 1956, and the display in New York harbor on July 4, 1976, but no one had seen anything as intense and immediate as this. It was not so much fireworks bursting high above, but the sky full of white light, staggering, overwhelming bursts of color.

On and on it went, the acrid smoke drifting across the water, the noise at times like an artillery bombardment, again and again the West Palm Beach skyline illuminated like full noon. Many of these buildings across the water had not been there a decade ago, office buildings and half empty condominiums, teetering on the verge of bankruptcy. And behind them ghettos as dangerous as any in America, and beyond that Latino slums, with handguns going off in the air to celebrate *Año Nuevo.*

Finally, after twenty-two minutes, in one immense burst of light and noise, the display ended, and most of the Coconuts left a party that had in some ways never begun.

The Everglades emptied out about the same time. Brownie drove a few blocks away to the Colony Hotel, where an old acquaintance of hers, Jim Kinnear, a Canadian oil billionaire, was giving a sixtieth birthday bash. He spent a reputed million dollars on Brownie's kind of party, flying in many of his guests and providing them with endless Dom Perignon and caviar, and eighties rock and soul from Daryl Hall and John Oates singing their hits, including "Rich Girl."

When Brownie left at four a.m. most of Palm Beach had long since gone to sleep.

29

The Entitled

I had been living in Palm Beach for fourteen years, and working on this book for at least two years, and still I had not managed to reach the central core, the island within the island.

From the day I set out on this project, people told me it would be incomplete if I did not talk to Pauline Pitt, that she was the queen of the old Palm Beach. Soon after I began my research, I wrote her a letter and tried in many ways to reach her, only to be put off. That did not surprise me. When an anthropologist visits a remote village, it is usually the local drunk or the least favorite ne'er-do-well who greets him or her at the outskirts. It takes a long time to meet the people who truly run the village, and I had almost finished my research when I drove over to Pauline's lakefront home to interview her.

Pauline could have been a character in an Edith Wharton novel, an elegant woman trying to reach out beyond the impregnable walls of class, scaling to the top in daring ascents, looking beyond but always falling back. She is a woman with an intelligence and moral energy beyond the circumscribed walled city of privilege in which she lives.

She is sixtyish, and looks far younger, not in the way that so many Palm Beach women do, with their face-lifted and Botoxed features creating dramatic advertisements for their supposed youth.

She probably has had work done too, but if she has, it is faultless, leaving her a gentle, youthful countenance. There is something almost Oriental in the wrinkleless softness. She also has the voice that Marylou Whitney would like to have had if she had not turned her accent into a theatrical announcement that she is upper class.

For four years in a row, from 2004 to 2007, Pauline chaired the Preservation Ball. It was a perfect fit, for it has become practically the last overwhelmingly WASP event, raising money to preserve the architectural and cultural heritage of Palm Beach. Besides her charity work, Pauline is also an interior decorator working primarily for her friends. In her own house, she has created a bold, eclectic décor: Oriental pieces mixed with antiques, contemporary pieces, family portraits, and artifacts all set together. The rooms do not shout professional decorator, stamping one obvious personal style on everything.

Her maternal grandfather, Charles A. Munn Jr., was one of the founders of the Everglades. He was known as "Mr. Palm Beach" in part because each Christmas he sent out a list of the three hundred people in Palm Beach who mattered, the defining social register of the island. During most of that time there were only a few hundred houses on the island, and he was less like Mrs. Astor naming the four hundred who represented true New York society than the compiler of a fairly obvious directory. When Munn died in 1981, the list was taken over by the Cuban-American sugar magnate Alfonso Fanjul, who bequeathed it to his son, Pepe. It is a far more difficult task to make the list these days, and if the Fanjul roll does not have quite the imprimatur of its early incarnations, it is still a primary social arbiter. The 2007 list is an eclectic one that contains the names of six Fanjuls and two convicted felons, Alfred Taubman and Conrad Black.

Pauline's bloodlines go back in the American and Palm Beach elite a long way on her father's side as well. Her paternal grandfather, George F. Baker, helped found the First National Bank in 1863, when he was only twenty-three years old. He was number four on the first Forbes list of the wealthiest people in America.

His son, George F. Baker Jr., followed his father working for what is now Citibank.

Pauline was brought up with a kind of wealth and privilege more common to the Gilded Age than to women of her generation. The Bakers had a complex of mansions at Park Avenue and East Ninety-third Street that originally had a railroad spur in the basement connecting to tracks beneath Park Avenue. On Long Island her father built two summer homes from which he commuted to Wall Street by sea plane. In Georgia there was a plantation that Pauline remembers with special fondness. And then, of course, there were the winter visits to Palm Beach.

The wealthy are probably no unhappier than anyone else, but their misfortunes often seem to stand out more. For her first husband, Pauline married Dixon Boardman, a man many felt was beneath her, not in wealth but in character. "My beef with Boardman is not his womanizing—it's probably the only good thing about him—but the way he treated a wife to whom he owed everything," wrote the columnist Taki. "To be a cad one has to be a gentleman first, and in my book Boardman gave us cads and womanizers a bad name."

The couple divorced and Boardman imparted further malice, at least in the eyes of observers, in marrying a much younger woman. For her part, Pauline married a man far older, seventy-three-year-old William H. Pitt, who had been married forty-five years to his late wife. There was little danger that he would wander, but six months after they married in 2000 he died. Then five years later, her older brother, sixty-six-year-old George Baker III, died flying his private plane to Nantucket. In 2008 her other brother, Anthony, died flying an experimental plane that he had just purchased.

Pauline had grown up among people who had held their fortunes for several generations, and she had seen so many of them dissipate, if not financially, then psychologically. She had seen how inheritance is often more burden than glory and how without some struggle for meaning life becomes nothing but one flaccid indulgence after another. "I tried with my two children, to say, 'You never know what can happen,'" Pauline says of her two daughters,

Samantha and Serena Boardman. "I sent them to work for a magazine in New York when they were sixteen, not that they were struggling. The idea was you have to get up and do something. And that's been the problem, I think, in a lot of my generation of WASPs and maybe my older brother's generation. So many of them just didn't have any reason to do anything and therefore died of alcoholism or something."

Pauline had been brought up thinking that publicity is something unseemly, a display that has nothing to do with the lives of ladies and gentleman. "I remember my family was horrified, at least, when there was somebody they knew very well who hired a publicist," she recalls. "It just was not heard of." And yet for a time her daughters were princesses of the gossip columns in New York, their exploits as stylish single women followed as avidly in certain circles as the Yankees were in others.

Many of Pauline's contemporaries in Palm Beach are overwhelmed by the money and vulgar energy of the new arrivals to the island. She could have retreated into her shrinking world, dividing her time between the B&T and the Everglades and using the Fanjuls' Christmas list as the only telephone book she ever needed. But like the décor of her house, her friends are an eclectic lot.

When Pauline thinks of wealth, she assumes everyone has a plane. "Mostly today, anybody who's got much has a private plane, right?" she asks, and according to her definition of "much," she is right. She does not have to worry about traveling commercial on what is "said to be the worst leg for any airline, New York to Palm Beach, for any stewardess because it is just the worst behaved people possible." And when she arrives to New York and goes to Michael's or Swifty's or any of the most exclusive restaurants, she does not have to wait for a table either.

One of her close friends is Emilia Fanjul, who had taken a passionate interest in the plight of the people who live in Pahokee and work the sugar fields that allow her family to live in immense wealth in Palm Beach. "I've been out there many times and we've given to her school that she's building, but I mean, they are so poor out there," Pauline says with conviction. "I mean, it's just like a different world. It's like going to Darfur, and it's only an hour away."

I wanted to know whether she thought there is a connection between her friend's family and their business and the way these people are living in this Darfur in the midst of America. And is there something unseemly about the millions of dollars in charity money going to hospitals in Boston, art museums in New York, and research centers in L.A. when ten minutes away lies desperation.

These were the kinds of pesky, imponderable questions that I was asking Pauline. She was clearly not used to thinking much about such matters, and she struggled with them as if they were riddles that could somehow be unlocked.

"A lot of very nice people live here, and those are the ones I focus on," Pauline said, in what could be her motto. As she spoke a lovely little girl in a school uniform from the Day School came walking into the living room.

"Hi, Julia," Pauline said as she walked up and began speaking.

"Tonight it's going to be between thirty-five and forty degrees Fahrenheit," Julia Pitt said matter-of-factly.

Julia looked like Pauline and even acted like her, but she had not always been Pauline's child. Pauline's divorced friend Hethea Nye had adopted Julia shortly before she developed terminal breast cancer. Before she died in 2006, Pauline promised her friend that she would adopt the seven-year-old child. She does not appear to have pondered endlessly over a decision that would change her life the way nothing had in years. It was just what one did.

Pauline went on to talk about Julia's ninth birthday party held in the garden the previous Saturday. She spoke with vivid detail and pleasure the way she had not about the complex contradictions of life in Palm Beach.

"We had, what, over forty kids," Pauline said. "We closed the main gate and we got a big blow-up slide that's about sixty feet high in the air. Giant thing. And a climbing wall. And we had a cotton candy maker. And then we have a little garden over there with a playhouse, a trampoline, and swings. And we had the table loaded with all kinds of sandwiches."

THERE WAS ANOTHER PERSON whom insiders said I had to talk to if my book was going to be authoritative, and that was Stanley M. Rumbough Jr. Even if his first wife had been other than Dina Merrill, daughter of the empress of Mar-a-Lago herself, Marjorie Merriweather Post, Stan has done enough on his own to be considered by some the unheralded, uncrowned king of old Palm Beach, even if he would cringe at such a title. The octogenarian public citizen has been the chairman or the cochairman of the Palm Beach Civic Association for a decade. It is by far the most important civic group on the island and Stan has been involved in most of the crucial issues in the town for a generation. He also has played a nonpareil role in the development of Planned Parenthood in Palm Beach County.

Despite his age and the fact that he lost an eye on the golf course, there is still an exuberant impish quality to the man. He loves Palm Beach with passionate loyalty and devotion. He loves the island the way he loves women, the sheer lines of Palm Beach, the nuances, the subtleties, the grace.

Stan was a student at Yale when the Japanese bombed Pearl Harbor. By 1943 he was a marine fighter pilot flying a Mustang against Japanese islands in the South Pacific. Captain Rumbough flew over fifty missions and some of his friends did not come home. He won two Distinguished Flying Crosses and eight Air Medals.

America won World War II in the scrappy hollows of West Virginia, and the asphalt streets of New Jersey, but the country also won it on the football fields and gyms of Yale. Five hundred and fourteen Yale men died in World War II

These days in Palm Beach honor guards of young marines back from Baghdad escort elderly matrons into the charity ballrooms, and when Iraq veterans are introduced, it is usually amputees or other disabled. But the younger men on the island have rarely served in combat, and neither have their sons and grandsons.

As soon as the war was over, Stan married the twenty-one-year-old actress Dina Merrill, by any definition one of the most desirable women of her time. Not only was she an heiress to a major fortune, but Dina was an accomplished actress whose archetypal blond looks left her stereotyped in roles as a cold, upper-class beauty. She was named to the best-dressed lists, and they were a stunning East Side couple, the epitome of the sophisticated world of New York in the fifties.

Stan was a natural Republican and he was one of the founders of the political movement that worked to draft General Dwight D. Eisenhower to run for president in 1952. When Eisenhower became president, Stan went to Washington to work in the White House as a special assistant.

Although Stan's great-grandfather was one of the founders of the Colgate Company, he is not the toothpaste heir that people often call him. He inherited about $250,000, a large sum to most people, but not the basis of a great fortune. He had to work, and work he did, founding various companies, putting together various deals, and making his own not immodest fortune.

Stan's marriage to Dina lasted nearly two decades, his ex-wife marrying movie star Cliff Robertson after the divorce became final. In 1973 Stan's and Dina's son David died in a boating accident. Stan's second wife, Margaretha, was a Swedish artist, whom he divorced in 1988. His third wife, Janna, whom he married two years later, is a prominent Danish American horsewoman who has won numerous dressage competitions.

When Stan and Janna moved down to Palm Beach permanently, they first purchased a house in midtown in 1990. Five years later, they bought a house on Everglades Island, one of the most exclusive parts of the estate section, for $3.7 million.

I only got to Stan toward the end of my research. The first time I met him, I went to his office at the Palm Beach Towers. He did not talk about his war record or many of his other accomplishments.

"I want to keep Palm Beach the way it is, which is the way I know it," he said firmly. "And so I'm chairman of the Palm Beach

Civic Association, which has over two thousand members and really devote themselves to all types of trying to help keep this town the way it's always been." To Stan the great villain and emissary of unwanted change is Donald Trump, who, by manipulating and threatening, turned a temple of the old Palm Beach into a beachhead of the new.

Stan stays close to his former wives, and Trump had apparently done the unthinkable and the unforgivable by insulting Dina Merrill in one of his innumerable autobiographies. The impresario of the new Mar-a-Lago called Dina "Mrs. Post's arrogant and aloof daughter, who was born with her mother's beauty but not her brains," and described her living in Palm Beach in a "terribly furnished" condo. Stan has never entered the portals of Mar-a-Lago since Trump turned it into a club, and as long as he lives he will never go there.

To Trump publicity is a kind of currency and you can never have enough money in the bank. To Stan it is something repulsive and garish, an ostentatious display of oneself, unseemly and unnecessary. "Most of the people I know do not want to be in the Shiny Sheet unless it's something that they feel is very worthwhile," he said. He was a true amateur athlete and most of his appearances in the papers were when he was in some major competition, playing tennis in an exhibition at the National Doubles Championships in 1951 or golf in the Pebble Beach National Pro-Am in 1986. Other than that, he had no use for publicity. He was only talking to me because of his love of Palm Beach and his hope that I would not get it hopelessly wrong.

"I don't think Palm Beach has changed that much," Stan reflected. "I think there have always been people in Palm Beach that don't fit a gentlemanly mold, or are ostentatious. The population of Palm Beach has not grown, and basically this town is a lot like it was twenty-five years ago. You've been here. What do you think?"

"I think it's changed more in the last fifteen years than in its whole history," I said. "There's immense new money coming in here that doesn't care about the old world of the Everglades and the

B&T. Beyond that, nobody wants to talk about it, but the majority of the town is Jewish, and it's becoming more that way all the time."

"Well, my world hasn't changed at all," Stan replied. "Just let me tell you."

"Stan, listen to me," I said. "Fifty years ago the Jews lived in a ghetto in Palm Beach, going from one hotel to one beach club to one country club. Okay? Now you and your fellow WASPs are in a ghetto. You mainly live in the estate section. You travel between the Everglades and the B&T, and you throw private parties at your clubs for three hundred or so people, and that's everybody in the world that matters."

Stan did not like what I was saying, and he profoundly disagreed with many of my views. "Well, I'm delighted to have met you," Stan said at the end of the interview. "I enjoy your conversation. I enjoy your questions. And I think you probably will write a very interesting book. I won't necessarily agree with some of the aspects of what you write about in Palm Beach. I don't know those aspects because most of the people that I know steer clear of it."

Stan and I saw quite a bit of each other in the next few months, and not for more interviews. One evening he and his wife Janna took me to dinner at McCarty's, a midrange restaurant that is as close to a WASP hangout as there is on the island. Afterward, we attended a Palm Beach Pops concert at the Kravis Center. Stan was cochair of the development committee for the cultural center, and we had the best seats in the house and at intermission took the elevator up to the patron's lounge for champagne.

Then one day in the mail came an invitation for a dinner party at the Everglades. The invitation did not say so, but it was a celebration of Stan's eighty-eighth birthday. I was astounded that we were invited. The Everglades and the B&T are so journalistically restricted that the Shiny Sheet does not even cover events at the two clubs.

I had been to numerous dinners, lunches, and private parties at the club, but when I entered the Everglades that evening, I knew that this was an extraordinary moment. There were about fifty people and it was one of those rare events where nobody asks you who you are or what you do. You are there. That says it all.

During the evening Stan told me the party was off the record. I had finally fallen upon the one event that encapsulated the best of the old Palm Beach, and I could not even write about it. Perhaps that is just as well, for I don't know how well I would have captured the evening. It was not that the conversation was always witty or memorable, but everyone was at such profound ease, and there was such a feeling of warm regard for Stan and the decades of his life. He stood for something, and he was being celebrated as much for that as for his birthday.

There is another man in Palm Beach who brilliantly exemplifies a certain Palm Beach. That is Jimmy Barker, who because he is gay is rarely mentioned as part of the old elite (and was *not* on the Fanjuls' 2007 list!). Whether encountered at his gallery or at a party, he has always been a charming, vibrant presence. During the course of my research, I had talked to him and found him a blithe spirit, a joyous, ebullient man who elevated the spirit of anyone who came within his presence. I had talked to him a few times, about his Kentucky childhood, his decades on the island, and his life as a gay man, and as I was finishing my book I wanted to talk to him again.

I was still seeking some answers, and I thought he might have them. A hundred years ago Henry James made this same writer's journey that I had made. As he looked up at the Royal Poinciana Hotel, he found "it hard to express without some air of extravagance my sense of the beauty." The hotel is long since gone, but the beauty of the island is manifest in a thousand new ways, and I am a witness to that as much as I am to the lives of Palm Beach.

Like James, I too found that few of the lives have the beauty of the surroundings, or the depths of the artistic vision that inspired this island. Everything is larger here, not only the homes, but the opportunity that money brings. Everything is larger here, the disappointments, the unhappiness. Life opens up each morning on a sunrise full of promise, and few set out on glorious journeys to fulfill that promise. There are some who grasp the joy in each moment. There are some who understand how blessed they are, and I thought of Jimmy as one of those.

I kept calling asking for Jimmy and every time a man answered, "This is Jimmy." Each time I had to go through this lengthy dialogue to realize the man on the phone was not James Barker, but rather James Heyman, the sixty-five-year-old mildly disabled friend who for the past eighteen years had lived with Barker and his partner, and had breakfast with him each morning. He was a man reminiscent of the movie character Forrest Gump, painfully slow at times, and then capable of the most astounding insight or perception.

It was a pain to figure out which Jimmy I was talking to, but it was curiously affecting that neither man had taken some other derivative of his name, and everyone had simply to figure out which Jimmy was on the phone. I was not quite sure if Jimmy Heyman was passing my messages on to Jimmy Barker, and almost every day I called, each time I was told that Jimmy Barker was out of town.

Barker was indeed out of town in Louisville for the Kentucky Derby on May 3, and the day after my last call, he had flown into Miami and was driving back to the island when he talked to Jimmy Heyman at the house to tell him he was on his way. About a half hour later, he received a phone call saying that his house was on fire.

It was a major blaze, and when Jimmy Barker arrived, firefighters from Palm Beach and West Palm Beach were pouring water on the fire. They had been there for close to an hour, and nobody had gone inside.

Jimmy Heyman was a man of habit. This time of day, he was likely in the upstairs front west bedroom. The Palm Beach firefighters may go a lifetime without a moment like this one where there may be a living person in a flaming house. They say that they acted with the highest professional standards, but the people on the sidewalk wondered why they did not even try to enter the house. The police and at least one onlooker told the firefighters the room in which Jimmy Heyman might well be found; but they did not raise a ladder and break through the wooden shutter with their axes to see if he was there.

Barker did not know if Jimmy Heyman had gotten out. He did not know if the two dogs, Holly Golightly and Annabel Lee, had gotten out. And when he sought to go inside the house, he was told that was impossible, and he should stand with the other onlookers until the fire was fully put out. Jimmy Barker is not a firefighter. Jimmy is an eighty-year-old man. He knew nothing about fires, but he knew about his friend and he knew about his dogs, and he ran around the block and jumped over a six-foot fence and entered the backyard. He pulled open the sliding kitchen door and entered the smoky kitchen and hunted futilely for the two dogs. Water poured down and he was soaked with sooty water. He walked into the dining room and up the stairs. The air was heavy with smoke, but there was no longer any fire in the main rooms, though the attic was still in flames. Climbing over debris, he hunted for his friend. He moved to the front bedroom, where the fire had not entered and there was only smoke damage, and he knew that if his friend was in the house, this was where he would be. The water was so intense that the roof had fallen on top of the twin beds and Jimmy saw nothing. And then one fireman on a ladder saw Jimmy and yelled at him to leave by the back door, and Jimmy yelled back that he would leave, but he would leave the way he wanted to leave.

And so he came down those stairs, and opened the front door and walked out to where scores of people stood watching. And as he walked into the sunlight, the police say he pushed one of them. Two police officers tackled him, knocking out one of his false teeth, and when they had him down they handcuffed him, and took him to the police station. And though a uniformed police officer went into the house and found the dogs, Holly Golightly died soon after, and the firefighters did not find Jimmy Heyman's body until the next day in the unburned front bedroom.

What is left of Jimmy Barker's house is like a black cave, with shards of memory everywhere, a melted brass statue, a burned remnant of a painting, a few threads of a curtain. He had no insurance, and everything he had collected in a lifetime is gone, yet Jimmy Barker smiles as he always smiled, and walks with a lilt to his gait. Unlike many people on the island, he had always lived beneath his means, and he is far from impoverished. He owns ten acres of land in Nantucket, and he will sell that now and rebuild his house. He had always transcended the games of money and prestige that consume the lives of so many in flames no less brilliant than those that had destroyed his house. He had always lived for his friends, his dogs, and his art, and he lives for them still. He is one of those characters who once lived often within the world of wealth who rarely any longer walk the streets of Palm Beach.

30

Epilogue: Crimes and Misdemeanors

At 7:30 p.m. on the fourteenth of December, 2007, guests began arriving at Club Colette in Palm Beach for a charity dinner/dance for Boston's Brigham and Women's Hospital. The splendidly attired couples left their Rolls-Royces and Bentleys with the valet parkers and entered behind the high hedges to the private precincts. The 144 guests included a veritable social register of the island's elite Jewish families, an overwhelming number of them members of the Palm Beach Country Club.

In her column in the Shiny Sheet, Shannon had dubbed the evening one of the half dozen or so most special events of the season, and so it was. Profoundly thankful to the doctor and the hospital for saving his life, club owner Daniel Ponton decided to celebrate the twenty-fifth anniversary of his club with a $2,500-a-ticket benefit to raise a million dollars for the hospital. Ponton personally gave half a million dollars, and he ensured that every element of this evening was beyond first class.

For months I had been going out almost every night researching my Palm Beach book, and these social occasions had grown increasingly enervating and endlessly redundant. The conversations had been tedious, nothing but mindless politesse—but this evening was different. Those at my table were constantly questioning, probing, analyzing, and challenging in ways that WASP society would have considered impolite, but which I found just the opposite. The conversation was so fascinating that I barely observed the Argentinean tango dancers and half listened to the performance by En Vogue.

At a nearby table sat ninety-four-year-old Carl Shapiro, one of the most revered figures in Palm Beach. It is tempting to conclude that Shapiro's beneficence and generosity helped to give him a good, generous life far beyond the biblical three score and ten. Well into his nineties, the philanthropist walked with the posture of a young man.

At another table this evening sat Shapiro's daughter, Ellen, and her husband, Robert Jaffe. Shapiro had two other daughters, but Ellen was the spoiled one, with a sense of entitlement that affected almost everything she did. Her greatest treasure was her husband Robert. He wore a black dinner jacket tailored to his tall, lean frame.

There was endless Dom Pérignon this evening and by rights a toast should have been made to Bernie Madoff, who was not even in attendance. After all, the philanthropist had mentored the young Madoff, and the latter had reciprocated by managing Shapiro's money in Bernard L. Madoff Investment Securities; it was Madoff, not Shapiro, who was the savvy investor with the Midas touch. Out across that room that evening there were any number of people whose money, or much of it, was with Bernie, silently and certainly increasing in value as they danced the evening away.

Almost a year to the day after that evening at Club Colette, I was about to go out to dinner, when the phone rang. It was a member of the Palm Beach Country Club, telling me extraordinary news. Madoff had just been arrested. Bernard Madoff Securities was said to be nothing but a Ponzi scheme and almost all of the fifty billion dollars in investments was gone.

I drove to Echo, an Asian-fusion restaurant on the island, where one of my close friends, Herb Gray, was hosting a dinner. Herb is from Boston. He is worth about twenty million dollars. Herb's father was a factory worker and he went to New England College of Pharmacy, which later became the Northeastern Pharmacy School. When I had mentioned him to the other guests at Club Colette the previous year, none of them knew who he was. He wasn't rich enough and he didn't belong to the right clubs. He had no interest. He was immensely philanthropic himself and a collector of Boston Impressionist art, but he wasn't one of their kind.

When I mentioned the Madoff scandal to the group at Echo, Herb jumped up from the table. "My God!" he exclaimed. "I've got to call Bob Lappin."

I used to play tennis at the Breakers with Bob and his sons Andrew and Peter. Lappin was a lean, bearded, modest man who spent the winter season at the Breakers, the rest of the year in Swampscott, twelve miles north of Boston. After serving in the Navy in World War II, Lappin made his fortune as the inventor of the Shetland vacuum cleaner, selling it to small appliance stores. I knew little about him except that he had a reputation as an extremely shrewd investor.

Lappin wasn't part of the publicity-seeking charity/social world of the island. He dressed like he was there to fix the plumbing. He played chess outside at the Breakers most afternoons, and for his eighty-fifth birthday in February 2007, his two sons gave him an afternoon playing chess with Susan Polgar, one of the greatest players in the world. It might have been Bob's birthday, but Polgar destroyed him in twenty minutes.

When Herb got off his cell phone, he was ashen-faced. "Bob had his entire charitable foundation and his company's pension plan all with Madoff, and it's gone now, every cent," Herb said. "He's going back to Boston to walk through the wreckage."

The collapse of Madoff took down the entire $8 million of the Robert I. Lappin Charitable Foundation, and Bob immediately terminated the staff and closed the doors. He does not fault himself for gullibility. "I do not berate myself for investing with Madoff," he says. "Over seventeen years, we received confirms of his trades, timely and accurately. Withdrawals were overnight. Nothing suspicious. Two SEC examinations gave him a clean bill of health. And, of course, Madoff was among the most highly respected members of the financial and philanthropic communities.

"In my view, there is no great lesson here. In every generation, from time immemorial, evil people, disguised as paragons of virtue and knowledge, have emerged to take advantage of innocents. Thus spoke Zarathustra, and so it shall be."

THAT EVENING AT ECHO was the first inkling I had of the devastating impact of Madoff's humongous scam. In my sixty-four unit ocean-front building, two owners shuttered their apartments and headed north. In the building across the street, a friend said that he had suffered a "nicking." Only in Palm Beach is a five or ten million dollar loss a "nicking."

I know another Palm Beach man, like Lappin a Jewish veteran of World War II, who had a major fortune. He intended to give almost all of it charity, and now his plans are ashes. There will never be a groundbreaking for that hospital wing, never the cancer research that he planned to fund. He feels he has let people down. He feels a tragic sense of loss, of failure, of shame, of embarrassment.

Every day I kept hearing more stories of devastating losses, of an island home put up for sale for $6.5 million and overnight dropped to half that, of a CEO cleaning out his locker at the Trump International Golf Club never to return, of dreams destroyed and aspirations ended. It's all out there, finished, gone, done.

Among the guests at the Colette party, Shapiro lost an estimated $135 million in his charitable foundation plus over $500 million more of his personal wealth. Scores of the guests had suffered losses, which most of them have tried to keep out of the media.

Beyond the unprecedented fraud that has brought Madoff's investors to their knees, there are the charitable losses, the foundations that are no more, the gifts that have dried up or will never come.

. . .

When Bernie entered the Palm Beach Country Club, he clearly targeted his wealthy religious kin and moved in to pluck away the money of perhaps as many as a third of the three hundred members. These mega-wealthy members have suffered financial losses the implications of which are only slowly being absorbed.

At dinner Christmas Day at the Palm Beach Country Club, there were two sittings and an almost unprecedented turnout. It was as if to say, things are the same, but they are not and everyone knows it. There were some people at the club that evening whose anguish was not over their personal losses, but what would happen to their charities. They were of an age when they had no consuming desires for new luxuries but had reached a stage where they truly wanted to give back.

"I was sitting next to somebody who is going to be fine," recalls one member. "But she lost her charitable trust. And that's all she cares about. That's what's killing her, that she cannot give. Another friend lost fifty million in his charitable trust. That was his whole life. This one man, he is like an angel. That's all he does is give. He does not live a lavish life. He lives well, but that is what his life is about. He's not one to exaggerate, and he said that he's just going to continue with those obligations with whatever he has."

Since his exposure, Bernie had been under house arrest or in jail, but his lieutenants and shills still walk the same streets as his victims. One of Jaffe's oldest friends asserts that his boyhood buddy is far too dumb to have been involved in such a masterful scheme. Even if he had not a suspicion, Jaffe may find himself in serious legal trouble for taking commissions for bringing people into the investments. That is especially true since Jaffe is not currently registered in Florida with FINRA (Financial Industry Regulatory Authority) as a broker, nor has he been since at least 2007.

Jaffe has reportedly tangled physically with a disgruntled investor at Mar-a-Lago, and although the Jaffes were planning to give an elaborate engagement party for their son, Steven, on the second Saturday after his patron's arrest, they cancelled. At least one of the guests thought better of sending a gift to the son and future daughter-in-law of a man who had become a mega-loser. She called the shop on Worth Avenue from which she had bought an exquisite crystal piece and said that if her gift hadn't been shipped yet, she wanted it cancelled.

That was not the end of Jaffe's humiliations. He and his wife stepped down from chairing the Dana-Farber Cancer Institute Ball. Another mega-wealthy Boston couple, Michele and Howard Kessler, took over as honorary chairs. In a sign of public mourning, the event, though not the ticket price, was downgraded from formal dress to cocktail wear, though mourning wear would have been more appropriate.

Shapiro faces the possibility that everything he has stood for and accomplished may turn to nothing but retribution and pain. It is not simply that he has lost over half a billion dollars, but that the hundreds of millions of dollars he has given to charity may have been largely ill-gotten gains. Almost nothing is certain any longer.

A member went up to Shapiro at lunch at the Palm Beach Country Club and commiserated with him over his enormous losses. Shapiro looked out from his plate full of food and said, "I'm still eating." Perhaps that is the only sure pleasure he has left.

The overwhelming response of the victims was immense, inchoate anger that spilled over on anyone or anything that came into their purview. Jaffe seemed not to care or notice but went out night after night, often to Club Colette or to his favorite restaurant, Bice. When *20/20* came down to the island doing a major piece on Madoff, producer Anna Schecter stood outside the Italian restaurant with her small camera in her hand. When Jaffe emerged, Schecter says she asked Jaffe if she might film him. "You're a bad girl," Jaffe said, and knocked the camera to the ground.

AND DESPITE JAFFE'S continued patronage, the restaurants on the island were often half empty, even though the proprietors were offering dinner specials that they previously had offered only in the off-season. The stores on Worth Avenue had 40-percent-off sales, which they had never had before—and still the customers did not come.

The perfect metaphor for the profligate life of the island was Trillion, a store on Worth Avenue that proudly announced it was about money, and would have sat comfortably between establishments named Ostentatious and Indulgence. Trillion was one of Bernie's favorite stores, and shortly before his arrest, he purchased a pair of cashmere slacks for two thousand dollars. It was excess beyond excess and suggested how money had become God and squandering money a form of worship, a public ritual that only the anointed could pursue. Bernie had not picked up his slacks, and now he was in jail and the slacks were back on a rack with other goods that suddenly seemed wildly excessive and foolish.

Part of the problem was Bernie and part was the recession. It was a time of reckoning, but the diminished Shiny Sheet stepped around the crisis like some unpleasantness on the sidewalk. And everyone seemed to turn inward, especially at the Palm Beach Country Club, where members talked about the Madoff disaster in whispers and subtle asides.

Many of the women in the club attended a luncheon lecture series at the Kravis Center, an enviable occasion to get away from the endless talk of the merciless con. In March, Lee Wolf, who is a member of the country club, gave a talk on Woody Allen's classic film, *Crimes and Misdemeanors.*

Wolf had seen her fellow club member Madoff over the years and knew any number of people who had lost fortunes to the con artist. For months, she had observed the change in the lives at the club, and in her lecture she compared Madoff to Dr. Judah Rosenthal, the film's main protagonist, and turned the twenty-year-old movie into a metaphor for the world in which Madoff operated.

As the film opens, the distinguished ophthalmologist is being honored at a charity event. The setting could easily have been the ballroom of the country club, the guests largely indistinguishable from those in the Kravis Ballroom. And the praise and self-satisfaction and adoring family could have been Madoff's, not Rosenthal's. The good doctor has a loving wife (Claire Bloom) who knows nothing about his airline stewardess mistress, Dolores (Anjelica Huston).

Dr. Rosenthal has tired of his brash, emotionally demanding mistress, but Dolores refuses to give up the relationship and threatens to tell his wife and to expose his misappropriating money from his own charity. With the help of his lowlife brother Jack (Jerry Orbach), Dr. Rosenthal hires a hit man, who murders Dolores. Before the body is discovered, the doctor returns to her apartment to retrieve love letters and other incriminating evidence. In the end, the crime is pinned on a drifter with other murders to his credit, and Dr. Rosenthal's life goes on as before.

Crimes and Misdemeanors is the story of upscale Jews brought up with a belief in a moral God who holds their every action up to higher scrutiny. In the film, the bearers of this biblical wisdom are old or dead or commit suicide. They speak with the heavy accents of Central and Eastern Europe. Everyone else in the film speaks in an American idiom and lives in a morally denatured world, where they may mumble their prayers and speak the truths of an ancient faith, but these are mere homilies devoid of meaning.

"There is no God, no adjudicator, no purpose," Wolf said. "Madoff is not an anomaly. These are the poisonous butterflies that are born from this toxic chrysalis. Madoff is the by-product of all this moral decay. We live in a world that by and large is designed to protect material wealth at all cost. And human values are so subordinate to what you accumulate. You see it in the killing in the film. What is she but an insect, a poor nobody to be stamped out? She got in the way of the doctor protecting his ownership of his terrain. His wife looked upon him as a God, and he played God.

"I think that's what Ruth Madoff saw in Bernie. He provided her with everything. He brought her into the mega–American dream. People looked at him as a demigod. That's what he was and he had to keep producing for them. Bernie was the only God we truly worship now, God, the creator of wealth, the ultimate value. And God did what he had to do."

When Wolf finished, there was a long silence followed by sustained applause and a raft of questions, hands waving all over the ballroom. Some people spoke to the subject of the talk. Others had no inkling that Wolf was talking about this world of Palm Beach as much as she was talking about Madoff or Woody Allen's film. And some people were bewildered by this strange talk.

"What's the big deal?" one woman asked, her voice charged with irritation. "The doctor got away with it. He got away with it. What's the big deal? Why are we even talking about it?"

On the island, two days after Christmas, the New York Rabbi Marc Schneier spoke to a standing-room-only crowd at the New Synagogue. No one had to announce the topic, for there was only one subject on people's minds.

"This is the greatest financial devastation in the history of Jewish philanthropy," the forty-nine-year-old rabbi said. "The scam of the century, orchestrated by one man, Bernie Madoff. In response to this unparalleled Ponzi scheme, I say shame on us, shame on our community, and shame on our society, for promoting valuables at the expense of values, for elevating men and women to positions of prominence based on their wealth rather than their worth. We need to take a hard look at ourselves, at our materialistic society."

It was a lesson not only for those in the synagogue that evening, but for everyone in Palm Beach.

Acknowledgments

When Hyperion's new editor in chief, Will Balliett, said that he would be editing my manuscript, it was as if Bill Gates were coming over to fix my computer. I was honored that I merited such attention but wondered if he would be able to stay long enough to do the job. Not to worry. Will found time at dawn and midnight, and did an extraordinary job. He was joined in this process by executive editor Leslie Wells. Will's assistant, Bijani Mizell, was a tiger for details, as is her succesor, Nina Shield. As the compelling cover makes obvious, Phil Rose is a creative director where the emphasis is decidedly on the adjective. The new president of Hyperion, Ellen Archer, has been a strong force behind this book. Beth Gebhard, executive director of publicity, proved her acumen immediately by signing on Sally Anne McCartin to work on this book. I also must tuck in a thank-you to Will Schwalbe, the former editor in chief, and Bob Miller, the former president, who brought this project to Hyperion.

Madness Under the Royal Palms has my name on the cover, but it could not have been written without the assistance of many people. A number of my sources asked that their contributions remain anonymous, and I also want to thank them. Some of those mentioned may have sat for several interviews, and to those whose names do not appear in the main text, I offer my apologies and sincere appreciation. Others mentioned below were not interviewed, but provided other sorts of assistance. I would like publicly to thank: Abe Gosman, Agnes Ash, Alexandre de Bothuri, Allan Reyes, Allen Maines, Anneli Ganger, Arianna Comstock, Arnold Scaasi, Ashley Swain, Barbara Cohn, Barbara Wainscott, Beatrice Cayzer, Bennett Cohn, Bill Toulouse, Bob Andrews, Bob Keifer, Bob Moore, Brian Bohlander, Brigitte Keil, Bruce Bent, Bruce Sutka, Bruce Zeidel, Cathleen McFarlane Ross, Celia Lipton-Farris, Chief of Police Michael S. Reiter, Chris Ruddy, Clifford Klenk, Craig Bachove, Cynthia Friedman, Dale Coudert, Dagmar Lowe, Dan Ponton, Dan Swanson, Dennis Gallo, Deputy Fire Rescue Chief Brodie Atwater, Detective Peter Hardiman, Diana Stanley, Dick Cowell, Dick Nernberg, Dimick Reese, Don Earhardt, Dorothy Sullivan, Dr. Frank Vaccaro, Dr. Gregory Boyajian, Dr. Stephen Alexander, Dr. G. Heath King, Eddy Louis, Eles Gillet, Eric Purcell, Etonella Christlieb, Evalena Holgren, Frances Fisher, Frank Carruth, Fred Keller, George Kerr, Gunilla von Post, Harvey Oyer III, Henry Mehlman, Herb Gray, Hillie Mahoney, James Barker, James Fadiman, James Sheeran, Jan West, Jasmine Horowitz, Jean Tailer, Jeffrey A. Cloninger, Jeff Diamond, Jeffrey Fadiman, Jesse Newman, Jim Anderson, Jim McCann, Joe Idy, John Blades, John Herring, John Hendrickson, John Sullivan, Jonathan Berger, Judy Schrafft, Kate Ford, Kelly Layman, Ken Thompson, Kyle Zimmer, Larry Gold, Larry Keller, Leslie Keller, Leslie Spero, Lydia Crozier, Mae Bell Lin, Marilyn Riseman, Mark Brentlinger, Mark Kupic, Martin Haines, Marylou Gray, Marylou Whitney, Mildred McLean, Mimi Landau, Mort Kaye, Mrs. John Volk, Nanci Hewitt, Natalie Kalinka Paavola, Parker Ladd, Pat Cook, Pat Kocak, Patrick Flynn, Patrick Park, Patti Spero, Patty Myura, Paul Rampell, Paula Roth, Pauline Pitt, Pene Latham, Peter Rock, Pierre David, Renee Fadiman, Robert Ganger, Robert Montgomery, Rose Sachs, Sally Roche Higgins, Shannon Donnelly, Sharon Keller, Sheila Johnson, Sherman Adler, Steve Ross, Stan Rumbough, Stephen Richardson, Steven Stolman, Sumner Kay, Susan Markin, Susan Nernberg, Terri Vaccaro, Tony Legett,

Tony Senecal, Tyler Buchanan, Vicki Bagley, Walter Ross, Warrington Gillet III, and Wolfgang Keil.

I would especially like to thank several of my fellow authors who read parts of the manuscript: Kai Bird, Nigel Hamilton, Burton Hersh, Dr. G. Heath King, and my brother Edward Leamer. Several other friends also read parts of the manuscript, including my daughter Daniela Mantilla, and Kristina Rebelo Anderson. My wife, Vesna, not only read the manuscript at every stage, offering her own unique insights, but took care of all sorts of matters that allowed me to focus on writing this book. My agent, Joy Harris, watched over the project with the detailed concern that is her trademark.

I must also thank Susan Swiatosz, the archivist at the Flagler Museum, and her equally dedicated colleagues, Kae Jonsons and Debi Murray at the Historical Society of Palm Beach County. The Palm Beach County Library was highly helpful, as was the Library of Congress. I also would like to acknowledge a few people in Palm Beach who had nothing to do with this book but in various ways have helped me: Alice Hodach, Jorge Quezada, Paula Lannoti, Rose Carnicelli, Mary Flynn, Linda McDonald, and the late Theresa Tacoma.

And then there is the late James Jennings Sheeran, publisher of *Palm Beach Society*. During most of my research, we had lunch once a week and he was immeasurably helpful to me. Nobody knew Palm Beach as well as he did or loved it so deeply. I am dedicating *Madness Under the Royal Palms* to his memory.

Notes

Chapter One

5 Barbara Wainscott blew out: Interview, Barbara Wainscott.

10 "a marvel indeed . . .": William James, *The American Scene*, (1907), p. 426.

11 "the inordinate desire . . .": Ibid, p. 434.

12 "It is not a good sign . . .": *Palm Beach Daily News*, February 28, 1898.

Chapter Two

14 Barbara and David had already: Interview, Wainscott.

14 "refugee rags": *Chicago Tribune*, April 19, 1941.

16 William alleged: *Wichita Eagle*, March 8, 1998.

17 He had charged: Interview, Dan Ponton.

18 "Strong contender . . ." *Palm Beach Post*, December 10, 1989.

19 "Prince Edward plans . . .": *Palm Beach Daily News*, March 5, 1997.

21 "used to utterly utter . . .": *New York Times*, January 30, 2000.

Chapter Three

27 "we of northern European . . .": Fred Keller gave me almost complete access to his personal and legal files including the various, largely unpaginated versions of his memoir.

27 "I simply felt . . .": Fred Keller memoir.

28 One evening Fred stood: Interview, Fred Keller.

28 "slapped me in the head . . .": Paul Keller, *Isthmus*, unpublished manuscript, p. 139.

29 Brian was the only son: Interview, Brian Bohlander.

29 "I was going to lose my kids . . .": Interview, Fred Keller.

30 He told with relish: Ibid.

31 Fred ended up suing: Interview, Fred Keller and Paul Keller manuscript.

32 "Palm Beach Millionaire . . .": *Palm Beach Post*, November 12, 2003.

33 On one of the sheets: Document courtesy of Pene Latham.

33 "I am hoping . . .": Ibid.

34 "You're not ever . . .": Interview, Pene Latham.

34 I've never been . . .": Ibid.

34 He told her he would pay: Ibid.

35 Fred studiously observed: Interview, Fred Keller.

Chapter Four

36 "They see the old masters . . .": Interview, Eddy Louis.

38 In Beirut, his father: Ibid.

39 Before the couple moved: Interview, Eddy Louis.

40 "I wasn't really a": Interview, Eric Purcell.

40 His mother shipped: Ibid.

41 "It's a big mistake . . .": Ibid.

42 Eric's father was technically: Ibid.

43 One evening in February 1995: Ibid and court documents in the State of Florida v. Eric Pfenniger.

44 "We should talk, . . .": Interview, Eric Purcell.

44 "Well, actually, I did, if the truth . . .": Ibid.

44 She was diagnosed: Consultation Report, Kendell Eye Institute, Miami, November 7, 1995.

45 Eric declared himself insolvent: Interview, Eric Purcell and State of Florida v. Eric Pfenniger.

Chapter Five

47 "an albino raccoon . . .": William Wright, *Ball:A Year in the Life of the April in Paris Extravaganza* (1972), p. 11.

47 that was what she said: Interview, Mildred McLean.

48 Brownie is the only invitee: *Palm Beach Post*, December 30, 2002

50 "Leave it alone . . .": Interview, Mildred McLean.

50 "I was a big girl . . ." Ibid.

51 "She and I . . ." Ibid.

53 May 1953, she married: *New York Times*, May 7, 1953.

53 the interest on the fortune: Evalyn Walsh McLean, *Queen of Diamonds* (2000), p. 222.

54 sent to Hewitt School: *New York Times*, June 12, 1966.

54 "Men are lost here . . .": Interview, Mildred McLean.

Chapter Six

57 Addison was the seventh: Caroline Seebohm, *Boca Rococo* (2002), p. 23.

57 One day in 1917: Ibid., p. 150.

57 Singer was the next to youngest son: Peter Kurth, *Isadora: A Sensational Life* (2001), p. 249.

58 "What do you see . . .": Ibid, p. 157.

60 He was a gay man: Ibid., p. 201.

60 "Say anything you want about me . . .": "The Florida Home" in *Arts & Decoration* (undated), Courtesy Historical Society of Palm Beach County.

60 "I aim to please . . .": *Palm Beach Post*, January 27, 1926.

61 "unlawful for anyone . . .": *Chicago Daily Tribune*, April 15, 1945.

61 There was genial applause: Cocoanuts of 1924" in *Palm Beach Life*, undated, p. 17, Archives of Palm Beach County Historical Society.

62 One year Brownie: Interview, Mildred McLean.

63 Three years later, in 1975: *New York Times*, July 8, 1975.

63 James Sheeran, the witty publisher: Interview, James Sheeran.

Chapter Seven

66 Eddy said that touching: Interview, Eddy Louis.

67 Vera had told her closest: Interview, Mimy Laudau.

67 "Okay, that's my face . . .": College project by Renee Fadiman.

67 "three or four glances . . .": *Palm Beach Daily News*, March 9, 1997.

69 The four-times-married cereal heiress: Nancy Rubin, *American Empress: The Life and Times of Marjorie Merriweather Post* (1995), pp. 348–9.

70 Fadiman was an austere: Interviews, Jeffrey and James Fadiman.

70 "You'll never be pretty . . .": Interview, James Fadiman.

70 "My mother equated . . .": Interview, Jeffrey Fadiman.

71 They could not abide: Interviews, Jeffrey and James Fadiman.

73 In October, after the death: Interviews, Eddy Louis and Jeffrey and James Fadiman.

75 "I want the pills . . .": Interview, Jeffrey Fadiman.

75 "Oh please . . .": Interview, Meaghan Karland.

76 "Get the fuck out of the way . . .": Palm Beach Police Department Incident Report, May 2, 1998.

76 "I've got more balls than you! . . .": Interview, Eddy Louis.

76 Sergeant Diana Burfield drove: Palm Beach Police Department Incident Report, May 2, 1998.

76 "CIVILIAN CHAPLAIN ARRESTED . . .": *Palm Beach Daily News*, March 31, 1999.

76 The following Sunday, the editorial cartoon: Ibid., April 9, 1999.

Chapter Eight

79 David picked Barbara: Interview, Barbara Wainscott.

80 Jonathan could not conjure: Interview, Jonathan Berger.

80 Three times a day: Interview, Barbara Wainscott.

81 Lehmanns, Warburgs, and Seligmans: Stephen Birmingham, *Our Crowd* (1967), p. 402.

81 Jewish entrepreneur, A.M. Sonnabend: *New York Times*, May 14, 1944.

81 "We must at any cost . . .": *Palm Beach Life*, April 1979, pp. 71–2.

81 "We must at any cost . . .": *Palm Beach Life*, April 1979, pp. 71–2.
82 The following year: *New York Times*, February 12, 1964.
82 In early 1965, the Anti-Defamation League: *New York Times*, March 13, 1965.
83 "You guys have a lot . . .": Discussion, Richard and Susan Nernberg.
85–96 Please go to Leamer.com/endnotes to read the additional notes for this revised edition.
92 eight million dollars, plus three million: Donald Trump, *The Art of the Comeback* (1997), p. 64.
93 "You don't understand the demographics . . .": Interviews, Paul Rampell and Robert Moore.
94 suing the town for fifty million: *Palm Beach Post*, November 6, 1997.
96 "One . . . two . . . three . . . four . . . five . . . six . . .": Interview, Nanci Hewitt.

Chapter Nine

98 Tony has seen the movie: Interview, Tony Senecal and *Charleston Daily Mail*, May 30, 1997.
99 Just before the club opened: Interview, Tony Senecal.
100 "concentration": *Miami Herald*, April 22, 1998 and Robert Frank, *Richistan* (2007), p. 116.
101 He was picking up the phone: Interview, Tony Senecal.
101 The story got into the newspapers: Interview with B&T member, OTR.
101 became the company's best-selling perfume line: Interview, Michael Gibbons.
102 One day a woman arrived: Interviews, Steve Greenwald and David Day.
103 a tacit agreement: Interview, Tony Senecal.
103 Trump's own Boeing 727: *Miami Herald*, April 8, 2007.
103 sue Palm Beach County: *Palm Beach Post*, June 15, 1995.
103 The county promised: *Palm Beach Post*, September 4, 1996.
104 Nothing pleased them: Interview with caddy, OTR.
104 killed the rare bird: *Palm Beach Post*, January 13, 2001.

105 In February 2007, club: Interview, Tyler Buchanan and Tyler Buchanan, Plaintiff, vs. Irving Stein, Defendant in the court of the Fifteenth Judicial Circuit of Florida.

Chapter Ten

106 his two Mercedes-Benz 560Sls: *South Florida Sun-Sentinel*, April 2, 1990.
107 Until the last few years: Interview, Eles Gillet.
107 "When the Whitneys get here . . .": "Weddings, Parties and People," by Earl Blackwell, *Town and Country*, April 1965, p. 20.
107 One evening she rode: "Gentlemen Prefer Marylou" by Michael Shnayerson, *Vanity Fair*, August 1995, p. 155.
108 The day after: *New York Times*, September 14, 1963.
108 Marylou was such a socially unacceptable match: *New York Times*, November 25, 1967.
108 "at least five press agent . . .": *Vanity Fair*.
108 "You know you have to let a man . . .": Jeffrey L. Rodengen, *The Legend of Cornelius Vanderbilt Whitney* (2000), p. 123.
108 "He loved for me to . . .": Interview, Marylou Whitney.
109 "If he was morose . . .": Ibid.
109 "I know you're a friend . . .": Rodengen, p. 137.
109 "the frightening spectre of old age . . .": C.V. Whitney, *High Peaks* (1977), p. 103.
110 Late at night, she had: Interview, Eles Gillet.
110 seventeen gowns: *Palm Beach Daily News*, February 16, 1992.
110 "I feel like this is a Cinderella world . . .": Ibid.
110 a hundred or so porcelain dogs: *Miami Herald*, May 25, 1998.
111 At the 1992 Red Cross Ball: *Palm Beach Post*, February 1, 1992.
111 "Marylou, if you get": Interview, James Barker.
111 "My oldest son said, 'You . . .": Interview, Marylou Whitney.
112 "Nice *nothing*! . . .": Interview, Barbara Wainscott.
112 $2.8 million: Palm Beach County Property Appraiser Public Access System.
112 nine hundred thousand dollars more: Ibid.

Chapter Eleven

114 "All I'm asking for, Fred . . .": Interview, Fred Keller.

115 Flagler had initially come: Edward N. Akin, *Flagler: Rockefeller Partner and Florida Baron* (1991), p. 72.

115 In January 1891: Susan E. Tifft & Alex S. Jones, *The Patriarch: The Rise and Fall of the Bingham Dynasty* (1991), p. 58 and David Leon Chandler with Mary Voelz Chandler, *The Binghams of Louisville* (1987), p. 23.

116 He vested a million and a half: Tifft and Jones, p. 59.

116 generous to Mrs. C. W. Foote: David Leon Chandler, *Henry Flagler* (1986), p. 115.

116 "rather plain of face . . .": Misstatements and inaccuracies in Prof. Sidney Walter Martin's book *Florida's Flagler* (1949) as notated by Harry M. Flagler in his copy of the book. Courtesy Flagler Museum.

117 the most authoritative researchers: Chandler and Voelz Chandler, p. 214 and Tifft and Jones, p. 66.

117 "young, beautiful, the whole world . . .": The deposition of Rosemarie Keller, January 24, 2003, in Re: the Marriage of Fred Keller and Rose Keller.

118 He said that he fought: Fred Keller memoir and interview, Fred Keller.

119 "likely to become a public charge": Antenuptial Agreement between Rosemarie Keil and Fred Keller, July 1, 1992. in Re: the Marriage of Fred Keller and Rose Keller.

120 "How's that cunt marry . . .": Transcript of recorded message on Fred Keller's answering machine, June 28, 1993 in Re: the Marriage of Fred Keller and Rose Keller.

121 She also convinced: Interviews, Wolfgang and Angela Keil.

122 The event was for charity: Interview, John Herring.

122 "Rose ended up . . .": Interview, Jeff Diamond.

123 "Lawsuits are Fred's . . .": Interview, Bennett Cohn.

123 squeezed a pool table: Interview, Dr. Stephan Alexander.

124 "I'm a German wife . . .": Interview, Fred Keller.

125 "That was the first time . . .": Ibid.

125 "I misled her, no . . .": Ibid.

Chapter Twelve

128 It took a while for Shannon: Interview, Shannon Donnelly.
129 "I knew it was a step . . .": Interview, Barbara Wainscott.
129 named corporate chairman: *Palm Beach Daily News*, February 6, 1996.
130 "It doesn't matter . . .": *Washington Times*, February 6, 1996.
131 "So, which one will it be?" *Palm Beach Daily News*, February 6, 1996.
132 "He was not the kind . . .": Interview, Barbara Wainscott.
132 distinguished himself: Interview, OTR.
132 No one realized: Interview, Barbara Wainscott.
133 "I told her I wanted . . .": Interview, James Sheeran.
133 contemporaries tried to get: Interview, Dan Ponton.
134 Only David, Shannon: Interviews, Shannon Donnelly and Dan Ponton.
135 "Prince Philip says . . .": Interview, Barbara Wainscott.
135 One evening she was invited: "Driving Mrs. Whitney" by Charlotte Hays, *New York*, August 17, 1998.

Chapter Thirteen

138 "Expenses Edward": *Mail on Sunday*, January 21, 1997.
139 his fee a reported two hundred thousand dollars: *Mail on Sunday*, March 7, 1999.
140 "members and guests are . . . ": Bath and Tennis Rules and Members 2006-2007.
142 "Let me ask you a question, Larry . . .": Interview, Larry Gold.
142 "In the marquis's dining room . . .": Stendhal, *The Red and the Black*, translated by Burton Raffel (2004), p. 241.
143 Dixon had worked: *Philadelphia Daily News*, August 3, 2006.
144 "He's not going . . .": Interview, Barbara Wainscott.
144 Dixon said that it was: Interview, OTR.
145 "I've never in my . . .": Interview, Barbara Wainscott.
145 "Barbara called me . . .": Interview, Shannon Donnelly.

Chapter Fourteen

147 "I have no friends . . .": Ibid.

147 circulation of around 7,000: Bloomberg.com, August 12, 2008.

150 "Every single picture in the paper today is Jewish . . .": Interview, Shannon Donnelly.

150 "Which side is the better . . .": Interview, Agnes Ash. Mr. Gordon does not have specific memories of this but says that it might well be true.

150 Much of the Gordon family money: Discussion, Bob Gordon.

151 "I was still so unsophisticated . . .": Interview, Shannon Donnelly.

152 On Thanksgiving 1992, Shannon: Ibid.

152 she was making $47,210 a year: Shannon Donnelly provided her income tax statement.

154 Miller began by buying: *Palm Beach Post*, September 23, 1995.

155 "they laughed—they thought it was funny.": *Palm Beach Post*, March 16, 1997.

155 84,626-square-foot monolith: Palm Beach County Property Appraiser Public Records.

155 It takes two hundred thousand: *Palm Beach Post*, April 29, 2007.

156 "My intent has been to maintain . . .": *Palm Beach Daily News*, October 6, 2004.

156 "Knocking a building . . .": *Palm Beach Daily News*, October 17, 2004

157 "Maybe it was more a woman's . . .": Interview, Dan Swanson.

Chapter Fifteen

160 "The reason I like you . . .": Interview, OTR.

161 "Not only does she know . . .": Interview, Eric Purcell.

161 "Meaghan's always with me . . .": Interview, Ibid.

163 "I'm enjoying it . . .": Ibid.

163 "Terry Von Pantz has died . . .": Interviews, Meaghan Karland and Eric Purcell.

163 "Your Honor, I see the past . . .": Letter Eric Purcell to Judge Leesfield, November 24, 1997, in The State of Florida v. Eric Pfenniger.

163 In February 1998, after Eric agreed: Order vacating of sentence, February 1998 in State of Florida v. Eric Pfenniger.
165 "He wanted to care, and he could not care . . .": "Winter Dreams" in F. Scott Fitzgerald, *All the Sad Young Men* (1926), p. 90.
165 "spit in her face": Interview with Eric Purcell by Officer Thomas R. McLaughlin, November 2, 2006, Palm Beach Police Department Incident Report.
165 except for an item: *Palm Beach Post*, March 30, 2007.

Chapter Sixteen

168 "That's right—$1 million . . .": *Palm Beach Daily News*, February 18, 2001
169 "Young lady, do you know who I am? . . .": Interviews, OTR.
170 After pledging $750,000: *Palm Beach Post*, March 14, 2004
171 "The enemy I had was Shannon Donnelly . . .": Interview, Simon Fireman.
171 "I took the executive director . . .": Interview, Shannon Donnelly.
171 "the crowd was made up . . .": *Palm Beach Daily News*, January 31, 2005.
171 The Red Cross announced: *Palm Beach Post*, September 24, 2006.
173 "There's a lesson in . . .": *Palm Beach Daily News*, February 1, 2006.
173 "return to dignity . . .": Ibid., January 29, 2007.
173 "Woman of Distinction": Ibid., February 20, 2002.
174 Schur wanted to know: *Palm Beach Post*, May 19, 2002.
174 He picked up the phone: Ibid.
174 given ten years' probation: Ibid., November 27, 2002.
174 Even that was too onerous: Ibid., February 24, 2004.
176 "she and Heine . . .": Detective Michele D. Pagan interview with Abby Ruttenberg, November, 28, 2004. Palm Beach Police Department Incident Report.
176 "If we threw everyone . . .": Interview, OTR.

Chapter Seventeen

177 "invalid mother": *Boston Globe*, August 9, 2005.

178 turned one of the organizations: *Washington Post*, May 26, 1992.

178 "I must admit . . .": *Boston Globe*, November 15, 1995.

178 "I want to have a . . .": *Boston Globe*, November 29, 1995.

179 after only five dates: *New York Post*, February 20, 2001.

179 "one percent (1%) of the value of . . .": Agreement between William I. Koch and Angela B. Gauntt, November 22, 1996, part of Koch V. Koch, Palm Beach County.

180 punched her in the stomach: Angela Browder Koch's Motion for Temporary Relief, Koch v. Koch.

180 "to beat his whole . . .": *Boston Globe*, July 20, 2000.

180 her husband had not threatened: Angela B. Koch to William Koch, November 9, 2000, Exhibit A. in Koch v. Koch.

180 "Every marriage has its . . .": Ibid.

180 "absolutely scurrilous": *Palm Beach Daily News*, November 4, 2000.

181 "an alcohol abuse problem": Hearing before the Honorable John Phillips, Koch v. Koch, October 12, 2000.

181 "to preclude the wife from . . .": Husband's Response to Wife's Motion for Temporary Relief, Koch v. Koch.

181 "the resolution of the criminal charges . . .": *Palm Beach Daily News*, November 15, 2000.

181 buy an 8,986-square-foot mansion: Palm Beach County Appraiser Public Access.

181 He came to South Florida: *Palm Beach Daily News*, March 25, 2001.

182 "caused some jaws . . .": *Palm Beach Daily News*, January 6, 2002.

182 In 1991, she and . . .: *Palm Beach Post*, June 21, 1991.

182 couple was a public item: *Palm Beach Daily News*, December 26, 2001.

182 This evening was a 1970s: *Palm Beach Daily News*, May 5, 2002.

183 purportedly fourteen years old: *Palm Beach Post*, July 7, 2008.

183 Alan Dershowitz and Kenneth Starr: *Palm Beach Post*, February 13, 2008.

183 "The slow, dissatisfying resolution . . .": *Palm Beach Post*, July 7, 2008.
184 "fantasy world": *Palm Beach Post*, September 18, 2005.
184 "I liked looking at it . . .": *Palm Beach Daily News*, December 31, 2000.
185 35,000 bottles: *Chicago Tribune*, March 8, 2007.
185 "narcissistically titled": *Boston Globe*, September 2, 2005.
185 "unrepentantly lowbrow": *Boston Herald*, January 21, 2006.
186 planning to tear down: Interviews, OTR and *Wall Street Journal*, July 11, 2008.
187 The previous owner: *Miami Herald*, June 26, 1988.
188 131-foot yacht *Octopussy*: *Palm Beach Post*, April 27, 1989.
188 Four years later, he bought: *Boston Globe*, August 8, 1991.
188 he sold Mediplex once again: *Boston Herald*, January 5, 1994.
188 Abe pensioned off: *Boston Globe*, November 20, 1991.
188 He eventually settled: *Palm Beach Post*, May 18, 2004.
188 buying the Santa Anita: *Boston Globe*, March 31, 1998.
189 adding five Texas golf courses: *Palm Beach Post*, March 11, 1998.
189 bought the estate for $41.35 million: Ibid., November 16, 2004.
190 "Pop! I'm a dime a dozen . . .": Arthur Miller, *Death of a Salesman* (1999), p. 102.
192 "Nobody dast blame this man": Ibid., p. 108.

Chapter Eighteen

194 "How you doing?": Interview, Fred Keller.
194 The situation was only resolved: Proceedings before the Honorable Kathleen Kroll in Rosemarie B. Keller vs. Fred Keller, July 20, 2001.
195 He was a recovering: Interview, Brian Bohlander.
196 "Brian was more than a little disturbed . . .": Interview, Lois Yost.
196 "a bare butt whipping . . .": Paul Keller manuscript Isthmus, p. 23.
196 "the sole remaining connection": Ibid., p. 6.
197 "an inability to develop or": Evaluation of Fred Keller by Stephen R. Alexander, Psy.D., November 29, 2000 and February 5, 2001 in Fred Keller V. Rose Keller.

197 "Ms. Keller probably was . . .": Evaluation of Rosemarie Keller by Stephen R. Alexander, Psy.D., December 21, 2000 and January 25, 2001 in Fred Keller V. Rose Keller.
197 "You know and I know . . .": Proceedings before the Honorable Kathleen Kroll in Re: the Marriage of Rosemarie B. Keller and Fred Keller, October 14, 2004.
198 "My intention was to placate her . . .": Interview, Fred Keller.
198 She was doing his paralegal's: Interview, Martin Haines.

Chapter Nineteen
202 As she began restoring: *Sun-Sentinel*, March 19, 1995.
202 Cathleen chaired: *Palm Beach Post*, March 24, 1991.
205 "I was probably the only girl . . .": Interview, Cathleen McFarlane Ross.
206 "What do you do?": Ibid.
207 Both of his wives: Interview, Walter Ross.
208 There were 150: Palm Beach Charity Register 2007–2008.

Chapter Twenty
214 "How do you feel?": Interview, Barbara Wainscott.
216 Barbara apologized for the wildly: Ibid.
219 "Son of a bitch . . .": Interview, caretaker.
220 The supposed benefactors: *Palm Beach Daily News*, October 10, 2007.
221 "a one-horse ship . . .": *Time*, October 06, 1952.
221 In 1948 when his only son: Ibid.
222 "I was in Palm Beach and my . . .": Interview, Eles Gillet.
222 Warry feared that: Interviews, Warry Gillet III, and Eles Gillet.
224 "She was the chicest woman . . .": Interview, Dan Ponton.
225 "I did cancer three times": Interview, Eles Gillet.
226 "You don't marry a good-looking woman and then be hurting for money . . .": *New York Observer*, February 17, 2003.
226 "We are gonna blow . . .": *Miami Herald*, December 30, 1983.

Chapter Twenty-One

229 found that her husband: *Baltimore Sun*, May 16, 2002.

229 their son had served: *Chicago Tribune*, September 22, 1995.

229 "all funeral expenses be paid as soon as practical,": . Last Will and Testament of F. Warrington Gillet, Jr., August 2, 1993, Palm Beach County, Florida.

229 Warry III claims: *Palm Beach Post*, May 18, 2003.

229 But in 1993, Warry wrote a will: Last Will and Testament of F. Warrington Gillet, Jr., August 2, 1993, Palm Beach County, Florida.

230 The codicil signed eight years later: First Codicil to Last Will and Testament of F. Warrington Gillet, Jr., April 30, 2001.

230 Warry III and Susan: Interviews, Warry Gillet III and an attorney intimately involved with the matter.

230 "The silver is well protected": The dialogue is from Eles Gillet's memory of the exchange. Susan Chewning tells a similar story. *Palm Beach Post*, May 18, 2003.

231 "good friend": *Palm Beach Post*, July 8, 2005.

231 "She hurt us badly, so . . .": Interview, Warry Gillet III.

231 "Eles Gillet's friends are coming . . .": *Palm Beach Daily News*, January 25, 2004.

232 as "the story of a wealthy tobacco . . .": Interview, Warry Gillet III.

232 her forty-nine-year-old son: *Palm Beach Daily News*, October 17, 2006.

233 "dupioni silk in burnished oranges, reds and yellow": *Palm Beach Daily News*, March 12, 2008.

233 "I couldn't see anybody": Interview, Eles Gillet.

234 immortalized himself as one: Interviews, Mildred McLean and Jan West.

235 rammed his Red Chrysler into a Ford: Palm Beach Police Department Incident Report, March 1, 2006.

235 Peter tore the paraphernalia: Interview, Peter Rock.

235 Eles wrote out: Interviews, Eles Gillet and Peter Rock.

235 He started making excuses: Interview, Peter Rock.

236 "According to paperwork . . .": *Palm Beach Post*, April 4, 2008.

Chapter Twenty-Two

238 "I want you to know that": Interview, Dan Ponton.
239 "There are these people who join . . .": Ibid.
242 "But finally I realized that . . .": *Palm Beach Daily News*, May 25, 1979.
243 Roxanne and the psychic sued: *Miami Herald*, October 7, 1982 and *Sun-Sentinel*, July 15, 1987.
243 four female legs, a trumpet: *The Palm Beach Post*, July 13, 1990.
243 "I want the people to identify with what . . .": Ibid.
244 Three years later, he twisted poor Santa: Interview, Bruce Sutka.
244 Sutka put up another holiday house: Ibid.
245 The event came into its own in 1981: *Palm Beach Daily News*, January 3, 1981.
245 The leopard leaped upon a table: Interview, Bruce Sutka.
245 some of the guests decided: *Palm Beach Daily News*, January 31, 1981.
246 "Choosing one of the two events is a little": *Palm Beach Daily News*, January 2, 1991.
246 "It wasn't like a voice from . . .": *Palm Beach Post*, July 13, 1990.
246 "Fall of the Roman Empire": *Palm Beach Daily News*, January 2, 1990.
246 "Bruce will have to come up with something good next year . . .": Ibid., January 3, 1991.
247 "What do you want us to do?": Interview, Bruce Sutka.
247 One of the drag queens stood: *Palm Beach Post*, January 8, 1995.
247 "Oh my God . . .": Interview, Bruce Sutka.

Chapter Twenty-Three

250 a totally nude: Interview, Eles Gillet.
250 The gentleman in question arrived: Discussion, Alexander Gauderi.
250 "I don't have any problem . . .": Interview, OTR.

252 "In my whole life . . .": Interview, Arnold Scassi.
252 "Gays are never truly . . .": Interview, Parker Ladd.
253 "Most gay trophy guys . . .": Ibid.
254 but the $8,800,000 home: Palm Beach County Appraisers Public Access.
255 "There is so much . . .": Interview, Mark Brentlinger.
255 Two days before Christmas: Interviews Mark Brentlinger and Bryan McDonald and *Palm Beach Post*, January 11, 2008.
255 On his one visit . . . Ibid.
255 He came back: Interview, Bryan McDonald.
256 "People take their pen . . .": Interview, Mark Brentlinger.
257 "In the gay world . . ." Ibid.
257 He had a large collection: *Miami Herald*, May 25, 1998.
258 Jimmy loved Staffordshire Cavalier: *Miami Herald*, May 25, 1998.
259 "Well, you know, most artists . . .": Interview, James Barker.

Chapter Twenty-Four

265 punctuated with nightmares: Interview, Wolfgang Keil.
267 collapsed into abject despair: Interview, Fred Keller.

Chapter Twenty-Five

268 "My book will likely be . . .": letter author to Fred Keller, February 2, 2007.
269 "You talk about your love . . .": Taped hearing before the Honorable Edward A. Garrison in State of Florida Plaintiff, vs. Fred Keller defendant, April 13, 2007.
270 "is a kind of confidence man . . .": Janet Malcolm, *The Journalist and the Murderer* (1990), p. 1.
273 "He's still my dad, but there's no . . .": Taped conversation between Dr. Alexander and Fredchen Keller in re: Guardianship of Fred L. Keller, a minor.
274 "relocating to Florida, going . . .": Letter Fred Keller to Austin Keller, November 6, 2006.
276 "It was a tragic thing to see": Interview, Bennett Cohn.
276 Wolfgang insisted on seeing: *Palm Beach Post*, August 27, 2007.

277 The boy usually sits: Angie Keil Bovi's testimony in Fred "Fredchen" Keller's lawsuit against his father's estate, February 29, 2008.

277 "Fred Keller spent his whole": Interview, Dr. Alexander.

Chapter Twenty-Six

279 "Sonny, you know, I've been broke . . .": Interview, Eric Purcell.

280 One day in January 2003: *Boston Globe*, June 5, 2003.

281 Sonny decided to bid: *Boston Globe*, June 5, 2003.

281 "Who the hell is that?": Interview, Shannon Donnelly.

282 who said that if one can read: G. Heath King. *Existence Thought Style: Perspectives of a Primary Relationship Portrayed through the Work of Søren Kierkegaard* (1996), p. 13.

282 The psychoanalyst sensed: Interview, Dr. S. Heath King.

283 "Quite frankly, I suspect . . .": E-mail Dr. S. Heath King to Sonny Peixoto, March 3, 2006.

284 "You know, I'm not going to live very long . . .": Interview, Eric Purcell.

285 "Sonny says this is the best place": Interview, Ashley Swain.

285 She sidled away from Sonny and hugged King: Interview, Dr. S. Heath King.

Chapter Twenty-Seven

288 it troubled her to be dating: Interview, Natalie Kalinka Paavola.

290 "Amity said she needed the attention": Interview, Ashley Swain.

292 "looked like a mobster": *Atlanta Journal-Constitution*, June 5, 2007.

292 He had no money, so he borrowed: Interview, Eric Purcell.

292 "She said he made no noises . . .": Interview, Ashley Swain.

293 He realized that Sonny was doing: Interview, Dr. S. Heath King.

293 "In 2004, he pleaded guilty . . .": *Palm Beach Post*, March 4, 2007.

294 "Let's get together around eight o'clock . . .": Interview, Eric Purcell.

294 "Gee, this is nice": *Palm Beach Post*, June 6, 2007.
295 As Bruce stood there, Sonny fell: Interview, Bruce Sutka.
295 Eric decided that it might be: Interview, Eric Purcell.

Chapter Twenty-Eight

297 the late Philip Rauch: Palm Beach County Property Appraiser Public Access System.
298 "I needed a man": Interview, Jasmine Horowitz.
299 Sonny's brother Samuel: *Palm Beach Post*, April 25, 2008.
300 He took her to see: Interview, Marianne Strong.
300 On the morning of the fiftieth annual gala: Interview, Eric Purcell.
300 "built a billion-dollar fortune . . .": *Forbes*, October 13, 1997, p. 108.
301 "God has given us a lot": Interview, Patrick Park.
301 "the standouts were the high-drama": *Palm Beach Daily News*, February 18, 2008.
301 a 2005 Rocca Bernarda: Wine list provided by Palm Beach Cancer Society.
302 Dinner would start: Photographed by Robert Nelson, *Palm Beach Illustrated*, February 2008.
305 Dan was further diagnosed: Interview, Dan Ponton and *Palm Beach Post*, December 26, 2007.
306 David was born: Photo of tombstone, *Who's Who in America*, 2008, and interview, Barbara Wainscott.
308 He spent a reputed: *Palm Beach Post*, January 6, 2008.

Chapter Twenty-Nine

310 He was number four: *Forbes*, September 27, 1902.
311 "My beef with Boardman . . .": *Spectator*, May 11, 2002.
311 married forty-five years: *Palm Beach Daily News*, March 12, 2000.
311 Then five years later: *New York Times*, December 7, 2005.
311 In 2008 her other brother: *Palm Beach Daily News*, July 10, 2008.
311 "I tried with my two children, to say . . .": Interview, Pauline Pitt.

313 "A lot of very nice people live here . . .": Ibid.
314 marine fighter pilot: *Palm Beach Daily News*, January 2, 2005.
315 Stan's marriage to Dina: *Palm Beach Post*, April 24, 2005.
315 In 1973 Stan's and Dina's: *New York Times*, September 9, 1973.
315 divorced in 1988: *Miami Herald*, April 8, 1988.
315 married two years later: *Palm Beach Post*, March 13, 1990.
315 bought a house on Everglades: *Palm Beach Post*, December 17, 1995.
315 "I want to keep Palm Beach the way it is, which is the way I know it": Interview, Stanely Rumbough.
316 "Mrs. Post's arrogant and aloof daughter . . .": Donald Trump, *The Art of the Comeback* (1997), p. 64.
316 National Doubles Championships: *New York Times*, August 15, 1951.
316 Pebble Beach: *San Francisco Chronicle*, January 29, 1986.
316 "I don't think Palm Beach has . . .": Interview, Stanley Rumbough.
319 people on the sidewalk: Interviews, Jeffrey A. Cloninger and Gunilla von Post.
320 Barker did not know: Interview, James Barker.
320 police say he pushed one of them: Palm Beach Police Department Incident Report, occurrence date May 5, 2008.

Chapter Thirty

322–330 Please go to Leamer.com/endnotes to read the additional notes for this revised edition.

Bibliography

Akin, Edward N. *Flagler, Rockefeller Partner and Florida Baron* (Florida Sand Dollar Book). Gainesville, FL: University Press of Florida, 1991.

Amory, Cleveland. *Who Killed Society?* New York: Pocket Books, 1962.

Bender, Marylin. *The Beautiful People*. New York: Coward, McCann, 1967.

Birmingham, Stephen. *"Our Crowd": The Great Jewish Families of New York*. New York: Harper & Row, 1967.

———. *The Grandes Dames*. Thorndike, ME: G K Hall & Co., 1983.

———. *The Right People: A Portrait of the American Social Establishment*. Boston: Little, Brown, 1968.

Brenner, Marie. *House of Dreams: The Bingham Family of Louisville*. New York: Random House, 1988.

Brooks, David. *Bobos in Paradise: The New Upper Class and How They Got There*. New York: Simon & Schuster, 2001.

Chandler, David Leon, and Mary Voelz Chandler. *The Binghams of Louisville: The Dark History Behind One of America's Great Fortunes*. New Jersey: Random House Value Publishing, 1989.

Chandler, David Leon. *Henry Flagler: The Astonishing Life and Times of the Visionary Robber Baron Who Founded Florida*. New York: Macmillan, 1986.

Collier, Charles W. *Wealth in Families*. Cambridge: Harvard University Press, 2001.

Collier, Peter, and David Horowitz. *Fords: An American Epic*. New York: Summit Books, 1987.

Curl, Donald W. *Mizner's Florida: American Resort Architecture* (Architectural History Foundation Book). London: MIT Press, 1987.

Earl, Polly Anne. *Palm Beach: An Architectural Legacy*. New York: Rizzoli International Publications, 2003.

Fireman, Simon C. *No Justice*. Bulverde, TX: Omni, 1999.

Frank, Robert. *Richistan: A Journey Through the American Wealth Boom and the Lives of the New Rich*. New York: Crown, 2007.

Friedman, Lawrence J., and Mark D. McGarvie. *Charity, Philanthropy, and Civility in American History*. New York: Cambridge University Press, 2004.

Gilbert, Daniel. *Stumbling on Happiness*. New York: Vintage, 2007.

Grunwald, Michael. *The Swamp: The Everglades, Florida, and the Politics of Paradise*. New York, NY: Simon & Schuster, 2007.

Hays, Charlotte. *The Fortune Hunters: Dazzling Women and the Men They Married*. New York: St. Martin's Griffin, 2008.

Hemphill, C. Dallett. *Bowing to Necessities: A History of Manners in America, 1620–1860*. New York: Oxford University Press, 2002.

James, Henry. *Henry James on Culture: Collected Essays on Politics and the American Social Scene*. Edited by Pierre A. Walker. Toronto, Canada: Bison Books, 2004.

———. *The American Scene*. New York: Harper & Brothers, 1907.

Johnston, Alva. *The Legendary Mizners*. New York: Farrar, Straus and Giroux, 2003.

———. *Those Incredible Mizners*. New York: Hart Davis, 1953.

Jones, Alex S., and Susan E. Tifft. *The Patriarch: The Rise and Fall of the Bingham Dynasty*. New York: Summit Books, 1991.

Kasson, John F. *Rudeness and Civility: Manners in Nineteenth-Century Urban America*. New York: Hill and Wang, 1991.

King, G. Heath. *Existence, Thought, Style: Perspectives of a Primary Relation, Portrayed through the Work of Soren Kierkegaard.* Milwaukee: Marquette University Press, 1996.

Kurth, Peter. *Isadora: A Sensational Life.* New York: Back Bay Books, 2002.

Loring, John. *Tiffany's Palm Beach.* New York: Harry N. Abrams, 2005.

Malcolm, Janet. *The Journalist and the Murderer.* New York: Vintage, 1990.

Martin, Sidney Walter. *Florida's Flagler.* Athens, GA: University of Georgia Press, 1982.

McLean, Evalyn Walsh. *Queen of Diamonds: The Fabled Legacy of Evalyn Walsh McLean.* Franklin, TN: Hillsboro Press, 2000.

Miller, Arthur. *Death of a Salesman: 50th Anniversary Edition.* Boston: Penguin, 1999.

Mizner, Addison. *Florida Architecture of Addison Mizner.* New York: Dover Publications, 1992.

Ney, John. *Palm Beach: The Place, the People, Its Pleasures and Palaces.* Boston: Little, Brown, 1966.

O'Brien, Timothy L. *TrumpNation.* New York: Warner Business Plus, 2005.

O'Sullivan, Maureen, and Dianna Shpritz. *Palm Beach: Then and Now.* New York: Lickle Publishing, 2003.

Packard, Vance. *The Status Seekers.* Philadelphia: David Mckay, 1959.

Phillips, Kevin. *Wealth and Democracy: A Political History of the American Rich.* New York: Broadway, 2003.

Rodengen, Jeffrey L. *Legend of Cornelius Vanderbilt Whitney.* Fort Lauderdale, FL: Write Stuff Syndicate, 2000.

Scaasi, Arnold. *Women I Have Dressed (and Undressed!).* New York: Scribner, 2007.

Scaasi, Arnold. *A Cut Above.* New York: Rizzoli International Publications, 1996.

Seebohm, Caroline. *Boca Rococo: How Addison Mizner Invented Florida's Gold Coast.* New York: Diane Publishing Co., 2004.

Seward, Ingrid. *Prince Edward.* London: Arrow, 1999.

Sheeran, James J. *Palm Beach Power & Glory, Wit & Wisdom*. Palm Beach: Palm Beach Society Publishing Group, 2004.

Standiford, Les. *Last Train to Paradise: Henry Flagler and the Spectacular Rise and Fall of the Railroad That Crossed an Ocean*. New York: Three Rivers Press, 2003.

Stendhal. *The Red and the Black*. New York: Modern Library, 2003.

Stuart, Nancy Rubin. *American Empress: The Life and Times of Marjorie Merriweather Post*. New York: Villard, 1995.

Tocqueville, Alexis de. *Democracy in America, Volume 1*. New York: Vintage, 1990.

Trump, Donald J. *Trump: The Art of the Comeback*. New York: Crown Business, 1997.

Whitney, C.V. *High Peaks*. Lexington, KY: University Press of Kentucky, 1977.

Wright, William. *Ball: A Year in the Life of the April in Paris Extravaganza*. New York: Saturday Review Press, 1972.

Index

Addison Development, 157
Adirondacks, 113
Aga Khan, 84
Alexander, Stephen R., 196–98, 273, 274, 277
Allen, Woody, 328–30
Anderson, Loy, Jr., 244
Angiulo, Gennaro, 88
Anne, Princess, 12–13
Anti-Defamation League of B'nai B'rith, 82
Aradi, Nicholas S., 262
Ash, Agnes, 150–52, 246
Atkins, Robert C., 228
Avalon, Frankie, 172
Avello, Andy, 230–32, 234

Baker, Anthony, 311
Baker, George, III, 311
Baker, George F., 310–11
Baker, George F., Jr., 311
Ball (Wright), 46–47
Barker, James "Jimmy," 110–12, 257–60, 318–21
  house fire of, 319–21
Barker, Lex, 40
Barrett, Peter Charles, 149, 151, 152
Barron's, 92
Bath and Tennis Club (B&T), 8, 20, 61, 68, 69, 87, 94, 97, 100, 129, 133, 140–44, 234, 250, 256, 304, 317
  Combs at, 100–101
  gay community and, 255–56
  Jewish community and, 83, 127, 141–44
  rules at, 102, 140–41
Beach Club, 8, 122, 202, 225, 234
Beam, Phillip, 249–51, 253, 254
Beard, Marie, 179
Berger, Barbara Wainscott, 5–23, 78–80, 82, 106, 127, 129, 131–36, 139, 155, 214–20, 237, 305
  background of, 7
  Brownie McLean and, 47, 48
  David's divorce from, 218–19, 237
  David's engagement and marriage to, 134–36, 137–39
  David's illness and, 214–17, 219
  David's prenuptial agreement with, 134, 215, 218
  dinner dance for Prince Edward hosted by, 5, 6–7, 12, 14–23, 67, 133, 134, 177, 305
  Donnelly's friendship with, 128–29, 134, 139, 145, 147
  at Four Arts dinner, 143–44
  love life of, 133
  Marylou Whitney's invitation and, 106, 112–13
  Shiny Sheet and, 145–46

Berger, Barbara Wainscott (*continued*)
shopping of, 215, 217–18
weight of, 134, 305
Windsors and, 5–7, 12, 14–23, 67, 133–39, 216
Berger, Daniel, 19, 80, 214, 215, 217–19
Berger, David, 6–9, 12–15, 17–23, 78–83, 92, 106, 127, 129, 131–36, 139–40, 160, 168, 214–20, 237, 254, 305
background of, 7–8
Barbara's divorce from, 218–20, 237
Barbara's engagement and marriage to, 134–36, 137–39
Barbara's prenuptial agreement with, 134, 215, 218
clothing of, 132
death of, 305–6
drinking of, 214
fortune of, 8, 14, 17, 106, 134, 218, 219
at Four Arts dinner, 143–44
gifts to Barbara from, 132
illness of, 214–17, 219
Jewish heritage of, 7–9, 12, 80–81, 94, 127, 129, 132, 133, 143–46
love life of, 133
as Red Cross Ball chairman, 129-31
Shiny Sheet and, 127, 145–46
stinginess of, 79, 106, 132
Whitney estate purchased by, 112–13
Berger, Harold, 19
Berger, Jonathan, 80, 214, 215, 218, 219
Bernard L. Madoff Investment Securities, 85–88, 91, 323
Beth Israel Deaconess Medical Center, 90
Bice, 327
Billingsley, Sherman, 51
Biltmore Hotel, 81, 82
Bingham, Mary Lily Flagler, 115–17
Bingham, Robert, 116–17
Black, Conrad, 310
Blackstone Group, 78, 156
Blodgett, Alicia, 168
Bloody Social, 232
B'nai B'rith, 82
Boardman, Dixon, 311
Boardman, Samantha, 311–12
Boardman, Serena, 311–12
Bohlander, Brian, 26, 27, 29, 30, 269, 275
Bohlander, Ludwig, 196
Boston Globe, 177, 178, 185
Boston Herald, 185
Bourgault, Roy, 199, 200
Boykin, Robert Ingalls, 226–27, 232
Boykin, Samuel, Jr., 222
Boys Club Ball, 122
Brandeis University, 90
Breakers Club, 21–22, 82
Breakers Hotel, 21, 24, 82, 122, 129, 133, 160, 168–69, 202, 220, 233, 244, 324
Purcell and Peixoto at, 281, 282
Turquoise and Denim Ball at, 297–98
Breakers Row, 106
Brentlinger, Mark, 253–57, 306
Brigham and Women's Hospital, 305, 322
Bruce, Donald, 243–44, 246
Buchanan, Tyler, 105
Burfield, Diana, 76
Bush, Barbara, 252
Bush, Laura, 252

Cancer Ball, 168, 300–303
Castelbajac, Catherine de, 178–79
Castle, John, 212
Castle, Mrs. John, 212
Castre, Lin, 188, 189
charity events, 129, 141–42, 168, 208, 211
Boys Club Ball, 122
Cancer Ball, 168, 300–303
Eles Gillet and, 224–25
Ladies' Auxiliary of the Lord's Palace tea, 201–3, 211–13, 225
March of Dimes Ball, 281
Preservation Ball, 310
Red Cross Ball, 129–31, 139, 168–73, 244
Turquoise and Denim Ball, 297–98

Charles, Prince, 12–13
Chong, Dora, 173–74
Clinton, Bill, 183
Clinton, Hillary, 175
Club Colette, 17–18, 132, 153, 175, 224, 237–41, 304–5, 322–25, 327
Coconuts New Year's Eve Party, 48, 61–62, 245–46, 303–4, 306–8
Cohn, Bennett, 123, 268, 271, 273, 276
Colgate Company, 315
Combs, Sean, 100–101
Costner, Kevin, 182
Cowell, Richard, 108, 307
Cox, James, 204, 205
Crimes and Misdemeanors, 328–30
Croft, Frank, 181–82
Cuomo, Mario, 187
Custer, George Armstrong, 184

Daily Mirror, 52
Daily News Record, 88
Damone, Rena, 203, 211–12
Damone, Vic, 203, 211–12
Dana-Farber Cancer Institute Ball, 327
Day, Arthur, 305
Dean, Deborah Gore, 41–42, 163, 165
Death of a Salesman (Miller), 190–92
Democracy in America (Tocqueville), ix
Dershowitz, Alan, 183
Diamond, Jeff, 122
Dixon, Ellin, 144
Dixon, Fritz Eugene, Jr., 143–44
Doherty, Henry L., 81
Dole, Robert, 167
Donnelly, Ian, 152, 153, 181, 303–4
Donnelly, Shannon, 16–19, 67, 127–29, 131, 147–53, 168, 233, 281–83, 322
  background of, 127–28, 148–49
  Barbara Berger's friendship with, 128–29, 134, 139, 145, 147
  at Cancer Ball, 301, 302
  at Coconuts New Year's Eve Party, 303–4
  Eles Gillet and, 231
  Fireman and, 168, 169, 171, 173
  first marriage of, 149, 151, 152
  Koch and, 177, 183
  Schurs and, 173, 175
  second marriage of, 153
Douglas, Kenneth W., Jr., 257
Duncan, Douglas, 263, 265–67
Duncan, Isadora, 58

Easton, Michael, 199, 200
Ecclestone, Diana, 169–70, 300
Edward, Prince, Duke of Windsor, 14
Edward, Prince, Earl of Wessex, 138–39, 216
  at Barbara and David's wedding, 135, 136
  dinner dance for, 5, 6–7, 12, 14–23, 67, 133, 134, 177, 305
Eisenhower, Dwight D., 315
Elephant Walk, 6, 78, 112–13, 127, 133
  Donnelly at, 128–29
Elizabeth, Queen, 5
El Solano, 56, 63
Epstein, Jeffrey, 183
"Evening of Paradise" event, 245
Everglades Club, 8, 20, 59, 61, 81, 83, 87, 94, 100, 127, 129, 133, 204, 206, 208–11, 223, 256, 299, 304, 308, 310, 316–17
  Eles Gillet and, 233, 234
  gay community and, 250, 255–56
  Jewish community and, 21, 206, 207
  rules at, 209, 210
  Seven-Year Itch dinner dance at, 203–4, 208–10, 212

Fadiman, James, 70, 72
Fadiman, James, Jr., 70, 72, 73, 75
Fadiman, Jeffrey, 70–73
Fadiman, Renee, 67
"Fall of the Roman Empire" event, 246
Fanjul, Alfonso, 310
Fanjul, Emilia, 255, 312–13
Fanjul, Pepe, 255, 310, 318
Farris, Celia Lipton, 300
Fatio, Maurice, 57, 155
Ferraro, John, 205
Ferraro, Margaret Hart, 20–21, 204–5
Fiandaca, Alfred, 137

Fireman, Mrs. Simon C., 300
Fireman, Simon C., 167–73, 300
accident of, 172–73
Fisher, Jeffrey, 180
Fitzgerald, F. Scott, 164–65
Flagler, Harry, 116
Flagler, Henry, 115–17, 241
death of, 116
Flagler, Ida Alice Shourds, 115, 116
Flagler, Mary (Henry's first wife), 115
Flagler, Mary Lily Kenan (Henry's second wife), 115–17, 245, 246
Flagler Museum, 244–47
Flesh for Frankenstein, 41
Foote, Mrs. C. W., 116
Forbes, 300
Ford, Robert, 184
Four Winds, 155–56
Frankel, Lois, 293
Friday the 13th, Part 2, 226

Garrett, Ernie, 226
Garrison, Edward, 264, 269, 270
gay community, 249–60
Gillet, Eleanor Tydings, 222, 225, 232
Gillet, Elesabeth "Eles," 18, 107, 110, 129, 131–32, 220–26, 229–36, 250, 251, 304
background of, 220–21
first marriage of, 222–23
Rock and, 234–36
Warry's death and, 229–32
Gillet, F. Warrington "Warry," Jr., 18, 107, 110, 112, 131–32, 220, 222–24
background of, 223
death of, 229–32
first marriage of, 222–23
weight gain of, 228
Gillet, F. Warrington, III, 225–26, 229–32
Gillet, F. Warrington, IV, 226
Gillet, Susan, 229, 230
Gold, Larry, 141–42
Goldman, Laura, 91–92
Goldstein, Brad, 180
Gordon, Arlette, 150–51, 300
Gordon, Robert G., 150–51, 191, 300
Gosman, Abraham D., 187–91
Gosman, Betty, 188
Gosman, Lin Castre, 188, 189
Gray, Herb, 25–26, 323–24
Gray, Marylou, 25
Green's Pharmacy, 91, 95–96
Greenwald, Steve, 102
Gucci, Aldo, 237, 238
Gucci, Paolo, 238

Haig, Alexander, 209
Haig, Mrs. Alexander, 209
Haines, Martin, 193, 195, 198, 199
Hamilton, George, 247
Hardwick, Bob, 7
Hare, Channing, 257
Hart, Margaret, 20–21, 204–5
Hassan, King, II, 234
Hayworth, Rita, 70
Healey, James C., 205–6
Hebrew SeniorLife, 90
Heine, Leonard, Jr., 175–76
Heine, Sandy, 175
Hendrickson, John, 135–36, 235
Herald News, 152
Hewitt, Nanci, 95–96
Heyman, James, 259, 319–20
Hickel, Mrs. Walter, 135
Hickel, Walter, 135
High Peaks (Whitney), 107
Holmes, Oliver Wendell, 250
Homer, Winslow, 184
homes, 154–58, 186–87
Horowitz, Jasmine, 298–300, 304
Horowitz, Manfredo, 298–300
Hosford, Frank, 107
Howard, Teddy, 107
Hughes, Howard, 52
Hutton, E. F., 155–56

Idy, Joseph, 37
Iglesias, Julio, 130–31
Ingalls, Robert, Jr., 221
Ingalls, Robert Ingersoll, Sr., 221
International Centre for Missing and Exploited Children, 170
International Polo Club, 284–86
International Red Cross Ball, 129–31, 139, 168–73, 244
Isthmus (Keller), 196

Jaffe, Ellen, 88, 89, 323, 326–27
Jaffe, Robert M., 87–89, 91, 323, 326–27
Jaffe, Steven, 326
James, Henry, 10–11, 241, 318
James, Jesse, 184
James Hunt Barker Galleries, 257, 258
Janjigian, Robert, 182, 301
Jewish community, 8, 9, 18, 21, 81–83, 93–96, 106, 129, 139, 141, 206, 229, 233–34, 239, 252, 297, 317
  Bath and Tennis Club and, 83, 127, 141–44
  David Berger as part of, 7–9, 12, 80–81, 94, 127, 129, 132, 133, 143–46
  Everglades Club and, 21, 206, 207
  Mar-a-Lago and, 93–95
  Schurs as part of, 173, 175
  Shiny Sheet and, 150
Johnson, Don, 247
Johnson, Eastman, 257–58
Johnson, Richard, 231

Karland, Meaghan, 75–76, 159–66
Kaye, Danny, 20–21
Kaye, Sumner, 172
Keil, Angelika "Angie," 121, 262–65, 269–71, 273, 275–77
Keil, Brigitte, 121, 263–64
Keil, Klaus, 121, 124–25
Keil, Wolfgang, 26, 121, 194, 199, 200, 262, 269–71, 273, 275–77
  Fred Keller's shooting of, 200, 261, 263–66, 271
Keller, Austin, 274–75
Keller, Blanch, 26, 27, 28–30, 193
Keller, Eric, 28, 29, 30–31, 119–20, 124, 193
  cancer of, 262
Keller, Fred, 22, 25–35, 114, 117–26, 268–77
  arrest and trials of, 261–67
  author's interviews with, 268–72
  background of, 26–67, 196
  death of, 276–77
  divorce of, 126, 193–200
  lawsuits of, 123
  leukemia of, 118, 123, 194–95
  near-death experience of, 125
  prenuptial agreement of, 119, 123–24, 195
  in prison, 268–70, 272, 274
  property agreements of, 123–26, 198, 261
  Rose and Wolfgang shot by, 200, 261, 270–73, 276
  sentencing of, 269–70
  vasectomy of, 120
Keller, Fred "Fredchen," 26, 120–21, 123, 193–95, 197–98, 261, 262, 268–77
Keller, Ludwig, 118
Keller, Paul, 28, 29, 30, 31, 119–20, 124, 196
  cancer of, 195, 262
Keller, Rosemarie "Rose" Keil, 22, 34–35, 114, 117–26
  divorce of, 126, 193–200
  Fred's murder of, 200, 261, 270–73, 276
  Fred's properties and, 123–26, 198, 261
  grave of, 277
  prenuptial agreement and, 119, 123–24, 195
Keller Trust, 121–23, 194, 199, 200, 261, 263
Kennedy, Jacqueline, 148, 224
Kennedy, John F., 212, 224
Kennedy, Robert F., 212
Kennedy, Ted, 183
Kessler, Howard, 327
Kessler, Michele, 327
Khashoggi, Adnan, 247
Kierkegaard, Søren, 282–83
King, G. Heath, 164, 282–83, 285–86, 288, 289, 292–93
Kinnear, Jim, 308
Kissinger, Henry, 109
Knickerbocker, Cholly, 52
Koch, Angela Browder Gauntt, 16, 177, 179–82
  assault case and, 180–81
  Croft and, 181–82
  divorce of, 181, 182, 184

Koch, Angela Browder Gauntt (*continued*)
prenuptial agreement and, 179–81
remarriage of, 182
Koch, Charles, 177
Koch, David, 16, 177, 178, 183, 303
Koch, Robin, 180
Koch, William, 16, 177–86
art collection of, 184, 185, 186
assault charge against, 180–81
birthday bash of, 182–83
Castelbajac and, 178–79
divorce of, 181, 182, 184
home of, 183–86
lawsuit of, 16, 177–78
prenuptial agreement of, 179–81
Rooney and, 182
security guards of, 184–85
Kozak, Amity, 284–86, 287, 289–94
background of, 289–91
jewelry of, 292
Peixoto and, 284–86, 288–89, 291–94
Peixoto's murder of, 296, 298, 299
Kozak, John, 292
Kozak, Pat, 292
Kravis, Raymond F., 83
Kravis Center for the Performing Arts, 83, 89, 90, 317, 328
Kroll, Judge, 197–99, 261, 262

Ladd, Parker, 111, 251–53
Ladies' Auxiliary of the Lord's Palace, 201–3, 211–13, 225
Lambiet, Jose, 236
Landau, Mimy, 67
Lappin, Andrew, 324
Lappin, Bob, 324–25
Lappin, Peter, 324
Latham, Pene, 33–34
Lauder, Estée, 62, 101, 154
Lawrence, Joseph, 168
Leamer, Vesna, 2, 21, 48, 166, 172, 212, 288, 302, 307
Leesfield, Ellen, 163, 164
Lembcke, Bernd, 102
Lennon, John, 20, 63
Lindemann, Frayda, 229
Lindemann, George, 229
Lord's Palace, 201–3, 211–13, 225
Louis, Desirée, 38, 39, 66, 73, 77, 287
Louis, Eddy, 21, 22, 36–40, 65–69, 72–77, 158, 161, 164, 287–88
background of, 37–38
gun carried by, 76–77
Karland and, 75–76
Louis, Vera Lukin, 21, 36, 39, 65–75
automobile accident and death of, 74, 75, 78
background of, 68–69
sexuality of, 66–67
Louisville Courier, 117
Lukin, Philip, 71
Lukin, Vera, *see* Louis, Vera Lukin

McConnell, David, 42–43, 163
McConnell, Neil, 163
McDonald, Bryan, 253–57, 306
McFarlane, Melissa, 210–11
McFarlane, Norris, 20, 21, 206–7
McFarlane-Ross, Cathleen, 20–21, 201–12, 220, 222, 304
background of, 204–5
first marriage of, 206
and Ladies' Auxiliary of the Lord's Palace, 201–3, 211–13
second marriage of, 205–6
third marriage of, 20, 21, 206–7
Walter's marriage to, 207
McLean, Evalyn Walsh, 53, 55
McLean, John "Jock," II, 20, 47, 53–55, 56, 61–64
death of, 63
McLean, John R., 53–54
McLean, Mildred "Brownie," 20, 46–55, 56, 61–64, 107, 129–30, 220, 222, 251, 297, 304, 308
background of, 49–52
"troops" of, 63–64, 234
McLean, Ned, 53
McQuaid, Cate, 185
Madoff, Bernard, 3, 85–87, 89–92, 323–30
Jaffe and, 88–89, 326
Shapiro and, 89–90, 325, 327
Madoff, Ruth, 86, 87, 91, 329

Mail on Sunday, 138
Malcolm, Janet, 270
Mann, Jonathan, 294–95
mansions, 154–58, 186–87
Mar-a-Lago, 69, 84, 92–95, 97–103, 127, 141, 164, 233, 240, 251, 304, 314, 326
Cancer Ball at, 300–303
gay community and, 250, 256
Red Cross Ball at, 170–71
March of Dimes Ball, 281
MAR Hedge Fund Report, 91
Martin, Karen L., 273
Matrix Essentials Inc., 154
Medina, Maria Garcia, 43–45, 159–64, 280
Mediplex Group, 188
Merrill, Dina, 314–16
Meyer, Sydelle, 90
Miller, Arthur, 190–92
Miller, Sydell, 154–55
Mizner, Addison, 56–61, 155, 157, 201, 202, 204, 208, 209, 241, 242
Modigliani, Amedeo, 184
Moffett, Frank, 91
Muller, Alice, 154–55
Muller, Ralph, 154–55
Munn, Charles A., Jr., 310
Munn, Mrs. Gurnee, 61
Museum of Fine Arts, Boston, 90

NASDAQ, 85
National Bank, 244
Neiman Marcus, 281
Nernberg, Dick, 84
Newsmax, 172
Newton, Wayne, 302
New York Post, 231, 236, 243
New York Times, 305
Nixon, Pat, 7
Nixon, Richard, 7, 13
Norton Museum of Art, 83, 90
Nun, Terry, 249–51, 253, 254
Nye, Hethea, 313

Octopussy, 188
Ono, Yoko, 20, 63
Ostivich, Todd, 76

Paavola, Natalie Kalinka, 288
Pagan, Michele, 176
Palm Beach Art Gallery, 258
Palm Beach Civic Association, 314–16
Palm Beach Country Club, 8, 9, 82–84, 93, 189, 322
Madoff and, 86, 87, 92, 326, 328
Ruttenbergs and, 175–76
Schurs and, 173, 175, 176
Shapiro and, 89, 90, 327
Palm Beach Daily News (the "Shiny Sheet"), 12, 16–20, 25, 41, 48, 67, 83, 110, 114, 127–29, 131, 144–45, 147–53, 156, 168, 201–2, 241, 246, 253, 261, 282, 316, 317, 322, 328
Cancer Ball and, 301
Coconuts New Year's Eve Party and, 304
David Berger and, 127
Eddy Louis gun incident reported in, 76–77
Eles Gillet and, 231
Fireman in, 168, 169, 171, 173
Jaffe and, 89
Jewish events and, 150
Kochs and, 177, 182, 184
Madoff and, 87, 91
Schurs in, 173, 175
Sutka and, 242
Palm Beach Day School, 24–25
Palm Beach International Airport, 103, 226, 257
Palm Beach Post, 18, 60, 149, 165, 183, 235–36
Peixoto in, 293
Palm Beach Society, 63, 71, 133
Pandula, Gene, 156
Parish, Sister, 224
Park, Daniel, 300
Park, Kelly, 300
Park, Patrick, 300–302
Park, Raymond P., 300
Patterson, James, 282
Pavarotti, Luciano, 187
Peixoto, Helder "Sonny," 278–89, 292–95
Amity Kozak and, 284–86, 288–89, 291–94

Peixoto, Helder "Sonny" (*continued*)
 Amity Kozak murdered by, 296, 298, 299
 suicide of, 295–96, 298
 vehicular homicide charge against, 280, 293
Peixoto, Samuel, 281, 282, 299
Pell, Claiborne, 7
Peterson, Peter G., 78
Philip, Prince, Duke of Edinburgh, 5, 15, 17, 135–36, 137–39
Phipps Ocean Park Tennis Center, 25
Pita, Maria, 165
Pitt, Julia, 313
Pitt, Pauline, 251, 309–14
Pitt, William H., 311
planes, private, 256–57, 312
Planned Parenthood, 314
Polgar, Susan, 324
polo matches, 284–86
Ponton, Daniel, 17–18, 134, 224, 237–41, 304–5, 322
 brain tumor of, 305, 322
Post, Marjorie Merriweather, 69, 98, 99, 103, 314, 316
Powers, Keith, 185
Preservation Ball, 310
Preservation Foundation, 233
Pulitzer, Peter, 243
Pultizer, Roxanne, 243
Purcell, Eric, 21, 22, 40–45, 159–66
 dinner party given by, 288–89
 Horowitz and, 298–300, 304
 Karland and, 159–66
 Medina and, 43–45, 159–64, 280
 Peixoto and, 278–84, 292–96
 in prison, 162–64, 278, 280
 Tropics Party of, 287–88
 Van Pantz estate and, 163, 164

Queen Mother, 13

Racolin, Mendel, 68
Rampell, Paul, 93–94
Rauch, Philip, 297
Red and the Black, The (Stendhal), 142
Red Cross Ball, 129–31, 139, 168–73, 244
Reed, Martha, 161, 164
Reese, Claude D., 81
Reingold, Joyce, 183
Reiter, Michael, 183
Remains of the Day, 98
Remington, Frederic, 184
Renoir, Pierre-Auguste, 184
Rich, Denise, 159
Robert I. Lappin Charitable Foundation, 324
Robertson, Cliff, 315
Robinson, Dick, 169
Rock, Peter, 234–36
Rockefeller, John D., 115
Rooney, Bridget, 182
Ross, Cathleen, *see* McFarlane-Ross, Cathleen
Ross, Walter, 203, 204, 207–12, 304
 Cathleen's marriage to, 207
Roth, David, 263, 268–69
Ruddy, Chris, 172
Rumbough, David, 315
Rumbough, Janna, 315, 317
Rumbough, Margaretha, 315
Rumbough, Stanley M., Jr., 314–18
 birthday celebration of, 317–18
Russell, Charles M., 184
Russell, Jane, 70
Ruttenberg, Abby, 175–76
Ruttenberg, Reid, 175
Rybolovlev, Dmitry, 186

Sailfish Club, 8, 234
Scaasi, Arnold, 111, 224, 251–53
Schecter, Anna, 327
Schneier, Marc, 330
Schrafft, George, 47, 52–53, 54
Schrafft, Victoria, 53, 54
Schumpeter, Joseph, 155
Schur, Edie, 173–76
Schur, Matthew Henry, 174
Schwarzman, Stephen A., 78, 155–56
Scripps, Betty, 122, 154–55
Seaview Tennis Center, 24, 25
Senecal, Tony, 98–101
Seven-Year Itch dinner dance, 203–4, 208–10, 212

Shapiro, Carl, 88–90, 323, 325, 327
Sheeran, James, 63, 133
Shiny Sheet, *see Palm Beach Daily News*
Simmons, Desmond, 7
Simpson, Wallis, 14
Singer, Isaac Merritt, 58
Singer, Paris, 57–58, 59
Sitting Bull, 184
Sjostrom, Jan, 184
Skelly, Carolyn, 49
Slade, 294–95
Slater, Andrew, 263, 264
Smith, Lesly, 153
Smith, William Kennedy, 182
Social Register, 108
Society of the Four Arts, 139–40, 143–44
Sonnabend, A. M., 81–82
Sophie, Countess of Wessex, 216
Standard Oil, 115, 116
Stanley, Diana, 212–13
Starr, Kenneth, 183
Stein, Irving, 105
Stendhal, 142
Stockham, Angela, *see* Koch, Angela Browder Gauntt
Stockham, Doug, 182
Stone, Edward Durrell, 2
Streisand, Barbra, 251–52
Strong, Marianne "Mimi," 300
Strong, Mrs. John L., 6
Sullivan, Ed, 52
Sun and Surf Beach Club, 8, 9, 81, 82
Sutka, Bruce, 6, 242–48, 295
Swain, Ashley, 285, 286, 290–92
Swanson, Dan, 157–58

Taki, 311
Taubman, Alfred, 310
Thatcher, Margaret, 133
Time, 101
Titanic, 143
Tocqueville, Alexis de, ix
Todd, John J., 280
Town & Country, 107
Trillion, 328
Trump, Donald, 69, 92–95, 97–98, 100–102, 164, 170, 172, 233
  Combs and, 101
  gay community and, 250
  Gosman estate purchased by, 189
  lawsuits of, 103
  Rumbough and, 316
  Senecal and, 98–101
Trump, Ivana, 92, 255
Trump International Golf Club, 103–5, 256, 325
Turquoise and Denim Ball, 297–98
20/20, 327
"Twilight Zone" event, 247
Tydings, Eleanor (Gillet), 222, 225, 232
Tydings, Joseph D., 222
Tydings, Millard E., 222

Underwood, Mary, 131
Urban, Joseph, 57
USA Today, 33, 34

Vanity Fair, 231
Van Vooren, Monique, 40–41, 44, 159, 299, 300
Von Pantz, Terry, 163, 164

Wagner, Cyril, 104
Wainscott, Barbara, *see* Berger, Barbara Wainscott
Wainscott, Jeffrey, 7
Wallis, Duchess of Windsor, 14
Warhol, Andy, 41
Watermark, 189
Washington Post, 30
Wexner, Leslie, 187
Whitehall, 8, 9, 81, 82, 116
  Coconuts New Year's Eve Party at, 303–4, 306–8
Whitmore, Sue, 168–70
Whitney, Cornelius Vanderbilt "Sonny," 18, 107–12
  death of, 111
Whitney, Gail, 108
Whitney, Marylou, 18–19, 20, 106–13, 129, 220, 226, 251, 304, 310
  Hendrickson's marriage to, 135, 235

Winchell, Walter, 52
"Winter Dreams" (Fitzgerald), 164–65
Wolf, Lee, 328–30
Worth Avenue, 122, 131, 237, 238, 256, 281, 327–28
  James Hunt Barker Galleries on, 257, 258
  Sutka's window displays on, 242–44
Wright, William, 46–47
Wrightman, Stephanie, 242

Yost, Lois, 196
Young, Sally Fenelon, 244
Young Friends of the Red Cross Ball, 244–47